DELEGATES LEAVING CARPENTER'S HALL AFTER A SESSION

FROM THE ORIGINAL DRAWING BY H. A. OGDEN

COPYRIGHT 1896

THE BRITISH RETREAT TO BOSTON

Boston, the Red Coats, and the Homespun Patriots 1766-1775

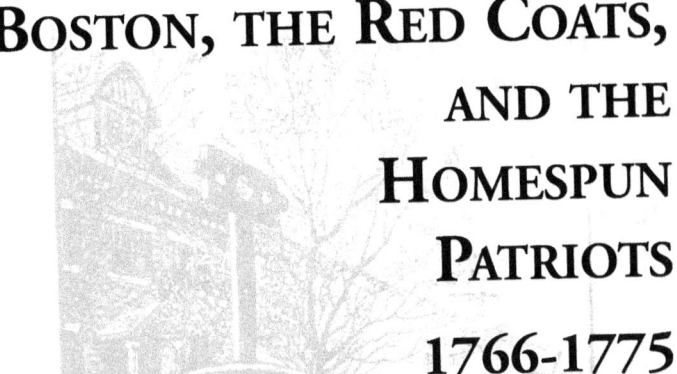

Armand Francis Lucier

HERITAGE BOOKS
2009

HERITAGE BOOKS
AN IMPRINT OF HERITAGE BOOKS, INC.

Books, CDs, and more—Worldwide

For our listing of thousands of titles see our website
at
www.HeritageBooks.com

Published 2009 by
HERITAGE BOOKS, INC.
Publishing Division
100 Railroad Ave. #104
Westminster, Maryland 21157

Copyright © 1998 Armand Francis Lucier

All rights reserved. No part of this book may be reproduced or transmitted in any form or by any means, electronic or mechanical, including photocopying, recording or by any information storage and retrieval system without written permission from the author, except for the inclusion of brief quotations in a review.

International Standard Book Numbers
Paperbound: 978-0-7884-0999-8
Clothbound: 978-0-7884-8225-0

CONTENTS

Forward..vii
Contributors..ix
Part 1: 1766..1
Part 2: 1767...45
Part 3: 1768...85
Part 4: 1769..133
Part 5: 1770..189
Part 6: 1771..235
Part 7: 1772..275
Part 8: 1773..317
Part 9: 1774..369
Part 10: 1775...421
Index...452

FOREWORD

All the articles in this book are taken from Colonial newspapers and presented as they were originally published and read by the elite as well as the populace in town and country, from the repeal of the Stamp-Act in 1766 to the start of the Revolution in 1775.

Sit down, and enjoy, consider the words printed at a time public print was the only source of information available to the Americans, and sense the influence it must of had in thier thoughts.

Get the true feeling of the people of Boston, and contemplate which side each issue would have best suited your lifestyle. Many items published were facts, exaggerations and fabrications to calm or excite the people of Boston and all American Colonies.

Included you will find extracts of sessions of the English Parliament concerning America, letters from tradesmen, merchants and gentlemen from London expressing their views pro and con on American affairs, speeches of Governors, sessions of Houses of Representatives in the Provinces, letters to the editors, and the day to day life of the inhabitants.

Relive the memorial events of the British occupation of Boston, the Boston Massacre, the Boston Tea Party, and the British march to the town of Lexington and Concord, and many other events that has played a part of our American history.

Armand Francis Lucier.

CONTRIBUTORS

The Boston Chronicle. Boston. Mein & Fleming.
1767-1770.
The Boston Evening Post. Boston. Thomas and John Fleet. 1766-1775.
Boston Gazette. Boston. Edes and Gill.
1766-1775.
The Censor. Boston. R. Russel. 1771-1772.
Connecticut Courant. Hartford. Thomas Green.
1766-1768.
Connecticut Courant. Green and Watsson.
1768-1771.
Connecticut Courant. Ebenezer Watsson.
1771-1775.
The Essex Gazette. Salem Massachusetts. Samuel Hall. 1768-1771.
The Essex Gazette. Salem Massachusetts, Samuel and Ebenezer Hall. 1772-1775.
Essex Journal. Newburyport Massachusetts. Isaiah Thomas, Henry & Walter Tinges. 1773-1774.
Essex Journal, Newburyport Massachusetts. E. Lunt & Henry & Walter Tinges. 1774-1775.
Rivington's New-York Gazette. New York. James Rivington. 1773-1775.
The Georgia Gazette, Savannah. James Johnston.
1766-1770.
The Massachusetts Spy. Boston. Z. Fowle and Isaiah Thomas. 1770.
The Massachusetts Spy. Boston. Isaiah Thomas.
1770-1775.
The New-York Gazette. New-York. Hugh Gaines.
1768-1775.
The New-York Journal. New-York. John Holt.
1766-1775.
Norwich Packet. Norwich Connecticut. Alexander & James Robertson, James Trumble. 1773-1775.
Pennsylvania Chronicle. Philadelphia. William Goddard. 1774-1775.

All articles are facsimiles as they were published originally in the Colonial newspapers with no mutations to their composition punctuation, capitalization or spelling. except for the sake of readability, consistency, and clarity.

1766

BOSTON Jan. 6. On Tuesday Night an Accident happened near Hanover-Square, South-End; it being a severe cold season, a Woman thinking to keep her Child the less exposed to the inclemency of it, put it in a cradle close to a Hearth, whereupon there was a small fire of coals, she herself lying at the other End of the room; but in the middle of the Night she was awakened by the crying of the Child and the room being full of smoke; a Spark of the fire having communicated itself to the cradle, and had burnt the foot of the same, part of the Blanket and a couple handkerchief that lay thereon, &c. but the Child escaped untouched.

Last Week one John Ward, a Journeyman Baker in this Town, was committed to Goal, for a rape on the Body of Elizabeth Allen, an Infant between 9 and 10 Years of age, and otherwise very much abused her.

BOSTON Jan. 13. Friday last Capt. Morton arrived here in a Brig from Newcastle, but last from the Downs in about 10 Weeks: He informs that on Thursday the 26th of December, in Lat. 41. 50. & Long. 60. he met with a Sloop from Fyal, bound for New-York, David Harriman, Master, who had been out 65 Days, and were in the most distressed Condition for want of Provisions, having had nothing to eat for 5 Days, and were almost starved. Capt. Morton intended to supply him with what he could spare, being himself at very short Allowance, but a violent Storm came on which separated the two Vessels, and 'Tis feared that the people on board the Sloop have all perish'd.

Our Harbour partly cleared of Ice, Yesterday Morning Capt. Hunter in a Ship for London, and several other Vessels got out and sailed.

BOSTON Jan. 20. Mr. Elijah Packard, (formerly Minister at Scituate) was froze to death in walking over the neck from Kennebeck River to Sheepscut.

Mr. Henry Lear, and one Mr. Renken an aged Man fell thro' the ice at Kennebeck and were drowned.

Two Negro Men being fishing in an open Boat near Falmouth, was froze to Death.

Last Week died at Dorchester, Mr. Benjamin Evereden, he was the only maker of Gun Powder in this Province, and for a Number of Years improved a Mill at Milton for that Purpose.

BOSTON Feb. 1. It being reported in this Town, that I the Subscriber am either appointed or to be appointed to the office of distributor of the Stamps within this Province; I hereby solemnly declare that I have never, directly made application for said office, to any person whatsoever: Nor had I even the least Knowledge of Expectation of any persons making, or intending any such Application in my behalf. And I further declare, that should I hereafter find an Appointment made to me to any Part of the aforesaid Stamp-Office, I shall think myself ill-treated thereby, and will instantly reject so much an injurious a designation.
Sam. Waterhouse.

Wednesday last a Young Man belonging to Dorchester named James Marshal, driving a Cart into Town, his feet accidentally slipping he fell down, and the Wheel of another Cart which was passing by ran over his neck, and wounded him in such a Manner that his life is despaired of.

BOSTON Feb. 3. From London, the Gazette Dated November 1, 1765.

Scarce are we delivered from a War in which we lavished with an unsparing hand such vast sums in defence of America, that we are repaid by an obstinate opposition to, or rather rebellion against, the British legislature, on account of laws made last session of Parliament, charging a few paltry stamp duties in their deeds, and law proceedings which in many years cannot amount to a considerable sum.

This law was passed by the unanimous consent of both houses, without even the contracting voice of one senator to the votes who introduced it. Both majority and minority concurred in the expediency of the usual prefatory resolution so that that measure cannot be regarded, as the work of faction, or estimate to be an opressive manuevre of the late administration. No, Sir, if this Stature contains any injudicious enactment, the error is the error of all concerned in our legislative assembly. So that the turbulent behaviour of the Americans upon this occasion, must appear to every man of sense, in the light of being a premeditated affront, wantonly thrown upon the whole British legislature. remonstrances not riots are the only arms with which loyal subjects combat grievances; and the coloring with which the Americans varnish their complaints, is of as bad a composition as the methods are based by which they try to get rid of this law. they sometime allege charters which contain no exemption from taxes laid on by Parliamentary authority. Upon other occasions they plead, that their birth right operates an immunity from the burden they never consented to by their representatives on Parliament; and of late they contend, that in a free country no taxes should be laid on but by those who bear a share of these taxes.
    Of these defences in order as they lie, Their charters, enable their provincial assemblies to make by laws, and raise money for provincial uses, under an expressed reservation of the sovereignty of England, and this reasonable condition, that the acts of their assembly shall shall not be made in contrary to one common statute law. Has not every corporation in England the same power? How come it then that a privilege, which in England was never understood to include an exemption from the taxes laid on by the parliament, should imagine to be extensive in America? But, Sir, the reservation of the sovereignty, so strongly inculcated in those charters, is wholly decisive as to this point. A power to say on taxes is inseparable from the legitimate rights of sovereignty.

Who ever heard of a sovereign who could not tax his subjects? wherever the sovereignty resides in any nation, whether in a collective body, or a single person, there, the power of raising taxes must necessarily center, or else we should have a sovereign assembly, which could not provide for the duration of the republic under its care; or, in other words, for the usual exigencies of the state. An American only could have tho't of so important sovereignty, a sovereignty which would be such only by name; but, like the log in the fable, might be insulted at pleasure by American frogs. We must therefore admit that our parliament, like all other sovereign assemblies is vested with an uncontroulable power of raising taxes all over the British dominions, and have unquestionable right to suppost their legislative jurisdictions, with its inseparable appendage, the power of raising taxes wherever the British empire extends.

Now, the American birthright come regularly in our way. But what is this birthright, Sir? a right to be esteemed denizens of Great Britain. Is this the right of a denizen of Britain to oppose the British law within the British dominions? or have our taxing laws less authority than the rest? But the Americans are not represented, it seems, in parliament. If this plea be good for any thing, it must oporate an immunity from all our laws, for no free subjects is bound by any laws to which he never consented. The taxing laws are of no different nature from the rest. Whoever claims the benefit of our laws, must take them as they stand, without picking one and rejecting another. There is no medium between the state of the subject, and that of a foreigner. A foreigner is bound by none of our laws, a subject by all of them. Whoever consents to live in a state of subjection to us, consents to be ruled by our laws, and to submit himself to the sovereignty of our parliament. But the first settlers in America by the acceptance of their Charters subjected themselves to every power exercised by our parliament, they consented to all our laws, and that there laws should bind their posterity; they also consented, that our parliament should continue to exercise in their acquisitions all rights of the sovereignty. America consent to all our laws, and must bind every person born in, or travel to British America. Acceptance of charters, containing a reservation of our sovereignty, is a full consent to be considered as subjects, and consequently as being bound by all our laws without any exemption. Whoever comes into America upon this plan, give his full consent to every law, which the wisdom of the British parliament dictates, and consequently of taxing laws among the rest.

I am now arrived, I think, that the last resort of the Americans; the futile pretence, that in a free country no taxes should be laid on, but those who bear a share of those burthen. It is true, Sir, But have the late taxation in America produced another arrangement in our state? Has parliament said on any taxes in America, which are not paid by themselves in a private capacity, as well as by every other subject of England? We know they have not. Why then this idle objection to this taxing statute. What subject of Britain is exemted from payment of the stamp duties, as heavy as those demanded of the Americans? Why then let up this absurd objections, which is in this case sole de se, and gives us an opportunity of turning the tables, and asking the Americans, why he should enjoy exemption unknown in Britain? Neither his original nor his charters entitles him any superior privileges; nor can he set up his poverty as a shield against the law, which cannot be considered as a grievance by the poorest subject; the exaction are too trifling to admit of such objections. But it is full time to have done with examining an argument, which carries so little appearance of reason in its bosom. I ought now to consider the American tumults in a political light, enquire what reasons they are to dread an open rebellion from that quarter; and whether in regard to the present state of America, we ought not to intercede for them with our legislature, or acquiesce in their proposals of sending representatives to our parliament; but as this letter already rather too long. I must reserve these disquisitions for another occasion.   Pacificus.

BOSTON Feb. 3. Friday last Capt. Hathorne arrived at Salem fron the Granades, and after he had been to the Custom House and entered his Vessel, it was reported his papers were stamp'd, upon hearing of which the Selectmen of the Town were applied to by a number of the Sons of Liberty, desiring them to send to the Custom House for those Marks of Slavery that they might see them, having nothing of the kind among them till then. The gentlemen at the Office readily delivered them up, when they were brought upon the Parade and there exposed to public View, then carried to the London Coffee-House, where were assembled a large Company of respectable People (on the occasion) who soon came to the following Resolution. Viz. 1. That these Marks of Tyranny were by no means to be lodged in a public Office. 2. That they together with Jack boot (out of which the devil was peeping) should be affixed to a long pole and carried thus between Heaven and Earth (as fit for neither) near the Common Whipping Post. But some objecting that they did not deserve so much an Honor as to be fixed to it; it was then agreed they should be burnt nigh it: which was accordingly done by a Bonfire prepared for that purpose, amidst the loud Huzzas of the assembly, and the ashes scattered in the Air. ——— After which the populace immediately dispersed without doing any harm or making any Disturbance, A number of the Gentlemen returned to the Coffee-House, Spent the Evening, and Drank several loyal Toasts, such as long life and prosperity to his Majesty King George the Third, Destruction to the Stamp Act, &c. &c.

BOSTON Feb. 10. For the benefit of those who intend to be Adventured in Faneuil-Hall lottery No. 5. We are desired to advertise in this paper, that the Tickets are all rolled up and the boxes completely prepared for drawing, which will commence very soon as the Town have voted to take their Account what Tickets may remain unsold at the Time fixed for drawing.

BOSTON Feb. 14. A Fine Healthy Male Negro Child to be given away. Enquire of the Printer.

Boston Feb. 17. Extract of a Letter from London December 24.

The Disturbances in North-America about the stamp's are very alarming, and cause great uneasiness to those Gentlemen who have large sums which are due them there; the stagnation of Remittance for a few Months may be attended with bad consequence. You are very right with regard to the Method of the Trade from this Body of Merchants trading to the several Provinces, who in Conjunction with those concerned in the trade thither intends to apply to Parliament for some redress with respect to the American Trade; and it's hoped the Government will repeal the Stamp Act, from a Conviction that the late Ministry have done wrong.

BOSTON Feb. 19. Messiers Edes & Gill. By Putting the following you will oblige me, who was formerly a Customer, tho' now reduc'd to poverty and want.

I was born in this Town, in the year 1719, and had the best Education of the Town: was an only Son, and a favorite Child. My Parents were in great Credit, and in very good Circumstances on which I placed my greatest Dependence. When I arrived at the Age of Nineteen, My Father dyed. Oh!

Of my tender Mother I took the greatest Advantage, and too, too soon, I threw off the Yoke, and that kind of Obedience that was her due. At Twenty one, I received Three Thousand Pounds, in old Tenor Paper Bills, left me by my Father, which found me many that I thought were Friends. At Twenty three I married well, and in the course of six Years had four agreeable Children, and kept along some Reputation till within these ten Years past: And I date my Ruin from too free Use of Spirituous Liquors, and acquaintance with several, that meet the Day (Sunday exempted) at Eleven o'clock and five, at a certain Place, in order to club for strong

Drink, so habituated was I to it that a shameful Neglect of my Business followed; and at length I became Sot, left my Business, and all Government in my Family; and poverty came upon me like an armed Man, and now, alas! what am I, a poor, despised, indolent Wretch, a very Nuisance to Society. But Oh! the Cutting Reflection —— The Adder's Sting I sometime feel. Have I ruined myself alone, Oh! No. A once virtuous Wife and poor Children, have catch'd the infection from me; from me —— who should have been their Guardian, Friend, and all. But! Oh! that fatal tho' slower poison too freely drank; call'd rum —— Pity me; oh ye pitying ones, can it be? —— Yes true it is to tell you, that I have seen some Children drunk; and more, their Parents with them; and pilfer for a Morning Dram: Drunk, with that to common Drink call'd Toddy; But I forbear. I could not be easy in my mind, until I have given the above Account; as from no other motive have I done it, than that if it should be any other so unhappy, as to be treading in some said Path, they may be early prevented, I earnestly recommend it to all Parents and Masters to prevent if possible their Children and Servants, fetching or using Strong Drinks; a likely pretty Lad from a good family, I know was ruin'd by living with a Man where the aforesaid Club resorted. Many will undoubtedly be curious in their Searches about the author of the above: What further I have to say is, that in a little Time, my condition is such that I must be known, unless some relief from an Uncle in a neighbouring Town (which God grant) prevent it.

BOSTON March 10. Last Thursday Night the Store of Thomas Lee, in Kilby Street, was broken open & two Pieces of Brakaded strip'd Lutestring, and about 30 Dollars in Silver stole from thence. Twenty Dollars Reward offered for the Discovery of the Thief.

We hear that the principal Inhabitants of this Town are subscribing an Agreement, that they will not purchase any Lamb this Season, they will not buy any any meat of any Butcher that shall expose Lamb for Sale; and will give all

Manner of Discountenance to such Butchers for the Future.

From a New-York Paper, The Resolution against eating Lamb before the first day of August, or employing Butchers that kill it having been so generally received in this Town, must give great satisfaction to all well-wishers to this Country, as it will both save Money, and employ our Poor, many of whom have been in starving Conditions for want of Material to keep them at work.

We hear that a Vessel arrived last Friday at Providence, in a short Passage from South-Carolina, and it is said, that the Sons of Liberty at Charlestown are in high Spirits, and determined to oppose again to the last Extremity the odious Stamp Act, should any again attempt to enforce it. ——— That there hath been a great Uneasiness amont the Seamen, who wanted their Wages paid them while their Vessels lay in the Harbour, not being able to receive Clearance; ——— but that at length, on petition of the Merchants and others, the Custom-House was opened, and Vessels cleared as usual. We also hear there had been a sharp Conflict between the Governor and the House of Common there, before the Office could be got Open.

BOSTON March 17. Between 10 & 11 o'Clock last Thursday Night came on as severe a Storm as any we have had the Winter past, Wind at N. W. and very high, which continued till Saturday Forenoon; during the Time, a great Quantity of snow fell, which render'd the Roads almost impassible, and it drifted very much, Several Chimeys were blown down, but providentially no lives were lost by their Fall, two of which were very remarkable Preservations, viz. sundry Persons who had just Breakfasted, had scarcely gone out of the Room, before the Chimney fell, and carried all before it to the Ground, and a Man at work in the Kitchen, had no sooner quited it that the Chimney fell and likewise carried all as it fell to the Ground. The Storm was so severe as to prevent the Thursday's Eastern Post crossing Charlestown Ferry before Saturday. We fear the Consequence of any Vessel that might have been on this Coast.

Messier' Printer. In a Late Act of Parliament against Mutiny and Desertion, which I find printed in the temporary laws of this Province, I observe a paragraph which empowers two or more Justices of the Peace to take up uninhabited houses, barns or other other buildings, to quarter soldiers, in those places where sufficient barracks or public houses shall not be provided. —— I wonder a little that this paragraph should be conceived in the same term, as far as the more general design of it will permit, with a paragraph of the law of this Province for quartering soldiers, pass'd in the year 1759. The concern I then had in military affairs brought the paragraph to my mind. I have since been informed, from good authority, that when the clause for quartering soldiers in private houses, which are still part of the bill in parliament, alarmed the friends to the Colonies, this clause or paragraph vas propos'd by Governor Pownall to the ministry and accepted and substitute instead of the other. I think it no more than doing Justice to this Gentleman to make it public. —— Boston March 22, 1766.

BOSTON March 24. On the 18th Instant, to the inexpressible Grief of her Father's Family, and greatly lamented by all her acquaintances, died at Barnstable, Miss Abigail Otis the youngest Daughter of the Hon. James Otis, esq; —— Her Funeral was conducted in conformity to the laudable and patriotic Example shown by the Inhabitants of the Metropolis, and now almost universally followed Tho' the Continent by retrenching the late Extravagancies in Mourning Apparel.

Capt. Javis, who was blown off this Coast last Winter arrived here Saturday last.

BOSTON March 31. Tuesday the 18th Instant, a Lad about 14 Years of Age, Son of the Late Dr. Nathaniel White of that Town, stepping out of the Way of some Oxen that were turning a Cart, fell backwards and his Head striking on a Piece of Ice, fractured his skull in such a terrible Manner, that his Brain came out, and he expired in about eight Hours after.

The Evening of the same Day one Tower going with several Persons from Nantasket to Cohasset heating himself from running the Beach, was suddenly seized with a Chillness, and expired as soon as he got to a House, which was about an Hour after.

A Girl about 4 Years old died last Saturday 7 night at the Alms-house, and was to have been buried on Monday last, but there being a Suspicion that the Child had been treated ill, a Jury of Inquest was called, and after Examination they found that the Blows and cruel Treatment the Child received from two Women who were in the same Apartment, was the Means of the Death of it. The two Women were immediately confined.

Last Thursday Night one Mrs. Banks was delivered at the Alms-house in this Town three Children, two Boys and a Girl which we hear are all like to live.

BOSTON April 3. Extract of a Letter from London January 16.

"The Manufacturers in England begin already greatly fell the effects of American resolution not to import any goods from England, several shipments, caulking, and every other branch of the shipping, down the river, not having employment even for the apprentices; and we are told that one considerable stocking manufacturer near the city has discharged no less than forty workmen within these few days.

BOSTON April 7. Yesterday Morning the Chimney of a House near the North Writing School catch'd on Fire and being a very windy Time the Sparks set Fire to several adjoining Houses, but having immediate assistance were soon extinguished. In the Afternoon the Town was again alarmed by a Fire breaking out in the Roof of the Dwelling House of the Rev. Mr. Checkley jun. nearly opposite the place where the Fire was in the Morning, which did considerable Damage to the upper Part of the House before it could be suppressed.

This Morning arrived here the Nova Scotia Packet from Halifax; also Capt. Nailer Hatch in a Sloop from the same Place. Capt. Hatch sailed from hence a few Days before the late severe Storm in which he lost his whole Deck Load, and was in imminent Danger of foundering.

Wanted Four Fishermen well skill'd in the Fishing Business, for further Particulars enquire of Henry Lloyd.

To be Sold, a Likely Negro Boy about 15 or 16 Years of Age. Enquire at the Heart & Crown.

It is Desired of the Corporation of Harvard-College, that all such Gentlemen as have generously offered to give Books to the Library of said College, would be pleased to send them to the Hon. Mr. Hubbard or the Rev. Mr. Eliot of Boston, or to the Library at Cambridge; and such Gentlemen as have Books in their Possession, belonging to the former Library, are desired to return them forthwith; the Committee for the Library being now engaged in disposing the Books for the immediate Use of the Students.

BOSTON April 14. The Select-Men have received with Pleasure the Account from Maryland, that the Repeal of the Stamp-Act was on the 8th of February Resolved by a great Majority in Parliament, and as soon as they shall receive certain Advices that an Act for the repeal had passed the usual Formalities, they will fix the Time for general Rejoicing, and give the Public timely notice thereof.

BOSTON April 14. Taken out of the shop of the subscriber, near the White Horse Tavern, South-end, last Friday, two Beaver Hatts, supposed to be stolen. Any suspicious Person offering the same for sale, it is desired they may be stopt.
———— any one who can give information, so that the Person who took them may be convicted, shall be well rewarded by Lazarus Le Barron. N. B. Hats of all Sorts made and sold at said shop.

We hear from Harwick, that a few Days Ago the Hon. Brigadier Ruggles being with a Number of Men he had employed to fell some Trees, one of the Trees falling sooner than expected struck the Brigadier before he could get out of the Way, whereby he was greatly bruis'd and had several Ribs broke, as also one of his Arms in two Places.

BOSTON April 21. Great George and the Patriot Pitt forever sing.

This is to certify all who it may concern, in Europe, Asia, Africa or America, that all Rejoicing and Exhibitions of Joy throughout this Continent on Occasion of the repeal of the Stamp-Act, be they general Illuminations, Ringing of Bells, Bonfires, Firing of Cannon, and other Fireworks, will be merely in Duty and loyalty to out most gracious Sovereign, in respect, Love and Gratitude to his wise and Patriotic Ministry, and Honor of the immortal Pitt, the Illustrious Five, and all those, and those only who are and were for repealing that detestable Act as unconstitutional, and in the highest Triumph over the contempt of an infernal, atheistical, Popish, Jacobite, and Tory Crew on boyh Sides of the Atlantic, who, by the Providence of Almighty God, are totally, and 'tis to be hoped everlastingly frustrated to the diabolical Purposes towards Great-Britain and all her Colonies.

P. S. All Printers throughout the Continent are desired to publish this Advertisement.

BOSTON April 21. For the Benefit of the Insurers. To-Morrow will be sold by Public Vendue, at the Exchange Tavern, in King Street, at one o-Clock: 70 Bolts (damaged) Duck, from No. 1 to No. 9. which may be viewed at the place of Sale.
J. Russell Auctioneer.

At Private Sale. A Strong well -built Sloop, Burthen 65 Tons, is not one Year old, extremely well sound, and prime sailor. for further particulars, Enquire of J. Russell of whom may be had inventory of her Stores. Also a Sprightly, active Negro Women about 24 Years of Age, who can do all Kind of House business and have a good Recommendation.

To-Morror Will be Sold at Public Vendue, at the Royal Exchange Tavern in King Street at one o'Clock (if not sold before at private Sale) 4 likely Young Negro Boys, two 19 Years of Age one of 15 and the other one 10 ——— All Lately from the Gold Coast. Any Person who is inclined to purchase at private Sale are desired to Apply
J. Russell Auctioneer.

BOSTON April 28. The Ship Boston Packet, John Marshal, Commander, owned by John Hancock Esq; Merchant, was the first Ship that cleared out this Port, without stamped Papers after the first of November and we hear was entered at the Custom-House in London without the least difficulty.

As some Persons may imagine that the Vessels which arrived here lately from England brought Goods for Merchants who had engaged to Countermand the Orders until the Stamp-Act was repealed. Such Persons are informed that the above Orders were sent in Captain Marshal who arrived in London the middle of February, and were not received until after the Goods now imported were engaged for, packed, and shipped.

Monday last the Freeholders & other Inhabitants of this Town of Boston, met at Feneuil-Hall when they were very well pleas'd with the Accounts which had been received from Home, in Regard, to the Progress of the Repeal of the Stamp-Act; whereupon they voted the Method to exhibit their Joy, when the Account shall arrive of the Bill for the Repeal has passed the whole Legislature.

At the said Meeting the following Vote also passed; Voted unanimously, that Magistrates of the Town, The Selectmen, Firewards, Constables and Engine-men be desired to use their utmost Endeavours, to prevent any Bonfire being made in any Part of the Town, also the throwing of Rockets, Squibs, and other Fireworks in any of the Streets in said Town, except the Time that shall be appointed for general Rejoicing; and that the Inhabitants be desired for the present to restrain their Children and Servants from going abroad on Evenings.

BOSTON April 28. On Friday last came to Town and was shipped on board Capt. Davis for England, a Ton of Pearl Ashes, made by Henry Barnes at Marlborough, a Sample of which was viewed by the dealers in this Commodity, who declared it superior to the foreign Pearl ashes usually imported here from England.

The same Night, Mr. Henry Price a young gentleman just setting out in Life as a Physician, was seized in his Bed with Apoplexy, and expired on Monday Night following.

BOSTON May 5. By His Excellency Francis Bernard, Esq; Captain General and Governor in Chief in and over his Majesty's Province of Massachusetts Bay in New-England & Vice Admiral of the same.

A PROCLAMATION

Whereas I have received advice from William Lightgow, Esq; Commander of Fort Halifax on Kennebeck River, that he hath been informed by an Indian and a Boy that they left a Chief Indian of the Norridgework Tribe named Noadgawwerremet, and his Wife, on the first Day of November last, in their Camp about fourteen Miles distant from the said Fort, on the shore of Cubbassuconte Pond, and with them twenty beaver Skins and other Furs, two Gund and two Traps with sundry utensils and Provisions: That twenty Days after they returned to the Camp which they found burnt, and that the Ruins thereof found the Bodies of the two Indians before mentioned almost burnt up; but that they found none of the Furs, Instruments or Utensils afore mentioned or even Part of the Iron work belonging to either of them, nor any other thing which they left in Camp, save a small Part of the Provisions at a little distance from it. And that the said Indians express'd a Jelousy that the other two were murdered by some English Person:

I have therefore thought fit by and with the Advice of his Majesty's Council, to issue this Proclamation, hereby calling upon all Officers, Civil and Military within this Province, and all other of his Majesty's good Subjects, to do their utmost Endeavouring to discover the Author or authors of this supposed Murders, that such atrocious Offenders, who by Act of Barbarity of this Kind expose the peace of the Government and the Lives of his Majesty's Subjects, may be brought to condign Punishment.

And I do hereby promise a Reward of One Hundred Pounds, lawful Money of the Province afore said, to any Person or Persons who shall discover the Author or authors of the said Mischief to be paid out of public Treasury upon the Conviction of any one or more of them.

I do likewise promise that any Person concerned and an Accomplice in the Crime, who shall first discover the Person or Persons who actually committed the said Murder, shall be admitted as an Evidence in Behalf of the King, be exempted from the Penalties of the Law.

Given at the Council Chambers in Boston, the 30th Day of April, 1766, in the Sixth Year of the Reign of our Sovereign Lord George the Third, by the Grace of God of Great Britain, France and Ireland, King Defender of the earth. By His Excellency's Command,   Fra. Bernard.
  A. Oliver, Sec'ry.

Thirty Dollars Reward

Whereas some evil-minded Persons on Friday Night last, broke into Trinity Church in this Town, and carried from thence the Church Bible, with other Books likewise of great Value, and threw them into a neighbouring Garden and Yard, whereby much damaged. If any Person will discover said Criminals, so that they be brought to Punishment, he shall receive a Reward of Thirty Dollars from the Wardens of said Church.
                      Rufus Green, S. Greenleaf.

Wednesday last at the Superior Court, John Ward, for attempting to ravish a Girl about 10 Years of Age, was sentenced to be set upon the Gallows for the Space of one Hour, with a Rope about his Neck and one end cast over the Gallows, to be whipped 20 Stripes upon his naked Back under the Gallows, to suffer one year imprisonment, and to pay Cost. &c.

BOSTON May 12. At the Meeting of the freeholders and other Inhabitants of this Town on Tuesday last, for the choice of Persons to represent them in general Court of Assembly for the Province the ensuing Year, &c. the Number of Votes were 746. The votes were as follows, For the Hon. James Otis, Esq; 642. Thomas Cushings, Esq; 676. Mr. Samuel Adams, 671. John Hancock, Esq; 437. John Rowe, Esq; 309. John Ruddock, Esq; 83. Whereupon the four Gentlemen first named were declared duly elected.

BOSTON May 17. A London Gazette being come to

Hand, containing the important News of the Repeal of the Stamp-Act. His Excellency summoned the Council to meet this Day, and acquaint them that he had given Orders for Firing the Guns at the Castle and the several Batteries in Boston and Charlestown, on this happy Occasion, which was very much to the satisfaction of the Council; and his Excellency also gave an invitation to the Gentlemen of the Council to drink the King's Health, on Monday Evening next, at the Province House, which the Council cheerfully accepted of. And it was Ordered that the Town-House and Province-House should be illuminated the same Evening.

At a Meeting of the Sons of Liberty held last Evening in Hanover Square, it was unanimously voted 1. That their Exhibition of Joy on the Repeal of the Stamp-Act be on the Common. 2. That the Fire-Works be play'd off from a Stage to be erected near the Work House Gate. 3. That there be an Advertisement published on Monday next, of the intended Exhibition, the place where, and the time when it will end.

BOSTON May 19. There has been a General Goal Delivery of all Debtors, this Day, by Subscription, on account of the Repeal of the stamp-Act.

BOSTON May 26. The Row of Trees opposite Mr. Paddock's Shop have of late received Damage by Persons inadvertently breaking of the limbs, of the flourishing. The Youth of both Sexes are requested, as they pass that Way not to molest them, ────── These Trees being planted at a considerable Expense, for an Ornament and Service to the Town. ────── Not one of the Trees was injured the night of General Rejoicing, but last Wednesday Night several Limbs were broken off.

BOSTON May 26. Whereas my Character has been greatly injured by several false Reports. ────── I think myself bound in justice to myself and Family, to take this Publick Method of declaring my innocence, which I hope will restore to me the Favour and good Opinion of all well-meaning and candid Men.   Samuel Summers.

Suffolk, ff, Boston May 8. 1766. Samuel

Summers of Boston, aforesaid, sailmaker personally appeared before me, and made Solemn Oath, that he never did, directly or indirectly, either by himself, or any for or under him, give any Information to any Custom House Officers, or to any Person whatsoever, relating to the concealing or running of any Goods or Merchandize whatsoever. Neither of his own Knowledge was he ever acquainted with any Person that was is call'd Informer, altho' some Time ago, some evil minded Person or Persons gave themselves the Liberty to report such Things of him greatly to his Damage, and the Hurt of his said Family. Sworn before me. John Steel Just. Peace.

BOSTON May 26. (In the Evening Post of the 13th January last, we gave an account of Capt. Morton's Meeting with a Sloop on the Coast the 26th of December, bound from Fyal to New-York, David Harrison, Master, who had then been out 65 days, and was in a most distressed condition for want of provisions, which Capt. Morton endeavoured to supply them with, that he was at very short allowance himself, but was parted from them in the night by a violent gale of wind, without being able to give them that assistance he intended. The following a late English Print is further and more particular account of the distress which the People on board the Sloop suffered, till they were taken up by a vessel bound from Virginia to London.

"On the 9th of Nov. in Lat. 39. 10. & Long. 32. he met with a heavy gale of wind, which carried away all his sails, and tore his rigging to pieces. Being in this miserable situation, he then put the ship's company to an allowance; that on the 25th day of Dec. all this stock of provisions was quite exhausted; they were then obliged to kill what living creatures they had on board, which were two pair of pigeons, a dog, and a cat, which served for that day and the following; they afterwards fed two days on barnacles, which they took from the Sloop's bottom. From the 28th of December until the 9th of Jan. they had nothing to subsist on; and being almost famished with hunger: it was resolved among the ship's crew to cast lots which one of them should be killed; they accordingly drew lots and it happen to fall on a negro man who they had on board, and he was immediately killed, whom they fed on for seven days; and from the 16th of January until the 29th, they had nothing to live on, when they resolved a 2d time to cast lots for another man to be killed, the lot fell on a foremast man, whom they allowed twenty-four hours to prepare himself for death; but on the 30th day in the morning (which was the day he was to be killed) they observed a sail at some distance; but having no canvas to spread, were unable to make towards her; but the ship observing their distress, stood for them, and hoisted out her boat and took them on board. She proved to be the Susannah of London. Capt. Thomas Evers, from Virginia, who behaved to Capt. Harrison and his distressed crew with great kindness and humanity. It must be observed, that Capt. Harrison had not the least food for forty-days, as he would rather have chose to die, than to have eaten part of the negro. One of the Ship's company died raving mad, occasioned as they imagined, by eating the negro's flesh raw. The other poor fellow whose lot it was to have died (had not providence sent Capt. Evers in their way) had been out of his senses ever since his lot was drawn.

The mate is dead since his arrival at Dartmouth, and another of them is now on the point of death. Capt. Harrison could not omit mentioning the great inhumanity of Capt. Morton, who commanded the snow from Newcastle, bound for Boston, which he fell in with the 26th of Dec. who promised to supply them with some provisions; but instead of doing so, immediately made sail again, without giving them the least morsel of any thing; and on the same day they were obliged to eat part of the cat and dog which they killed.

BOSTON May 29. The following Accident happened last Monday at Newmarket, to Lieut. Junathan Falson of that town ——— he having loaded a swivel that had lain buried 25 Years, it burst in pieces, one of which struck him in the breast and several others in one of his Legs which split his legs which split the Bone thereof to pieces on which the Surgeon thought proper to cut off above the knee.

BOSTON June 2. Extract of a Letter from Hartford May 26, 1766.

Last Tuesday was received the joyful News of the repeal of the Stamp-Act, the General Assembly then sitting, they appointed Friday last for a Day of General Rejoicing, and gave two Barrels of Powder to the Young Gentlemen of the Town, to prepare a set of Fire works; none understanding their Preparation but Mr. William Gardiner, and Col. Talcort's Son, they undertook and prepared near 500 Rockets in the Brick School-house here, in which was about 60 wt. of dry Powder, &c. The two Companies of Militia being ordered to be raised, and a Barrel of Powder given them at the School-house, the Soldiers in filling their Horns at the Door scattered much of it, which some Children around gathering and making a Train, put Fire to which run under the Door of the School-house and communicated to the Barrel of Powder within, and in an instant blew up the whole House; in the Chamber of which was Mr. Gardiner and 28 other young Gentlemen, three died in a few Hours; ―― every other much hurt, many compound Fractures: altho' 200 Men were immediately assisting, it was half an Hour before we could remove the Rubbish to get out the Distressed; Several who were outside of the House were considerably hurt. Many were so much burnt and disfigured that their Relatives did not know them. In short the scene of Joy was immediately changed to the most gloomy ever known in this Place.

We are not able to give the Names of all who were dangerously wounded. ―― It is said those who died, were one Knowles, about 26 years of age, one Lord about 12 both of Hartford, one Jones about 19 of Weathersfield. Mr. Gardiner the young Gentleman mentioned above, who served his Time here, had both his Legs broke: Dr. Ledyard both Thighs broke, James Tyler, Goldsmith his Collar bone broke, with many others to whom it will be proved mortal.

Strayed away from Boston, on the 28th ult. a red milch Cow, middling size, with good Bag. Whoever will inform the Printer, or Mr. Abijah Adams, Clerk of Farneuil-Hall Market of her, so this Owner may have her again shall be well rewarded.

BOSTON June 16. The following is a copy of a Letter from the principal Merchants in London trading to the Colonies, sent by express when the Act for repealing the Stamp-Act received the Royal Assent, which Express has not yet arrived that we have heard of.

To John Hancock Esq; and the rest of the Merchants in Boston. London March 18, 1766.

Gentle, We have now the satisfaction of informing you by Capt. Wray, sent by us Express in the Ship Dispatch, that the Bill repealing the Stamp-Act receive the Royal Assent this Day.

To enumerate the Difficulties which we have had in this Affair, would be disagreeable Talk to us; as it may seem calculated to enhance one of our Merit, at the expense of characters who we respect for their Situation, however they may have been induced to act a Part we could not approve, or thoroughly reconcile to the true Interest of the British Empire.

Nevertheless, we think ourselves entitled, from the pains we have taken to serve you to the privilege of imparting our Sentiments on your past and future Conduct, with that Freedom and Impartiality which Observation and Experience dictates.

You must know better, than to imagine that any well regulated Government will suffer Laws, enacted with a View to public Good, to be disputed by lawless Rioters, with Impunity.

There is no Government so perfect, but that thro' Misinformation, and the Frailty even the most elevated human Understanding, Mistakes, or at least the Appearance of such, may arise in the Conduct of Affairs, even the wisest Legislation ——— but, it is just, is it to be tolerated, that without Proof of Inconvenience, Tumultuous Force shall be encouraged by a Part, to fly in the Face of Power established for the good of the whole? We are persuaded, Gentlemen, that you cannot be of the Opinion, that you will exert your utmost Endeavours to cancel the Remembrance of such fresh flagrant Breaches of public Order, and manifest your Gratitude and Affection to your Mother Country, which by the repeal of the Act have given such incontestable Proof of her Moderation.

What Sentiments you ought to entertain on this Occasion, and what Conduct we would with you to observe, will sufficiently appear from our former Letter dated the 28th of February last, and sent the first Conveyance, The Moment we could inform you with any Degree of Certainty what was likely to be the fate of the Stamp-Act.

We shall only observe that under Providence, you are indebted for this Event to the Clemency and Paternal Regard of his Majesty for the Happiness of his Subjects, to the public Spirit, Abilities and Firmness of the present Administration; and to the Humanity, Prudence, and Patriotism of the Generality of those who compose the Legislature and the most considerable Persons of every Rank in this Kingdom.

We hope Gentlemen that this Conduct in the British Legislatures provoke by the most irritable Measures on your side, will forever be a Lesson to your Posterity; and it is the most convincing Proof, that if by any means, Laws are or should be, enacted detrimental or seemingly oppressive to any part of the British Subjects; the British Legislature will at all Times, with the utmost Tenderness consider every Grievance & redress then the moment they are known.

We cannot but acquaint you, that had the Americans endeavoured to acquiesce with the Law, and dutifully represent the Hardships as they arose, your Relief would have been more speedy, and we should have avoided many Difficulties as well as not a few unanswerable mortifying Reproaches on our Account.

Such however is the Patriotism and Magnanimity of those Powers, that, unaffected, by the conduct of many on our Side of the Water, and the Strenuous Efforts of an Opposition here to carry Measures of Lenity and Indulgence towards

America; they are endeavouring to establish its Commerce in particular, as well as that of the British Empire in general, upon the most solid Foundation, & the most extensive Utility.

On Your Part we hope that nothing will be wanting to obliterate the Remembrance of what is passed, by setting the Example yourselves, and promoting the like Sentiment in others; of a dutiful Attachment in your Sovereign and the Interests of your Mother Country, a just Submission to the Law and respect for the Legislature; for in this you are most effectually promoting your own Happiness and Security.

By this Conduct like this, Gentlemen you will both encourage and unable us to serve you with Zeal on future Emergencies, should any such arise; and to support our mutual Interests; the Interest of the Colonies, which are inseparable from the common Interests of Great Britain with Efficacy and Success.

We are Gentlemen, Your assured Friends and very humble Servants.
[Signed by 55 of the principal Merchants trading to North-America]

BOSTON June 16. On Wednesday last the Honorable House of Representatives voted that Galleries be fixed, to accommodate any Gentlemen that may be desirous of hearing the debate in the assembly, and the next morning the Gallery at the West End of the Representatives Room was opened, and the following order passed the house, viz. That no Person admitted to a seat in the Gallery without applying to and introduced by a Member of this House.

Monday Evening last one of the Town Fishing Schooners took up a canoe in Broad-Sound, and in it suppos'd some Person that had been in it, was drowned, there having been violent Gusts of Wind that Afternoon: ——— The Canoe is 18 feet in length, has but one Row-lock; there were two Fishing Lines over the Sides, the Lead on one mark'd C. the other mark'd S. a Hat bound with Ferret was in the Canoe.

Yesterday Afternoon about 7 o'Clock Fire broke out in a large Barn belonging to Dr. Clark at the North part of the Town, which consumed the same.

BOSTON June 23. Last Saturday Afternoon Capt. Dunn came to Town from Cape Ann, where he arrived in a Fishing Schooner, from the Isle of Sables, and informs, that he was passenger on board Capt. Qwin, in a large Ship between 4 & 500 Tons Burthen, richly laden, bound from Bristol to this Place, that on the 24th of May, at Nine o'Clock at Night, in thick Weather, they unfortunately ran ashore on the S.E. Part of the Island, about a Mile from the Bar, where they remained till the next Morning, when the Vessel went to Pieces, and 14 of the People unhappily perished; others, 12 in Number, with great Difficulty got safe ashore upon the Masts and other parts of the Wreck; ——— Capt. Dunn remained on the Island 11 Days after the Disaster, during which Time but very little of the Cargo came ashore; he thinks some of the Letters were taken up which, with what other things might be saved, Capt. Qwin intended to bring with him in Capt. Beal, who was there in a Schooner belonging to this Place: Among those unhappy Persons who were drowned by the Melancholy Accident, was the Mate Benjamin Blackman of this Town, Capt. Cahoun, a Passenger, a Boy of Capt. Dunn's and a Nephew of Capt. Qwin's also a Woman, wife of one of the Seamen. The Ship was about 60 Yards from the Shore she went to Pieces.

Capt. Dunn further informs, that a Schooner had been cast away on the Island some Time before, and that the Bodies of two of the Men, supposed to have belonged to her, were found dead on the beach, which by their dress appeared to be Fishermen.

We hear that several Merchants in this Town will be great Sufferers by the loss of the above Ship, their Interest on board not being insured.

BOSTON June 30. Monday last sailed for London the Ship Lion Capt. Binney on whom went Passengers, seven Indians of the Mohawk Tribe, so called, four Men & three Women, with complaints, it is said, that Part of their Land were taken possession of by Persons belonging to New-York Government.

BOSTON July 7. To be let, and enter'd upon this 25th of September next in good tenateable Repair, the Five Water Grist Mills, at the North Part of the Town of Boston with stabling for the Horses, Stores for Grain &c. ——— Any Persons inclined to hire may apply to William Hunt, in Hanover-Street, whom the Proprietors have empowered to let the same.

We hear from Hanover that the 16th Ult. as Mr. Studly and his Son were returning from his Wood Lot with a Cart of Wood, a Thunder Storm came on, and his Son taking a Tree for Shelter, was struck instantly Dead by a Flash if Lightning.

BOSTON July 14. Wednesday an Express came to Town from the Westward by whom we have the following Particulars: That the Inhabitants of a Place called Nobletown and Spencer-Town, lying West of Sheffield, Great-Barrington, and Stockbridge, who had purchased of the Stockbridge Indians the Lands they now possess, by virtue of an Order of the General Court of this Province, and settled about 200 Families: ——— That John Van Ranslear, Esq; pretending a right to said Lands, has treated the Inhabitants very cruelly, because they would not submit to him as Tenants, he claiming a Right to said Land by Virtue of a Patent from the Government of New-York, ——— that Ranslear some Years ago raised a Number of Men and came upon the poor People, and pulled down their Houses kill'd some People, imprisoned others, and have been constantly vexing and injuring the People: ——— That on the 26th of last Month said Ranslear came down with between 2 and 300 Men, all armed with Guns, Pistols and Swords; that upon Intelligence that 500 Men armed were coming against them, about 40 or 50 of the Inhabitants went out unarmed, except with sticks, and proceeded to a Fence between them and the Assailants, in order to Compromise the Matter between them: That the Assailants, came up to the Fence, and Hermanus Schuyler the Sheriff of the County of Albany fired a Pistol down upon them, and three others fired their Guns over them.

The Inhabitants there upon desired to talk with them, and they would not hearken; but the Sheriff it is said by some who knew him, ordered the Men to fire and killed one of their own Men, who had got over the Fence, and one of the Inhabitants likewise within the Fence ——— Upon this the Inhabitants unarmed as afore said retreated most of them into the Woods, but 12 betook themselves to the House from whence they set out, and there defended themselves with 6 Small-Arms & some ammunition that were therein; Two Parties here fired upon each other, the Assailants killed one Man in the House, and the Inhabitants wounded several of them, whom the rest carried off and retreated, to the number of 7, none whom by the last Account were dead ——— That the Sheriff shewed no Papers nor attempted to execute any Warrant and the Inhabitants never offered any Provocation at the Fence, excepting their continuing there, not had any one of them a Gun, Pistol or Sword, till they retreated to the House. At the Action at the Fence one of the Inhabitants had a Leg broke, whereupon the Assailants attempted to seize him and carry him off: he therefore begged they would consider the Misery he was in declaring he had rather die than be carried off, whereupon one of the Assailants said, you shall die then, and discharging his Pistol upon him, as he lay on the Ground, shot him through the Body, as the wounded Man told the Informant; That the said wounded Man was alive when he left him, but not like to continue long. The Affray happened about 16 Miles distant from Hudson's River. It is feared the Dutch will pursue these poor People for thus defending themselves, as Murderers; and keep them in great Consternation.

The New-York Account is as Follows, Viz. Extract of a Letter from Claverack, (near Albany) June 27.

"For some Months past, a Mob has frequently assembled and ranged the Eastern Part of the Manor of Renselear ——— Last Week they appeared at Mr. Livingston's, with some Proposal to him, but he being from home, they return'd to Mr. Renselear's Son's about ten Miles from Claverack, where not finding him at home they used some insulting Words, and left a Message for Mr. Renselear, that if he did not meet them next Day at the Rendezvous they would come to him. On the 26th, the Sheriff of Albany, with 150 Men under his Command, went to disperse the rioters who were assembled, it is supposed, to the Number of 60, in a House on the Manor. On the Sheriff's advancing to the House they fired upon him, and shot off his Hat and Wig, but he escaped unhurt. Many Shots were exchanged on both Sides —— Of the Militia one Man Mr. Conolius Tenbrook, of Claverack was killed, and seven wounded; —— of the Rioters, three were killed, (two of whom were Ringleaders) and many wounded, among whom was Capt. Noble (one of the chief instigators) in the back. The Rioters retreated to Capt. Noble's House, where they form'd a Breast Work and did not quit the House till the Sheriff's Party left the Place. Col. Reneselear's Horse was killed under him. He afterwards went to Poughkeepsie to get Assistance from the Regulars to disperse the whole; but the regulars were gone to the Pendergast House on the Philips's Patent."

We hear from Fredricksburg, in Dutchess County, that on Saturday last, as a Party of the Regulars, stationed there, under the Command of Major Brown, were crossing a Bridge, they were met by about 30 of the Rioters who were going to Join Pendergast, their Chief's Party —— a Skirmish ensued wherein two Regulars were wounded, and it is supposed a much greater Number of the Rioters, who generally dismounted, and fled to the Cornfields and Bushes leaving, some of their Horses and Guns, which were taken, and one Prisoner; several more were taken that night. The next Evening they sent a Flag of Truce with 50 followers, who were all lodged in the Meeting-House, and the next Day several more Parties came in. Pendergast's Wife was gone to persuade her Husband to accept of the Governor's Mercy, as were many more Wives of the Rioters. We hear of no Lives lost. —— It was reported that 300 of the Rioters lodged at a Quaker Hall, intended to attack the Regulars on the 30th ult. but the Report in uncertain.

BOSTON July 21. Last Friday Afternoon a Lad about 6 Years old, Son of Thomas Clarke, Goldsmith, fell from a Wharf at the South Part of this Town, and no Assistance being near, he was unfortunately Drowned. His Body was soon after taken out and some signs of life appearing, Methods were used for his Recovery but without effect.

The same Afternoon two Children being in great Danger of Drowning, near Wind-Mill Point, Mr. David Wheeler, Blacksmith in hastily jumping into a boat, in order to go to their Relief, unfortunately broke one of his Legs in two Places. The Children were taken up by some other Persons who came to their Assistance.

We hear between Kenderhook and Albany, there has lately been discovered a most valuable Spring of Water issuing out of a Rock, of the Hot Kind, the Bathing with which, and drinking the same has already cured many Disorders, and that great Numbers of People afflicted with different calamities resort thither daily.

Lost out of a Chaise, last Wednesday Week, between the Orange Three and the Prison, a crab-Tree Walking Stick, with a neat Carved Head.—— Whoever took up the same and will return it to the Printer shall be satisfied for their Trouble.

BOSTON July 28. The Workmen have begun to dismantle the Goal, in order to erect a more safe and commodious one in its Room.

On Wednesday last David Wentwort, a young man belonging to Stoughton, was found dead on the Road to Milton: It is Supposed he fell from a Cart that he was driving, and one of the Wheels going over his Neck, killed him instantly. The repeated Casualties of this kind, should make the Drivers more careful than they generally are.

Last Week as some Boys were sporting in the Water a Lad who was on Shore took a stone and jerking it among them, struck a Boy about eight Years of Age, in the Neck, which cut his Vein, whereby he bled to such a manner that he died soon after. —— A mischievous and Dangerous Practice Boys have of pelting each other with stones, which ought often to be cautioned against.

Wednesday a Child about 5 Years old was run over by a Wheel of a Cart at the North End, and one of his Legs broke.

The same Afternoon a Child about 3 Years old fell out of a Chamber Window at the upper End of Long Lane, and broke its Thigh in two Places.

And Yesterday Afternoon a Negro Fellow belonging to Capt. Doyle of this Town, having been on board a Brig lying in the Harbour, in getting out of her into a boat, he accidentally fell overboard and was drowned.

BOSTON Aug. 4. Ran Away from the Subscriber, on the 28th Instant, Abner Wade; an indented Servant, 19 years of Age, about 5 Feet 3 Inches high, light Complexion, brown Hair tied behind, looks very young for a Person his Age, by Occupation a Taylor; Had on when he went away a blue Coat with brass Buttons, light coloured Waistcoat, a pair of scarlet knit Breeches, he also took with him a light coloured Broad cloth Coat and Jacket, dark coloured Cotton velvet Breeches, blue Great Coat, a Chest with a Number of other Articles.

It is supposed he is gone or going to Kenne-Beck-River, as his Parents live near that Place. Whoever takes up said Run-away and return him to the Subscriber, his Master, shall have Twenty Dollars Reward, and all necessary Charges paid. Boston July 30, 1766.   John Wheatley.

All Masters of Vessels and others, are hereby cautioned against concealing, harbouring or carrying off said Servant, as they would avoid the utmost Rigour of the Law.

BOSTON Aug. 11. Since our last another Express has come to Town from the Westward with a Petition to his Excellency the Governor and Council, for a Number of the Inhabitants of Nobletown, who have been drove from their Settlement there; complaining of the cruel Treatment they have again lately met with from the Sheriff of Albany and others, and begging the Interposition of this Province, under whose encouragement they first settled there. ———
The Substance of their Complaint we have in the

following Letter from Egremont, to which Place many of the Inhabitants were obliged to flee for Protection &c.

Extract of a letter from Egremont in this Province, dated July 30, 1766.

"On Saturday the 26th of July Instant, Herman Schyler, Sheriff of the County of Albany, and Robert Van Ranslear, of Cleverack, attended with about 250 of General Gage's Light Infintry armd with Guns, Swords, Pistols and Field Pieces and three Swivels, came in a hostile Manner to Nobletown, to the House of Andrew Stalker, which they broke down; from thence they proceeded to the House of William Bever, broke down his House and robb'd him of 3 Guns and sundry other Goods and Tools, from thence they came to the House of Everet Comielkbaker, where they pitched their Camp; from thence said Schyler and others, on Sabbath Day the 27th, travelled 3 Miles to the House of Joseph Clarke and broke it open and robb'd him of all his Books, Arms, Cloaths, Provisions, and every Thing they could lay their Hands on, from thence they went to the House of Robert Mecher, and broke down the House, flung out and destroyed and carry'd away every thing that was therein; from thence they returned to their Camp; from whence in the Afternoon the said Schyler and others came to the House of Robert Noble, which House and Furniture they entirely destroyed, and set Fire to the Barn &c. which were consumed; from thence they proceeded to the House of said Clarke and Mercher, and carried off all they left in the Morning, then returning to Camp they took as Prisoner Thomas Millard, killing and destroying Swine, Fowls, &c. as they returned: On Monday the 28th the said Schyler and others came to the House of Robert Warren, which they broke open and plundered and rifled of every thing therein, killed 4 Sheep, 3 Hogs, 1 Calf and abused the Children, &c. thence they proceeded to the House of William Kellog and a Man who was in the House upon their Approach fled, but was pursued and had a Gun fixed on him, but he escaped; they then returned to the House which they robb'd of every thing, and much abused a Child there, killed 2 Hogs, ten Geese, &c. Thence said Schyler and others came to the House of Ed. Smith of Egemont, rifled it of every Thing valuable and light to carry away, and thence returned to Camp; and on Tuesday they drew off, threatening they would come again in a few Days and lay the whole Town in Rubbish, plant 3 Forts there, and tarry to keep off the Inhabitants. ——— This the Inhabitants of Nobletown drove away to their Neighbouring Towns, as Sheep by Wolves, to Egremont, Sheffield, and Barrington, with their Wives and Families, and are in the most distressed Circumstances, having nothing to support them but the Charity of the People."

BOSTON Aug. 11. The Granada Frigate Capt. Whitwood, who arrived last Week at Newburry-Port from Gibraltar, on the 12th of July spoke the Peggy Sloop, John Tillock, Master, Lat. 31. 30. Long. 66. 12. W. bound from Maryland to the River Mississippi, with 225 French Refugees, all well on Board.

BOSTON Aug. 18. Last Thursday Morning Mr. David Wheeler's Leg, which sometime since was broke, as been mentioned, was taken off to prevent the bad Effects of a Mortification, which had begun.

We hear from Falmouth, Casco Bay, that the Officers of his Majesty's Customs there have seized several Hogsheads of Sugar, &c. for illegal Importation, a Number of Persons in the Evening muster'd in a riotous Manner, insulted the Officers and rescued the Goods out of their Hands.

We hear from Lancaster, that on Monday last a Son of the Rev. Mr. Mellens, about 3 Years old, accidentally fell into a Tub of boiling Water, and was scaled in such a Manner that the Child died in a few Hours.

Last a Whaling Sloop arrived here from the Streight of Belleisle, by whom we learn, that there has been small success in the Fisheries this Season, not above 17 Whales having been caught among the many Vessels which were fitted out for the Purpose: ——— We also learn, that the Cod Fishery on the Labrador Coast has been greatly interrupted and broke up by one of his Majesty's Frigates, who pressed one Man out of each Vessel, and obliged them all to leave the Coast, and of others destroying the small quantity of Fish they had already catch'd, and beating and abusing some of the Skippers for demanding the Reason of the Treatment towards them, from whom they rather expected Encouragement and Protection.

"Tis said the Captain of the Frigate acted in Consequence of Orders from the Commanding Officer of that Station; and that one of his Orders was "Not to suffer any American Vessels to Fish for any other than Whales, in any of the Ports or Coasts of Newfoundland lying between Point Riche and Cape Bonavista."

BOSTON Aug. 25. To the Printer. Sir, The Account given of the last Boston Paper, of the Riot and Robberies committed in the Province of Massachusetts-Bay, by Herman Schyler, and Robert Van Ranslear, assisted by a Number of the Kings Troops, is very alarming. At it cannot be supposed that General Gage would lend the Force under his Command to such daring and abandoned Persons, to assist them in driving away his Majesty's peaceable Subjects from Habitations in destroying Houses, in robbing and Thieving; so it cannot be doubted but he will deliver upon the Offerders, upon the first Requirement of Civil Authority.

There are extraordinary Forces acting in the Colony of New-York. A Number of Men Claim to hold vast Tracts of Land there, under Title said to be good for nothing. There are great Number of quiet and industrious Persons on those Lands, who were not willing to submit to the violent Measures of the Claimants. Compulsory Means were the Consequence, which the interest of the Claimants, who have great influence with the Legislature and Executive Powers, easily brought about.

The Army Truly, was used on the Occasion, and after most scandalous treatment of these innocent People to screen their own Guilt, and to disguise the whole Matter, they are, with the Assistance of the Red-Coats, trying these

Inhabitants for High treason, as if defending their Persons and Properties against the Ravages and Plundering of a few Persons, who have unjustly attempted to appropriate to themselves those Lands, and levying War against the King. These are Mighty Men indeed. They are taking the same Steps, which have ever been taken to enslave a Country. If they can have military aid in support of their Claims and Intentions, farewell Liberty and Property! —— So saith my Spirit.

BOSTON Sept. 8. Since our last Accounts has been received of the violent proceedings of Ranslear's Party at Nobletown, &c. and of the distressed Condition of the Inhabitants were in. On Saturday the 19th of August a Party took Possession of the House of one Isaac Spoor, and all that was therein, and informed said Spoor that the House was in New-York Government. This House stands on a Grant of Land made by this Province, and had been a licensed House for a Tavern for many Years by our Courts; it stands about 4 Miles West of Great Barrington Meeting House but within the District of Egremont, near the East Part, and but a small distance from the West line of Great Barrington, and between two or three Miles East of the line that was formerly run for a twenty miles from the Hudson's River.

This Tavern the Party made their Head Quarters; a Deputy Sheriff with one or two Persons were admitted to pass the Guard in the Evening, who, having obtained Leave from the Commanding Officer, levied a Warrant of Robert Ranslear, upon this there was a terrible Bluster, the Soldiers under Arms, all their Bayonets fixed, and confined the Sheriff, as also the Justice who went to endeavour to settle the Matters, till almost Day break: This alarmed the whole Country; and in the Morning a great number of the People, with about 40 Stockbridge Indians, collected together to give the Party a Battle, but meeting with the Gentlemen who had been detained, it was happily prevented. The Regulars withdrew in the Morning, & the People returned Home.

We are further informed, that the Party who had Committed Hostilities at Egremont, had withdrew beyond the twenty Mile Line from the Hudson's River, and returned some of the Cattle they had taken from the People, and promised to make Restitutions for all Damages they had done to Egremont; it is added, they are leaving Nobletown; ——— as to the Crops of the poor people that belonged there they are mostly destroyed already.

BOSTON Sept. 15. This is to forewarn all Persons not to Trust Elizabeth Shaw, the Servant of me the Subscriber; for I declare that I will not pay one farthing that she shall contract from the Date hereof Boston Sept. 11, 1766.

Joseph Martin.

A likely Negro Girl about 19 Years of Age, that can do most sorts of House Work, fit for Town or Country, to be Sold for no fault. Inquire of the Printer.

Last Thursday Morning a sorrowful Accident happened to one Roach, a Carpenter, by means of a carelessness too common of that Occupation, a Scaffold on the Top of a House the Corner of Queen-Street, which he was shingling, being but slightly nailed, gave way, whereby he fell into the Street, and his Head coming on a Stone, fractured his Skull in such a terrible Manner, that he survived but two or three Hours and then expired.

BOSTON Sept. 29. We hear from Brookline, that a melancholy Affair lately happened in the Family of Capt. Crafts of that Town. Three of his Children, one of the Age of 6 Years going to School, gathered some Seeds out of a prickly Pod that grows upon Henbane, of which one of them eat a great Quantity and poisoned himself to a Degree that he died in a short Time after in great Agonies. Another much poison'd and in great Distress, but is likely to recover; the Third, and youngest, eating but a small portion was not so much affected. This Henbane is not what generally bears that Name: it grows in the High-way and is commonly known by the Name of Devil's-Weed; it has wide spread Stalk and a broad Leaf, bears a large round prickly Pod and is of a bad Smell; when the Pod opens, and the seeds are like small Coffee.

Monday last some Children near the Mill-pond, one of them, a Boy of about 6 Years of Age fell in; It was several Minutes before Help could be obtained, he was taken up from the Bottom as dead, but after rolling him on a Barrel and rubbing him well with Salt, then covering him with Blankets before a good Fire, recovered so far as to be blooded, and a potion of Physic administered to him, and is likely to do well.

We hear from Waymouth, that last Week two Brothers belonging to that Place, having some dispute, one of them being much provoked by the other, struck him a blow across the Face with his Hand, which knocked him backwards, 'tis said he died immediately.

Public Notice is hereby given, That a Concert of Musick is intended to be open'd on Tuesday the 7th Day of October next, to be continued every Tuesday Evening for Eight Months. Any inclined to be Subscribers may know the Terms by applying to Stephen Debloes, at the Concert-Hall in Queen-Street.

Next Thursday will be published, and sold at the Heart & Crown in Cornhill, The Examination of Benjamin Franklin, Esq; before an August Assembly, relating to the Repeal of the Stamp-Act, &c.

BOSTON Sept. 29. Wanted Scandal-Mongers of all kinds to abuse the New Administration. Any Gentheman well versed in Lying, perverting of meaning, making false reports, and raising doubts will be taken into full work for the ensuing year. They must be equally able to white-wash the blackest characters out of power, and to black-ball the fairest characters in power, They must have no scruples of conscience about setting the nation together by the ears, Persons who have the fear of the pillary before their eyes, or who do not hold the laws of their country at defiance, will not be treated with.

For further particulars, enquire of Mr. Mac Trickman, at the Scotch Arms, in Knave Acres; or of little Vamp, Bookseller, at his Scandal warehouse.

BOSTON Oct. 6. A Number of Vessels are arrived from their Whaling Voyages, which in general has not been very successful. One of them viz. Capt. Clark on Thursday Morning the 25th ult. discovered a Spermaceti Whale, near George's Banks, mann'd his Boat, and gave chace to her, and she coming up with her Jaws against the Bow of the Boat struck it with such violence that it threw a Son of the Captain's (who was forward ready with his Lance) a considerable height from the Boat, and when he fell the whale turned with his devouring Jaws opened, and caught him; he was heard to scream when she closed her Jaws and part of his Body was seen out of the Mouth, when she turned and went off.

BOSTON Oct. 13. Last Monday Night was committed to Goal, for Stabbing Mr. Isaac Townsend Man of the Town Watch a certain William Beach, (a Scotchman) who, 'tis said, about 4 Years ago received his Majesty's Pardon for the Murder of a man at Halifax. Mr. Townsend's Wound being only a Flesh one, 'tis said he will soon recover.

Fencing and Dancing Thought in a genteel expeditious and reasonable Manner, by William Pope who lately arrived in this City from the West-Indies: Any Gentlemen or Ladies inclineable to employ him, may be waited upon at the Houses of Lodgings, by sending a Line directed to him at Capt. Richard Trype's in Ann Street, near the Draw Bridge.

N. B. He will attend on a Number of Gentlemen or Ladies, at any Boarding School or Academy within Ten or 15 Miles of the Town, by directing as above.

BOSTON Oct. 13. Last Monday Night, a small coasting Vessel belonging to Piscatagua, John Hooker, Master, going round from this Place, loaded with English Goods, &c. was unfortunately cast away off Cape Ann Harbour, where we hear she is now lies in a miserable condition almost full of Water.

BOSTON Oct. 20. We hear from Stoughton, that on Monday the 6th a Barn almost full of Hay and Grain was struck with the Lightning, and soon consumed by the Fire, notwithstanding the Efforts of the People to extinguish it. The Owner and his Son was in the Barn at the Time when it was struck, and providentially were so little hurt that they got out onto the Yard before the Fire reached them.

We hear that a few Days ago a Person had both his Eyes put out by pouring some cold Lyes into a Kettle, to prevent the hot Lye from flowing over when boiling to make Pot-Ash.

We also hear that a Person in a Neighbouring Town, accidentally step'd one of his Legs into a Kettle of hot Lye that was fluxing to make Pot-Ash, which in an Instant burnt off his foot.

Last Sunday Morning, Mr. Benjamin Morse of Southboro was found dead in the Through of a Horse's Shed at Little Cambridge. ——— As he had a load with him, and coming to Market, tis tho't he lay down the preceding Night, in order to rest himself, and died in his Sleep. ——— The Jury of Inquest having sat on the Body, bro't in their verdict, Natural Death. 'Tis said he left a Widow and six Children.

BOSTON Oct. 27. Capt. Watts who arrived here last Wednesday from Newfoundland, on the 19th Instant in Lat. 43. 15. North and Long. 67. 20. W. Spoke the Brig Greyhound from Barbadoes bound to Portsmouth, out 28 Days, the People inform him, that on the 5th about 5 in the morning the Vessel was struck with Lightning, every Man on board knocked and stunned, all recovered again but one Man on board named William Molton Belonging to Philadelphia, who was killed, and one other wounded: The Mainmast was split from the Top to the Step, also both the Pumps; the lower Deck and part of the upper Deck was blown up, and the whole Vessel was full of Smoak and Sulphur for an Hour; the Lightning likewise spoil'd both their Compasses, and scorch'd the Cards so much that Capt. Watts was obliged to supply them with one. They had met with a hard Gale which split their Foresail in Two.

One Night last Week a Gentleman at South Kingston was robbed of 200 Dollars, in the following manner: The Money was in the Saddle Bags on his Horse, which he left at the Door of the Tavern and went into the House, where he staid a few Minutes; during which time, his Bags were cut open, anf the Money taken away. We hear he has detected the Thieves, & recovered most of the Money.

BOSTON Oct. 27. The Subscribers, Treasurer of Harvard College, Hereby notify Persons indebted to the College, either on Bond, Mortgage, Note of Hand, or otherways, and are deligent in their Interests that he shall (according to Order, and without Respect or Persons) put every such Obligation in suit next January Court; which should any oblige him to do, they must blame themselves therefor, and not him. Boston Oct. 16, 1766.   T. Hubbard.

N. B. The longest time allowed for the payment of Interest is 20 Days after it becomes due.

BOSTON Nov. 3. We hear from Mr. Paine who keeps the North Mills having had Suspicion of his Corn & Meal being stole from Time to Time, resolved one Night last Week to watch for the Thief, early on the Morning a Rat above 5 Feet in height came and took a two bushel bag full of Corn on his Shoulders and was carrying it off, when Mr. Paine discovered himself and rescued the Bag from him without any great struggling ——— Inserting the above may prevent such mischievous Vermine attempting to enter either the Mills or any other Places.

Last Friday a Man Travelling on Foot to Connecticut, with a Pack at his Back, was overtaken at Attlebourough by another Foot Traveler in Sailor's Habit, who, when they got to the parting Road at the Entrance of Seekonk Plain, demanded of him his Bundle, which the other not being willing to part with, a scuffle ensued, in which he got the better of the Robber, whom he left, after giving him a severe Drubbing, and proceeded on his way to Patuxet, where he informed some People of the Affair, who directly went in pursuit of the Fellow and apprehended him at Rehoboth, where he was carried before a Justice, and sentenced to receive 30 Lashes, which was immediately put in Execution; and 'tis said were well laid on, with good intention to deter him from any attempt of the like kind in the Future.

Drifted from the Snow Industry, John Kent, Master, Lying at Cape Ann, on Monday Night the 20th Instant, a Moses Boat, about 19 Feet, almost new. Whoever shall take up said Boat and return her to the Master of said Snow, or Isaac Smith of Boston, shall be paid for their Troubles.

BOSTON Nov. 3. On Tuesday night between 10 and 12 o'clock, a number of Soldiers with bayonettes went to several houses in the fields, where they were very noisy and abusive, to the great disturbance and terror of the inhabitants. This was occasioned, it is said, by the treatment, which some of the soldiers had received the night before, at some of the infamous houses, which to the great scandal of our wholesome laws, are suffered to exist as so many receptacles for loose and disorderly people.

On Saturday Night last, the Centry on his post near the Victualing Office, was knock'd down and had his skull fractured in such a manner, that it is doubted whether he can recover, It is not certainly known who was the person guilty of this cruel Action.

BOSTON Nov. 10. To be Sold, just Imported, a Stout able Negro Fellow, about 25 Years old: also a likely Negro Boy about 9 Years old; likewise a parcel of good Muscovado Sugar at Craft's Wharf. ——— Enquire of the Printer, or Daniel Parker, Goldsmith, near the conduit, where may be had a variety of Tools and necessaries for the Goldsmith, Jewellers and Watchmakers use, cheap for Cash.

BOSTON Nov. 17. In the House of Representatives, Nov. 13, 1766.

Resolved, that Mr. Speaker, Mr. Otis, Mr. Hancock, Capt. Sheaffe, Mr. Adams, Mr. Dexter, Col. Brown, Mr. Hall, & Mr. Bowman, be a Committee, in the Recess of the Court, to consider the Difficulties the Trade of this Province labors under, write to the Agent as they shall Judge necessary thereupon and Report.

The above Committee will meet at the Representatives room on Thursday next at 5 o'Clock, P. M. of which Notice is given that Merchants & others inclined may attend.

Last Monday the Body of a Woman named Blakey was found floating in the Channel opposite the North Part of Town: 'Tis said she was seen in the Street about 4 o'Clock that Morning almost naked, but no Person mistrusted her design she was suffered to pass unoticed. It is apprehended that the long absence of her Husband, and the care of Five Children, for the support of whom she has at times expressed the greatest anxiety, seeming somewhat destitute of means, threw her in a delirium, which ended in this rash Action.

BOSTON Nov. 20. Several large Flocks of wild Geese being on their Flight for a warmer Climate were so overborne by the weight of Ice and Snow, which congeal'd on their Wings, that divers of them were shot at and killed from the Wharves, and from on board the shipping in the Harbour.

BOSTON Nov. 24. Wednesday last a white Lad, named M'Clarey, and a Negro Boy were pelting at Snowballs, the latter in return threw a large brick bat, which striking M'Clarey on the Head, fractured his skull in such a manner, as that he now lies in a very dangerous State.

An Act of Parliament prohibiting the Exploration of any kind of Goods from America to Ireland, or any other place to the Northward of Cape Pinisterre, except to Great Britain takes Place the First Day of January next.

BOSTON Nov. 24. To the Printer. It is proper the Guardian of the people should know that there has certainly been Scene set on Foot in this Province, by designing and selfish Men, to raise a Revenue out of Duties on Trade, in order to make a military and civil Establishment in this Colony, as in Ireland. ——— A Trojan-Horse, by which the worst of Evil to both Contries ——— And That some Gentlemen, particularly a late Judge, has gone Home to procure a Slice of 300 Pounds Sterling out of it. ——— If this vigilant Assembly should meet and rise without instructing their Agents on this Head as the Parliament sits for Business in December, such a Delay may be attended with fatal consequences, ——— It is easier to prevent, than to remove Evil.

BOSTON Nov. 24. Stray'd or stolen from Benjamin Dolbeare's Stable in Boston, the 21st Intant a Mare almost Black, 13 Hands and a half High, with a whip slip down her Face, and one white hind Foot, a natural Pacer. Whoever will bring her to said Dolbeare's shall be well rewarded for taking her up.

Strayed or Stolen last Monday Night from a Pasture near the Common in Boston a Bay Horse, about 10 years old, his Mein & Tail black, and both cut, Trots all, about 14 Hands and a half High, whoever takes up said Horse, and brings him to the Subscriber, shall have two Dollars, Rewars, and all necessary charges paid.

N. B. If the Horse was stolen and the thief apprehended and brought to Justice, a Reward of Five Dollars will be given, and all necessary charges paid by   Nathanial Green.

BOSTON Dec. 8. Yesterday Morning between 3 and 4 o'Clock a Fire broke out in a Building near the Rev. Mr. Checkley's Meeting, at the South Part of Town, improved by Mr. Snow for the making of Pott-Ash, which had got to such a head before it was discovered that the whole Building was consumed before it could be extinguished: a Horse in a Shed adjoining was burnt to death.

BOSTON Dec 15. On Friday last Mr. Robert Waterman of Cambridge Carpenter, being an evidence at the Court of Charlestown in some Affair, just as he had finished his Deposition, bowed his Head to the Court, as it was tho't in order to retire, but instantly fell down in a fit, expired the next Sunday Morning. He was a young Man about 24 Years of Age, and sustained a good Character: Formerly belonging to Hingham.

The Select-Men acquaint the Inhabitants, That upon Application made to them, they have given orders to the several Watchmen of the Town to take up all such Negro, Indians and Molatto Slaves, as may be absent from their Master's Houses, and walking in the Streets after nine O'Clock at Night, unless they are carrying Lanthorns with Lite Candles, and can give good and satisfactory Accounts of their Business: that such Offenders may be proceeded with acording to Law.

BOSTON Dec. 22. Monday last arrived Capt. Valentine from Serrinam, on his Passage a young Man and a Cooper having had some Differences, they got to Blows; about two Hours after which the former died: Upon the arrival of the Vessel here the Cooper voluntarily surrendered himself into the Hands of Justice.

Boston Dec. 29. Two Guineas Reward, Deserted from the Ship Jean, John Ritchie, Master, a Seaman named William Thompson, about 24 Years of Age, born Scotland, wears his own black Hair, and much pitted with the small Pox. ——— Whoever will take up the said Deserter, and bring him on Board the Ship Jean, at Ritchie's Wharf, shall have two Guineas Reward, and all necessary Charges by   John Ritchie.

A Quantity of Second hand Rigging to be sold by said Ritchie.

The Treasurer of the County of Suffolk hereby notices the several Constables and Collectors of Taxes for the said County, that there are not only common Charges of the County to be Paid, but the additional Expence of Building a New Goal, and therefore it is expected, that those in a particular Manner, who have been long in arrears, as well as others, make their Payments to him with all possible Speed.

BOSTON Dec. 29. The new Stone Goal in this Town not being finished, Joseph Andrew who was committed for murder of the Capt. of the Sloop Polly, and several others onboard, in the West-Indies, was removed to the Goal in Charlestown; and on Wednesday last he made an attempt to kill himself by cutting his Throat, but his knife being very small he did not fully accomplish his design; and the Wound was dressed, and care taken to prevent any further attempt.

                    Cox and Berry
Just arrived from London, in the John Galley, Capt. Blake, Beg leave to acquaint the Public, That they have just opened at the Store of the late Messirs, Green & Walker, opposite the Rev. Mr. Cooper's Meeting-House, an assortment of

Plate, Jewellry, and Gold & Silver Lace. Also modern Books of all kinds, School Books, Bibles, Common Prayers, and Stationary Goods of every sort. And whom may be had the following very useful Books, viz.

1. Garrett's Designs and Estimates for Farm-Houses.
2. The Nobleman and Gentleman's Director and Assistant for the Choice of the Wheel-Carriage.
3. Abbott's Grand, Magnificent, and Superb Designs for Couches and Chariots, beautifully Coloured.
4. Every Man a complete Builder, or easy Rules and proportions for drawing and Working the several Parts of Architecture.
5. The Cabinet and Chair-maker's real friend and Companion containing upwards of 100 new and beautiful Designs of all sorts of Chairs.
6. Crunden's Joiner and Cabinet maker's Darling, containing 60 new and beautiful Designs for all sorts of Frets for Friezes, impost, Architraves, Tabernacle Frames, Tea stands, Stoves, Fenders, and Fan-lights over Doors.
7. The Manner of securing all sorts of Buildings from Fire.
8. The Carpenter's Companion, containing 32 new and beautiful Designs for all sorts of Chinese Railings and Gates.
9. The Carpenter's Complete Guide to the whole System of Gothic Railing.
10. The Smith's Right Hand, in all Branches.
11. Barett's new Book of Ornaments very useful for Cabinet-makers, Carvers, Painters, Engravers, Chafers, &c.

N. B. Those who please to favor them with their Commands, may depend on being served on the most reasonable Terms.

Last Week died Miss Abigail Perkins, eldest Daughter of Dr. Perkins of this Town. ――― A young Lady whose uncommon Understanding was only equalled by the Modesty of her Deportment and the unaffectedness of her Religion. Who in the reflective Hours of a retired Life found that Happiness which the gay and thoughtless vainly seek for in a constant Succession of new Objects. Whose Mind too active for the Delicacy

of her person, in the boundless pursuit of
Knowledge, brought upon her a Decay, that terminated so fatally. Fatal only as to this Transitory Scene, but a glorious emancipation to purer and far more exalted Enjoyment.

1767

BOSTON Jan. 5. Last Week we had here extreme Cold Weather, which entirely froze up the Harbour, so that many Vessels which were loaded and ready for sailing, are detained thereby; and People travelled to and fro from the Castle on the Ice.

Last Saturday se'nnight, in the Evening, Mr. John Waite, of Chelsea, was froze to Death in returning home from Lynn, where he had been catching of Eels.

THe same Night, one Mr. Bird, of Dorchester, in going home from Town, was also froze to Death.

We hear that several People belonging to the Country, had some of them their Hands and Feet and other their Noses, and Ears &c. froze in coming to or returning home from Market, in the extreme cold weather we had last Week.

The Weather being now something moderate, and an Easterly Wind Yesterday, had broke up part of the Ice in our Harbour; and are in hopes that in a few Days the whole will be entirely clear again.

BOSTON Jan. 12. At a Town Meeting held last Week, it was voted that a new Clock be purchased for the old Brick Church in this Town, the present being represented as not worth repairing.

For the benefit of Mr. Hartley, will be preform'd at Concert Hall, on the 15th Instant, A Concert of Vocal and Instrumental Music, consisting of select pieces by the most eminent Masters. To begin precisely at 6 o'Clock. Tickets to be had at Concert Hall, Brazzo Hand, Coffee House, Bunch of Grapes, and Mr. Hartley's Lodging next door to William Greenleaf's the Bottom of Cornhill, a Half a Dollar each.

BOSTON Jan. 19. Capt. Simms in a Schooner from Martineco, laden with Molasses, having put out frome the Vineyard on Monday the 29th ult. a thick Snow Storm came on at Night, which drove the Schooner on Sandy-Point, about 3 Leagues East of Nantucket: The People with great Difficulty saved their Lives, having near 8 Miles to travel, most of the Way up to their middles in Snow, before they could reach any Habitation: it is said the chief Part of their Cargo will be saved; but the Vessel lost.

We hear that in the same Storm a small Schooner belonging to Barnstable, bound from Connecticut, was drove out of the Hayeneas, (a Harbour near the Vineyard) and struck upon a Reef or Rock, by which Accident the Vessel, Cargo and all the Crew four in Number unfortunately lost.

BOSTON Feb. 2. On Friday last a Committee of the Honorable House of Representatives waited on his Excellency the Governor, with the following message.

May it Please your Excellency,
The House of Representatives beg to be informed by your Excellency, whether any Provisions has been made, at the Expence of the Government, for his Majesty's Troops lately arrived in the Harbour, and by whom? and also, whether your Excellency has Reason to expect the Arrival of any more, to be quartered in this Province.

To which his Excellency was pleas'd the same Day to send them the following Answer.

Gentlemen of the House of Representatives.
In Answer to your Message of this Day, I send a Copy of the Minutes of Council, by which Provisions for the Artillery Company at the Castle in pursuance of the late Act of Parliament was made.

I intended to lay the Matter before you, and had given Orders for an Account of the present Expence, to be made out for that Purpose, which having received since your Message came to me. I hereby communicate.

I have receiv'd no Advise whether of any other Troops being to be quartered in this Province, nor have I any Reason to expect the Arrival of such except from common Report, to which I gave little Credit.

BOSTON Feb. 2. As the Great and General Court of the Province is now convened, and the cries of the People against Quackery have continued Waxing louder and louder, the present paper presumes to lay before the Guardians of the public Weal a few further thoughts on the subject.

No county or township of our extensive province is insensible of the great importance of a wise and able Physician among them, who rightly distinguishing the peculiar nature of each disease, and happily understanding a just and rational method of cure, might be depended on in the doubtful and often nearly inscutable maladies, to which their most valuable members was daily obnoxious.

Few Men of any figure in life now believe that the knowledge of a few herbs and roots, and reading a dozens pages of Culpeper, can qualify a man from the safe practice of Physic; and yet it seems to be attended with uncommon difficulty to get a youth bred as he ought to be to this profession; the case truly this.

No profession in life is in itself so observed and intricate. ——— The very subject of his first enquiry is a world of wonder ——— A self moving machine of the most exquisite fabric, powers and prosperities, yet as far as traceable by human industry, under the same governing laws as the rest of the visible world. ——— These powers may be discovered innumerable ways, in the dark cells of the human body: and without to assistance of an uncommon genius, & improve understanding, the Symptoms of their disorder can never be sensibly noticed or properly conceived; and so hidden fire consume the vitals before a spark is suspected ——— The united labors of thousands has conspired to draw these important secrets out of their native obscurity and since they are now published to the world, may we not justly expect the pretenders to them should really possess them? Themselves complain, the thousands are lost by the ignorance of invaders of their province, and leach retorts on the other; we fear with too much reason, while we see every day Dunces as ignorant as the beasts of the field going as themselves soly to learn to be Doctors; of some Wizzard, the extent of whose sagacity never reached the distinction between a continent and remitting fever, and without even reading one page of Anatomy, Physiology, Materia Medica, Medical History of Diseases or any thing else, plunge right into practice, follow their master and give Fever-Powders, spirit of Hartshorn, pill-Cochia, or Jesuit bark as he does, without comprehending for what, more than the ravens of the valley comprehend the cause of the death of the carrion they devour.

The destruction of our species —— The augmented suffering of our languishing fellow creatures, imploring and expecting help from the hands of wretches, who like Pilate's officers, appease inflammatory thirst, if not with gall and wormwood, at best with tincture of Hiera-piera, or decoction of Virginia snake-root; and like the fiends in the infernal regions, deny a drop of water to cool parched tongues.

These things, O Fathers, awake our resentment alarm our fears, and draw forth our most passionate commiseration in favour of such general distress. —— Ye have nobly exerted yourselves for the preservation of our dear privilege, our lives now beg your protection! ye have done much to prepare the way to this salutary understanding. —— Go forward and establish professed teachers of the divine science at your respectable seminary, who may instruct our youth at least some of the outlines of a profession of which, alas! to few know the general division.

Publicola.

Boston Feb. 2. Thursday Morning the Goal in Town was discovered to be on Fire; a Criminal that was convicted a few days before for Stealing of Leather, &c. at Roxbury, and sentenced to be whipp'd at the Public Whipping Post, perpetrated the Crime in order to make his escape, which with another Person confined with him, he affected before discovery; A Hole being burnt in the Floor over the Room into the chamber thro' which they got out. But the next Day the fellow who was the chief Offender, was apprehended at Waltham and bro't back. ──── and will tis thought receive an additional Punishment to that he is now under sentence.

BOSTON Feb. 9. Tuesday night last a few Minutes after Ten o'Clock, the Bake House improved by Mr. George Bray (formerly Mr. Davenport's) nigh Mill-Bridge, burst into Flames, which immediately communicated to Mr. Bray's Dwelling-House, and other Buildings contiguous thereto: The Wind blowing hard, and not steadi- at one Point, the Flames soon drove on the Roofs of the Houses on every Quarter, and Water being scarce, for some time baffled the efforts of the Firewards, Enginemen, and of others; and as they were employed in extinguishing the Fire where it broke out, it was found necessary for many to attend at distant Places; and being uncertain what the course the Fire would pricipally take, a great Number of Families were obliged to remove their Goods and Furniture, none being safe on that Neighbourhood: A large brick House belonging to John Hancock, Esq; which was slated, in a great Measure stopped its Course Southward, and a Brick Wall of Mr. Bolfinch's prevented his House, and those on the South-Side of Mill-Creek from being burnt; but the Flakes of Fire then drove mostly North Eastward, passing over the Creek, and catch'd the House of Capt. Ball the Pilot, Mr. John Griffith, Mr. Jacob Emmons, with many others on both sides of Paddy's Alley (so called) and consumed all as far as Cross-Street, and Fore-Street, the back Part only of some of these were burnt, tho' all were on Fire several times; the large Mansion-House of Mr. Jonathan Williams, Merchant, was the last that was entirely consumed; many other Houses were on Fire several Times and considerably burnt, especially in Fore-Street; but the Tide coming up into the Docks the Engines were plentifully supplied with Water, by which they were prevented from being consumed, and the Fire spreading further. It was about Three o'clock in the Morning before the Flames were subdued! during so many hours the Inhabitants were indefatigably in supplying the Engines with Water, and helping the distressed, notwithstanding the Extremity of the Weather, which was so cold, that the Water which fell on the Cloaths immediately Froze. ——— Nothing seemed favorable at the first breaking out of the Fire, excepting the time, being before the Inhabitants were generally in Bed ——— the Weather had come on very severe in the evening, and the Wind high at W. at N. W. the Streets slippery, being covered with Ice, and low Water: ——— It was really distressing especially for those who had Children and sick persons to take out of their beds, and remove with their Goods to a great Distance: ——— Many Goods which were bulky and heavy were obliged to be left in the Street, whereby they were very much damaged. ———The loss to the several sufferers, we pretend not to estimate but certainly must be very great, and it is said above Twenty Dwelling houses, besides other Buildings, were consumed, and between Forty and Fifty Families deprived of their Habitations ——— But by a gracious Providence no lives were lost; nor do we hear of any dangerously wounded tho' many were exposed to imminent Dangers, confined to very narrow Passages, among the Flames of the Fire and the falling of Houses, Chimneys &c.

BOSTON Feb. 23. Last Thursday Night one Sharp (convicted for Stealing Leather out of a shop in Roxbury, and whom some time ago burnt a hole through the Wooden Goal and made his escape, but was next Day taken at Waltham and brought to Town, and afterwards Whipp'd at the Public Whipping Post, agreeable to his Sentence as had been mentioned) broke out of the new Stone Goal, which he accomplished by boring out a Square Piece of the Partition which led into another Room which the Workmen had not finished, and where the Door was left open, thro' which he went out and had not since been heard of.

BOSTON March 2. In the Debate in a very respectable Assembly, last Friday, an Extract of an anonymous Letter, said to be written in

England, was read, which concluded the following Words, "So that if your Assembly will suffer themselves to be by that very absurb, ignorant Firebrand, he may bring them into a worse Scrape than they can imagine." Upon which it was Resolved, That the Words were an high insult, and in Breach of Privilege, and that the Person who wrote them was an Enemy to this Province.

BOSTON March 2. Messeurs Printers. The following is said to be a genuine Copy of a very dirty anonymous Extract, said to be taken from a letter from one _____ in London, to another _____ in Boston. dated December 13, 1766.

"There is a spirit rising in Parliament very different from that of the last Session. It was then made shibboleth of Party to support all American claims, and Mr. Pitt's Extreme animosity against his Brother, led him to condemn everything he had done merely because it was his doing. He now seems to be recovering himself, and one of the first offers of Lord Chatham made in his negotiation the other day with the Duke of Bedford, was to maintain the King's authority in all his Dominions.

Yesterday he spoke a language of the same sort in the House of Lords. The rioting against the custom house officers in your province, was mentioned in the House of Commons early in the Session, when chancellor of the Exchequer declared in the strongest terms that so long as he was in office, he would not suffer the authority of the King's laws to be trampled upon, and that he thought it the highest injury to the nation to suffer the acts of the British Parliament to be broken with impunity. And that the whole house seemed animated with the same spirit, for that if your assembly will suffer themselves to be lead by that very absurd ignorant Firebrand, he may bring them into a scrape that they can imagine."

BOSTON March 9. As you by a long claim of poisonous suggestion and gilded falsities, have most assiduously attempted to inflame the minds of the people of the province, and irritate them against the Governor, whose firmness and mind despises such means of arts, painting him in the most odious colors, representing his public character in the most infamous light, without bringing one single fact which which can with certainty be relied on in proof of such uncharitable and ungenerous assertions: I do as a man, as a hater of falsehoods, as a lover of my country, and for the sake of the peace of this province. (which you have so long disturbed) call upon you to show me, and prove beyond a doubt, (as in what you have already advanced, in my opinion, you fall very much short of it) one single fact, which can render him worthy such unrestrained licentious abuse. —— If you refuse me this reasonable request, then I and every other man must look upon and esteem you as a Firebrand, an incendiary, who would set your country in a blaze in order to satisfy your ambitious and wicked purposes by the horrid general conflagration.

A Friend of to the Province.

Messiers. Fleets, Please to insert the following Appeal to all who it may concern.

It is not surprising, That such Numbers of Lads should be encouraged to act in characters unbecoming their calling? Does it not tend to take their minds off from their business an instead of making them good Taylors, Shoemakers, &c. render them nothing more than strolling Players? it is not detrimental to their Master's interest, as well as their own health, to have their shews at such unreasonable hours, when so many children are obliged to steal from their homes as to be of the party? But especially it is not unaccountable that a place erected for encouraging Industry, &c. should be so prostituted, as to be employed as a School for Idleness, and the vices consequent thereon? I am Friend of Family Order, and a sufferer by such performances.

BOSTON March 16. We hear that last Week the General Assembly, now sitting here, made choice of the Hon. Thomas Hutchinson, Esq; the Hon. William Brattle, Esq; and Capt. Edward Sheaffe, to be Commissaries on the Part of the Province, to join with those to be appointed from New-York to run the Boundary Lines between the two Provinces.

This is to give Notice, That the Feast of St. Patrick is to be celebrated at Capt. Bennett's in Boston To morrow, the 17th of March Instant at One o'Clock P. M. Where all Irish Gentlemen are expected to give their Attendance, Also all Gentlemen Well-wishers to Ireland.

BOSTON March 23. Wednesday the 18th Instant, a Day sacred to the Liberties of America, being the Anniversary of the Repeal of the Stamp-Act, was celebrated with excessive Joy; and every Token expressive of Gratitude and supreme Satisfaction —— The Morning Sun was saluted with a Thunder of applause bellowing from a Number of Cannon, and a regular and beautiful Parade of the Sons of Liberty thro; the great Street of the Town, with Musick preceding a cannon, adorned with the loyal Flag waving above it; the venerable Elm of Liberty was variegated with multitudes of Streamers most beautifully disposed among it's Branches, and in the Houses of many of the Inhabitants were distinguish'd by The same Trophy. —— The Burst of Joy reverberated from one Part of the Town to the other the whole forenoon from the busy mouths of the well-fed Cannon —— In the Afternoon, by the Vote of the Town, a Profusion of Wines and other Liquors were prepared in Faneuil-Hall, to collect the genuine Sons of Joy, to celebrate the happy Festival; accordingly a large Company of the principal Inhabitants crowded the spacious Apartments, and with loud Hurras and repeated Acclamations saluted the glorious and memorable Patrons of America, particularly those who distinguished themselves in the cause of Liberty, while we were groaning under the Iron Hand of Oppression —— at the close of the Day, the Company retired to different Houses in Town to conclude the Festivities with a collation supplied by private expence of some oppulent Gentlemen —— when Faneuil-Hall was beautifully Illuminated, and the several Houses where the Companies were collected blazed with Profusion of Candles —— But the Tree of Liberty chiefly attracted the

Notice of the Town, being richly shaded with the Splendour issuing from 108 Lanthorns, disposed in beautiful Order. —— Nothing could possibly exceed the Granduer of its Appearance; and throughout the Town, Musick and Mirth, Gratulation and Joy betrayed the exulted Satisfaction which took place in every Breast on this thrice happy Occasion.

BOSTON March 27. Messeurs Edes & Gill. "I was very sorry to find that the bill which brought into the General Court the last Session, for the prohibiting the African Slave Trade, had miscarried for the present, I say, as I trust the House, in some future Period will not fail to resume the consideration of so important a subject.

The most popular and plausible Excuse for the Slave Trade is, that the Africans are bro't from a Land of Darkness, to a Land of Gospel-light. They who advance this in Justification of this Business, are guilty of the most abominable Hypocrisy, in making a religious Concern for the Salvation of immortal Souls, a Cloak for the basest Perfidy, Avarice and Barbarity. Shew me the Merchant or Captain, whose Conscience in a Serious Hour tells him that he ever understood a Voyage to Africa, with a benevolent Desire or Design of bringing poor Negroes to the Knowledge of Christianity. Is it consistent with such a Design to use the most inhumane, unchristian, infernal Methods getting them away from their native Land? It is consistent with such a Desire, to foment perpetual Discord and War among the unhappy Nations? Is it consistent with such a Desire, to crowd so many Hundreds together in a Ship, that a great Part must inevitably perrish on the Voyage, and when they are brought to Port dispose of them in such a Manner as to put them under a great Disadvantage on account of Religion, as before they came from their own Country? Suppose a Ship-load of immortal Souls brought to Market, one of them appears superior to the rest, and equally attracts the liking of two Men who appear to purchase; That one of these is a sober, religious Man, and known to be so, he offers 20 Pounds. The other a notorious profligate, abandoned wretch, he offers 24 pounds ——— Now Mr. Conscience under which of these two Masters is the poor Soul likely to gain that divine knowledge, the love of which was moving cause of sending to Africa, that these poor Creatures might obtain equally with thee? And which of these shall be Purchaser? Can there be the least Struggle between Interest and Religion? I cannot help recollecting a line or two I have somewhere met with.

   Spain in America had two Designs,
   To Spread Religion, and to seize Mines,
   For where there is no sure supply of Wealth,
   Mens Souls are never worth the Charge of Health.

If These Men have any sincere Desire that the Africans should be benefited by the Gospel, why do they not take the nearest and most effectual Method to accomplish this End? Why don't they either send English Missionaries among them, or else instruct those Negroes who are already here and send them back on this benevolent Errand? The Truth is the Plea of benefiting their Souls is nothing but a vile, detestable, hypocritical Artifice to smooth over their antichristian, diabolical Covetousness, cruelty and Murder; for that they are guilty of these sins is glaringly evident to the view of Mankind; and why they should escape the Gallows, is beyond the Power of the most able Civilian to prove confident with our natural Ideas of Justice.

   BOSTON April 6. Messiers, Fleets. It is notorious that acting of Plays and Tragedies in this town is now practiced with impunity: whether the law prohibiting Theatrical Entertainment is insufficient to put a stop thereto, or those whose proper business it is to see such laws enforced, neglect their duty, is not for me to determine.

   I well remember a few years since, when a number of credible young gentlemen entertained some of their friends with a noble and decent Comedy or Tragedy, a method was soon found to put a stop to them: With more propriety should those of so insignificant a character be prevented acting in such a high life. It certainly concerns the parents & masters of the youth to discountenance such; for give me leave to inform them, that those entertainments are chiefly designed for assignations, which in the end may be of sorrowful consequence: I am certain they little suspect those assignations, & would highly resent the choice of their daughters companions, especially to gallant away at such unreasonable hours as from eleven o'clock at night to four in the morning: ———This I judge of by an adventure the other evening, for having had business which detained me pretty late, I was returning near the Cornfields, two Misses ran out, and with their Sparks passed me, very merrily relating how they had bilk'd their parents after they had gone to bed, & were concern'd least some others, whom they nam'd pretty loud, had not succeeded so well: ——— As I am a great admirer of the fair Sex, I choose not to be more explicit at present, tho' they could be easily pointed out.

I would just add, that it would not be forreign from the office of our teachers to exort the youth against such immoralities: I am very sure had a late worthy Divine survived to this time, the present place of resort would nor have passed unnoticed; for he embraces every opportunity to discountenance those vices which reproach to youth, and to inculcate those virtues that are an ornament to them; at the same time be allowed sundry diversions to be consistent with Christian Sobriety, which may of his Order would not chuse publicly to recomend.

P. S. It is apprehended that when the American Company of Comedians, who are now in New-York or Philadelphia, hear there is so great an inclination for such entertainment in this place, they will endeavour to introduce themselves, and certainly with more justice than these bunglers and coblers in every business.

BOSTON April 13. Jean Day begs leave to inform the public, that she intends to open a School for young Ladies, on the first Monday of May next in her House the Corner of Queen-Street; where she will teach all kind of Needle Work as usual.

BOSTON April 13. Messiers Edes& Gill. Since

the ever-memorable Repeal of the Stamp-Act, it has been the unwearied endeavour of a few uneasy & factious persons, disappointed at the happy event, to destroy the tranquility of this province: They have ben perpetually representing us in a disagreeable colour to our brethren and fellow subjects in England, to the ministry, and to Parliament: their malicious whispers have penetrated even the Royal Ears: It has been expressly said by a minister of state, a friend and patron of the colonies, that, "his Majesty is entirely sorry to observe any degree of ill-temper remaining in his colony of Massachusetts-Bay," &c. The Nobility have been told that "it is the intention of the Americans to bring the authority of the Parliament into contempt": Every trifling adventure of a Customhouse officer, has been carefully recorder, and whenever little altercations have arisen, not worth the notice of a common constable, to serve the darling point, they have arrested the attention even of the men in exalted stations; and to make the best appearance, depositions have been taken and sent home, and all the sordid interest has been used to get them laid before the Parliament; We have a notable instant of this the well-known affair of Capt. Malcom.
────── Two or three custom-house officers would fain have enter'd forcibly into Capt. Malcom's house, but he would not let them; and two or three boys in the street, or men if you please happened to smile at the scene, or perhaps laughed aloud, for the town was all in perfect good humour, and so the matter ended. Some folks it is thought, were greatly mortified, that it did not end in pulling down Houses and Bloodshed; but the people knew better then to do such things: However enough happened to work up a sad narration; the tale is made, and eagerly the first opportunity is snatch'd to hasten it to the other side the water to be told there. ──── But lo, the ungrateful return!: Your tale is an idle tale, and ye are a set of impertinent folks; the town have given no offence, and let us hear no more of such matters. Sadly mortifying indeed! what, no whips and scorpions, no

rods of iron to chastise this insolent rabble! But in vain do they call; the people are now viewed in that light —— ye have spit your venom to no purpose —— We dare to tell you, and we know it will make your teeth chatter, and perhaps your tongues too, you have done your worst —— you cannot any longer wound the character of a loyal people. —— We know also what you have wrote —— and we chuse you should go on to write —— your letters are harmless to this people —— yourselves will fell the ill effects of them. —— Thanks to the late patriotic house of assembly —— they have also wrote —— this town have wrote —— and thro' favor, their letters have been well receiv'd —— We have reason to hope that his Majesty's displeasure, incurred by your slander, such was your baneful influence then, is happily appeas'd; and we doubt not but the foundation of a mutual confidence between Great-Britain & her Colonies, in so solid and firm, as to be out of the power of your malice and envy to destroy it. Populus.

Boston April 27. Extract from a Gentleman in London to has Friend in Boston Dated Feb. 14, 1767.

The affair of the Opposition to the Custom House Officers, and the proceedings in your Town-Meeting, with some other transactions on your side of the water, will probably be attended with disagreeable consequence; I mean to the violent and seditious only (some who have been the principal are already mark'd out) for I am sure no measures will be taken here but such as tend to secure the future peace and tranquility of the colonies & the protection of every ones person and property (who conform themselves to the laws of their country) against a set of rabble, encouraged and abetted only by a set of enthusiastic madmen, who under the cloak of liberty have done such things as would not have been suffer'd in any state Christian or pagan upon the earth. —— I am glad to find that the victims to the sons of riot, are to receive some satisfaction for the injuries they have received, I say some, for I cannot call it full, as the authors of calamity are to indemnified for what they have done: however it is certain, that e'er long such measures will be taken tho' ever so contrary to the opinion of some among you, that they will find the Parliament of Great Britain have not only a right to make laws respecting the colonies, an all cases whatsoever, but they will also find they have power to carry such laws into execution, and to punish all violators of the same, and all disturbers of the public peace whatsoever.

The People may depend upon it that the Report wickedly propagated of the Troops being to be sent to and new Taxes laid upon America, are entirely without Foundation —— That the Conduct of this Province and of the late House of Representatives has been highly approved of by the great ones in Parliament, from many of the Letters have been received expressing the same, and their great affection for the People.

BOSTON April 30. By the February Packet arrived at New-York, a Letter has been receiv'd from Mr. De Berdt, directed to the Speaker of the late House of Representatives, dated the 14th of February last. The following Paragraphs are extracted therefrom.

Sir. "The Government are about to call home the Troops from America and place others in their Room the preparing for the embarking of which has occasioned much speculation here, and the Report runs that there are fresh Troops going to America, which has occasioned my particular Application to Lord Shelburne on that Head, who was So condescending and obliging as to assure me, I might satisfy all Friends that there was no Intention or augmenting the Forces in America but a mere exchange.

BOSTON May 4. As a Report has been propagated by some Persons, that the Letter published in our last, dated London, February 14th, was wrote in Boston. —— The Public may now be assured, that it was absolutely wrote at the Place from whencce it was dated; The Publishers having been favored with the Original Letter by the Gentleman to whom it came directed, in order to satisfy them with Regard to that Point.

BOSTON May 4. Messiers Edes & Gill, Please give the following a Place in your next. about this time annually, or sooner, somewhat, has been committed to your faithful and impartial press (by which the public are, and have been much oblig'd, benefited and edify'd) relative to the choice of Representatives through the Province. ——— And to a modest man, what formerly was said on that head seem quite sufficient ——— Nor should I now have said a word, had it not been I plainly perceived that the Philistines were upon thee Sampson ——— I mean the many under-handed, under-ground letters lately wrote, purely on account of one man, and to satisfy his boundless ambitious mind. ——— How industriously has the stale old doctrine been propagated! ——— not two pence better, better did I say? may infinitely worse, if possible, than that of non-resistance and passive obedience ——— I mean that of worshipping graven images ——— expressly forbidden by certain Commandments coming from higher and greater authority, that which is for the time being ——— and which I dare not break or disobey; and I thank God I can't find in my heart any thing prompting me therein. However my dear brethren, as this time of the day I trust we do not behold men (or things) as merely thro' a glass darkly, but face a fact, as one man seeth another, ——— for sure I am, we have had recent instances of glaring conduct! ——— and which if desired, I may in future explain. ——— I am of no partyman ——— but a well-wisher to my King and country, and would seduously avoid or rather despise that man, who should attempt only to fawn & flatter the one, or injure the other, be his mask of modesty ever so large. ——— I could say many things ——— but if i could, provoke to love and emulation. But I cannot help saying, I stand astonish'd and amaz'd to see any of this people so blind to their own interest. ——— Have not your tools and sycophants (not to say any thing worse) merely by low art and management, heretofore been in some towns elected Representatives, while worthy, honest and truly qualified men have just stood by neglected. ———

and all to satisfy the same man. In a word, may
our decent firmness, stability, & manly resolution, touching our most unquestionable rights
and privileges, be as conspicuous as our unshaken and remarkable loyalty and dutifullness
to the best Sovereigns ——— I say it, (and
I glory in it) I say it, and will repeat it,
as conspicuous at our unshaken and remarkable
loyalty and dutifulness to the best Sovereigns
——— then will even Majesty itself (if not
misinformed) look down upon us with royal paternal smile. ——— Touching the approaching
Election, (the cob-web essays which have been
made behind the door notwithstanding) rouse my
dear countrymen, and with one voice, let us
chuse for the ensuing year, the honest, the
prudent, the knowing, the wise and the just;
ever set these men upon your high watch-tower.
——— These men shall descry danger from afar,
and wicked design at a distance ——— these men
shall scatter iniquity with their eyes ———
and these men shall, under God, preserve use
from the base intrigues of the rascally time-
server, and the most poltroon forker.   Modus.

   BOSTON May 18. A report prevails in London,
that a congress was to be held in New-York in
May, but deputies from the several provinces and
colonies in America; upon which it was said that
orders were sent to Sir Henry Moore, Governor
of New-York, to put a stop thereto.

   BOSTON May 25. King's Arms Tavern. William
Goodhue, acquaints the Public that he was lately
opened as a Tavern, a large commodious House
very pleasant and conveniently situated in the
Center of the Town of Salem, and known by the
name of King's Arms. Where all Gentlemen Travellers and others, who please to favor him with
their Custom, may depend on the best entertainment and heartiest Welcome.

   BOSTON May 25. To the free independent Electors of the Week, Gentlemen, Could you pass over
the infinite Insults the People of this Prov-
vince have in the Course only of last Year receiv'd from those who are dead to the ties of
Nature and the Gratitude, permit me to ask.
What has these men ever done for this Country?

Rather what have they left undone against her? was there ever, can they ever be a Minister so abandoned that they would not rejoice to carry his measures into execution? Your invaluable Rights and Charter Privileges must depend on a steady, resolute and uniform Conduct at the ensuing Election. Should you not attend to the noble Example of Connecticut, but suffer yourselves to be intimidated by the Threats of a Governor, and replace your confidence in Stampmen, or the promoters and favorers of the stamp-Acts, you will point a Dagger at your own Breast, which your implacable Enemies will not fail to push to your Heart.   Cato.

   BOSTON June 1. Wednesday last the Anniversary Day appointed by the Royal Charter for the Election of His Majesty's Councillors of the Province met at the Court House in this Town: After the usual oaths were administered to the Gentlemen who were returned to serve as Members of the Honourable House of Representatives, and the Declaration Subscribed by them, they elected the Hon. Thomas Cushing Esq; for their speaker, who being presented to his Excellency the Governor for his Approbation, according to the Direction of the Royal Explanatory Charter, His Excellency was pleased to send a Message in Writing to the House, signifying his Approbation of the said Election: The House then made choice of Mr. Samuel Adams, for their Clerk.

   Ran-away the 21st Instant, from his Master Stephen Harris, junr. a Servent Boy, named John Major, 14 Years old, about 4 Feet high, had a light Cloath Pea Jacket, a blue Waistcoat, Leather Breeches, light rib'd Stockings, a blue mill'd Cap, a Cotton & Linnen Shirt, and square Brass Buckles. Whoever takes up said Servant, and bring him to his Master, shall have two Dollars Reward, and all necessary Charges paid by me,   Stephen Harris, junr.
   N. R. All Masters of Vessels and others are hereby caution'd against Harbouring, concelling or carrying off said Servant, as they would avoid the penalty of the Law.

   BOSTON June 1. Last Saturday Night some daring William went on board two Ships in the

Harbour and took away the Captains Breeches from under their Heads while they were asleep, & robbed them of their watches and Cash to a considerable amount.

This is to give Notice to all Gentlewomen and others, that David Burnet makes all sorts of Stays; likewise any that are deformed in the Body he makes them appear straight, as he has done to many, Any that wants, let them come to the Sign of the Stays, at New-Boston, just below the West Meeting-House, where they shall be supplied with the best at a reasonable rate.

BOSTON June 8. The Subscriber hereby informs the Publick, that he has provided a Stage Coach that will carry 6 Passengers, and is ready to carry Persons to the mineral Spring at Newton. The Coach will set out on Wednesday the 17th Instant, at 5 o'Clock in the Morning to return at Noon, and go out again at 2 in the Afternoon to return at Evening, and will proceed regularly every Day in the said Manner if suitable Encouragement be given. Each Person to Pay 4 s. Lawful Money to be carried and returned the same Stage. Those intended to go in the Morning, to leave their Names and Places of abode, at the Sign of the Lamb the evening before, and for the Afternoon Stage, the Morning of the same Day they shall be waited on.
John Wood.

BOSTON June 11. We hear from Bridgewater, that last Thursday se'nnight, after a Number of Men had erected a Frame for a Dwelling-House and secured it in the usual Manner, there of a sudden came up a black Cloud, which soon vented itself in violent Gusts of Wind, and which, to the astonishment of all, immediately crushed the whole Frame to the Ground, and destroyed a considerable part of the Timber.

BOSTON June 18. Last Wednesday 7-night as Seth Pittee a young Man in his 21st year of age belonging to Dedham, was returning from this Town with his Team, was taken with bleeding at his Mouth and Nose, and immediately carried into a House, where he died in another Hour.

BOSTON June 22. Extract of a Letter from a Son of Liberty, now in London, to his friend in New-England, dated the 11th of April.

"The House of Commons have appointed the first Thursday after the Holidays to enter upon the Consideration of American Affairs. New-York is said, will certainly receive some Chastisement, for refusing to Billet the Troops: and Massashusetts-Bay for their warm Addresses, Resolutions, &c. in their Squabbles with Governor Bernard. And many intend to have something done that may reach all the Colonies. The only chance for us seems to be, that it is now so late in the Session, that they will hardly find Time to ripen any Plan replete with so much difficulty and delicacy as they will find much attend any measure they will choose to adopt.

BOSTON July 4. Last Week sundry Robberies were committed in Town, and some very Large ones: only one of the Villains is as yet apprehended, who stole 16 half-Johannes, 21 Guineas and some Silver from Capt. Wier in the Quebec Trade, and is now in Goal, and 'tis hoped he will meet with his Deserts. People would do well to see that their Windows and Doors are secure before they went to Bed, as this Town seem at present to be infested with a Number of Vagrants.

BOSTON July 6. Captain Lyde left London May 14th, Just as he came away some Gentlemen, at the New-England Coffee House, wrote the following Article, and gave to some of the Passengers viz. "The Parliament met the 13th of May upon American Affairs, and resolved that a Bill be brought in after the following Manner.

That a Tax be laid on Painters colours, Paper, Glass and China. That the Americans may have Liberty of importing Lemons, Wine, Fruit & Oil directly from Spain and Portugal, subject to a Duty, the Duty of Wine to be 7 Pounds per Ton. That the Duty on Tea remaining in England be taken off, and a Duty of 3 d. per lb. be laid on the importation in America. That there be a Board of Customs, as also a Court of Exchequer in New-England. That the Legislative Power of New-York cease until they comply with the billeting Bill. That the Governors and Judges be made independent by increasing the salary which is to be paid out of the revenue of the Customs.

"George Greenville made a Motion to oblige the Americans to take oath of Allegiance and Obedience to the Parliament of Great Britain, which was put to Note ----- for the Question 90, against it 180 odd."

BOSTON July 6. A Fellow who work'd his passage in Capt. Wier from Quebec, stole a Purse of Money from one of the Passengers the Day they arrived, with which he made off, with an intent for New-York, but being pursued, he was taken at Worcester with the Purse and most of the money upon him, which being sworn to by the owner, he was brought to Town and committed to Goal on Friday Evening.

BOSTON July 13. Messieurs Edes and Gill, One Evening last Week arrived in Town from the Southward, a certain American Judge, who to shew his Love for his Country, discribed the Colonies in print, and deserving to have their Laws written in Blood. But it is with Pleasure observed his Reception (except by those few who think as he does) was not very agreeable to him.

BOSTON July 27. Adino Paddock, and his shop in Common-Street, Has to sell several second-hand Chaises, and he carries on the Coach and Chaise-making Business, as usual, in all its branches: and will take old Chaises in part pay for the new. ——— Neat's Foot Oil, and Horse Nets to sell.

BOSTON Aug. 3. This Town is favour'd with many good regulations to prevent Fraud in Weight and Measured, but after all I strongly suspect injustice is not wholly banished; what I have in particular Respect to this Time is the Tin-Pots, Quarts, Pints, &c. by which we buy Milk, Fruit of all sorts, any Thing that looks like a Quart is used, and tho' the buyer suspects that it is short Measure, yet the Value of the purchase small he for quiet sake passes it, as I have done many Times: but when I think that these get their whole Living by handling out of these Pots, their Cheating must amount to a very considerable Sum, this Profit is tempting, and no Notice being taken of it by Authority, it is to be fear'd many People pall all their Days in Breach of the sacr'd Law of Justice, and from these People we cannot expect any internal Regard to any moral Duty. In some Measures to prevent this Evil I apply to the Tinmen, or makers of Tin Ware, and propose to 'em as they'd consult the Good of the Publick, that they should not upon any Occasion make any Vessels but except, Gallons, Quarts, Pints, &c. And Tho' I am sensible that many Vessels of Measure are made of other Metals than Tin, yet as that is the most prevailing for its Cheapness and lightness could I gain this Point with my Brethren Tin Men, I shoulf have the Satisfaction to think I had done some Service to the Publick ―――― Could I think of being heard by the Legislature, I would humbly propose having a Law to destroy the Distinction between Beer and Wine Measure; for I am persuaded having two measures occasions much Iniquity, and many great Mistakes, which are too obvious to need pointed out; But I can't conceive one possible Advantage that can arise to any honest Man from our present Distinction of Beer and Wine Measures. Your's

A Tin-Man.

The publishers of this Paper begs Leave to inform the Public, that they have remove their Printing Office to the other Side of Queen-Street, opposite to that they lately occupied ―――― Where Articles of Intelligence, Advertisements, &c. are received for the Gazette, & all other Printing carefully and expeditiously performed.

Tuesday Morning last Mr. Samuel Collsworthy, Shipwright fell from a Stage at the Nort Part of Town, and his Back coming across a Piece of Timber, bruis'd him in such a Manner that he died in the Evening of the same Day.

BOSTON Aug. 10. To the Publishers of the Boston Evening-Post.

As the most communicative way of delivering an injured person's sentiments to the public is thro' the channel of a News Paper, I Therefore take this method to deliver mine.

My aunt Mrs. Alice Quick, was one and a heavy one of the sufferers in the great fire in Boston in 1766, and as there were large collections made for them and deposited in the hands of several Gentlemen duly appointed (and I don't know but sworn) to equally and justly distribute the same among them, accordingly to such accounts as should be truly exhibited to them, the very poor to be first assisted; and the rest to be alike in proportion to their loss.

Now Mrs. Quick was greatly a sufferer. She lost her mansion house in the most public Street in the town, together with a great part of her shop goods and furniture —— so great a part of her shop goods that she was obliged to write to England for a large quantity to make an Assortment.

She timely gave in to the Gentlemen so appointed as near an estimate of her loss as possible, but within what she really did lose.

Proper application was made to them, either by herself or her friends, for her proportion of the money collected, and repeated promises that she should have her part in due time. I Was once myself a witness to such a promise to her —— She died without receiving a farthing —— I was made her residuary legatee, in consequence of which, finding the Gentlemen were about to close their distribution upon them at Col. Phillips's, who was one of them, and where they met. —— Col. Phillips treated me very politely and asked me to sit; immediately Mr, Samuel Dexter or Mr. Royal Tyler or both, who were also distributors, in a rough manner ask'd me who order'd me there? I told them no one, but as I understood it was their last distribution of the money collected for the sufferers, I came to see whither there was any for Mrs. Quick's estate. I was rudely answered by Mr. Dexter or Mr. Tyler —— not a Farthing. —— The reason I could not remember which of them answered me was the great surprise I was there in their ill treatment, and being a stranger in the town.

Upon the whole I have never to this day got a farthing, nor does it seem at present likely I shall, tho' the town has taken away one and a half foot of my land and made me pay a large tax besides for widening the street.

And now what shall I say? What shall you, my

fellowmen, tho' I be a stranger, say at such (to me seeming) injustice? You surely will not laugh at my calamity, but I hope and doubt not you will rather mock those who have thus injured me, if I can get no other redress this will be some satisfaction.

The candor of the public I hope will excuse this narrative as it appears so late, nor should I have thus related it, but being often told my aunt relinquished her right, all my certainly knowing she never did.   Thomas Knight.

BOSTON Aug. 10. Stage-Coach No. 1. Kept by Thomas Sabin, sets out every Tuesday Morning, from the House of Mr. Richard Olney, innholder at the Coffee-House the Sign of the Crown in Providence, to carry Travellers to Boston, and the most expeditious and cheap Rate. ⸺ while in Boston, he puts up at Mr. John Burrow's, at the Sign of the Lamb, where he will be ready to wait on all those who maybe pleased to return with him on the Thursday following ⸺ Said Sabin has provided himself with several sets of good Horses for the said Purpose, and intends following the Business all the Summer Season. ⸺ All Gentlemen and Ladies may depend upon the most ready Observance of their Desires, by their humble Servant.   Thomas Sebin.

BOSTON Aug. 31. This is to Notify the curious, That there is to be seen a Variety of Curiosities, of different Sorts of animals in Bottles, to the amount of 90 odd, at Six Coppers a sight, at Barker's Shop opposite the New-North meeting House at the North End.

BOSTON Sept. 7. A Letter of the 13th of June, from a Gentleman in London to his friend in Boston, says, It is Lord Mansfield's Opinion, that the authors of riots and seditious pieces in America, should be sent for to England and there tried for Treason; particularly the writer of Pamphlets, some time since published in Boston: ⸺ against which Author there is particular Evidence for his seditious and treasonable Speeches in an American Assembly.

At the Superior Court held last Week, a Negro Fellow belonging to Mr. Durant of Newton, was tried for the Murder of a Man with whom he differed on the road some time since, but as a doubt remains upon the Minds of all the Jury whether the blows given by him were the sole Occasion of his Death, he was acquitted.

BOSTON Sept. 14. Messiers Edes and Gill. I am an old Man, and have numerous Offsprings. ——— I cannot be silent, when I see the Liberties of my Country struck at. ——— It appears to me that the State of Slavery will soon succeed the blessed Liberty fought out and obtained by our famous Forefathers. unless we exert ourselves with Spirit and Firmness to avert the Blow. which is meditating against us. I Inherited a fair Estate. which hath descended to me from my Ancestors; but what I Prize infinitely more, they left me in the Enjoyment of the Liberty which is the Right of every Man, and which is so perfectly consistent with our civil Government. that it is the great Object of its institution. That no other see all my Progeny dead or that leave them in Slavery. I dread the Consequence of a Paliamentary claim to tax us.
Roger Martum.

BOSTON Sept 21. It is rumoured, and some say with great Probability, that a Body of Troops are ordered to be in Readiness at Halifax to embark to any Part of the Continent of America, upon the first Notice of Uneasiness at the Novelties we daily expect. ——— It is as certain that America is also in readiness to defend their Liberties at the Risque of every thing else ——— there can be no Hesitation whenever the Alternative shall be Slavery or Death ——— If therefore they wait to know whether we will tamely submit to Slavery, the sooner the Matter is bro't to a Crisis the better. ——— But while we have any opinion of the Integrity and the good Sense of the Parliament of Great Britain such Reports will not easily gain Credit.
Deteaminatus.

BOSTON Sept. 21. Messiers Fleets, If you think the annexed Piece is worth Publishing I must desire you'll insert it as sent you.
To the People in this Province.   Syez Sage.

I am extremely grieved to see those who pretend to pride themselves in the love and prosperity of their country, and stile themselves patriots (at this critical juncture) endeavouring to poison the minds of the people of this province (with their inflammatory publications) who naturally incline to moderation and prudence: What can they mean or drive at? Can they be so blindly led away with political enthusiasm as not to perceive their inability to oppose the mother country? Can they imagine that the same kind of horrid bluster and parade too lately exhibited in this part of the world capable of intimidating a British Senate? or can they be presuming enough to imagine themselves equal to the task of opposing their strength to that of Great Britain? Surely no, these designing men must know better: Believe me, they are the only enemies we have in our country, who propagate such notions; and be assured that the only true friend we can justly boast of, are those cool, deliberate, sensible men that abhor and detest the ridiculous parade and poisonous performances of those people; if you are aggrieved; strive by all prudent means to obtain redress; these you most certainly have in your power and that without risking any thing, or requiring the ill-timed zeal of the Blue-Coats, who not only serve by their violent measures to sower the minds of the unwary and ignorant at this side of the water; but by their atrocious arrogance and indelicacy to their mother country daily hasten on those very burdens they themselves so grievously complain of: I will dare to say, that those very Blusterers that appear as if they at all times carried about the fire & faggot, to burn and destroy all those who presume to differ with them (in their enthusiastical political notions) are the very people who upon an emergency would be the foremost to flip their necks out of halter: and leave others by no means so culpable as themselves to pay the score.

Do not mistake me, my country men, I do not want you to be slaves; I detest the name, and would go as far as to drive it from off the coast (and I am persuaded much farther) than those mighty Hosts (or rather Ghosts) of

Patriots: But think well; in this same Liberty that you so greedily run after to be found by sheating the sword in the bowels of your fellow subjects? is it by inflammatory ill-wrote and worse judged pieces, daily crowded into the Papers; that you expect redress? Surly it cannot be: —— Resolve them, my countrymen, to discourage all inflammatory publications; all indecency of expression, and above all discountethose canker worms of the state; they must be men of desperate fortunes, who know they cannot be suffered let the game play as it will, or they would never conduct themselves with so small a share of discretion.

A True Patriot.

BOSTON Sept. 21. By our latest Advice from London, which come down to the 8th and 9th of July, we are informed that the King has established the Admiralty-Office for the New-England Provinces, and appointed Robert Auchmuty, Esq; Judge, with 300 Pounds Sterling per Annum, and to have no fees; Jonathan Sewall, Advocate-General, and Mr. Arodi Tayler, Marshall. —— That his Majesty hath likewise settled a Board of Customs in consequence of an Act of Parliament for that purpose, their Residence to be at Boston: —— That the appointment of the aforementioned Officers had not been declared, nor their respective Salaries; the Salaries were to be settled by his Majesty out of the Revenue arising from the Duties laid by the Act of parliament which were devolved to the Crown, as therein set forth, for the paying of Officers of Government: it is however said that they were determined on, tho' not declared.

BOSTON Oct. 5. Whereas various reports have been spread in news-papers and otherwise, That a court of exchequers was to be established in America: —— The act of Parliament respecting the same is now come over, and contains nothing more than conforming an act of this province, past in the 11th year of King William the third which may be in the same province law-book page 97, without the least addition of any power whatsoever.

BOSTON Oct. 12. Messieurs Edes & Gill. Please

insert the following.

That no man ought to be allowed to judge in his own case, is founded in reason; because human nature not so perfect as to judge impartially on both sides. In some instances taken there are some exceptions, but such I take it are because of necessity. If man attacks another with a drawn sword, and puts his life in hazard, and there be no possibility of his fleeing from the danger, in reason he ought to be the judge of the expediency of enduring the risque any longer or putting an end to the life of the assailant. —— In this case there is no opportunity of appealing to an indifferent judge. The law of self preservation can be the only rule.

As no individual can be presumed to be the equal judge in his own case, so neither any united body of men, by what name or character soever distinguish, in cases which concern them as a body —— Do we not often see inhabitants of towns or corporations taken off from juries in cases where those towns or corporations are interested —— The evidence of witnesses are not taken, if they are remotely concerned if be the cause, and even judges themselves are removed from the bench —— It sensibly is the natural principle of self-love felt, and the prejudice arising therefrom.

Perhaps the design of civil government, next to the security of merit persons, was this constitution cool dispassionate, disinterested, and in that sense an by independent judges, in all cases when individuals or bodies of men shall think themselves injured by others and complain. —— I am of opinion that the latter, considering the human make, argues the necessity of government & laws as much as the former. —— If a man is so void of the exercise of reason, as to do an injury to another, especially if he does it deliberately, it is not likely that he will be so indifferent afterwards as to judge and condemn himself for it. So if a man, or body of men, think they are abused, affronted, or in any wise injured, it is a difficult thing for an impartial by-stander to persuade them, however true it may be, that no injury was design'd much less that in fact none is given. Wise and honest men will always chuse to leave matters of controversy the the decision of indifferent persons: And whenever so reasonable a method is declin'd especially when the men refusing it, has by bodily strength situating it or other circumstance, and briefly the advantage of his opposer, it favors too side of ill-nature and a desire of revenge.

I ever admired that part of our civil constitution, which puts it out of the power of any man whatsoever to improve such advantages —— All controversies tho' the greatest and the meanest may be the opposite parties are determin'd by a jury of neighbours, which tho' not so summery a method of deriding them, ought by no means to be accounted piteous. —— And I am persuaded no man would be depos'd in the least to verge from this method, who has the principles of the British constitution in his mind.   Civis.

BOSTON GOAL Oct 17. Whereas I the subscriber, Surgeon and Oculist, &c. from London, beg Leave to inform the Public, that being confin'd in this Place from the public Practice, propose to furnish as usual these excellent Waters for the use undermention'd, which have given great satisfaction in Boston, and other places on the Continent. This excellent Water has all the virtues of other elaborate Compositions, and is derived from solid Experience, which confirms it excellent, rather than pompous, for its Virtues, it takes off felms of long standing, strengthens weak Eyes, helps old People to strength of sight: It is also for external uses, Inflammations, Burns, cutaneous Eruptions, tho' Erysipelas, old Ulcers, Gangrenes, &c. It is also famous for its Virtue in Catarrhs, Phthistic, Dropsy, Diabetes, and particularly Scurvy —— Shall be proud to serve Gentlemen and Ladies in Town and Country, either by their waiting on him; or sending their Orders to the above mentioned Place.   William Elliot.

N. B. The Price is 3 s. the single and 3 s. 6 d. the double Viol.

BOSTON Oct. 26. The Freeholders and other Inhabitants of this Town are notified to meet at Faneuil-Hall on Wednesday next, at Ten o'Clock in the forenoon, in order, among other things, to consider and agree upon some effectual Measures to promote Industry, Occonomy, and Manufactures, thereby to prevent the unnecessary Importation of European Commodities, which threaten the Country with Poverty and Ruin: —— That the Mind and resolution of the Town may be taken with respect to the Expedience of an humble Request to his Excellency the Governor, that he will convene the General Assembly as soon as may be; and the giving proper Instructions to the Representatives of the Town for their Conduct at this very critical Conjuncture of our public Affairs; —— Also to consider of some Measure for Employing the Poor of the Town of Boston, by reviving the Linen Manufacture, and in such other Ways as shall be thought most beneficial.

BOSTON Nov. 2. At the Meeting of the Freeholders and other Inhabitants of the Town of Boston, legally assembled at Faneuil-Hall on Wednesday the 28th of October 1767.

The Hon. James Otis Esq; Moderator, A Written Adress to the Inhabitants subscribed Phile Patria, recommending Occonomy and Manufactures, was, by the order read ——

The Town then took into Consideration the petition of a Number of Inhabitants, "That some effectual Measures might be agreed upon to promote Industry, Oconnomy & Manufactures; thereby to prevent the unnecessary Importation of European Commodities, which threaten the Country with Poverty and Ruin:" Whereupon in a very large and full Meeting, the following, Votes & Resolutions were passed unanimously.

Whereas the excessive Use of Foreign Superfluities is the chief cause of the present distressed State of this Town, as it is thereby drained of its Money; which Misfortune is likely to be increased by means of the late additional Burthens and Importations on the Trade of the Province, which threaten the Country with Poverty and Ruin:

Therefore Voted, That this Town will take all prudent and legal Measures to encourage the produce and Manufactures of this Province, and to lessen the Use of Superfluities & Particularly the following enumerated Articles from Abroad, viz. Loaf Sugar, Cordage, Anchors, Coaches, Chaise, and Carriages of all sorts, House Furniture, Men and Women's Hatts, Men and Women's Shoes, Sole Leather, Sheating and Deck Nails, Gold and Silver Thread Lace of all sorts, Gold and Silver Buttons, wrought Plate of all sorts, Diamond, Stone and Paste Ware, Snuff, Mustard, Clocks and Watches, Silversmiths and Jewllers Ware, Broad Cloths that cost above 10 s. per Yard, Muffs, Furrs and Tippets, and all sorts of Millenary Ware, Starch, Women and Childrens Stays, Fire Engines, China Ware, Silk and Cotton Velvet, Gauze, Pewterers hollow Ware, Linseed Oyl, Glue, Lawns, Cambricks, Silk of all King for Garments, Malt Liquors and Cheese. ——— And that a Subscription for the End be hereby recommended to the several Inhabitants and Householders of the Town: and that John Rowe, Esq; Mr. William Greenleaf, Meletiah Bourne Esq; Mr. Samuel Austin, Mr. Edward Payne, Mr. Edmund Quincy, Tertius, John Ruddock, Esq; Jonathan Williams, Esq; Joshua Hensaw, Esq; Mr. Henderson Inches, Mr. Solomon Davis, Joshua Wonslow, Esq; and Thomas Cushing, Esq; be a Committee to prepare a form of Subscription to the same.

And whereas it is the Opinion of the Town, that divers new Manufactures may be set up in America, to its great Advantage, and some others carried to a greater Extent particularly those of Glass and Paper.

Therefore, Voted, That this Town will by all prudent Ways and Means, encourage the Use and Consumption of Glass and Paper, made in any of the British American Colonies; and more especially in this Province. [Then the Meeting adjourn'd till 3 o'Clock Afternoon]

III o'Clock Post Meridien.

The Committee appointed in the forenoon to prepare a form of Subscription reports as Follows.

Whereas this Province labours under heavy debt,

incurred in the Course of the late War; and the Inhabitants by this Means must be for some Time subject to very burthensome Taxes: ——— And our Trade has for some Years been on a decline, and is now particularly under great Embarrassments, and burthened with heavy Importations, and our Medium very scarce and the Balance of Trade greatly against the Country.

We therefore the Subscribers, being sensible that it is absolutely necessary, in Order to extricate us out of these embarrassed and distressed Circumstances to promote Industry, Occonomy & Manufactures among ourselves, and by this Means prevent the unnecessary Importation of European Commodities, and excessive Use of which threaten toe Country with Poverty and ruin ——— Do promise and engage, to and with each other, that we will encourage the Use and Consumption of all articles manufactured in any of the British American Colonies, and more especially in this Province; and that we will not from the 31st of December next ensuing, purchase any of the following Articles, imported from Abroad, viz Loaf Sugar, and all other Articles enumerated above: ———

And we further agree strictly to adhere to the late Regulation Representing Funerals, and will not use any Gloves but what are manufactured here, nor procure any Garments upon such Occasion, but what shall be absolutely necessary.

The above Report having been considered, the Question was put, whether the same shall be accepted? Voted unanimously in the Affirmative. ——— Ant that said Committee be desired to use their best endeavours to get the Subscription Papers filled up as soon as may be. Also, Voted unanimously, that the foregoing Vote and Form of a Subscription relative to the enumerated articles, be immediately published; and that the Selectmen be directed to distribute a proper Number of them among the Freeholders of the Town; and to foreward a Copy of the same to the principal City and Town Officers of the Chief Towns in the several Colonies on the Continent, as they may think proper.

That Clause of Warrant, "That the Mind and resolution of the Town may be taken with Respect to the Expediency of a humble Request to the General Assembly as soon as may be," was read, and considered: Whereupon, Voted unanimously, That the Representatives of the Town having already made humble Application to his Excellency the Governor for the purpose above mentioned, the Town do approve of their Conduct therein; hereby declaring their Sense of the Importance of the Measure, and expressing their Hopes that his Excellency will be pleased to favor it, by convening the General Assembly as soon as conveniently may be.

The Clause in the Warrant, viz. "To consider of some Measure for employing the Poor of the Town of Boston by reviving the Linnen Manufacture, and in such other Was as shall be thought most Beneficial," was read ——— Whereupon voted, that John Barret, Esq; Mr. Edward Payne, Middlecot Cook, Esq; Mr. Henderson Inches, Malatiah Bourne, Esq; Jonathan Williams, Esq; Ezekial Goldthwart, Esq; be a Committee for the proposed aforesaid, to Report as soon as may be.

Upon a Motion made, Voted That the Town will take all proper Measures by keeping in their Children and Servants, and other Ways, to prevent such Disturbances as have sometimes happened on or about the 5th of November;

Attest   William Cooper, Town Clerk.

BOSTON Nov. 2. It is with pleasure we can inform our readers, that within the last Year, Thirty thousand Yards of Cloth were manufactured in one small Country Town in this Province; so far does this spirit of industry begin to prevail among us, and we hope will in this way, assisted by the Frugality and Occonomy, daily afford us a more promising prospect of emerging from our present alarming scarcity of Money, and consequent stagnation of Trade; and from the almost universally increasing complaints of Debt and Poverty.

BOSTON Nov. 9. We hear the Subscription paper for increasing our own manufactures, and laying aside certain enumerated articles, fill up surprizingly; and that the said measure is so well approved of in the country, that town meetings are now calling in order to agree upon similar measures ——— The Public papers and private advises acquaint us, that Rhode Island, Connecticut, New-York, New-Jersey, Philadelphia, &c. are steadily pursuing measures for lessening their foreign imports, by encouraging frogality, and their own manufactures. ——— It cannot be disputed that the colonies are greatly in debt, for whatever is drawn from us by way of duty, must be those monies which would go to Britain, as pay, and to procure more goods. Necessity is laid upon us, to be industrious and frugal, and who be to unto us, If we are extravagant.

BOSTON Nov. 12. Mr. Draper. Please to insert the following Extract of a Letter from a Gentleman in the Country, to his Friend in Boston, Dated November 7th 1767, and you'll greatly oblige your humble Servant. P. B.

"I have lately taken a Tour thro' most populous Parts of the Province and can assure you the people in general are highly pleas'd with the new Measures, which the Parliament of Great Britain have taken for raising funds for the support of Civil Government in the Colonies by which means they will be eased of a considerable Tax. ——— They cannot conceive at what the Faction in Boston would be after ——— but are apprehensive their tedious Publications will be a Means of bringing on the resentment of the Mother Country; the Consequence of which will undoubtedly be that the whole Province must suffer for the Disobedience of a single Town: ——— But should this be the case 'tis to be hop'd the resentment will be chiefly confin'd to Boston; I am certain that no People on Earth are more Loyal and pay more Regard to Authority than the People in the Country."

BOSTON Nov. 30. Whereas on John Gowdy, of this Town Carpenter, a slender bodied, tall young Man, 23 Years of Age, wears light Brown curl'd Hair, and is much Pock broken, was suspected of Stealing and carrying away sundry Goods out of a certain Warehouse in this Town, and a Warrant thereupon procured to search said Gowdy's Lodging or any other suspected Place or Places; and part of said Goods having been Yesterday found in the Chest of said Offender, which Chest was discovered under a Warehouse on Gray's Wharf; And Whereas a diligent search has lately been made, &is now making for said Offender who is supposed to be now concealed in some Part of this Town, or on board some Vessel in the Harbour bound to sea. ―――― This is therefore to caution all Persons whatsoever from harbouring or concealing said Offender, as they would avoid the Penalty of the Law in that case provided.

If any Person or Persons shall apprehend the said John Gowdy and bring, or cause him to be brought before any of his Majesty's Justices of Peace. or shall make discovery of the Remainder of the Goods Stolen as abovesaid, or any Part thereof, so that the right Owner thereof may have the same returned to his possession shall be handsomely rewarded for his or their trouble, by applying to Joseph Otis of said Boston, Deputy sheriff; Nov. 20, 1767.

BOSTON Dec. 14. Last Week died in the Alms-House Mrs. Magaret Pratt, said to be upwards of 100 Years of Age: ―――― She was formerly remarkable for her constant Knitting; of which Employment she was so fond of, that she always practiced it as she walk-d the Streets.

BOSTON Dec. 21. A Guinea Reward. Whereas three Malevolent Demoniacs, between the Hours of XII & I o'Clock of the Night preceeding the 19th Instant, sally'd up Fleet-Street, at the North End, and beat in Eleven Squares of Sash Windows in a certain House in that Street, purely for Mischief Sake, as the Owner is not concious of his giving any other Occasion for such Treatment if any one will give such information to the Printer hereof; as that the Aggressors may be legally prosecuted and convicted, he shall receive a Guinea Reward upon Conviction.

BOSTON Dec. 21. Most certainly it is that where Luxury and Extravagance are the prevailing Character of a People, (and that it is ours every Man must acknowledge) the final issue must necessarily be unhappiness ―――― Strange Information! unhappy State of Things! We all

see our woful extravigance of the Times ——
We all condemn it —— and yet we are all
carried away with it! Such is the Prevalence of
Example —— such the Force of Custom and habit
—— such in short, the fatality which bears
down even a wise and sensible People before it.
  O ye illustrious Patriots! ye darling Guardians of America! You who have so nobly exerted yourselves in the Cause of Freedom; who have bravely stem'd the Torrent of arbitrary Power, rescu'd your Country from the Slavery, pity, wretched America, still exert those abilities which lately preserv'd her Liberty, in convincing your Countrymen of their present Situation; rouse them from that supine Negligence which possesses them; paint the Miseries which threaten them in their true Colours; represent the dreadful consequences that must ensue fron that Luxury and Extravigance so universally prevailing; rekindle those dormant Sparks of Public Spirit which lately broke forth in Defence of their Darling Rights, into a glorious Blaze. You will then preserve your Country from Ruin (The conciousness of which must excite the most rapturous Sensations) lay a Foundation for the Happiness of inborn Millions, and transmit your Fame to the remotest Posterity.
  My fellow Citizens and Friends, would you preserve your Country from many Calamities which threaten us, banish from your Houses (for the present at lea't) those superfluous Attendants Luxuries and Prodigality; contribute every Thing for the Encouragement of Frugality, Occonomy and Industry —— How Intoxicated have we been, bless'd by kind Nature with a most fertile country, capable of producing not only every necessary of Life, every thing that might render it useful and delightful, but what might satisfy the most boundless vanity and Extravagance, to be indebted to distant Reagions for almost every Thing which might by Industry and a proper Management be produc'd amongst ourselves!!!!
  —— For Shame my Countrymen! Exert youselves, show that you have some Spark of Patriotism still left, that you have so much British Blood as to scorn being always dependent: Rise, and

encourage every laudable Attempt towards Industry, set upon manufacturies, and by your example Ability, Zeal, and every noble, patriotic Venture, bear down all opposition to the public Good, ―― If ever there was a Time when Unanimity, Industry and Resolution were necessary. It is now; our present wretched Condition loudly demands the Execution of these public virtues from every Man who truly loves his Country.

Think not American fair ones that you are excluded from Contributing Part towards the public Good ―― Your Country demands the exertion of all you gentler Faculties ―― Scorn to let such trifling Subjects as Dress, Scandal and Detraction engross your thoughts while the noblest Pursuits demand your utmost Attention; such Topics show Meaness of spirit, such depravity of Nature and scandalizes any, much more so the most beautiful Part of the Human Species: But rather show you have Souls capable of feeling for the Miseries of your Country, show that you will do every Thing to preserve it from ruin; lay aside those Gaities which ill suit the Circumstances of your Country; wear nothing but what is manufactured in America; this will be the greatest Encouragement of Manufactures and Industry, this will be acting worthy your charming selves.

In Line, let each Individual exert himself and encourage the Mechanic Arts, Manufactures, Agriculture, in short every Thing that might tend to the Emolument of America, we shall then find Employment for our Industrious Poor, we shall have a source of Riches almongst ourselves; Honour, plenty and happiness will be the Reward of our Industry, and the Consciousness of our having acted worthy the Descendents of our brave Progenitors, must afford a pleasure a delight that will Crown our greatest Toils.

A Young American.

BOSTON Dec. 21. Appeared in the Evening Post and reprinted in the Boston Gazette.

"The last Edes and Gill News-Paper is a turrent of envious Calumny, poured forth from a sink of meanness and Defamation. The foulmouthed Trumpeters of Sedition, bellow and rave and drivil like Mad-dogs and clumsy Cur-dogs, under a dying Man's Window, or like, any Thing and every Thing. At all this no Gentleman is at all surprized or moved, yet Persons of all Ranks and Parties are beyond Measure scandalized, astonished and frightened out of their Senses, that in these, even in these Times, such ebullient Envy and Malice should display itself, and that such a junto of everlasting Miserable of execrable Poetasters, Politicasters, poor Daubers and Dirtcasters, should be suffered to strut and stalk about so really, very and verily impudently, in the very presence of the Public, in all the Pages and Columns of the Edes & Gill News-Paper, as well as in the Holes and Corners and other private Purlieus of the Evening Post and Circulating Gazette It is my prerogative to insult and abuse who I please with Impunity, and they shall know, 'tis their Duty, after I have called them all the Dogs & dirty Souls in the world, to respect me for my Condescension in looking down on them with ineffable, Contempt. Characters the most respectable of the most distinguished Integrity and Ability, the sincerest Steadiest friends to the Province as well as I have been most Illiberally, scandalously and atrociously traduced, standered and willified in that uncommonly infamous Gazette. The Grub-street Powers would fain, tarnish my really very reputable Reputation, but I am already too Weather-beaten to suffer from lawless Cur-dogs. I was a little afraid of them once, but they are a Pack of toothless, cowardly Curs, that never bite. The Evening Post is in Comparison of this Paper, as clean, and free from Blots and dirt, as the Charlestown and Dedham Job Papers were, when bought at the Milton Manufacturery. I will continue to advertise my Countrymen with every Circumstance that I think may be of service to them, and myself even if I should ruin an hundred such Countries as this. And in Spite of those respectable Authors the respectable selectmen of Boston, for whose Persons, Performances and Town, I have no Respect, since they detected my Falsehood and Deceit, which was long since: I the true patriot repeat it with a loud Voice, that there never was a Yard of Cloth made in Dartmouth nor a pair of Shoes ay Lynn. There's pro bono Publico, there's Patriotism for you now! respectable sense keep your Moderation, and don't suffer the Liberty of the Press to be infringed on, nor the Cobal touched in their Monopolies of Corruptions, Treachery and Scandal. I have been writing and scribbling in the same Evening Post these seven Years with and for my Friends, and should never have been suspected, had it not been for the long-winded Cur Tacitus, who bro't out a galling offence that rouzed all the Kennel. Since that there has been such a Bustle, that I'd almost as soon run the Gauntlet from Albany-gate to Boston barefooted, as lead the Life I have. If they would confine themselves to guessing, and firing their Vollies at random, and let me fire from the Bushes. I could be cuntent. There has been great Pains taken to persuade the Town, that will Honeycomb Will ____e, or some sweet Tit, is the true Patriot, but it won't take. One has sworn off, one can't write his name, and the other, if he had been dabbling in one of two Papers, is soon going into the Country to his old trade of Tooth-pick and Pipe Stopper making other knick-knacks for his Friends."

BOSTON Dec. 28. To the Printers.

As several Pieces have lately been published giving Accounts of the ill Effects of Tea, we supply to please the Gentlemen; We therefore hope you will give the following Piece a Place in your next, by which you will oblige a Number of The Ladies.

Not long since we were present at, and terribly shocked with, the Cursing, Damning, and horrid Blasphemies of a Gentleman (so called) whose attendants imputed his Outrageousness to the pernicious effect of spirituous Liquors!
———— Wives left whole Days, and, what is worse, whole nights alone, loss Appetites, ———— Dreary Fortunes, ———— giddy Head, ———— confused Ideas, ———— Loss of Reason, ———— no government of Passion, ———— relaxed Nerves, and trembling Limbs, ———— miserable low spirit,

and Qualmishness, then the heat of the Liquor is over! ——— Add all these, Head-aches, ——— Fever, ——— Rheumatism, ——— Goats, ——— Oaths, ——— Exertion, ——— Blasphermies, ——— with ten Thousand unnatural Deaths and Horrid Murthers! Place all to Account of Spiritous Liquors, or hard Drinking: And then judge where the Reformation ought to begin; whether among the Gentlemen at Taverns & Coffee Houses, where they drink scarcely anything but Wine and Punch; or among the Ladies, at those useful Boards of Trade, called Tea Tables; where it don't cost half so much to maintain half a Dozen Ladies a whole Afternoon, as it does to entertain one Gentleman only one Evening at the Tavern.

However we are willing to give up our dear & beloved Tea, for the Good of the Publick, provided the Gentlemen will give up their dearer and more beloved Punch, renounce going so often to Taverns, and become more kind and loving Sweethearts and Husbands.

Most gladly we aside our Tea wou'd lay,
Could we more Pleasure gain so other Way.

1768

BOSTON Jan. 4. Wednesday last the Great and General Court or Assembly of the Province of Massachusetts-Bay met at the Court-House in Boston, when his Excellency the Governor was pleased to make the following Speech to both Houses, viz.

Gentlemen of the Council and Gentlemen of the House of Representatives.

I Have appointed this Session rather earlier than usual, that you may take into Consideration the proceedings of the Commissaries appointed to settle the Boundary-Line between this Province and that of New-York. For this Purpose you will have before you the Report of the Gentlemen employed in the Business on the part of this Province. I shall also lay before you a Letter upon this Subject which I have received from his Excellency Sir, Henry Moore, Governor of New-York, with its Enclosure thereto belonging.

From these it will appear how very inconsiderable the Difference in which has prevented the Commissaries from coming to a final Agreement; and how desirable it ought to be to the both Parties that Adjusting so trifling a Difference should not be made a Cause of Trouble to his Majesty and his Council. And yet as the Proposal of the Line adhered to by our Commissaries has the authority of the Opinion of the Board of Trade to support it, I cannot myself propose any Departure from it. But I shall with great Pleasure consent to any Concessions which you shall yourselves think fit to offer for the sake of an amicable Agreement and a speedy Determination of this interesting Dispute.

I Have also communicated to you a Letter which I have received from his Excellency Governor Wentworth, with several Inclosed relating to the Dispute concerning the Boundary Line between the Part of this Province called the Province of Maine and the Province of New-Hampshire. I must desire that you will give these due Consideration as soon as you well can; as the Business is of a long standing.

I have nothing in immediate Command from his Majesty to propose to you, I shall communicate at proper times by separate Messages. At present I have only to ask, that you may be assured that as well in the Business before-mentioned as in all others which shall come before this General Court, I shall be always ready to assist in all Measures which shall appear to me to be conducive to the true Honor and real Interest of this Province.   Fra. Bernard.

Council-Chamber. December 20, 1767.
The Senior Class of Scholars at the University in Cambridge, has unanimously agreed to take their next Commencement, dressed altogether in the Manufactures of this Country ——— A Resolution which reflects the highest Honor on the seat of Learning.

BOSTON Jan. 21. We hear that at the Meeting of the Inhabitants of this Town last Wednesday at Faneuil-Hall, the Scene proposed by the Committee for employing the Poor Woman and Children of the Town was unanimously agreed to; and the Thanks of the Town was voted the Committee for the Service.

BOSTON Jan. 25. Extract of a Letter from a Gentleman of Family, Fortune and great Abilities, in a remote Southern Colony, to his friend in this Town, dated December 5, 1767.

"The Liberties of our common Country appear to me to be of this Moment exposed to the most imminent Danger. But whenever the Cause of American Freedom is to be vindicated, I look toward the Province of the Massachusetts-Bay. She must, as she has hithers done first kindled the sacred Flame that on such Occasions must warm and Illuminate this Continent. Words are wanting to express my sense of the Vigilence, Perseverance, Spirit, Prudence, Resolution and Firmness, whith which your Province has distinguished herself in our unhappy Times. May God ever grant her noble Labours a successful Issue. Our Cause of the highest Dignity. It is nothing less than to maintain the Liberty with which Heaven itself hath made us free. I hope it will not be disgraced in any Colony by a single rash Step. We have constitutional Methods of seeking Redress, and they are the best Method."

BOSTON Jan. 25. We have the pleasure of informing the public, that several of his Majesty's council, and many of the house of representatives, now sitting, appear completely cloathed in the manufacture of this country; a number of the clergy are also cloathed, and cloathing themselves therewith —— such example cannot fail to excite the imitation of others, at a time when it is universally agreed, that the political salvation of this continent depends upon promoting frugality and manufactures.

BOSTON Jan. 25. Within 18 months past 487 Yards of cloth, and 36 pair of stockings, have been spun and knit in the family of Mr. James Nixon of Newport.

We are credibly informed that many other families in the Colony, within the year past have each manufactured upwards of 700 yards of cloth, of different kind.

These instances of Industry are mentioned with a view to demonstrate how easy it will be for these Colonies, in a short time, to be independent of any other country for cloathing, and at the same time to excite others to imitate examples so highly beneficial to themselves and the community.

BOSTON Feb. 8. We hear that James Scollay, Son of John Scollay, Esq; of this Town, comimg from on board a Vessel in the Evening, it is supposed fell between that and the Wharf, and went under the Ice, his Hat being found the next Day; he is still missing; —— This young Gentleman was deservedly esteemed by his acquaintances, and promised to be a worthy Member of Society.

We hear that a Boat belonging to his Majesty's Schooner Hope now laying in Nantasket, was broke so with the Ice, that the People in the Boat, said to be the Doctor, Mate, and two Hands perished in the water.

BOSTON Feb. 8. Extract from a Letter from a New-England Gentleman dated London, October 21, 1767.

"I have no Politicks; only I can assure you, that Governor Bernard's Mountain stands strong: This I don't say without good Authority, and I may add very greatly: And from the same Authority I am sure that it never entered into the minds of the present Ministry to invade our Liberties of Privileges, so far from that, I am persuaded they are the best Guardians of both ——— How often have you and I bewailed the nonsensical and inflammatory Pieces so frequent in our Papers, which can't do us good, but have done us harm! Where there is no intention to do wrong the insinuation of it is an Insult, ——— I am persuaded that at present we stand in as favorable a light as any of the Colonies: I wish a prudent, discreet and temperate Conduct may long continue in this Situation."

BOSTON Feb. 15. The Act for preventing Fraud in Debtors, and for securing the Effects of insolvent Debtors from the benefit of their creditors, is now in force until the 12th of March next, and no longer: Several Insolvent Debtors having already taken the Benefit thereof, and appears by the last Massachusetts Gazette, Feb. 11, 1768.

Bankrupts.

Benjamin Hammet, of Boston, Merchant. John Furnass, of Boston, Merchant. Moses Pitcher, of Boston Clazier. Jonathan Hall, Roxbury, Potter. Benjamin Joy, Sherburn, Yeoman and Trader.

BOSTON Feb. 15. It is said the House of Representatives now sitting in General Assembly, have presented a humble, dutiful and loyal Petition to the King; imploring his Majesty's gracious Protection of the Constitutional and Charter Rights, which are thought to be infring'd by several Acts imposing Duties to be levy'd on their Constituents, without their Concent in Parliament: and that they have forwarded Letters to the Rt Honorable the Lords S_____n, R_____m, C_____m, C_____n, and to Mr. Secretary C_____y, &c. representing the Grievance, and earnestly asking their Aid and Patronage: It is moreover added, that their committee have reported a Letter; which is attended by the House, directed to the several Houses of Representatives and Burgesses on the Continent; communicating in decent Terms, their Sentiments and Proceedings, on this Common Concern. And to prevent the Enemies of the Colonies misrepresenting this Measure, we are inform'd the House have ordered a Copy of the last mentioned letter to Mr. De Berdt, to be by him produced as Necessity may require. It is further said that for the Sake of cultivating, as far as lies in their Power a Harmony in the General Assembly, a Committee from the House waiting on the Governor of the Province, to acquaint him, that the House was ready to lay before his Excellency their whole Proceedings in the important affairs, if he desired it: which committee was directed humbly to request his Excellency that he would be pleas'd to favor the House with a Copy of the Letter from Lord Shelburne, which had been read the House by the Governor's Orders; and also Copies of his own Letter to which it referr'd. We are assured, that while the House have been sitting forth the Unspeakable Grievances of Subjects being Taxed Unrepresented; the greatest Care has been taken to show, that an equal Representation of this Province in the British Parliament is utterly impossible: This was undoubtedly a wise Precaution; for who will undertake to say, that a partial Representation of the People would be a less Evil, than over a Taxation without their Concent: It requires some considerable Dexterity at this time to steer right; otherwise it may happen that every vigorous and prudent Step ought most certainly to take to avoid both.

BOSTON Feb.15 . Bankrupts

John Mills, of Boston, Housewright. Dingly Wing, of Boston, Boat-builder. Pool Spear, of Boston, Taylor. Samuel Bayley, of Boston, Feltmaker. Increase Blake, of Boston, Trader. Paul Baxter, of Boston Cooper. Joseph Remick, of

Newbury-Port, Ship-Carpenter, William Alford, of Newbury-Port, Victualler, Dr. John Newman, of Newbury-Port, Physician.

Boston Feb. 15. Messiers Edes and Gill;

The Pretended "Extract of a Letter" published in the last Evening-Post, and said to be "from a N. E. gentleman, dated October 21, 1767", was in my opinion, neither written by a gentleman a N. E. man, nor in London. I think it was composed in Boston, and that between Wednesday, and Thursday noon, of the week before ─── The circumstances are very strong that "True-Patriot" is the real author of the same. The least of those circumstances in the striking similarity of style. The strongest is a very severe censure, on two respectable houses in Town, rapidly lead off without having a copy of the accusation, the names of the informers, or of the sentence of condemnation ─── The Pretended extract of which begins thus "I have no politick" Who does not know that? "Only I can assure you that Governor B_____d's mountain stands strong", &c. I know of no mountain his Excellency is possessed of but M_____t D____1. They can be no tend of necessity, of so often advertising the public, that "Governor B_____d's mountain stands strong". All good navigators know full well, that on the eastern coasts of the ocean are as they term it, iron-bound. 'Tis also certain that the rocks on the shore are as impenetrable as "True Patriot's" heart, and as perfect as solid as his head, And all others, if they please, may know by these presents, that nothing short of his Majesty's Negative of the grant can shake the title to; and that nothing less than a thunder-clap or an earthquake can overturn "Governor B____d's Mountain." But as either of those and worse events may happen in an evil hour when little expected; and as some mountains have been judged to stand strong impregnable till the very instant of tottering to their fall, it is at least advisable that the "True Patriot" and his most obedient servant should walk very humbly all the days of their Pilgrimage.   Moses Meek.

BOSTON Feb. 20. To be sold cheap for cash, a

Likely well-built Brigantine, burthen'd some 115 Tons near 2 Years old, now lying at Pulling's Wharf.   Enquire Edes & Gill.

BOSTON Feb. 22. Messieurs Edes & Gill.

Liberty is so natural to all men that it exerts itself upon particular occasions in the most slavish countries. To this are owing the revolution in Turkey, Persia, & Morocco, tho' the Government in those countries are so absolutely despotic that the People seldom gain any more by their struggles than the pleasure of being revenged on one Tyrant, and making him give way to another. But in Europe such struggling have often ended in the establishment of a proper liberty.

Liberty and prosperity are not only join'd in common discourse, but are in their own Natures ally'd that we cannot be said to possess the one without the enjoyment of the other; and yet there is this distinction to be made between them:

All men in their natural and primitive state had an equal right to possession, but when mankind were increased and formed into civil communities, and the whole mass of property became unequally divided among them according to every ones industry and merit they made laws unanimously for securing each other in their respective acquisitions. Hence it came about, that all men have a right to whatever property they can by the laws of a free country; and the principle on which this is founded, is the common good of mankind.

But liberty, the source and pillar of all true property cannot be preserved in society while the members possess it unequally. It can no longer exist but in its original and native capacity. All men are equally entitled to it. He who assumes more than his just share of liberty becomes a Tyrant on proportion to what he assumes, and he who loses it, becomes to many degree a slave.

BOSTON Feb. 22. From the Public Ledger, London. The late Resolution of Boston in New-England considered.

As the hard Applications of Rogues and Rebels

have within this few days been very plentifully bestowed on the inhabitants of Boston, and as the Public may be desirous to know on what this cruel Treatment is founded, I will inform them.

The Inhabitants being in great distress for want of money, and being fully convinced that a foreign and luxurious trade is the cause of their Poverty and Ruin, they have therefore resolved, in order to check such a destructive trade, not to import, 1. any Men or Women's Apparel ready made, and they have Taylor's and Manufacturers of their own. 2. To use no Gold, Silver or threadlace; because they cannot afford it. 3. To use no Gold or Silver Buttons, for the same reason. 4. No Diamonds, Stones, Paste or Jewllery; their Poverty is such that many of them never saw a Guinea; is it not a laudable resolution then not to import Diamonds. 5. Nor any Snuff or Mustard, their own Fields affording both, shall we be angry then that they make use of them? 6. Muffs, Furs and Tippets: would you prevent them, after killing a Boar, for turning his skin into a Muff?

7. Millinary: and do you think the Ladies too, because they resolve to make their own capes? 8. China ware: It would do honour to the People of England to follow this Example. 9. Linseed Oil: Why their fields are covered with Flaxseed, would you refuse their pressing a little for their own use. 10. Lawns and Cambricks, they deserve a vote of thanks for refusing the manufacture of our Enemies, but which the people of England wears in defiance of the Laws of the Land. Expensive funerals, they also prohibited, and are they not right, and are they not also right, and they not also right in the resolving not to wear cloth above 20 s. per Yard, because they cannot pay for it.

Finally they determine to establish a Linnen manufacture. This is so far from being any prejudice to England, that I, as a Linnen Draper, think they ought as well as Irish have a bounty on it for if New-England could remit their Linnens to England it would be a very fine remittance for our Woolen manufactury and hard ware, when we should no longer have occasion for linnen of Austria, Silesia, Hamburg, Holland, and Russia.

Thus much in answer to all the clamour and dirt thrown at New-England, a people, whose loyalty is unimpreached, notwithstanding the late unhappy difference, &c.   A linnen Draper.

BOSTON Feb. 22. Whereas the Carcasses of several Horses which have died of a contagious Disorder now prevalent, have been carried into the Common and other Parts of the Town, and left unburied, whereby some ill Consequence are apprehended. These are therefore to acquaint the Inhabitants, that such persons as may so hereafter have the dead Bodies of Horses, or any other creature so exposed above Ground, will be prosecuted for such Offences according to Law.

By order of the Select-Men.
                     William Cooper Town Clerk.

The Subscriber (now residing at Capt. Conner's near the Mill-Bridge) hereby acquaint the Town and Country, That he will undertake to cure all Distemper incident to Horses, (if curable) both external and internal. He is so confident of his Judgement, no cure no Pay. And further doth say, that he can relieve any Horse of the Distemper now rise among them in twenty four Hours, so that they may be fit for Business in three Days afterward.   Malchy Field.

Boston Feb. 29. Messieurs Edes & Gill.
May it please your _____, We have for a long time known your Enmity to this Province. We have full proof of your Cruelty to a loyal People. No age has perhaps furnished a more glaring instance of obstinate perseverance in the Part of Malice, then is now exhibited in your _____. Could you have reaped any Advantage from Injuring the People, there would have been some Excuse for the manifold Abuses with which you have leaded them. But when a diabolical Thirst for Mischief is the above Motive of your Conduct, you must not wonder if you are Treated with apex Dislike; for it is impossible, how much favor we endeavour it, to fell any esteem, and marks of guileful Treacherous Mad-Hater for Disgust and Infamy.

Nothing has ever been more intolerable than

Your insistence upon a late Occasion, when you had by your unsuitable Insinuations induced a worthy Minister of the State, to form a most unfavorable Opinion of the Province in general, and some of the most respected Inhabitants in particular. You had the Effrontery to produce a Letter from a Lordship, as a proof of your success in conformulating us. ——— Surely you must suppose we have left all feeling, or you would not have thus tauntingly to display the trophies of your Slander, and upbraidingly to make us sensible of the unoppressable misfortunes which you have brought upon us. ——— But I refrain, lest a full Representation of the hardships suffered by this to long insulted People, should lead them in an unwarrantable Revenge.

We never can trial good and Patriotic Rufers with too great Reverence ——— But it is certain that Men totally abandoned to Wickedness can never mark one Regard, be their Station ever so high.

"If such Men are by God Appointed,
The Devil may be the Lord's anointed."

A True Patriot.

BOSTON March 3. Tuesday last his Excellency the Governor was pleased to send the following Message to the Honorable His Majesty's Council.

I have been used to treat the Publication in the Boston Gazette with the Contempt they deserve, but when they are carried to a length, which is unnoticed, must endanger the very being of Government, I cannot consistently with the Regard to this Province which I profess and really have, excuse myself from taking Notice of a Publication in the Boston Gazette of Yesterday beginning at the Top of the second column of the second Page of the Supplement. I therefore consulted you in Council thereupon, and have received your unanimous Advice that I should lay the said libellous Paper before the House of Representatives.

In pursuit of which Advice, I have ordered the Secretary to communicate to you the said libellous Paper, that you may take the same, together with all the Circumstances attending it, into your serious Consideration, and do therein as the Majesty of the King, the Dignity of the Government, the Honor of the General Court, and the true Interest of the Province shall require.

Council Chamber, March 1, 1768. Fra. Bernard.

In answer to which, there being the full Number of the Council present excepting three Gentlemen, the Board unanimously Voted the following Address to his Excellency.

To His Excellency Francis Bernard, Esq; Captain-General and Governor in Chief, in and over his Majesty's Province of the Massachusetts-Bay in New-England, and Vice-Admiral of the same.

The Address to His Majesty's Council of the Province aforesaid.

May it Please your Excellency,
The Board have taken into serious Consideration your Excellency's Message of the first instant, with the Boston Gazette communicated therewith.

The Article in said Gazette, refer'd to by your Excellency gave the Board a real concern, not only as it is mischievous in Tendency, but as it is false, scandalous and impudent Libel upon your Excellency.

Altho' the Author of it may endeavour to screen himself by the Omission of a name, yet as it refers particularly to a Transaction so lately had in the General Court, there is the highest presumption, the Intention of it could be no otherwise than to place your Excellency in the most odious light.

Such an insolent and licentious Attack on the Chief Magistrate (the King's Representative in the Province) involves in it an Attack on Government itself; as it is subversive of all order and Decorum; and manifestly tends to destroy the Subordination, that is absolutely necessary to good Government and the Well-being of Society. It would have flagitious at any Time but being perpetuated while the General Court is sitting, and a Transaction in the court the alleged Occasion of it, it becomes from these and other Circumstances, in the highest degree flagitious; and may justly be deemed, not only an insult on the General Court; not only an Insult on the King's Authority, and the

Dignity of his Government, but as it concludes with the most unwarrantable Profaneness, and Insult upon the King of Kings.

The Board therefore cannot but look upon the said Libel with the utmost Abhorrence and Detestation: and they are firmly persuaded the Province, in general view it in the same light: The Threats therefore implied in the said Libel cannot be the Threats of the Province, but the Libelers.

The Board takes this Opportunity with one Voice to assure your Excellency that, to the utmost of their Power, they will always defend and support the Honor and Dignity of the King's Governor: and will be ever ready to do, in this affair, as in every other, whatever the Majesty of the King, the Honor of the General Court, and the Interest of the Province shall require.

In the House of Representatives, March 3 1768.

Ordered, that Mr. Hancock, Mr. Otis, Col. Ward, Mr. Spencer and Capt. Bradford, be a Committee to wait on his Excellency the Governor with the following Answer to his Message of the 1st Instant.

May it please your Excellency,
In Duty and great Respect to his Majesty's Representatives and Governor of the Province, this House have given all due Attention to your message of the first Instant. You are pleased to recommend to their serious Consideration, a publication in the Boston Gazette of Monday last as "being carried to a length, which if unnoticed, must endanger the very Reign of Government." In this View, your Excellency, in the Notice you have taken of it, without doubt, acted "consistently with the Regard to this Province which you profess."

We are very sorry that any Publication in the News Papers, or any other Cause, should give your Excellency an Apprehension of Danger to the Being or Dignity of His Majesty's Government here. But this House, after Examination into the Nature and Importance of the paper referred to, cannot see Reason to admit of such Conclusion as your Excellency has formed. No particular Person publick or private in named in it: And as it doth not appear to the House, that any thing contained in it can affect "the Majesty of the King, the Dignity of the Government, and the Honour of the General Court of the true Interest of the Province," they think they may be fully justified in their determination to take no further Notice of it.*

The Liberty of the Press is a great Bulwark of Liberty of the People: It is therefore the incumbent Duty of those who are constituted Guardians of the Peoples Rights to defend and maintain it. This House however, at our branch of the Legislature, in which Capacity alone they have authority, are ready to discountenance an abuse of this Privilege, whenever there shall be Occasion for it: Should the prejudice of Individuals of the Publick; it is their Opinion at present, that Provisions is clearly made for the Punishment of Offenders in common Course of the Law. This Provision the the House apprehend, is the present State of Tranquility in the Province, is sufficient, without the interposition of the General Assembly; which however, it is hoped, will at all Times be both ready and willing, to support the executive Power, in the due Administration of Justice, whenever any extraordinary Aid shall become needful.

*The Division upon the Question was 56 to 18. The Divisin of the House upon this message was 39 to 30.

BOSTON March 3. Bankrupts

James Green, of Maldon, Husbandman. James Hayes, of Reding, Leather-Dresser. Joseph Smetburst, of Marblehead, Trader. John Rand, of Newbury-Port, Chaise-Maker. Gidion Parker, of Ipswich, Shipwright, Natanial Conants, Of Beverly, Yeoman. John White, 3d, of Haverhill, Gent. William Rhodes, of Boston, Mariner, Benjamin Parker, of Rutland, Innholder.

BOSTON March 10. Bankrupt

Jeremia Parker, of Haverhill, Gent. Henry Spring, of Worcester, Gent. Phineas Butler, of Lanenburg, Husbandman. Richard Skinner, of Marblehead, Merchant. Samuel Bradley, of Haverhill, Trader. Daniel Canant of Beverly,

Husbandman. Peter Thurston, of Lancaster, Feltmaker, Joseph Convers, of Cambridge Victualler.

BOSTON March 14. We are inform'd that previous to the Dismission of Capt. Timothy Folgier from the Employment he held in Customs, which has been the Subject of Speculation, he was asked by one of the Board of Commissioners, whether the Name Timothy Folgier, with a Yea, affix'd to the late Resolve of the House of Representatives, for encouraging Industry and Suppressing Vive, and for the discountenancing foreign Superfluities, and promoting the Manufactures of the Province, was his name, and whether he voted in favor of the Resolution; and upon the Question's being answered by Mr. Folgier in the Affirmative, he was told, that he was not a fit Person to be employ'd as an Officer in the Revenue: and it is said that he was dismish'd without further Ceremony.

BOSTON March 26. Saturday Evening last died after a lingering illness, and Yesterday was decently interred, Mr. Samuel Draper, Printer, one of the Publishers of the Massachusetts Gazette. His exemplary Behaviour in Life renders his Death a loss to his Relatives and Acquaintances.

BOSTON April 4. Last Saturday Morning the Roof of a House near the Draw-Bridge having catched on fire by some Sparks from an adjoining Chimney, a Seafaring Man, named Doyle, a native of Ireland, being at the top of a Ladder endeavouring to extinguish it, accidentally fell from thence into the street, and fractured his Skull in such a shocking Manner that he expired immediately.

BOSTON April 4. Wednesday last the Governor was pleased, by proclamation, to dissolve the Great and General Court of Assembly of this Province.

Friday and Saturday last we had extremely high Winds, with Snow, which we imagine hindered the Southern Post from crossing the Ferries, as he is not arrived at the Publishing of this Paper.

BOSTON April 11. We hear Joshua Howe, the famous Money maker, was lately taken at Cohass, and committed to Goal in New-Hampshire Government with one John Snow, on suspicion of their being concerned in counterfeiting Dollars, &c. It is said there is a Clan of these Gentry of at the least 500 who correspond thro' all the Colonies as far as No. Carolina. Howe denies his being concerned in manufacturing any money but acknowledges he let out certain Tools at two Dollars per Day.

Last Week one Lue Tease a noted Dutch Sawyer in Town, was committed to Goal, charged with receiving from a Gentleman's Servant, at sundry times, a large Quantities of Goods, knowing them to be stolen.

Several small Articles have lately been stolen out of the Grocery Stores on the Long Wharf, in the Day Time, supposed by some of those Lazy Rogues which have lately swarmed among us, who prefer Pilfering to honest Labor; which may serve as a Caution to the Storekeepers to be a little more watchful, that so by detecting some of them, an Example may be made to others.

BOSTON April 11. Last Tuesday Evening died at Cambridge, after an Illness of four Days, Shute Bernard, the fourth Son of his Excellency the Governor, in the 16th Year of his Age. ——— His Genius, and his Understanding were good. His Excellency worthy of imitation. His Remains were decently interred at Cambridge last Friday Afternoon.

BOSTON April 25. We hear that the Superior Court of Judicature, &c. held at Boston last March one Leonard McIntire was convicted of uttering two false and counterfeit Pieces of Coin made in the imitation Quarters of Dollars knowing them to be counterfeit; for which he was sentenced to be whipped 20 stripes and pay cost &c. And one Joffrey Cotter was convicted both of counterfeiting and uttering one such piece. for which he was sentenced to be set in the Pillory one hour, to be whipped 20 stripes, and pay cost &c. which was executed last Thursday.

At the Superior Court &c. held at Charlestown last week one Jonathan Goodanow was convicted of unlawfully cohabiting with a Woman not his Wife, viz. one Elizabeth Everden, for which he was sentenced to pay a fine to the King of .25

pounds and cost, and to give bond for his good behaviour for 12 months: She to pay .3 Pounds and cost.

One William Smith for breaking into a store at Cambridge belonging to Mr. John Dennie, and stealing from thence to the value of 358 Pounds was sentenced to be branded in the forehead with the letter B and to pay treble damages and cost.

One John Johnson for escaping out of goal to suffer one month imprisonment and to pay cost; and upon two indictments against him for stealing, was sentenced to be whipped 30 stripes, to pay treble damages and cost.

One Bonker, who was indicted for assaulting and abusing his own daughter (of about 17 years of age) in a most shameful manner, pleaded guilty, As his crime was quite new specie, it is said that the Court has respited his sentence till next term, that they may have opportunity to consider what kind of punishment will be suitable to it.

One Ichabod Smith of Natick, being convicted of barratry, was sentenced to pay a fine to the King of 30 Pounds, to give bond for his good behaviour for 12 months, and to pay cost, &c.

We also hear that the last mentioned Court upon an action for damages brought by one Dougherty against one Thomas Little of Shirley, for unlawfully cohabiting with said Daughety's wife in his absence, a verdict was given against Little for 400 Pounds lawful money damage and cost; ——— and that is a final trial.

BOSTON May 2. Last Thursday came to trial at His Majesty's Interior Court in Suffolks, an action of Trespass wherein Mr. John Gill of this Town Printer, was Plaintiff, and Mr. John Mein Bookseller Defendant, for Assault & Battery; when after a long Hearing the Jury found a verdict in favour of the former, of one Hundred and thirty Pounds Lawful money Damages, and Cost of Court. From which Judgement we hear both Parties appealed to the next Superior Court.

BOSTON May 7. Whereas it has been reported in Town, that Edward Taylor has been concerned in tempting my Negro to steal Goods from me at

sundry Times ——— I declare That I have no reason to believe he has ever been guilty of such Crime; but on the contrary, has Reason to believe that he is a very Honest industrious Man.
W. Molineux.

BOSTON May 9. At a Meeting of the freeholders and other Inhabitants on Wednesday last, the following Gentlemen were chosen by a large Majority to represent them in the General Assembly the ensuing Year. viz. Hon. James Otis Esq; Mr. Thomas Cushing, Esq; Mr. Samuel Adams, and John Hancock, Esq.

The Town pass'd a Vote, nomine contridicente directing the Selectmen to refuse the Use of Faneuil-Hall to his Excellency the Governor and Council, on ensuing Election Days; unless they shall be assured that the Commissioners of Customs will not be invited to dine there on that Day.

BOSTON May 9. Messieurs Fleet,
When war was with all its terror, threaten'd us with extirpation, how oft have I with fervent zeal and unwearied perseverance animated my fellow subjects to defend the cause of their God, their King and their Country! What noble source had I then for the most natural and pathetic harangues! Religion, Loyalty and Liberty were sensible objects to a virtuous people; Superstition (hierarchy) Tyranny, & Slavery were dreadful sounds, and death itself was only looked upon as a casualty that might happen in securing the former and repealing the latter,

——— The Prints inform us that France is industriously equipping her marine, Portugal does not seem to use with the Complaisance we think ourselves entitled to by treaty; Spain has not yet discharged the Manilla ransom; and no considerate man will assure us we have the fairest prospect of a perpetual peace with all nations.

Now suppose the family compact of any other such powerful alliance to engage against Great Britain and threaten her with destruction, and we Americans should look upon it out duty and interest to support our mother state. I who never could be easy to such seasons, would be much obliged to all or either of those Gentlemen lately arrived from the Capital of the empire, and doubtless instructed in the secrets of government would they publish the general outlines of an effectual plan of persuasion to inspire the soldier with an equal ardor for glory and contempt of death in its pursuit as appeared under the old charter of King Edw. I. as to the late story defending and securing his Majesty's dominion in America, tho' every penny raised (without consent) should be spent in the colonies, it seems a very flat subject for declaration.

Probus.

BOSTON May 9. We hear from Newport, that on Tuesday the 3d about midnight a fray happened at a house of bad fame there, between some of the officers of the Senegal man of war on that station, One Nichols a Dutchman a shoemaker, and one Dexter a sailor, both belonging to Newport. ——— It began in the house with high words, during which Dexter put out the candle, and a scuffle ensuing one of the officers had his nose cut off, then Nichols and Dexter went away, and the people belonging to the man of war, went to a doctor's ——— soon after their departure, it is said, Dexter having changed his dress, came back to the house with a club struck with nails, threatening to search it, but on being answered there were not there, after some time departed, they however unluckily met again in the street, came to blows when Nichols and Dexter were both run through the body. ——— The Dutchman immediately ran home, called out that he was a gone man, and died in a few minutes. Dexter was alive when the post came away, but it was thought could not long survive.

Next day application being made to Capt. Cookson, of the Senegal, he expressed much surrow for what had happened, accompanied the sheriff on board his ship, and delivered up his officers to the civil authority; a vast concourse of people attended their landing, and threatened to dispatch them; but by the prudent management of the sheriff, they were safely conducted to the court house, followed by the crowd where they were examined, and afterward committed to goal. During the examination several of the crowd behaved with such indecency to the judges, that they ordered the sheriff to carry them to goal, but the mob prevented him from putting their orders in execution.

BOSTON May 16. We learn by letters from Capt. Jarvis. That the latter end of February, a Bill was brought into Parliament to continue the Bounty on Greeland Ships to the Year 1770, where the Act favourable to the American Fishery expires; The Bill was supported by Administration. The Ministry declared their Idea to be, that both Acts might expire together, when they could take the Matter up the whole, and give the preference to the British Ships as would weaken and lessen the American Fishery. —— Mr. G-m-le said that he intended to have thrown that whole Branch of Business into the Hands of the Americans, considering there too, as part of the British Empire, and as such subject to the Supreme Legislative Controul of Parliament; but since the Americans had denied the Supreme Power —— since they held opinions the most dangerous, the most traitorous to this Country, —— since even some in England had doubted the Supreme Power of Parliament over them, —— he had changed his Views and thought every Encouragement, every Preference ought to be given to the British Ships: —— he also declared in the House, that the Americans had no right at all, none, to the Fishery, it was conquered by our Arms, and protected by our Power, and that all the Privileges of Fishing which America had, was by Favour, Indulgence, and Kindness of Great Britain; When Mr. G-v-de mentioned the Fishery, he extended it to all Fisheries; and it is said, that it has been in contemplation to lay an heavy Duty upon every Fishing Vessel belonging to this Province.

BOSTON June 6. Messiers Edes & Gill. This Day I received great Satisfaction of observing an assiduity of the Officers of the Militia in the Town, which convinced of their solitude to render the Regiment respectable, yet I was much disgusted to find so many of the Inhabitants, by Law called upon to appear in Arms, absenting themselves from their Duty, and neglecting to get acquainted with the manly & frequently useful art of war.

But nothing could give me more Pleasure than the regular Soldier-like Behaviour of the Gentlemen of the Train of Artillery; the great expense, and unwearied Pains they must have been of, before they could have arrived to such Perfection, place them in a very agreeable Point of Light, and they are universally esteemed at a very great Military Ornament, to the Town, and likewise an Honor to the Province. It is to be hoped the greatest Applause do deservedly bestowed on them, will induce others to emulate their Merit.   A Spectator.

BOSTON June 13. Last Friday Evening some Commotion happen'd in this Town, in which a few Windows were broke, and a Boat was drawn thro' the Streets and burnt on the Common; since which Things have been tolerably quiet; it being expected that the Cause of this Disturbance will be speedily removed.

Tuesday last as some Carpenters were repairing the New-South Meeting-House, they discovered under the Floor a black Coffin, with a Child therein, which had lain a long time, as the Infant was greatly emaciated.

BOSTON June 20. Friday the 10th Instant towards Evening the Officers of Custom of this Port, made a Seizure of a Sloop belonging to and at the Wharf of John Hancock, Esq; which Vessel was improved as a Store to put some Barrels of Oil on board, there being no room in the Owner's Stores on the Wharf's. After the Officers took Possession of the Sloop. one of them made a Signal to his Majesty's Ship Romney, then lying off in the Harbour, whereupon the Boats belonging to said Ship, were immediately maned and armed, and made towards the Wharf. Several Gentlemen resent advised the Officers not to move her as there would be no Attempt allowed by the Owner to rescue her out of their Hands; but notwithstanding this Declaration, the Fast was cut away, and she was carried under the Guns of the Romney: ——— This conduct provoked the People who had collected on the Shore and in the Dispute, the Collector, the Comptroller of his Majesty's Custom, and the Comptroller's Son, were roughly used and pelted with Stones, none of them much hurt. The noise bro't together a mixed Multitude, who followed up to the Comptroller's House, and broke a few Squares of Glass, but withdrew by the Advice of some of the prudent Gentlemen that interposed; they were joined by a Number of Sailors, and vagrant Persons who were suspicion of an Intention to put them on board the Ship. These went in search for one of the Man of War's Boats, in their way met with the Inspector of Exports and Inports, him they attacked, broke his Sword and tore his Cloaths; but by some assistance he with difficulty escaped to a House on King-Street. No boat being ashore, about 10 O'Clock they went to one of the Docks and dragged out a large Pleasure-Boat belonging to the Collector, this they drew along the Street with loud huzzaing all the way, into the Common, where they set Fire to it, and burnt it to Ashes; they also broke several Windows of the Houses of the Collector and inspector-General which were nigh by the Common: No other outrage was committed that Night.

There were some Occurrences respecting the Officers of the Romney preceding this Affair which raised the Resentment of the Populace: On the Sunday Evening before a Press Gang went on board a Vessel just arrived from Glasgow and which came to anchor off the Long-Wharf, the impress'd Men took an opportunity while the Man of War's Men were furling the Sails from them, and got into the Ship's Boat and rowed ashore; it being after Sun-set several People had assembled on the Wharf in the Cool of Day, who made way for the men to run up; The Press gang as soon as they could get to their Boat pursued them, crying, stop Defectors, but no heed being given thereto, an Officer on the Wharf resented it, which raised a clamour, and prevented the Gang from Landing: ——— A few Days after a young Man that had served an Apprenticeship in this Town was impressed out of an inward bound Ship; Application made to the Captain (who it is said promised not to detain any Inhabitants of these Provinces) and he engaged to deliver him up, if an able-bodied Man was brought in his Room; such an one was procured for three Guineas, but upon his being carried on board the Romney, was refused, as the Officers of the Ship had been insulted, in the above Affair; many Things were said to the person who went to get the young Man released, reflecting on the Town and not without Threats: —— the Day following a Man was taken out of an Eastern Vessel, by an Arm'd Schooner that was bound for Halifax; —— These Transactions, with the Prospect of the Trade and Business of this and other Towns being in a Manner ruin'd, raised spirit of Resentment in the People, that the Board of Commissioners (these of them that arrived last November from England) and their other Officers, together with the Collector and Comptroller for this Port, and also the Officers of the Romney, thought it most prudent to repair on board the Ship.

On Monday the People in Town were in great Agitation; but lest any Tumult might arise at Night, the Consequences whereof would be very prejudicial, a Notification was posted up in divers Parts of Town, requesting the Sons of Liberty to meet at Liberty Hall on Tuesday the 14th at Ten o'Clock in the forenoon; the expectation of this Meeting kept the Town in Peace: Early on Tuesday Morning the Colours were Flying on Liberty Tree; and at the Hour appointed vast Numbers of the Inhabitants appeared at and near the Hall; but the Weather being wet and uncomfortable in the Street, they adjourned to Faneuil-Hall; where it was proposed to have a legal Meeting called; accordingly a Warrant was Issued by the Select-Men to the Constables to warn a Meeting of freeholders and other Inhabitants of the Town at three o'clock, and several Gentlemen were nominated to prepare a Draft of some Matters proper to say before them; At Three o'Clock the Inhabitants met, but so great was the Concourse that they were obliged to adjourn from Farneuil-Hall to the old South Meeting House.

It has been reported the Sloop was seized because no Permit for Loading was taken out at the Custom House before the Oil was put on board; others report that it was for Breach of the Act of Trade in her last Voyage, which was from Madeira; but which of the Reports is right we are not able to inform the Public.

BOSTON June 20. We are authorized to inform the publick, that Captain Conner, Commander of his Majesty's Ship Romney, in case he should want any more Men, he will not take any belonging to or married in this Province, nor any employed in the trade along shore, or the neighbouring Colonies.

And we are further authorized to assure the Public, that the Man pressed out of Captain Waterman, is dismissed, and will be ashore this Day.

Boston June 20. On Friday the Town meet by adjournment, and received a Report from their Committee, and unanimously voted the following Instructions to the Representatives, viz.

To the Hon. James Otis, ant Thomas Cushing Esq'rs; Mr. Samuel Adams and John Hancock, Esq;

Gentlemen,

After the repeal of the late American Stamp-Act, we were happy in the pleasing prospects of a restoration of that tranquility and unanimity among ourselves, and that harmony and affection between our parent country and us, which had generally subsided before that detestable Act. But with the utmost grief and concern, we find that we flatter'd ourselves too soon, and that the root of bitterness is yet alive. ——— The principle on which the Act was founded continues in full force, and a revenue is still demanded from America.

We have the mortification to observe our Act of Parliament after another passed for the expressed purpose of raising a revenue from us; to see our money continually collecting from us without our consent, by an authority in the constitution of which we have no share, and over which we have no kind of influence or controul; to set the little circulating cash that remains among us for the support of our trade, from time to time Transmitted to a distant country, never to return, or what in our estimation is worse, if possible, appropriated to maintenance of swarms of Officers and Pensioners in idleness and luxury, whose example has tendency to corrupt our morals, and whose arbitrary dispositions will trample on our rights.

Under all these misfortunes and afflictions, however, it is our fixed resolution to maintain our loyalty and duty to our most gracious sovereign, a reverence and due subordination to the British Parliament as the supreme legislative in all case of necessity, for the preservation of the whole empire, and our cordual and sincere affection for our parent country; and to use our utmost endeavours for the preservation of peace and order among ourselves: Waiting with anxious expectation, for a favorable answer to the petition and solicitations of this continent, for relief. At the same time, it is our unalterable resolution, at all times, to assert and vindicate our dear and invaluable rights and liberties at the utmost hazard of our lives and fortunes; and we have a full and rational confidence that no design formed against them ever prosper.

That such design have been formed and are still in being, we have reason to apprehend. A multitude of Place men and Pensioners, and an enormous train of Underlings and Dependents, all novel in this country, we have seen already: Their imperious tempers, their rash inconsiderate and weak behaviour, are well known.

In this situation of affairs several armed vessels, and among the rest, his Majesty's ship of war Romney, have appeared in our harbour, and the last, as we believe by express application of the Board of Commissioners, with design to over awe and terrify the inhabitants of the town into base compliances and unlimited submission, has been anchored within a cable's length of the wharves.

By passing over other irregularities, we are

assured, that the last alarming act of that ship, viz. the violent, and in our opinion illegal seizure of a vessel lying at a wharf, the cutting her fasts and removing her with armed force in hostile manner under the protection of the King's ship, without any probable cause that has yet been made known; no libel or prosecution whatsoever having yet been instituted against her, was by express order or request in writing of the Board of Commissioners to the commander of the ship.

In addition to all this, we are continually alarmed with rumours and reports of new revenue Act to be passed, new importations of Officers and Pensioners to suck the life-blood of the body politick, while it is streaming from the veins: fresh arrived of ships of war to be a still severe restraint upon our trade; and the arrival of a military force to dragoon us into passive obedience: orders and requisitions transmitted to New-York, Halifax and to England, for regiments and troops to preserve the public peace.

Under the distresses arising from this state of things, with the highest confidence in your integrity, abilities and fortitude, you will exert yourselves, Gentlemen, on this occasion that nothing be left undone that may conduce to our relief; and in particular we recommend it to your consideration and discretion, in the first place, to endeavour that impresses of all kind may if possible be prevented. There is an Act of Parliament in being, which has or even been repealed, for the encouragement of trade to America. We mean by the 6th Ann. Chap. XXXXVI, Sect. 9. it is enacted "That no mariner or other person who shall serve on board, or be retained to serve on board any privateer, or trading ship or vessel that shall be employed in any part of America, nor any mariner, or other person being on shore in any part thereof, shall be liable to be impressed, or taken away by any officer or officers of or belonging to any of her Majesty's ships of war, impowered by the lord high admiral, or any other person whatsoever, unless such mariner shall have before deserted from such ship of waw belonging to her Majesty, at anytime after the fourteenth of February 1707, upon pain that any officer or officers so impressing or taken away or causing to be impressed or taken away any mariner or other person, contrary to the tenor or true meaning of this act, shall forfeit to the master, owner or owners of any such ship or vessel, twenty Pounds for every man he or they shall so impress or take, to be recovered with full cost of suit in any court within any part of her Majesty's Dominions," So that any impresses of any mariner, from any vessel whatsoever, appears to be in direct violation of an act of Parliament. In the next place, 'tis our desire that you inquire and use your endeavours to promote a parliamentary inquiry for the author and propagators of such alarming rumours and reports as we have mentioned before; and whether the Commissioners or any other persons whatsoever have really wrote or solicited for troops to be sent here from New-York, Halifax, England or elsewhere, and for what end: and that you forward, if you think it expedient, in the House of Representatives, resolution, that every such person who shall solicit or promote the importation of troops at this time, is an enemy to this town and province, and a disturber of the peace and good order of both, Then the meeting was dissolved.

   BOSTON July 4. Messieurs Edes & Gill. Please insert the following short Narrative, and you'll oblige your humble servant.

   On Thursday last we the subscribers being out on a Party of Pleasure on the Water, on our Return about 9 o'Clock being two Guns short of the Buoy of the King's ship the Romney, commanded by Captain Corner; having a small Arm on Board, which we carried down for the sake of Game; and it being at the Time loaded, we thought it proper to discharge her for fear of an accident: This it seems gave great Offence to Capt. Cornor who ordered us on Board. Upon our coming on Board, we treated him with much civility as we were capable of. He ask'd us whether we knew it was contrary to the Custom of the King's Ships

to suffer a Gun to be fired within their Buoys?
to which we answered, we were not within the
Buoys ——— that it was usual for People out
on their Pleasure to fire after Game anywhere
in the Harbour, and even on Castle Island,
without giving offence; but that we were not
acquainted with the Custom of the King's ships,
as it was not common for them to be here. ———
He said it was high Time they were, and attempted in a rude Manner to strike off Simion Poley's
hat. ——— He told us we were both drunk, and
bid us to be gone. ——— He told us that he had
twenty-five Small Arms continually kept loaded,
and then he ordered a Gentleman, who appeared
to be an Officer to fire a volley on the first
Boat that should hereafter fire a gun within
the Buoys.

    This we relate, to give warning of this de-
clared Intention and Order of Capt. Corner, to
all Persons who may be concerned; and also to
leave it to the Consideration of the World,
whether he is that high good-humoured and well
bred Gentleman, which he has represented by some
to be. July 2, 1768. Simeon Poley, William Miller.

    BOSTON July 11. His Excellency Governor Ber-
nard hath issued his Proclamation, dated the
!st instant, for desolving the Great and General Court of this province in substance as
following viz.

    In obedience to his Majesty's Command signi-
fied to me by his Secretary of State, I dissolve
the Great and General Court or Assembly, is
accordingly Dissolved, and the Members thereof
are hereby discharged from all further attendance.

    BOSTON July 11. The Beaver Sloop of War Capt.
Belew, arrived here the beginning of the Week
from Halifax, and anchors now between Dorchester
Neck and Castle William near where the Gaspee
lately anchored, which has since sailed.

    Wednesday last came into this harbour, his
Majesty's armed Schooner Hope, and Little Romney.

    The next day arrived here his Majesty's Ship
Senegal.

    BOSTON July 18. At Anchor off Castle William
in Boston Harbour, His Majesty's ship Romney of

50 Guns, Capt. Corner; Beaver of 16 Guns, Capt. Belew; Senegal of 18 Guns, Capt. Cookson; and two armed Schooners.

The Province not having been favoured with a Station Ship during the last War were at a prodigious Expence to build and maintain Ships to protect this our Coast. We now behold Five parading in out Harbour, —— and what is very diverting, hovering round Castle-William as if there was the greatest Danger of its being attacked at a Time of Profound Peace.

BOSTON July 25. However meanly some People think about the Populace or Mob of a Country, it is certain that the Power or Strength of every Free Country depends entirely upon the Populace; and by their Affection only it is that the Magistrates can be protected and supported, in the exercise of that Power which the People have entrusted them with: The Governors and People of any Single Town or Province, may sometimes differ in their Sentiments, and the People may be kept in Obedience to their Governors, or at least prevented from breaking out in any Violences, either by the Hope that the Community would join together against them, and punish them, if they should commit any Violence against their Magistrate; But when this happens to be the case of the whole Country; when the Governors and the People in general are of different Sentiments, when the People, either openly or secretly rejoice at the Disappointment of the Governors meet with, the Liberties of that Country must be at an end, or their Government must be speedily changed; for it is impossible for those Governors, who are hated by the People to support themselves by the People; they must look out for some foreign, or some artificial Aid, they must provide for supporting and protecting themselves, either by foreign Alliance, or by standing mercenary Armies; and if they can support themselves by either of these methods, the Liberties of the People are surely at an end.
M. M.

BOSTON Aug. 1. Publick Notice is hereby given that Nathaniel Thayer of Boston, Sealer of Wood within the Town of Boston, has filed Information in the Inferior Court of Common Pleas, setting forth, that the Twenty First Current, he seiz'd on the Wharves improv'd by Benjamin Phillips, a common Warfinger and seller of Wood, in said Town, about Thirty-seven Cords of Wood, as forfeited, not being four Feet in length, praying that the same Wood may be adjusted to remain forfeited, on moiety to the use of him the said Nathaniel.

All Persons claiming Property in the same Wood, are hereby to appear before the Inferior Court on Tuesday the Ninth of August (if any they have) why the said Wood should not be Adjusted to remain forfeited as prayes for. July 26, 1768. By Order of the Court.

       Ezekiel Goldthwart, Clerk.

It has been asserted last Week that two regiments lay ready at Halifax to be embarked for Boston on the first application from the Governor. I wish it were ascertained, if they come whether they are to be employes in street-firing, or Walkerizing, the Inhabitants, or in both?

BOSTON Aug. 1. Extract of a Letter by Capt. Price from a Gentleman in London to his friend in Boston.

We too have firebrand, but much more and much more profligated and abandoned than yours. Upon some accounts I could wish we could change, for yours would be abhorred with you for his profligate and blasphemy; not but that he can at times play the Hypocrite, and might hang out a shew that might suit your taste.

BOSTON Aug. 8. The following is a copy of a petition reported to the house of Representatives by the Committee, and under their Consideration, when the Assembly was dissolved.

We your Majesty's most dutiful Subjects, the Representatives of your ancient and loyal Provinve of Massachusetts-Bay, impressed with the deepest Sense of Gratitude to Heaven, for calling to the British Succession your Majesty's Illustrious Family, and so firmly establishing your Majesty on the Throne of Royal Progenitors: And being abundantly convinced of your Majesty's Grace and Clemency, most humbly

implore the Royal Favour, while we briefly represent the Grievances we labour under, and which, under God, your Majesty alone can redress. ——— It is with inexpressible concern, that we are constrained thus publickly to complain of the Administration of his Excellency Francis Bernard, Esq; your Majesty's Governor of this Province; who has betrayed an arbitrary disposition. ——— He early attached himself to a Party, whose Principles and Views we apprehend, have ever been repugnant to your Majesty's real Service. -——— He has both in his Speeches, and other public Acts treated the Representative Body with Contempt. ——— He has, in an unwarrantable Manner, taken upon himself the exercise of your Majesty's Royal Prerogative in granting a Charter for a College, without even with the Advice of your Majesty's Council.
——— He has openly attempted to make himself sole Judge of the Qualification of Members, returned to serve in the House of Representatives. ——— We have also Reason to apprehend, that he endeavoured to persuade your Majesty's Ministers to believe, that an Intention was formed, and a plan settled, in this, and the rest of the Colonies, treasonably to withdraw themselves from all Connections with, and Dependence upon Great-Britain; and from their natural Allegiance to your Majesty's sacred Person and Government. ——— He has indiscreetly, not to say wantonly exercised the Prerogative of the Crown, in the repeated Negative of Councellors of unblemished Reputation, and duly elected by a great Majority of both Houses of Assembly. ——— He has declared that certain Gentlemen his Favorites, shall be so-elected. ——— He has unconstitutionally interfered with, and unduly influenced Elections; particularly in the Choice of an Agent for this Province. He has very abruptly displayed divers Gentlemen of worth, for no apparent Reason, but their voting in the Assembly against his Measures. ——— He has practiced the sending over Depositions to the Ministers against Gentlemen of Character here, without giving the accused the least Notice of his Purpose and Proceedings.

────── He has enacted divers new and unconstitutional Offices ────── He has drawn divers Warrants on the Treasury, for the Payment of monies, against the express Appropriations of the Assembly. ────── He has, at this Session, presumed to threaten the General Assembly, upon the Non-Compliance of the House of Representatives with a certain Requisition, not only to dissolve them, but to delay to call a new assembly, which is beyond your Majesty's Orders.

────── By the Means aforesaid, and many others, that might be enumerated, he has not only rendered his Administration disagreeable to the whole Body of the People, but entirely alienated their Affection from him; and thereby wholly destroyed the Confidence in a Governor, which your Majesty's Service indispensably requires. ────── Whereof we must humbly intreat your Majesty , that his Excellency Francis Bernard, Esq; may be removed from the Government of this Province: And that your Majesty would graciously pleased to place one in his Stead, worthy to represent the greatest and best Monarch on Earth. ────── And as is Duty bound, we &c. shall ever pray.

BOSTON Aug. 15. It has been currently reported that the Commissioners are soon to have a force whether Naval or Military, is not yet known. Strange it is indeed, if those few Men have such an extensive and unlimited Powers as to order Forces here, just to satisfy their Humours and Avaricious Ends. ────── It is to be hoped that the Extent of their Power will soon be known, by the publication of their Commissions, which we hear is now in the Press.

BOSTON Aug. 16. Last Wednesday Afternoon, between 4 and 5 o'Clock Mr. Paul Spier of this Town, coming by the Romney man of war in his lighter, which he certainly plies between this place and Nantasket for Ballast, was fired upon with a Musket from the Ship, which was repeated to 4 Times, and one Cannon, the Officer calling to him to lower his peak, Mr. Spier answering he had no peak ────── halyards, the Lieutenant and 6 other got into their Boat and rowed after him with all Speed, firing three Musket shot, some of which came very near him, but he still keeping head of the Boat ran his lighter aground, within a few Yards of Mr. Rowe's Wharf and left her: The Man of War's Men directly seiz'd on her and were endeavouring to haul her off, when the People gathering on the Wharf, saw one of the Lighter's men's Face bleeding, occasioned by a Stroke he had got by an Oar, and concluding he had been wounded by the firing, grew much enraged, and threw Stones at the Man of War's Men with much Violence, on which they in a few Minutes left the lighter and went off in great fury.

BOSTON Aug. 22. All the Advice from England agreeing, that nothing could contribute more to our obtaining a Redress of our Grievances, than the breaking off all Commerce with Britain, at least for the Season; the Merchants of this Metropolis have of themselves alone, with greater unanimity than in the Time of the Stamp-Act come into agreement not to import any Duty Goods, until the Repeal of those Acts, nor any other Merchandize, with a few exceptions from January 1, 1769 to January 1, 1770. May the Merchants of all other Provinces do themselves the Honor, to act with as much patriotic Disinterestedness, and America will still be free and happy.

BOSTON Sept. 8. Yesterday sailed from this Port his Majesty's Sloop of War Senegal, as also the armed Schooners, supposed to be bound for Halifax. There now remains in this Harbour, with their pendents flying, his Majesty's Ship Romney, of 50 Guns, and the Sloop Liberty.

The above Sloop Liberty was sold at Public Auction last Tuesday, and was struck up to the Collector of his Majesty's Customs for this Port, and it is said is now to be improved as a Cruiser for the Protection of Trade.

BOSTON Sept. 12. Whereas many persons are so unfortunate to lose their fore-teeth by Accident and otherways, to their great Detriment, not only in Looks, but speaking both Public and Private: ——— This is to inform all such, that they may have them replaced with false Ones, That looks as well as the Natural, and answers the End of Speaking to all intent, by Paul Revere, Goldsmith, near the Head of Dr. Clarke's Wharf, Boston.

All Persons who have false Teeth fixed by John Baker-Dentist, and they have got loose (as they will in Time) may have them fastened by the above, who learnt the Method of fixing them from Mr. Baker.

BOSTON Sept. 19. We hear that Saturday sennight two Informers, and Englishman and a Frenchman, were taken up by the Populace at Newbury-Port, who tarred them; but being late they were handcuffed and put in custody until the Sabbath was over: ——— Accordingly on Monday Morning they were again tarred and rolled in Feathers, then fixed to a Cart with Halters, and carried through the principle Streets of the Town, to the view of the Gallows, but what further we do not hear.

BOSTON Sept. 22. Saturday evening last his Excellency the Governor received a Letter from his Excellency General Gage, Commander in chief of his Majesty's Forces in North-America, advising him that in Obedience to his Majesty's Command, he had directed two Regiments, viz. the 14th and 29th, under the command of Lieut, Colonel Dalrymple, to embark at Halifax, and proceed to Boston as soon as possible, one of at present to be at Castle William, and the other in the Town; and the provisions be made for them agreeable to Act of Parliament. On Monday morning the Governor laid the same before his Majesty's Council.

His Excellency also laid before the Council, an Extract of a Letter which he had received the day before by Capt. Bruce from London, for the right Honorable the Earl of Hillsborough, his Majesty's Principal Secretary of State for the Colonies, setting forth that his Majesty had thought it fit to signify his Pleasure, after taking the opinion and Advice of his Principle Servants, that the Troops intended for the relief of North America in the next Spring, consisting of two Regiments, from Ireland should be immediately sent to America and landed in Boston. ——— That Transport Vessels were now preparing with all possible Dispatch, in order to proceed to Cock, to take on board said Regiments, which are to be augmented by Draughts to 500 Men each.

BOSTON Sept. 26. We hear Workmen for some Days past have been preparing the Barracks in Castle William for the Reception of the Troops which are hourly expected to arrive from Halifax; and don't learn of any Preparation are making to Quarter them in any other Part of the Town, the Barracks there being thought sufficient to contain them.

From Thursday Afternoon till Yesterday Noon, we had here a very severe Storm of Wind, attended with Rain and 'tis fear'd if any Vessels were on the Coast that they must have suffer'd thereby.

On Saturday Evening the Report of 13 Guns were heard, by which it is tho't some Ship of War was in Distress; ——— a Topsail Schooner was seen in the Bay the Afternoon before, and it is not unlikely to be an Armed Cutter bound hither, one or two of them being daily expected.

Whereas a Person belonging to the Militia in this Town did, on Thursday last about 2 o'Clock P. M. designedly and maliciously, as appeared to several By Standers discharge his Musket against the Legs of a Gentleman then passing thro' the Town-House and thereby hurt him so much as to occasion his Confinement: This is to give Notice that if any Person then present, or any other, will discover to the Printers the Name of the above Offender, so that he may be apprehended, he shall receive of the Printers One Guinea, and no Use shall be made of his Name.

BOSTON Sept. 26. By his Excellency Francis Bernard, Esq; Captain-General and Governor in Chief of the Province of Massachusetts-Bay, and Vice-Admiral of the same.

To the Gentlemen of the assembled at Funeuil-Hall, under the Name of Committee of Convention.

As I have Orders to support his Majesty strict Orders to support his Constitutional Authority within this Government. I cannot sit still and see so notorious a Violation of it, as the

Calling of an Assembly of the People by private Persons only. For a Meeting of the Deputies of the Town in an Assembly of the Representatives of the People to all Intents and Purposes; and it is not the calling it a Committee of Convention that will alter the Nature of the Thing.

I am willing to believe that the Gentlemen who so hastily issued the Summons for this Meeting were not aware of the high Nature of the Offence they were committing; and they who have obeyed them have not well considered of the Penalties which they will incur if they should present it continuing their Sessions and doing business therein. At present Ignorance of the Law may excuse what is past; A Step farther will take away the plea.

It is therefore my Duty to impose at this Instant, before it is to late. I do therefore earnestly admonish you that instantly and before you do Business, you break up the Assembly and separate yourselves. I speak to you now as a Friend to the Province, &c. a Well-wisher to the individuals of it.

But if you should pay no Regard to the Admonition, I must as Governor assert the Prerogative of the Crown in a more public Manner. For assure yourselves (I speak from Instructions) the King is determined to maintain his entire Sovereignty over this Province; and whoever shall present in usurping any of the Rights of it, will repent of his Rashness. Fra. Bernard.

BOSTON Sept. 27. In the last Paper it was mentioned that an Englishman and a Frenchman had been ill used at Newbury-Port for making Information against a vessel there; Since which the Englishman has complained to Authority of his ill-treatment, at the same Time cleared himself by the Deposition as under, besides some Evidence that may hereafter appear.

Joseph Vickery of Newbury, Ship-Carpenter, declares in Substance as follows viz.

That on Saturday the 10th of September current, he was in a riotous Manner assaulted in the King's High-Way in Newbury-Port, seized and carried by Force to the public Stocks in the said Town, where he sat from three to five o'Clock in the Afternoon, most of the Time on the sharpest stone that could be found, which put him to extreme Pain, so that he once fainted: ——— That he was afterwards taken out of the stock put into a Cart and carried thro' the Town with a Rope about his Neck, his Hands tied behind him till Dusk of the Evening, during which Time he was severely pelted with Eggs, Gravel and Stones, and was much wounded thereby, he was then taken out of the Cart carried into a dark Warehouse, and hand-cuffed with Irons, without Bed or Cloathing, and in a Room where he could not lay straight, but made the edge of a tar-pot, served as a Pillow, so that when he arose the Hair was torn from his Head; he was confined to this Place the whole of the Lord's Day, with a Guard that prevented any of his Friends visiting him excepting his Wife, who with Difficulty obtained Liberty to speak to him: ——— On Monday the 12th in the forenoon he was taken out and the Rioters upon their being well satisfied of his being innocent of what was laid to his Charge, compelled him only to lead a Horse Cart about the Town, with Francis Magno therein, who was stripped naked. tarred and then committed to goal for breach of Peace.

  Essex County, September 12, 1768.
Then Joseph Vickery of Newbury, personally appeared before me the Subscriber and made solemn Oath, That he never did directly or indirectly make or give any Information to any Officers of Custom nor to any other Person either against Captain John Emery, or any other Man whoever; that he was no ways concerned with Francis Magno in his Information nor even wrote on Line for the said Francis on account nor ever knew of the said Information until Saturday last. Signed by Me,   John Brown, Just. Peace.
  The Suspicion that Vickery was concerned in this Information arose from his going to Portsmouth on some Business, and took the Frenchman with him, the said Frenchman seeing the Vessel coming into the Harbour, and having had a previous Difference with the Master or Owner, gave Information when he got to Portsmouth ——— He

Declared repeatedly that Mr. Vickery was not concerned with him in the Information.

BOSTON Oct. 3. Friday last about two o'Clock the Romney and the rest of his Majesty's ships of war and armed schooners, with the troops from Halifax on board, consisting of the 14th regiment, commanded by Lieutenant Colonel Dalrymple; the 29th, commanded by Lieutenant Colonel Carr; and a detachment of the 59th, commanded by Capt. Wilson, with a company of the train of artillery and two pieces of cannon, came to anchor before the Town.

On Saturday forenoon, the troops were put on board an armed schooner, and the boats belonging to the men of war, and at 12 o'clock were landed on the long-wharf: From the wharf, they marched into King Street; and from thence into the Common: ——— about three o'clock a company of the train, with 2 pieces of cannon, joined them in the Common, where the 29th regiment encamped: the 14th regiment marched in the evening to Faneuil-Hall, and after waiting for some hours were admitted into the hall. On Sunday night part of the 14th regiment were quartered in the Town House. The detachment of the 39th, and the train are quartered in some stores of Griffin's Wharf.

BOSTON Oct. 17. A Proclamation published on Thursday last says, ——— Lieut. Col. Dalrymple has contracted for the building a Guard-House near the Fortification in the Town of Boston, in order to prevent the Desertion of the Troops under his Command, the Frame of which Building was, by some evil minded Persons, on the Night on the ninth Instant, cut to pieces or otherwise destroyed, to the Detriment of his Majesty's Service.

BOSTON Oct. 24. Last Wednesday forenoon it was said the high sheriff of the county of Suffolk has orders to clear the province manufactury-house in the town of Boston, for a number of years superintended by Mr. John Brown in behalf of a certain Company, and lately on his own account. Mr. Brown being informed the order was to be put in execution that day, detained some persons to serve as evidence of the transaction.

About 2 o'clock the sheriff came attended by Lieut. Governor, and approaching the hall windows of which the people leaned to receive them, the sheriff said he was sent by the authority of the province to demand possession of the house, and require Mr. Brown to clear it forthwith for the reception of his Majesty's troops; and observed that he had brought his Honor along with him that his advice might have the more weight in moving Mr. Brown to resign the house quietly. Mr. Brown questioned the sheriff with respect to his warrant, which he said was an order from the Governor, founded on a resolve of the council, whereby the Governor was empowered to clear the house; said he had never had any lawful warning to leave the house, and did not look upon the power of the Governor and council sufficient to dispossess him; and finally, that he would not surrender his possession to any till required by the general court under who he held, or was obliged thereon by the law of the province, or compelled by force.

His Honor replied that Mr. Brown was tenant at the will of the province, that the Governor and council were the remaining authority of the province, which he looked upon sufficient to warrant the proceeding; observed that Mr. Brown must be very ill advised to think of withstanding that authority and wished him to consider better than to involve himself in consequence so disagreeable as must attend his refusal. Mr. Brown to him replied, that his council were of the ablest in the province, and he should adhere to their advice be the consequence what they would. ——— Mr. sheriff then left the windows and walked up the easternmost stairs, rap'd moderately at the door, and nobody answering, soon returned, acquainting Mr. Brown he had done enough for the whole in the steps taken with him. The sheriff on his return took out and read a paper to Mr. Brown, containing as he said a transcript of a minute of council and instructions from the governor to clear the factory forthwith. Mr. Brown first requested and afterwards demanded repeatedly a copy of his order, which he refus'd and refer'd Mr. Brown to the secretary's office, where after divers applications he was there first put off and finally denied. —— Mr. Brown still retaining apprehension of violent measures, kept his doors and windows shut, and suffered none to come in without caution. This caused the men working in the cellar to keep one of the lower sashes moveable, to pass from the cellar to the yard.

Thursday in the forenoon the sheriff with Dr. S. Gardner were seen reconnoitering, and between 12 and 1 the sheriff came from Gardner's gate to the east of the factory, where was the window aforementioned, at which one of the weavers had just gone out —— the young man seeing the sheriff approach the window turned hastily to prevent his entering. The sheriff attempted to get his fingers under the sash and the young man to keep it down, till a square of glass being beat in and the weaver haled a little off by the much superior strength and formidable appearance of the sheriff, whose drawn sword, menacing speech and actual violence surpris'd and overcome him in such a manner that the sheriff returned to the sash, forced it up, and entered feet foremost with sword in hand, Mr. Brown at some distance in the cellar hearing the scuffle and the glass break, hastened to the window, but a loom intervened, the sheriff had fully forced entry before Mr. Brown could oppose him.

A small scuffle happened between them, in which neither party received much harm. Two of the sheriff's deputies with his servant followed, he sent one of the deputies to the office of the piquet with a written order to come with his guard to the factory immediately. On his arrival the sheriff ordered him to place two centinels at each door, two or more at the gate, and ten in the cellar, then read him a paper, giving him full possession of the yard, charging him to let any one come out of the house, but none go in. Finding the people gathered fast about the gate, he issued orders for another company, the posting of which gave the compleat idea of a formal blockade.

Friday morning bread and water was denied,

and no person allowed to speak to them for several hours. The sick were denied the visit of their physicians, and Dr. Church's apprentice in the afternoon had several pushes with bayonets as he was attempting to convey them medicine.

Some of the gentlemen deploring the emminate ruin of their country and fearing some ill consequence from the resentment of the people, who had been insulted by the guards, kept with them to moderate 'em, while others laid before the members of his Majesty's council the distress and danger they conceived the people subjected to by the unprecedented action of the sheriff.

The council assembled, and after some deliberations waited on his Excellency, and signified that their advice to clear the factory intended no more than to clear it by law. His Excellency said it appeared to him to impower him to clear it as he most conveniently could: However, it seems the consequence of this meeting was a recall of the troops about 7 in the evening, leaving only a small guard in the cellar, and one or two at the window.

It is wished and expected that the principal officers may for the future admonish all Subalterns and private men to speak with respect to the laws of the country, as a contrary behaviour must inevitably introduce that anarchy and confusion it was pretended they were sent to suppress.

BOSTON Oct. 24. Messieurs Fleets,
The large revenue arising from the article of Tea, and the design of the disposal ought in my opinion to be sufficient reason for every American to detest it, as a most deadly poison, tho' bread and water alone were to supply its place; but when we consider how many an easy substitutes this vast continent already does and by culture may produce, stupidity or downright madness will be found its only advocate. The Tea plant we most certainly have; it has been transplanted in the middle of August yet grown and flourished, no shrub is more easily propagated, and may affirm it grows wild thro' the colonies. The cure has been so well performed

in this town that age and package in a quantity seem only wanted to give a flavor equal to any import.

BOSTON Oct. 24. Extract of a Letter from a Gentleman of Distinction in New-York, Oct.15.

"Letters have been received in Town from New-Hampshire, Boston, Rhode Island, and Connecticut, which advise that the inhabitants are filled with rage and indignation at the villainous proceedings of the British Ministry to oppress his Majesty's loyal subjects on the continent, and bring them into base and mean compliances; and that they are determined, in general, to assist one another, when it shall become necessary, in defence of their just and constitutional rights and privileges, at all events; and though the southern colonies will have more virtue and spirit than to be tame spectators of the ruin of their country. I assure you the inhabitants of this city highly approve of the conduct of the brave New-England men, and seem resolved to risk their lives and fortunes in the common cause, if the infatuation of an abandoned ministry or a wicked Governor shall reduce them to that necessity."

BOSTON Oct. 31. Last Sunday Night se'night as Mr. Turner the Coxswain on the Pinnace belonging to his Majesty's Ship Romney was coming from the ship to Long-Wharf, with three other Men in a small skiff, they accidentally overset when the Coxswain and two of the Men were drowned: the other Man was taken up by a Boat that went off to their relief.

BOSTON Oct. 31. Province of Massachusetts-Bay Court of Vice Admiralty, October 27, 1768.

All Persons claiming Property in 33 Hogsheads and 4 Tierces of Molasses, seized on the 6th Day of September last by Joseph Dowse Esq; Surveyor and Searcher for the Port of Salem and Marblehead for breach of the Acts of Trade, and hereby notified to appear (if they see fit) at a Court of Vice Admiralty to be holden at Boston on Monday the 7th of November next, at 9 o'Clock before Noon, to shew cause (if any they have) why the said Molasses should not be adjudged to remain forfeit, pursuant to the Information

Filed in said Court for that purpose, By order of the Court   Ezekiel Price, D. Regr.

BOSTON Oct. 31. Richard Ames a Soldier of the 14th Regiment, who was tried for desertion on the 22d instant by a General Court Martial, has received a sentence of Death, and ordered to be shot on the Common this forenoon, between the Hours of 8 and 12 o'clock, ——— all Troops in Town were ordered into the Common this Morning by 6 o'clock, to attend the execution.

On Tuesday last the part of the 14th Regiment which, since its Arrival, has been quartered in Faneuil-Hall went into a Store on Pitt's Wharf, belonging to Justice Stoddard of this Town; and on Saturday, the 29th Regiment broke up their Encampment on the common and took up their quarters in a large Store by Green's-Lane, Major Green, Distiller and in a House in New-Boston belonging to Mr. Forrest: The remaining Part of the 14th Regiment, the detachment of the 59th, and the Train of Artillery, are quartered in the Town-House, in a House lately possessed by James Murray, Esq; and in a Store on Griffin's Wharf, hired of Mr. William Molyneaux, Attorney for Mr. Apthorp the Proprietor of 300 Sterling a Year, and it is said are now preparing for the reception of the Troops expected from Ireland. ——— The above mentioned Houses and Stores were hired by the Barracks-Master-General.

BOSTON Nov. 7. Last Tuesday upon complaint made by Selectmen of this Town before Richard Dana and John Ruddock, Esqs; two of his Majesty's Justices of the Peace for the County of suffolk, a Capt. of the 59th Regiment mentioned in a warrant, and others unknown, stood charged with advertising several Negro Slaves in the Town to beat, abuse and cut their Master's Throats, promising them a Reward, if they would appear at the Place of Parade, to make them free. Upon Examination of the Witnesses, the said Justices order'd the Captain to give Bond with Surity to appear and answer at the Court of Assize in March next, and for his good Behaviour in the mean Time.

It is said that the Selectmen have given it in Charge of the Town Watch to see that Good order is observed in the Night, and that they take up all Negroes who they shall find abroad at an unreasonable Hour.

It is said that the Deputy Sheriff, who by Law of the Constitution a Conservator of his Majesty's Peace, was opposed by the military in his attempting to serve a warrant from Mr. Justice Dana and Ruddock ——— a sufficient number of Town Inhabitants were at the same Time, as they always have been, ready and willing to assist the civil Officer in the legal Discharge of his Duty.

BOSTON Nov. 7. Messieurs Edes & Gill, It is not to be wonder'd at, that the Enemies of Great-Britain and the Colonies, who have too long discover'd their malicious Disposition in protecting whole Provinces, should busily employ themselves in attempting to vilify particular Characters. If a Gentleman appears to exert his Influence in Support of the constitutional Rights of his Fellow Subjects when they are invaded, he may be sure to become the Object of the malevolence of these Wretches whose Aim is to ruin his Fortune, if possible, or at least, to destroy his Influence, and prevent his serving the common Cause of his Country for the future. Such Instances must give Pain to every ingenuous and humane Mind. I have lately heard from good authority of an Attempt of this kind to sully the Reputation of a Gentleman of great Means as well as superior Fortune in the Town: A Gentleman who has the entire Confidence of his Fellow Citizens, in various Publick Stations; who has repeatedly serv'd them in the General Assembly, and that last May had the Honor of being chosen a Member of his Majesty's Council by a great Majority of the Suffrages of the two Houses of Assembly, tho' it must be Acknowledg'd he was negativ'd by Governor Bernard.

An Insinuation that Mr. Hancock was at the Head of a Mob in the Town of Boston, and that the Scene was concluded "before his door," might answer a wicked Purpose, at the Distance of a Thousand Leagues, while Britain seems too much inclin'd to harken the Tales of the Prejudice of her honest Friends and Fellow Subjects the

Colonists: But what could induce a Scribler to forge a Letter and publish it in a Coffee-House in New-York, under the Name of that Gentleman requesting, G. Gage that he might supply the Troops now in Town, or expected, (unwelcomed to the Inhabitants, considering the Errand on which all agree they are come), unless it was to induce in the Minds of the Gentlemen in New-York that from a sordid Love of Gain he had counteracted his profess'd Sentiments, and so to render him ridiculous there? I doubt not but both the General and Mr. Hancock know it to be a Falsehood: In this Province where he has the universal Esteem of good Men, there can be no Danger of its having the Effect which he the Author intended; but to remove any ill Impressions that may possibly he made on the Minds of our Brethen of New-York, and to prevent Jealously that the common cause of America has been in the least deserted by a Gentleman, who has so much to his Honor espous'd and defended it, I cou'd heartily wish that Mr. Hancock would condescend publickly to disown the Letter, no candid Man, it is presum'd, can doubt but it may be done with strict Truth. —— The Defamer may perhaps hereafter be as publickly expos'd to the Contempt he justly deserves. Your Humble Servant,
                                      Veritas.

    BOSTON Nov. 14. Messieurs Edes & Gill, I observed in your last Paper a Piece signed Veritas; the Writer of which says he had it from good Authority that a Letter under my Hand was published in a Coffee-House at New-York, requesting his Excellency General Gage that I might supply the Troops then expected, and which have since arrived in this Town. If such a letter has been produced there or any where else, I declare it to be a Forgery; for I have never made Application to any one for the Supply of said Troops, nor did I ever desire any person to do it for me. —— The Person who produc'd the Letter could have no other design but to injure my Reputation, and abuse the Gentlemen of New-York, —— I therefore desire you would give Place in your next, in which you will oblige. Your Humble Servant,   John Hancock.

BOSTON Nov. 14. Last week arrived six of the Transports from Cork, the two others, with the Hussar frigate, are hourly expected.

Yesterday arrived the Viper Man of War from Halifax.

The 14th and 29th regiments, with one of those from Ireland, are to be quartered in town, and the other to be quartered at the Castle till Spring when it is said, it is to be sent to the principal sea port towns in New-England.

That part of the 14th regiment, which since their arrival have been quartered in the town house, removed on Wednesday last to the Barracks.

The Hon. the Commissioners of the Customs, and the gentlemen belonging to the Board, are now come up to town, and the Board will be held as formerly at the Concert-Hall.

The Commissioners have offered a reward of Fifty pounds sterling, for discovering to justice any two or more of the principal offenders, who, on the 11th of September last, at Squam, forcibly confined the officers if his Majesty's Customs, who had possession of certain goods seized by the Surveyor and Searcher of the port, whilst the goods were feloniously carried away.

BOSTON Nov. 27. Monday arrived here from Halifax the Romney of 50 Guns, Capt. Corner; with Commander Hood and his Excellency Lord William Campbell on board.

Yesterday the 64th regiment, commanded by Colonel Pomeroy, disembarked, and went into the Barracks on Wheelwright's Wharf.

BOSTON Nov. 21. The public may be assured, that the Senior Sophister Class of the Havard College in Cambridge, have with a Spirit becoming Americans, & warmed with a truly patriotic Flame, agree to take their Degrees the next Commencement in the Manufactures of their own Country.

BOSTON NOv. 28. We hear that a young man belonging to a Connecticut Vessel inward bound, who was pressed some time ago by one of the arm'd schooners bound to Halifax, was last week discharged upon the first application made to Commodore Hood.

BOSTON Dec. 1. Last week a court martial was

held on board his Majesty's ship Mermaid, for the trial of some sailors for desertion; two were sentenced to be flogged from ship to ship. and another condemned to be hanged.

Thursday last a man was tried here before the Superior Court, for seducing a Soldier to desert, and was acquitted.

Thursday last arrived here one of the transports, with troops from Cork. ——— Another with Colonel Maclay, and other field officers of the 65th regiment is still missing.

BOSTON 5. Province of Massachusetts-Bay, Court of Vice-Admiralty, Boston November 18, 1768

All persons claiming property in the Schooner Friendship and Appurtenances, seized on the 31st day of October last by Robert Trial, Esq; Comptroller for the Port of Portsmouth for Breach of the Act of Trade, are hereby notified to appear (if they see fit) at a Court of Vice Admiralty to be holden at Boston on the 7th of December next at 10 o'Clock before Noon, to shew cause (if any they have) why the said Schooner and Appurtenances should not be adjudged to remain forfeit, pursuant to an information filed in said Court for that purpose.

By order of Court,   Ezekiel Price, D. Regr.

BOSTON Dec. 8. Friday last being the day appointed for the Execution of the Sailor on board the Mermaid (as mentioned in our last) a Yellow Flag was displayed on the Fore-top-mast of the Commodore's Ship, after which the Boats from the other Men of War in the Harbour rowed alongside of the Mermaid. At 11 o'clock the Rope was put round his Neck, and every thing prepared for his Execution, when the Commodore was pleased to send him a Pardon.

BOSTON Dec. 19. On the 7th inst. at Newport, Mr. Dudley Collector, and Mr. Nichol Comptroller of the Customs there, having seized a sloop for breach of act of trade, immediately after the seizure, a number of armed men obliged the officers, who had charge of the vessel to quit her, and then carried her off. The Governor of that colony, has published a proclamation requiring all officers of the justice, to use their utmost endeavours to discover and apprehend the persons guilty of the said offence and the Collector and Comptrollers offer one hundred dollars reward, to be paid in conviction, to any person who will inform against one or more of the offenders, and a further reward of one hundred dollars, to any person who will discover where, the vessel is carried, so that she may be recovered.

BOSTON Dec. 19. His Majesty's Ship Romney, Mermaid, Rose, Viper, and Beaver, are unrigged, and are to remain in our harbour the Winter.

Mr. John Curtis, Jun'r of Worcester, was journeying last night to Boston with his Team, and riding 'tis supposed, on the Tongue of the Cart (so called) he fell off and was instantly kill'd by the Wheel's crushing his Head. —— An alarming Providence to his Parents and his Widow, who is left with six young Children. —— A caution this, against the impudent Manner of riding as above mentioned!

BOSTON Dec. 24. Last Thursday Capt. Sweaney, of the Schooner Betsey and John arrived here from Halifax with the remains of the 14th and 29th regiments, including a number of women &c. belonging to the army quartered here. By him we hear that Capt. Duncan Campbell, in the schooner Providence with military stores, was cast away the 19th ult. on Betty's Island in Prospect Harbour, and one man was drowned.

BOSTON Dec. 26. On Sunday the 18th inst. in the afternoon, a quarrel happened between some soldiers and sailors belonging to an armed schooner lying at Peck's Wharf: a drummer had his scull fractured, one of the sailors was knocked off the wharf and it being high water, would have drowned, had he not been assisted by a gentleman on the wharf.

Saturday a soldier was detected in stealing some leather out of a shop at the south part of the town, when several people collected together, a comrade of his struck a person that stood by with a bayonet and slightly wounded him, in the mean time the thief went off, and the other was committed to Goal.

BOSTON Dec. 26. We hear from Newwalk that last week one Graham, late Quarter-master to the 16th

Regiment, was tried for willfully firing a Gun into a Barn there, which set it on Fire & burnt two valuable Horses. A Verdict was given against him with full Cost.

Last Friday last one Jones, a Labourer in this Town was committed to Goal for stealing a Quantity of cloth which was bro't by a Country woman to Market for sale.

Last Friday Morning a Soldier belonging to one of the Regiments here, was found dead in his bed; it is said he had drank three Pints of Rum the evening before, which, it's tho't, was the Occasion of his Death.

BOSTON Dec. 26. Three Dollars Reward. Made his escape last Friday from the Work-house in Boston, where he had been confin'd 5 or 6 Days for running away some Time since from the Schooner Sally, Abraham Van Bebber, Master, Peter Dyer, an indented English Servant Boy 14 or 15 Years of Age, well sett, short light-colour'd bushy head of Hear; had on an old slopt Hatt, green outside Jacket much faded, an under Jacket made of Floor Carpeting, Ornbrigs Shirt, narrow long Trowsers, blue Stockings, Shoes much worn. Whoever takes up said Boy, and will send him to the Printers hereof, shall have the above Reward paid by said Printers.

1769

BOSTON Jan. 2. Notwithstanding it had been industriously reported by some Persons concerned in the Manufactures at Home, that the Merchants at New-York had, contrary to the Agreement, given Orders for Goods; we can assure the public by authentic Advises received from thence, that the Merchants there who subscribed the Agreement by which they restricted themselves from importing Goods from Great-Britain, will be strictly adhere to the same, and that there is not any Reason to apprehend that any of the few, who refused to subscribe, will order any Goods ——— And we can assure the Public that we have the greatest Reason to believe that the Merchants of this Place will likewise steadily and persevringly adhere to the Agreement for the like Purpose.

On Monday last in the Afternoon was found Lying at the Foot of a Soldier's Grave in the Common Burying Place, an Infant Male Child wrapt in part of a Shirt with a course Ruffle round the Bosom. A Jury of Inquest sat on the Body and had several Persons under Examination. Their Verdict was, That the said Child came to his Death by being greatly neglected immediately on it being born, or having violent Hands laid on it soon after by a Person or Persons unknown.

BOSTON Jan. 9. Extract of a Letter from London to his Friend in Boston, on the 4th of October, by the Packet.

"Your Troops you may depend on it, will soon be called away in the Spring, and the Ships too. Doctor Franklin has given it his Opinion that the Colonies will obtain all that they can desire or wish for, if they behave with firmness. ——— Your Commissioners stand here exactly in the Character that they have established for themselves in America; and it is the Opinion of everyone, that the Board will be recalled, and a new Governor appointed for your Province. Lord Hillsborough himself says, he entirely dislikes their Conduct.

BOSTON Jan. 16. Whereas between Forty and Fifty Seamen have deserted his Majesty's Service from the Ships in the Harbour, under my Command since the forth of last Month, many of which are harboured and concealed in the Country, not twenty Miles from Boston. ——— This is to give Notice that whoever will apprehend any of the said Deserters, and bring them to the Commodore, shall receive a Reward of Forty Shillings sterling for each; and such as may be disposed to return to their Duty within Twenty Days of the date hereof, shall be pardoned.
Romney, in Boston Harbour, January 16, 1769.
                                        Samuel Hood.

BOSTON Jan. 16. It is desired that the inhabitants of the Town would not buy Wood or even Ashes of the Soldiers, ——— as there have been great Quantities of Wood stolen of Late; and it has been acknowledged by some that would steal Wood and carry it a good distance to burn for the sake of Ashes: ——— It is computed that the Ashes of 5 pounds worth of Wood will fetch 5 Coppers.

BOSTON Jan. 25. Extract of a letter from London November 14, 1768.
"The news of the defience of the King's authority came just before the meeting of the parliament, to open the eyes of the nation and to let them see the desperate length which your incendiaries would lead your people into. ——— Nothing could have been done to give the government here such an advantage over the colony as their separating and distinguishing their case from that of all the other colonies, and then the town of Boston from all the other places as none but Boston Selectmen have assumed to themselves the royal prerogative of calling a convention; and none but the province of the Massachusetts have dared to meet in direct contradiction to the King's authority. ——— The King's speech and the addresses will give

you the best idea of the sense of government.
───── I was in the house of Lords when their addresses was proposed; not a single Lord objected against it, I afterwards heard Mr. Greenville's speech. Much of it was levelled against Lord Camden's and Lord Chatham's denial of the right. As to the colonies, he did not at all wonder at it, nor could conceive the least resentment against their conduct. All men dislike taxes, and will oppose them, if they think that they can thereby get off from paying them: Even the county of Middlesex, (said he) where we now sit, if they had been told by the same authority the same things about the beer tax, that parliament had no right to such a tax, and that the people were not bound to pay it, would have rioted for their porter, in the same manner; but that nevertheless where the execution of the laws is opposed by force, there they must be supported by a superior force. In general tho' there were some differences of opinion in some lesser matters, yet I heard nothing, while I was in the house, except Mr. Bernard but what was clearly for maintaining the King's authority, and the full legislative power of parliament.
───── The language in one house, was "I will not say it of the province, but the behaviour of individuals have been traitorous and rebellious."

BOSTON Jan. 26. Extract of a letter from a Merchant in London, Dated Nov. 18th, 1768.

"Affairs look very unfavourable for Boston, Before matters were carried so far there, Government was disposed to repeal the duties on glass, paper, and colours, but by reason of the misconduct of the Assembly, the Junta, Selectmen, Convention, &c. there is now a determination to require obedience to the revenue laws, the sense of both houses of parliament is clear on this head; all agree that government cannot give up the point of right which they as generally asserts here an in America they deny. The Merchants trading to America having met with no returns for the pains they took, and 1500 pounds expence in entertainments, &c. in obtaining the repeal of the Stamp-Act, their letters not haveing been answered, nor their advice followed, will again appear in its favour, nor are they alarmed at the combination against the importation of the British Goods. Agreements entered into from a spirit of resentment, gives great offence."

BOSTON Jan. 30. Extract of a letter from London, Oct. 13, 1768.

"The prudent conduct and public virtue of America may save this distracted nation, whose council and credit are uncertain and inconstant as fickle wind, and whose power and dignity are almost annihilated by the rage of party, and love of inordinate wealth."

BOSTON Feb. 6. Monday Night last about ten o'Clock, the large new County Goal in this town was discovered on Fire: The first Attention was to preserve the Prisoners from perishing; But by the Hurry and Consternation of the People nigh at Hand, the Keys of some of the Doors were mis-placed, whereby they were obliged to have recourse of Axes, &c. to break through, which with great Difficulty was done, and the Prisoners pulled through very small Passages, their Flesh considerably tore by the Iron Spikes in the Doors; however they were all taken out alive, one or two scourched by the Fire, one elderly Man who was in the Room where the Fire began, was burnt.

The Fire began in an apartment on the middle story at the Northwest Corner of the Building, and proceeded with great Violence from one Apartment to another until the whole of the inside of the House was in Flames; The Thickness of the Partitions and Floors made the Heat intense, and the Walls and Iron Bars prevented the Water from the Engine doing much toward Extinguishing the Flames. When the Fire broke from its Confinement thro' the Roof, great Danger was apprehended from the Flakes, but their being little Wind, by a good Providence, it was prevented from spreading: The Night was very cold, the Fire wards exerted themselves the whole Time, also the Enginemen and other Inhabitants were very vigilant; The Officers of his Majesty's Regiment now here, attended with a Number of Soldiers, who were likewise Active and Serviceable in assisting the relieving the Inhabitants; About 5 o'Clock the Fire was got under. Two of the Prisoners escaped in the Night, the others were secured in birdewell, and in the Goaler's Dwelling-House until Morning: at ten o'Clock Examination was made before several Magistrates; It appears that Mr. Young the Keeper had been in the Goal, and was his Practice to see all was safe, about Nine in the Evening, and saw no Appearance of Fire: Upon examining the Prisoners who were in the Room when the Fire was first discovered, it was evident that these were determined to get out by burning the Door of their Apartment; accordingly in the Evening they put some Chips under the Door, and set Fire to them; they put the Shutters to their Windows to prevent the Light being discovered; the Door kept burning two or three Hours, till the length the Smoak and Heat increased so much, they were obliged to repair to the Window at the Windward for Air, when they gave the Alarm —— These Matters appearing full against two of them, one a Soldier the other a young Lad, who were confined for Stealing, they were both hand cuff'd, and by Habeas Corpus committed to the Goal in Charlestown —— The Loss of the County and the Town must be very great.

BOSTON Feb. 6. The loss to the county, by burning of the goal, is estimated at 3000 pounds sterling. The prisoners in the room, where the fire first broke out, were Abel Badger, a Cooper's apprentice, imprisoned for several burglaries, Bryan Donnelly, a soldier, for stealing leather, and Thomas Carmichael an old man. —— Badger declared, on examination; that the door of their room was set in fire by Donnelly and Carmichael, by means of some pieces of wood which Donnelly cut up with his knife; That he advised them not to set it on fire, as it would endanger their lives, upon which Donnelly threatened to knock out his brains, with a bar iron if he made any noise, or attempted to alarm the jail-keeper, and brought a Bible and obliged him to take an oath of secrecy. Carmichael also toke the oath; they then closed the window shutters, and Donnelly and Carmichael set fire to the chips, under the door, with an attempt to make a hole large enough to let them through, and then force the lock of the prison, and together with the prisoners in the next room, make their escape: but when the flames had spread out the outside of the door and up the stairs, he was going to cry fire, when Donnelly said it had not burnt enough, and again threatened to knock him down, however, when the flames burnt into their own room, that he was first who cried fire and gave the alarm.

Badger taken out of Court.

Bryan Donnelly was brought in, and said, that the jail was set on fire designedly by Abel Badger, Thomas Carmichael and himself; that he put in the first stick of fire to the door, and that the shavings and sticks were conveyed into the prison by Badger's fellow apprentice, between seven and eight o'clock of the evening of the fire, that Badger having beat Carmichael that evening, afterwards told Carmichael, to make up with him, that he would set fire, that Carmichael might escape; that then Carmichael told him (Donnelly) that Badger was such a sad villain, that he would tell the jail-keeper unless they made articles with him, upon which they took a Bible, and swore by it never to make any discovery; that their intentions were nothing more than to make a hole in the door to convey a bottle of rum to one Kemp, a soldier in the next room; but when the flames spread, the thought they might as well make their escape. That the fire was lighted about eight o'clock, that he went to bed and about half an hour after, Carmichael said that there was not wood enough, when he got up, and cut some splinters from the window, and put them on. —— That after the fire had communicated itself to their room, he was the first who alarmed the keeper, by crying fire, though he had been once, prevented by Badger, at which time he said, he would put an end to his own life with a knife he then had in his hand, to save himself from being burnt to death.

The court then thought proper to send for Badger's fellow prentice, when he came, Donnelly was then asked if he knew him to be the lad who brought the shavings &c. he believed he was, but was not certain, however, on Donnelly's asking him if he was the lad, he replied he was, that he came at the time Donnelly mentioned, and gave Badger the shavings and chips as he had complained to him before, of it being very cold, and of having little fire, that he did not know there was any harm intended; (on which the court mentioned there was no harm in giving the shavings;) He further said, that Badger seemed to make himself easy, as he had heard he would be released next morning to go to sea. ───── This lad being then ordered to sit down so as not to be observed, Badger was again ordered into court and asked who procured the shavings and cut the sticks to set fire to the door, he again said it was Donnelly and Carmichael and repeated much the same as his first examination, and that Donnelly said, he wanted to get out before the court sat, then he might escape by going on board the Romney man of war and which Donnelly said was a damned lie, and a very foolish thing for a soldier to think of making his escape, by going on board a man of war.

THe court asked Badger, if he recollected any person's coming to him at half past seven that evening? He said no. ───── if any fellow prentice had been there at that time? no, ───── If he had not asked anyone at that time to give him some shavings or chips? no, ───── If any one had at that time told him that he should be taken out of prison next morning? He said, a fellow prentice had told him so: being asked what time he told him so; and when he saw his fellow prentice; he said; not since Friday or Saturday. ───── The lad then confronted him, and said, you know Badger I was at half past seven, you said you was cold and begged me to give you some shavings and chips, which I did. ───── You was much discontented, and I told you, that if you would make yourself easy, you would be taken out in a day or two. ───── Badger then said, he was drunk all the time, and did not recollect it; ─────vowed his innocence and cried. ─────
As Carmichael was so much burnt, he could not

be brought to court for examination: ——— Badger and Donnelly were remanded back; and two of the justices went to take Carmichael's examination in the prison.

In the afternoon, Mr. Justice Foster Hutchinson related to the court the examination of Thomas Carmichael in prison to the following purport. That Carmichael went to bed early and that he knew nothing at all of the proceedings of the other two prisoners, nor even of the fire till the room was in flames. That he never had any agreement with them about it, that they were two sad villains, and that Badger had often vowed to set the jail on fire; that he knew he should be hanged, and would do something worth carrying him to the gallows. ——— Kemp, the soldier, in the next room; said, he never saw the face of Donnelly in his life, and never conversed with him, so that burning a hole to convey a bottle of anything else to him, was utterly false, besides there was a passage betwext their door to take any thing that they said was to be conveyed. ——— Some woman likewise in prison have overhead Badger swear he would set the jail on fire. ——— Therefore it is very evident that the mischief was concerted and executed by Badger and Donnelly only.

Donnelly the soldier's behaviour is very surprising, he escaped out of jail, but instead of runing away, he placed himself among the people who were handling the water buckets, where he continued till he was apprehended.

BOSTON Feb. 6. Messieurs Edes & Gill.
It is the opinion of many persons who attended the fire last Monday evening, that its progress might have been sooner stop't if the Piquet Guards had not been order'd out with their Firelocks and Bayonets: The mind of the people seemed to be disturbed, and their attention to business taken off, by such an unusual and needless military appearance, at a juncture of time when a vigorous effort might have had a good effect. The gentlemen of the army would do well to consider that this town is to be governed upon these and other occasions by its own regulations according to the laws of the province.

It is said that the General was fully informed of those regulations by the Firewards some time ago; and that the turning out of the Guards was not agreeable to their just expectations. It is however to be observed that the Officers marched them off, as soon as they were properly spoke to by the Town Officers, and that afterwards by the joint endeavours and activity of the inhabitants and the soldiers unarm'd, the fire was happily extinguished. Ubamus.

BOSTON Feb. 20. As a Correspondent in a large Paper had desired to know upon natural principles, why the Summer of late years have been so wet and winterly, and the weather in every part of the twelve months so uncertain and variable? I would just beg leave to hint, that most things are worse with wearing. The world grows old as well as you and I, and our Mother Earth is subject to diseases, and must have an end to her present state of existence, as well as we her children; and we can tell with certainty the particular disorder of which she will die, which is more than any of us can tell for ourselves. She has of late been afflicted with various disorders which shew her to be in the decline. A few years ago she had some violent convulsion fits; of which Lisbon, and a few other places are eminent witnesses: She had since been troubled with a grievous sickness at her stomach, which has gone off with violent vomitings at Mount Versuvius, &c. Sometimes she has been the Dropsy, at other times the fever, then the shivering ague: she is very often troubled with wind; at present she is much troubled with a diabetes; but I am positive this distemper will not prove mortal to her; for the very contrary viz. an inflation of her bowels, and burning fever, will at last carry her off. These Phenomena are only a conformation of the prophesy that was wrote by a person Of great veneration, some thousand years ago, viz. "That the Heavens and the Earth, yea, all of them shall wax old like a garment."

BOSTON Feb. 20. On Friday Evening one Mr. Soden, of Cambridge, who usually brings Milk from thence, and returning home in his Wherry on the Ice, his Horse fell in, towards the mouth of the Cambridge River, and, as it is tho't in his attempting to get him out, was himself unfortunately drowned, as the Horse was found dead in the Ice next Morning, but the Man has not yet been heard of.

BOSTON Feb. 23. The Sledding we have here sometime since, did not reach above 50 Miles on the Westward Road; so that many Farmers beyond Worcester, who depend on sledding to bring their Flour, Corn, and Provisions, was disappointed; the plenty of Flour, in those Parts have been very great; and large Quantities would have been brought to the Market had the Snow been as usual that way in the season.

BOSTON Feb. 27. Last Saturday a young Man who was pressed out of Capt. Holme's Ship, attempted to swim ashore from one of the Men of War, but was found dead next Morning, near the Steps at Long-Wharf. ——— "Tis supposed, that being cold and weary he wan unable to go over some ice that unhappily for him lay thereabout ——— "Tis said his name was Cochran.

Saturday last several Soldiers were apprehended by Civil Authority and bound over to the next General Sessions, for some disorderly proceedings at a House at the North-End, the Evening before.

BOSTON March 9. By order from home, the regiment quartered in Town are to encamp on the Common, as soon as the weather permits.

Last Tuesday the officers of the customs for this port. made a seizure of a ship of 200 tons, Capt. M'Cowen, belonging to London, lately from Ubes, and also a sloop from Virginia,

BOSTON March 13. Messiurs Fleets. I am informed that next Tuesday Night two plays are to be performed in this Town by Soldiers now here. ——— I should be much obliged to any one to inform me what right the commanding Officers have to give leave to their Men to perform any such Entertainment here? Whether we are to govern by Military Law; Or the Military by Civil? I hope the same spirit of Piety reign now as did in former times.

Monday the 27th ult. the Post-Rider with the

Mail for Rhode-Island, New-London, New-York, Philadelphia, &c. was assaulted on Boston-Neck, just after Sun-Set, as he was setting out for his journey by 4 or 5 Persons who appeared dress'd as Officers, one of them took his sword from his Belt, and with the small End in his hand struck the Rider on the Head with the Hilt with such violence that it forced the Sword out of the Scabbard and went a considerable Distance: ——— The Rider recovering himself, informed them he was on his Majesty's Service, whereupon they all ran off. The Rider would have return'd to Town, but they had been stoppage of late, occasion'd by the bad Travelling, he was determined not to be the means of the Mail returning out of Season, he went on, and at the first Stage had his Head bath'd, which considerably swelled with the blow, he reached Newport on Wednesday, from whence he employed another Person to perform for him these two Weeks past.

BOSTON March 13. Messieurs Edes & Gill. By inserting the following, taken from a good old Book, entitled, English Liberties, to the Free-born Subjects Inheritance, you will certainly oblige one, and perhaps all your readers.

"Amongst other Devices, to undermine the Rights of Juries, and render them insignificant, there has as Opinion been advanced, That they are only Judges of Facts, and are not at all to consider the Law. So that if a Person be indicted for a Fact, which really is no crime in itself by Law, but is work'd up by word of form, as treasonable, Seditiously, &c. it the Fact be but proved to be done, though the said wicked Circumstances do not appear, that they shall be supplied by Law, which are not to take notice of, but find the Bill, or bring the Person guilty, and leave the consideration of the case in Law to the Judges, whose Business it is. ——— This some People argue, but it is an apparent Trap, that once to perjure ignorant Juries, and render them so far from being of good use, as to be only Tools of Opppession to ruin and Murder their innocent Neighbours with the greater Formality: for though it be true, that matter of Fact is most common and proper Object of a

Jury's Determination, and a Matter of Law that the Judges, yet, as Law arises out of, and is complianced with Fact, it cannot but fall under the Jury's Consideration, Sect. 368. teaches us, That the Jury may, at the Election, either take upon them the knowledge of the Law, and determine both the Fact and Law themselves, or else find the Matter of Fact and Law together, and from their due Consideration of, and right Judgement upon both that a Jury brings forth their Verdict."

BOSTON March 20. Extract of a letter from a Master of a Vessel Dated London Dec. 10, 1768.

"I arrived here the 21st November, and am now discharged, and ready to take on board; but I cannot learn that there is any goods but your own, as there is not one order for the least thing. I never knew such dull times here before, and what will be the event God only knows. —— All trade seem to be at a stand. I am sorry to see I must tarry so long at this season as 'tis almost all night here; I hope to get into fresh air, here is nothing but smoak, fog, and rains. This is the first opportunity since I arrived."

Extract of a letter from London, Jan. 4, 1769.

"In short, it is impossible for you on the other side of the water to judge the opinion the People in this country have of America. —— There is a Number of vessels here put up for Freight for Boston, New-York, Philadelphia, &c. and not one Merchant in this city dare comply with their Orders, unless the Act of Parliament imposing Duties on America is repealed; which there is not the least prospect of at present. —— Many Ships are ordered to be sold and others to return in Ballast. I have nothing new to tell you, only that a report prevails, that a Rupture between England and France is soon expected."

BOSTON March 20. Extract of a Letter from a Gentleman of Distinction in Maryland to a Merchant in this Place. Feb. 8, 1769.

"The gentlemen in this Town being inform'd that there are some men with you that understand the making of Engines for Extinguishing Fire, and as we choose to give our countrymen the preference to that of our ungrateful Mother —— they requested me to write to my friend there, to procure one, and send it in the John, when she comes, it it can be got ready, and if that pleases, we shall send for two more."

BOSTON March 27, Resolves of the Right Honorable the House of Lords, relating to American Affairs; The following we here were proposed but not then agreed to by the said House, viz.

Resolve, That it appears that the Council for the said Province of Massachusetts-Bay not only refuse to give their Assistance to his Majesty's Governor for the suppressing the Riots and Tumults, and for supporting the Civil Power in the execution of the Law, although repeatedly called upon so to do, but did, at a time when the Town was in such a State of Disobedience to all lawful authority, and when the officers of the Revenue were compelled to seek Shelter from the fury of the People on board one of his Majesty's Ship of War, concur and join with the House of Representatives in a Resolution to enquire into the Grounds and reasons of the Peoples Apprehensions that Measures had been taken or were being taking for the Execution of the late Revenue Act of Parliament by Naval or Military Force.

Resolved, That it appears that the said Council for the Province of Massachusetts-Bay did at a time when it was evident that the Commissioners of his Majesty's Customs could not safely resume their functions in the Town of Boston, not only decline to propose or advise any measures for giving them such protection, but did contrary advise the Governor not to accept any offer from Gen. Gage to send Troops, and did declare that if any person had made application for troops to come thither, they deem'd them in the highest degree unfriendly to the peace and good order of that Government, as well as to his Majesty's service and the British interest in America.

BOSTON April 3. The prosecution, which have been for some time carried on, in the Court of Admiralty here against John Hancock, Esq; Capt. Malcom, and some other gentlemen of this town, we hear, were last week dropt by the Council for the Crown.

BOSTON April 10. On Tuesday last came on before the Superior Court of Judicature for this Province, the Trial of Badger, Donnelly, and Carmichael, for willfully setting Fire to the Goal in this Town, with an intent to burn it, when they were all three acquitted. ——— They were next day tried for Misdemeanor, for setting fire to it, with intention to make their Escape, and found guilty.

BOSTON April 17. On Friday the 14th Instant in the Morning was found Dead near Hollowell's Ship-Yard, James Petty, belonging to his Majesty's Schooner Halifax, now lying in Boston Harbour. A Jury of Inquest sat on the Body, from sufficient Evidence, found the following verdict, viz. "That the said James Petty came to his Death by a violent Blow, he received on the Head the last Evening, with a rough Stave from James Leat, Seaman, belonging to his Majesty's Schooner Halifax." The said James Leat has since absconded. Warrants were immediately issued to apprehend the said Murderer. It is supposed he is gone toward Marblehead, as several Gentlemen have seen a Person on the 14th Instant in the Forenoon passing thro' Medford, who seemed shy of Travellers, and answered the following Discription, viz. The said James Leat is about 5 Feet 6 Inches High, thick made of a swarthy complexion, his nose flatish, speaks very thich, wears his own Hair. Had on when he went away a Dutch Cap, an outside brown Jacket, an inside light color'd one, trim'd with black Tape and black Bottons, and wore a pair of long Trousers. It is Hoped that all Persons will use their utmost Endeavours to apprehend said Murderer, in order to his being brought to Justice.

BOSTON April 24. Extract of a Letter from London.

"Governor Bernard's letter have been read in the House of Lords, full of the most inflaming accounts of the riotous disposition of the people of Boston. And address of thanks have been voted to his Majesty for his care and vigilence in sending troops over to suppress them; strick enquiry is ordered to be made into the first Convention held in Bostom, and affidevits are to be taken, and the persons found guilty are to be sent over here to be tried for their lives. What mercy can be hoped for when our accusers are our Judges?

BOSTON April 24. The Merchants and Traders of this Town, at their Meeting of Friday last, appointed a Committee of seven Gentlemen to examine the Manifests of the Cargoes of the vessels lately arrived, or that arrive this Spring from any Part of Great Britain, and to take such other Steps as may be necessary, to determine whether there have been any Goods Imported contrary to the late Agreement of the Merchants, and by whom, and report at the Adjourning Morning; and also to make Enquiry whether any found contrary to said Agreement have been Imported from other Colonies, and by whom; and to make Report of the same at Adjournment.

BOSTON April 24. Extract of a Letter dated London February 4, 1769.

"You have, doubtless, seen several accounts of numbers of journeymen manufacturers having been dismiss'd on accout of the small demand for our Goods. Vast numbers begin to fell the effect of your Resolutions; and you stick to your text of Non-Importation, the Manufacturing for Yourselves, be assured the Parliament will either relpeal the late disgusting, impolitic, and unconstitutional acts, or send another large army and fleet to cut your wheels of Peace, and bombard your looms: But I believe they will be ashamed of the latter; and therefore you may depend of seeing the former accomplished, if you can but be unanimous, resulent, and persevering, for a short time.

BOSTON May 1. The following is an authentic account of the unhappy death of Lieutenant Panton of the Rose man of war April 22, 1769.

"At six in the morning the Rose man of war being five or six leagues off Cape Ann, ——— saw a sail, (the Pitt packet, Thomas Power master, from Cadiz to Marblehead) and fired two swivels and a gun before she was brought too, on which the cutter was sent off with the Lieut.

and two officers. When the Rose's boat came along side the brig, Mr. Panton went on board and enquired for the master, and went down into the cabin with him, and asked where the brig came from, and for his papers, &c. who replied that he was loaded with salt from Cadiz, had neither bill of lading or clearance, only a bill of health, which he produced; and on the enquiring how many men he had on board, was told, eight. Mr. Panton then asked for the log book, and said, he would order his people into the hold to search for unaccustomed goods, and for that purpose desired the hatchway and scuttles to be opened, which the master said should be done. Mr. Panton then went upon deck, leaving the master in the cabin, and there ordered one of the officers (a midshipman) and two of the Boat's crew to go bellow and search; after coming out of the main-hold, and going forward, one of the boat's crew saw a scuttle, which one of the officers ordered two of them to take up, here they found four men, and desired them to come up, but the brig's people swore bitterly, that they would cut off the limbs of the first man who dared to approach them, at the same time shewing a hatchet, a harpoon, a fish gig, and a musket; the officer after putting the question again, and they having refused in the same manner, informed Mr. Panton —— Mr. Panton then went forward with the officer and mildly desired them to come up, which they refused to do; swearing that they would die in the hold rather than go on board a man of war. Mr. Panton informed them he wanted to search the hold and asked them to allow him to come-down for that purpose; they repeated their threatnings, and shewed their weapons. Mr. Panton desired them a second time to cone out, adding that if they persisted in refusing, he must oblige them as his duty, on which one and all of them declared that if he brought arm against them, he should be their mark, and that they would put his lamp out first. —— The boat was then sent for assistance, and Mr. Panton continued endeavouring to persuade the people to come out, representing to them the impossibility of escaping, the folly of their obstinacy; and promising them good usage; but they declared, if they were fifty armed men, they would not be taken, and told he he should lose his life first, he replied, it was his orders. —— This conversation was repeated more than once, Mr. Panton gave a candle which he had in his hand, to one of them, (the place being very dark) desiring, that they would let him see thro' the scuttle what sort of a place they were in, the man who took the candle, moved it about the place where they stood; Mr. Panton said, he could not see it, and wanted to go down; they answered, he should not, and if he attempted it, they would that moment shoot him, presenting their musket, which they told him was loaded with slugs; and primed, and returned the candle. Mr. Panton said, "Aye, will you shoot me," and in a joking chearful manner added, "I will take a pinch of snuff first." Just at this time the boat returned; and soon after Panton ordered his men to open the bulk-head of the place where the brig's people were; but as soon as they began to work upon it, the people within declared, they would shoot the first man who made a hole; one of them advised the others to shoot the Lieutenant first, and divide themselves, two to defend the scuttle, and two defend the bulk-head; one of those at the scuttle presented a musket, another a fish gig, and one from within called out to fire; the gentleman with him, struck the musket downwards of its direction at Mr. Panton, who ordered the scuttle to be put down, and went to see what the boat's crew had done at the bulk-head. —— The master at arms having made a small opening with a crow, one from within presented a musket through it, threatening to shoot him, and while the bulk-head was breaking down (one called) Corbet said; Mr. Lieutenant, I will murder you first, and you may be certain of death if you do not go about your business, and presented the musket; on which the master of arms desired them to point at him, and not the gentleman who done them no harm. Corbet snapped the musket several times at them, all others calling out to fire, and damning it for not going off; one of the boat's crew got hold of it, but could not keep it. Immediately after one of the crew fired a pistol loaded with powder only at Corbet's face, hoping it would make them submit. Corbet desired Mr. Panton to observe what one of his men had done, who replied, when he surrender'd, he would show him the man when he came on board, (meaning to give satisfaction) and took away the pistol from him, and ordered his men not to fire upon any account. He asked the brig's people to lend him their ax, to knock down the bulk head a little faster; they assured, they would lend it to scalp him. Mr. Panton during all this, frequently begged them to submit, or he must clear his way to them; but all them said, they would shoot Mr. Panton first, and the master of Arms after, before they would be taken. —— The Master of Arms being pushed at, called out he must fire to save his life which Mr. Panton strictly forbid him on his peril to do, took the pistol from him, and blew out the priming. The boat's crew continued to break down the bulk head, on which Corbet made a pass at Mr. Panton with a harpoon, who stood upon his feet a few seconds, and said, "the rascal has stabbed me in the jugular vein." Immediately after the Lieutenant was wounded, one of Rose's men fired a pistol which wounded one of the brig's people in the arm. An officer with the assistance of two men, conveyed Mr. Panton to the brig's cabin, where he soon expired. The Rose was immediately hailed, and the Commander being informed of this unhappy accident, mann'd and arm'd the barge, and sent her immediately, and also a guard to take care of those who had committed the murder. About noon two of the people delivered themselves up, and soon after they seized Corbet. —— They were all carried on board the Rose. It must be observed that the man who was wounded came out soon after Mr. Panton was killed.

N. B. It has been said the Brig's men were drunk, but they did not appear to when they when they were carried on board the Rose.

The two men belonging to the brig not Mentioned on the account, were Americans, they remained on deck the whole time the Rose's people were on board her; the commodore, out of his great goodness, having given orders, that no Americans or persons married to Americans should be pressed."

Saturday April 29th, His Excellency Sir. Francis Bernard Baronet, Governor, Commander Hood, his Honour the Lieut. Governor, Hon, A. Oliver, Secretary, and Hon. Robert Aucmuty, Esq; Judge of Admiralty; went on board the Rose man of war, to take the steps previous to the trial of the men concerned in the death of Lieut. Panton, Capt. Caldwell of the Rose, received and entertained them with the greatest politeness. We hear the trial will come on within fifteen or sixteen days.

BOSTON May 1. Last Week Capt. Molesworth, of the 29th Regt. was married to Miss Sukey Sheaffe, Daughter of William Sheaffe' Esq; Deputy Collector for this Port.

Last Thursday three Deserters from the Regiment quartered here, which were lately taken up in the Province of New-Hampshire, were brought to Town guarded by a Party of Soldiers sent there for that purpose.

The same Day Badger, Donnelly, & Carmichael, the three persons convicted of setting Fire to the Goal here, and lately mentioned were set upon the Gallows during the space of one hour, and afterwards whip'd 20 stripes each, pursuant to their Sentence.

BOSTON May. 3. Last Friday the Freeholder and other Inhabitants of this Town, legally warned, met at Faneuil-Hall, and there made their choice of the following Gentlemen to represent them in the General Assembly at the approaching Sessions. The no. of votes being 508. The Hon. James Otis Esq;; 502. The Hon. Thomas Cushing, Esq; 502. Mr. Samuel Adams, 503. John Hancock, Esq. 505.

BOSTON May 8. We hear from Brooklyn, that on Monday last, the first Instant, there was a Spinning Match at the Dwelling-House of Isaac Gardner, Esq; of Weston, where Forty six Ladies met and spun Sixty Skains if Linnen Yarn, each Skain containing Twenty Knots; and they Carded and Spun Forty-five Skains of Cotton and Tow Yarn, and generously gave their Work.

BOSTON May 15, A Letter from New-York, Dated April 29, 1769.

"Last Friday at two o'clock P. M. one of our London Ships arrived, and had some Goods on board although the Quantity is small it makes a great deal of noise in this Place. ——— Saturday last the Merchants met and came to a conclusion to put the Goods into public Warehouse, which being done, the People were satisfied ——— A meeting of every Inhabitant of the city is called, and by what I can see the Merchants and others seem to be determined to ship back, as we look upon it they are only sent for bait, it is lucky that no body here will bite. ——— You will soon have a Letter from our Committee to acquaint your People what is done with the Goods, ——— in order to prevent any more Goods coming in the Fall Ships, they will be an agreement signed this day by the Merchants not to Ship any Goods on board any Vessel, or by any Commander of a Vessel, that should take Goods on Freight in Great-Britain contrary to the agreement the Merchants have entered into. ——— It gives us a good deal of alarm to hear you have so many goods ship'd for your Place, and we are afraid you will not take the necessary Steps as the Soldiery is among you, but if you are dragooned by them you are forever undone."

BOSTON May 22. The trial of the Persons charged with the Murder of Lieutenant Panton of his Majesty's Ship Rose, is to be at the Court-House in the Town Tomorrow at Nine O'Clock in the Forenoon.

BOSTON May 22. On Monday the 15th Instant, Mr. Jacob Parsons, Deputy Sheriff for the County of Essex, having arrested a Prisoner for debt ——— One Samuel Fellows, Commander of one of his Majesty's arm'd Cutters, then riding in the Harbour of Cape-Ann, with a Number of his Men, forcibly rescued the Prisoner from the Sheriff, carried him on board the said Cutter. In Consequence of which the Sheriff came immediately to this Town, and presented the following Memorial to the Governor and Council ——— And we hear that they took this heinous Offence instantly into Consideration, and proceeded to act on the same.

Province of the Massachusetts-Bay, to his Excellency Sir Francis Bernard, baronet, governor and commander in chief, in and over his Majesty's said Province, and the honorable his Majesty's Council of the Province aforesaid.

Jacob Parsons of Gloucester, in the County of Essex, and one of the Deputy-sheriffs for the same County, humbly represents to your Excellency and Honors,

That on the 15th day of May current at Gloucester, your memorialist, as one of the Deputy-Sheriffs of the county aforesaid by virtue of a due process of law, had duly taken and legally, held in custody the body of one Josiah Merrill, as a prisoner; ——— That, while your memorialist, was, then and there, in the due execution of his office aforesaid, one Samuel Fellows, a commander of one of his Majesty's armed cutters, then riding in the harbour of Cape-Anne, with four of his men, with fire-arms, cutlasses and other weapons of death, came, from on board said cutter, with a boat, on shore, and said Fellows immediately accosted the said Merrill, by asking him ——— "What he did there?" Upon which Merrill replied that ——— "an officer had taken him in custody for debt," ——— That in consequence of this reply, said Fellows, in an authoritative voice, commanded said Merrill; to come away to him, and that he would protect said Merrill; ——— That on this engagement, said Merrill broke away from the Memorialist, and ran towards said Fellows; ——— That your memorialist instantly commanded, in his Majesty's name, several persons, who stood near, to assist in seizing and stopping his said prisoner; ——— That obedience to the command of your memorialist, in his capacity aforesaid, several of his Majesty's liege subjects, unitedly with your memorialist, seized and held said prisoner ——— That said Fellows, who while this passed was within four rods from your memorialist and his prisoner, instantly on said Merrill's being seized and held, as last-mentioned, ordered his four men to fire; ——That on this order two of said Fellow's men leaped upon the beach, and run towards your memorialist and his said assistants, till they had got within four rods, when they presented their arms directly to your memorialist an his assistants, and fired; the shot and ball scarcely missed us, and entered a store within a few inches of where we stood; —— That the said prisoner taking advantage of the surprize and consternation your memorialist and his said assistants were then in and of the protection offered by one of his Majesty's officers, immediately broke away and run towards the said Fellow's boat; —— That during the whole of this time, said Fellows and his men, altho' they were reportedly told, that your memorialist was a King's officer, kept a constant round of oaths and imputations upon your memorialist, and his assistants; damning the King's officers and all who belong to him; swearing that they would blow the brains out, of the first man, who offered to touch said Merrill, or come towards the boat; —— That they would take better sight next time, and the like; —— That as said Merrill came nearer to the boat, said Fellows as his men kept firing at your memorialist and his assistants, till said Fellows commanded his men not to fire any more yet; but to keep a reserve, for any who should attempt a retaking of said Merrill; —— an that after said Fellows and his men had fired 6 or 7 times, by which your memorialist and his assistants were in the most emanate hazard of their lives, and the said Fellows and his men still defending said Merrill, returned on board the boat, and still kept firing, as they left the shore; and your memorialist had never since been able to retake his said prisoner, and bring him back to justice.

    BOSTON May 29. The Court was formed for the Trial of Michael Corbot, Pierce Fanning, William Conner and Joseph Ryan, charged with being concerned in the Murder of Lieutenant Panton, of his Majesty's Ship Rose; but some doubt having arises whether the Prisoners were entitled to a trial by Jury, the Court was adjoined to Nine o'Clock last Thursday, who, in the mean Time took under Consideration the Prisoner's Rights to a trial by Jury as aforesaid. The Court adjourned to this Day.

BOSTON June 5. The Court for Trying Piracies, Felonies, &c. committed on the High-Seas, which sat here for the Trial of several seamen charged with the Murder of Lieutenant Panton, mentioned in our last to be adjourned, met again Monday last, when the Prisoners, by their Council, filed a plea against the jurisdiction of the Court: Upon Court tho't proper to take the same under consideration and adjourned to the 14th Instant.

BOSTON June 5. Major-General Mackay being informed, that many of the Soldiers who have deserted from his Majesty's Troops that are quartered here, being sensible of their Crime and Error, would gladly return and join their Regiments, had they any hopes of Forgiveness: He hereby offers, and assures a Free Pardon to every Man that surrenders himself on, or before the last Day of June next, excepting, Edward Raynolds, John Cameron, Hugh Watkins, Robert Gaines, William Beetle, and Thomas Hubbard, of the 14th Regiment: James Nagle, Thomas copper, Daniel Rogers, Patrick Denmison, John Reddish, and John Crofts of the 29th Regiment; Robert Jones, Mathew Coleman, Ralph Bridge, Thomas Sullivan, Archibald Emtroistle, amd Michael Clifford of the 64th Regiment: whose Crimes are such a nature, as to oblige him to exclude them from any Promise of Pardon: And a Reward of three Guineas each offered for apprehending and securing them in any of the Public Goals.

Such Men who take the Benefit of the above pardon are desired to go to the nearest Justice of the Peace or Military officer, and get a certificate of the Day of their Surrender, and a Pass to come to Boston, as they may depend every Man who is taken up, on Deserts from this Date, will be brought to a General Court Martial. Boston 23d May, 1769. by order of Major General Mackay. C. Fordyke, Major of Brigade.

BOSTON June 12. On Tuesday last 95 Soldiers arrived here from New-York, these Men lately belonged to the 34th Regiment (which is soon to embark for England,) and are now incorporated into the 14th, 29th, and 59th Regiments.

On Tuesday Afternoon the beautiful seat of Major Bayard at Ruxbury, accidentally cought Fire, supposed by a Spark from the Chimney, and was entirely consumed.

Extract of a Letter from Albany May 28. "I fear we are on the Eve of an Indian War; Letters from Detroit advise, that the Indians are assembling that the Inhabitants are returning to the Fort; and such traders as had not left Niagara and Owego, when the account came, remain there."

BOSTON June 19. We are assured, that the order for Sir Francis Bernard, Bart. to return to England in Express to be to attend the King as Governor to report to him the present State of the province; that it contains directions for the present administration of the government during his absence; and that there is no intention at present of superseding his commission. We hear that he proposes to embark about the end of July.

BOSTON June 19. On Wednesday next the 21st Instant at One o'Clock, will be Sold by Public Vendue, at the Bunch of Grapes, in King Street, 5 stout able-bodied Negro Men, that are healty and strong, Also a Negro Boy about 17 Years of Age, and 2 Negro Women, suitable for Town and Country. Any Persons minded to purchase any of the above Negroes at private sale, before the time fixed for public, may apply to

J. Russell Auctioneer.

Boston June 19. From the Providence Gazette, Dated June 10, 1769.

Custom-House Boston June 2, 1769.

Whereas on the 18th of May last, in the evening, a great number of People riotously assembled in the Town of Providence, in the Colony of Rhode Island, and violently seized Jeffe Saville, a Tidesman belonging to the Custon-House of the said Port, who was the attending his Duty there and having gagged and put him into a wheelbarrow almost strangled, they carried him to a Wharf, where they threatened to drown him if he made the least Noise; tied a

Handkerchief round his Face cut his Clothes to Pieces, stripped him naked, covered him from Head to Foot with Turpentine and Feathers bound him Head and Feet, threw Dirt in his Eyes, and and repeatedly beat him with their Fists and Sticks, then threw him down on the Pavement, cut his Face, and bruised his Body, in a most barbarous Manner; during which inhuman treatment, which lasted an Hour and a Half, but was near expiring and now lies dangerously ill.

For the better bringing to Justice and condign Punishment the Authors of this Daring & atrocious Outrage, the Commissioners of his Majesty's Customs do hereby promise a Reward of Fifty Pounds Sterling for the Discovery of any of them, to be paid upon his or their Convictions. By order of the Commissioners,

Richard Reeve.

BOSTON June 19. Tuesday last his Excellency Governor Wentworth arrived in Town, with a great Retinue, from New-Hampshire; several other Gentlemen also arrived here, being Officers included in the Commision for the Trial of Piracy and Felonies on the High-Seas: The Court was opened according to Adjournment last Wednesday for the Trial of the Persons charged with the Murder of Lieut. Panton of his Majesty's ship Rose: The plea against the Jurisdiction of the court was not admitted, and the Evidence, and the Trial was continued from Day to Day till Saturday Noon, when the Court unanimously acquitted the Prisoners.

BOSTON June 22. On Tuesday, June 20, Major General Mackay, reviewed on the Common, the 29th regiment, which made a very fine appearance, and performed the manual Exercise, firing and evolutions with such exactness, as does honor to Colonel Carr, and the other Officers. ——— Commodore Hood, Brigadier General Pomeroy, the field Officers of the regiments quartered here, and a numerous company of Ladies and Gentlemen were present.

BOSTON June 22. On Friday last the cannon at the Main-Guard of the King's Troops opposed the Court-House, were removed, and shipped on board one of the cutters as were also the other stores belonging to the detachment of the Royal Train of Artillery: ——— the company having since embarked, and are sailed for Halifax.

BOSTON JUne 26. Soon after the acquaintance of the persons charg'd with the murder of Lieut. Panton, of his Majesty's Ship Rose, a Deputy Sheriff in this County went on board said Ship and arrested Mr. Peacock, a Midshipman in the Action of Damages, for firing upon and wounding in the Arm, one of the Men who had been charged as an Accessory: to which Mr. Peacock gave Bail in the Sum of 300 Pounds lawful Money.

On Wednesday the 65th regiment began to embark from Castle Island, on board the Rippon and Rose man of war, and on Saturday they also sailed for Halifax. ——— The 64th regiment is soon to follow them. ——— The 29th is to move to the barracks at the Castle, and the 14th regiment perhaps will remain here.

BOSTON July 3. On Saturday last Michael Carter, a Native of Ireland, was driving a Cart in Back-Street, loaded with coal. and attempting to turn the Corner of a said Brick building, the upper corner of the Cart taking his Head, and the under Corner his Breast, by which means his skull was fractur'd, and the body violently pressed, so that he immediately expired: he was about 20 Years of Age.

BOSTON July 6. The Embarkation of the 64th regiment is posponed it is said for ten days.

BOSTON July 10. Tuesday last at launching a Vessel near the South Battery, one of the Workmen Mr. Samuel Sloper, of this Town, aged about 50 Years, in cutting away, the Wale Shores, one of them fell on his Head, and fractured his skull: He was taken up senseless, and died the same Evening.

BOSTON July 16. The Representatives of this province have in a large House of upward of an hundred members unanimously remonstrated against the administration of Sir Francis Bernard, baronet, of Nettleham, Governor of this Province, as having been corrupt and arbitrary; and humbly petitioned the King that he may be for ever removed from this Government. It is said that above a dozen articles are therein exhibited against him, with authentick proof, taken from own letters and speeches of former and later days.

BOSTON July 17. We hear the Rippon is to sail from this Port for England the 25th of July, in whom it is said his Excellency Sir Francis Bernard, Bart, and the Hon. Brigadier General Mackay goes Passenger.

BOSTON JUly 24. By a Gentleman from Rhode-Island and by Mr. Mumford the Post-Rider, we have the following account;

On Saturday the 16th instant, Capt. Reid in the armed sloop Liberty, seized a brigantine belonging to New-London, Joseph Packwood Master, from Hispaniola with a cargo of mollasses and Sugar on board, and a sloop, where belonging and from whence, unknown, having on board brandy, wine, &c. which Captain Read says, he had information were taken out of the brig. —— Capt. Read immediately carried both vessels into Rhode-Island, and with the sloop Liberty came to an anchor off the Long-Wharf in New-Port: Capt. Parkwood on his getting ashore at Newport, reported his vessel at Custom-House, and made a declaration; that he had no contraband goods on board. On the Wednesday following, Capt. Parkwood went on board the brig to get his clothes to be washed, and asked for his sword, all which, the commanding Officer on board refused to deliver him; but which after some altercation, he took possession of and put into the boat, and was rowing to shore, when the people on board the brig hailed the sloop Liberty, and told the Commanding Officer, (Capt. Read not being on board) that Capt. Packwood had used them very ill, and desired him to bring the boat too, on which some person on board the Liberty fired a musket with a brace of balls at Capt. Packwood, one of which went but a few inches over his head, and the other over the head of some of the people standing on the wharf, they afterwards attempted to fire a swivel, but it only flashed, and Capt. Packwood pushed on shore. By this time a number of people assembled, who with Capt. Parkwood went in search of Capt. Read, who they soon meet in the street, when they demanded the reason of the insolent behaviour of his people! Capt. Read told them that he was ignorant of this affair, was extremely sorry for what had happened, that he would deliver up the people who had fired, to be punished according to law; and proposed to go himself on board and fetch them to shore: ——— This the people would not permit, but insisted on his going to hail the sloop and order them to be immediately sent on Shore. ——— This was complyed with, and a boat was sent off for them, which soon returned with two of the sloop's hands, but the people declaring there were not the persons who had fired; the boat was sent on board a second time, and brought two others, but these likewise being declared not the persons, the boat was again set off and brought others, till there were only two left on board belonging to the sloop, soon after which, some people who had tarried on board the sloop, cut her cables and ran her on shore, threw the guns overboard, cut away the mast, rigging &c. and scuttled her: the boat they dragged to the upper part of the town and burnt: They also set fire to the sloop, but it being nigh a warehouse and some vessels where she was run on shore, they extinguished it for fear of the flames spreading.

During the affair, the sloop with the wine, &c. on board was carried off. ——— On Friday Capt. Packwodd demanded permission of the officers of the Custom to proceed on his voyage, or he would throw the vessel and cargo on their hands, and sue them for damages; on which, it is said, the vessel was suffered to depart.

Yesterday afternoon, sailed his Majesty's ship Senegal it is said for Rhode-Island.

BOSTON July 27. Yesterday sailed for Halifax, his Majesty's ship Romney, and Viper, having on board, the remaining five Companies of the 64th regiment. ——— Commodore Hood, his Lady and family returned to Halifax in the Romney.

Saturday se'nnight died at Newport Mr. Samuel Munford, formerly post-rider between that place and this town.

BOSTON Aug. 7. Thursday last embarked on Board his Majesty's Ship the Rippen, Sir Francis

Bernard, of Nettleham, Bart. who for nine Years past, has been the Scourge of this Province, a Curse to North-America, and a Plaque to the whole Empire. He having sagely fixed on the First of August, the Day of the Elevation of the House of Hanover to the British Throne, for the Time of his Departure, there were four Cause for the public Rejoicing. 1. The Accession of the present Royal Family. 2. That the King had been graciously pleased to recall a very bad Governor. 3. The sure and certain Hopes that a very that a very good one will be sent out, and placed in his Stead. 4. That a worse cannot be found on this side ———, if there. ——— On Monday Evening the Baronet, being unwilling to give himself a friends, if he has any, the Trouble of a formal Leave or the people Opportunity to hiss him off the stage, sneaked down to Castle William, where he lay the Night. The next Morning he was toated on board the Rippon, in a Canoe, a Tom-Cod Catcher, or some other small Boat. The Ship was soon under sail, but had not proceeded a League, before the wind Shifted, she came to Anchor, and lay Wind-bound 'till Friday Noon, when she sailed again with a fair Wind after her: The Captain, Thompson, and the Ship, both worthy a better Cargo. Should the Jonas, on the rising of the first Storm, sign a Round Robin to the Captain to throw the Baronet overboard for fair Weather, and he find his way into a Whales Belly, it is hoped he will not be cast out. ——— So soon as the Rippon was under sail on Tuesday, the Cannon of the Castle were fired with joy ——— The Union flagg was displayed from Liberty-Tree, where it was kept flying 'till Friday. ——— Colours were also flung out from the top of Houses in Town. ——— The Bells were rang, and Cannon fired incessantly 'till Sunset. In the Evening was a Bonfire on Fort-Hill, and another on the Heights of Charlestown. The general Joy of our City was found defused through the neighbouring Towns, who gave similar Demonstrations of it. There was not the least Disorder committed, and the night was the most quiet the Town had enjoyed since August 1760, the Time of the Baronet's Arrival here.

His Excellency upon embarking, having delivered the Province Seal to the Lieutenant Governor, Wednesday his Honor in Council took Oath required by Act of Parliament, in order to take upon him the Administration of the Province.

BOSTON Aug. 7. We hear from Newport, that last Saturday se'nnight the remains of the Sloop Liberty was drifted ashore on Goat Island, very near the place where the Pirates were burried; where she was afterwards set on Fire and totally consumed.

Tuesday Afternoon a sad Accident happened near the Town-Dock, a Negro Lad having loaded a Pistol with Powder & in putting two large Charges was afraid to fire it, a Sailor took it out of his Hand and discharged the same; the Negro then loaded the Pistol again, but before he took the Rammer out of the barrel, a Soldier flipped the Pistol out of his Hand and fired it off, and the Rammer went into the Belly of a young Lad that was passing, which put an end to his Life the day following about two o'Clock. The Lad was between 13 and 14 Years of Age, named Seth Billings belonging to Milton or Stoughton, and was Apprentice to Mr. Joseph Billings in this Town. The Jury of Inquest bro't in their Verdict, of Accidental Death.

We hear that the Collector's Boat at New London was lately burnt, and one Wilson, an informer pretty roughly handled by the Populace there.

BOSTON Aug. 14. At a Meeting of the Merchants at Faneuil-Hall, August 11, 1769.

Voted, That the Names of the following Persons be inserted in the Publick papers as importers contrary to the Agreement of the Merchants, viz. Richard Clarke and Son, John Bernard, Nathaniel Rogers, Theophilus Lillie, James McMasters and Comp. John Mein, Thomas Hutchinson, jum'r and Elisha Hutchinson.

Voted, That Mr. Cyrus Baldwin, Mr. Gilbert Deblois, and Mr. John Avery, jun, be a committee to prepare an Agreement for the Vendue Master in this Town to sign, restricting them from selling either publickly or privately, any Goods that have been or may be imported contrary to the Agreement of the Merchants, and the Committee be and hereby are directed to publish in the News-Papers, the Names of such who refuse to sign the same: And if any person or persons shall take the Advantage of this Restriction and establish a new Office or Offices for the sale of such Goods, that they be waited upon by the Committee to sign the Agreement afore mentioned; and upon their refusal, that their Names be likewise published.

It having been suggested of the Meeting, that Mr. John Greenlaw had broke the Agreement of Merchants, he was sent for, and appeared, when he made the following Acknowledgement, which was voted to be satisfactory.

Whereas I John Greenlaw having purchased Goods of Persons who have imported contrary to the Agreement of the Merchants which I Subscribed. I do now declare that I am sensible of, and sorry for my Misbehaviour in that Respect; and that I am now ready, and do hereby engage to the Committee of Merchants such goods as I have now by me, which I purchased contrary to the Agreement; and also all of those which I may hereafter receive in Consequence of any Orders I have forwarded, to be then kept, till a general Importation takes Place: And that for the future, I will strictly adhere to the Engagement I have entered into in August last.

John Greenlaw.

The Goods are delivered to the said Committee and accordingly received into the public store.

BOSTON Aug. 28. Messieurs Fleet, Please to insert the following and you will oblige Your's.

W. P.

In The Boston Chronicle on Monday last, Mr. Mein has taken upon him to publish Mr. Hancock's Name in a list of Importers, and that, in such an artful and evasive Manner, as was evidently intended to mislead People (especially those who are ignorant of the Nature of British Manufactures) to conclude that the Non-Importation, by importing an Article not excepted in the Agreement. As Mr. Hancock is now out of the Province, I thick it my Duty to inform the Public in general, and those who are unacquainted with the Nature of English goods in particular, that the 100 Pieces of British Linen mentioned by Mr. Meins as imported by John Handcock, Esq; in the Lydia, Joseph Hood, Master, is neither more or less than one hundred Pieces of Russian Duck, and Article particularly excepted in the Agreement, and which is frequently mentioned as British Linen in the Cockets.

In the same artful evasive Manner Mr. Mein conducted through the whole Course of his late extraordinary Performance; but I leave it to the respectable Body of Merchants to detect and expose his Fallacies. Sure I am, those Gentlemen can, and will vindicate their own conduct to the Satisfaction of the whole Continent.

It would be a ridiculous Task for anyone to attempt a Vindication of Mr. Hancock's Character, even if the Demand was made by a Person of any Consequence: The Gentlemen's Reputation as a Patriot and a Merchant (notwithstanding Mr. Mein's sarcastical Sneer) is too well established to suffer any injury from the Aspersions of Mr. Mein or any other of his Clan. Their "good Disposition" toward him is to notorious to escape Observation: The Man who seeks the Welfare of his Country cannot fail to render himself obnoxious to those who are using every Artifice in their Power to enslave it.

Wm. Palfrey.

BOSTON Aug. 24. Last Friday Trial was made of the Brigatine, Rising Liberty, belonging to John Hancock, Esq; and lately built by Mr. Walker of this Town. ——— At the Invitation of Mr. Hancock, a Number of Gentlemen among whom were several of Distinction from the Southern Colonies, embark'd early in the Morning in a Party of Pleasure on board the Brig. On Her Departure she discharg'd a Round of Cannon, which was answered by three full cheers from a great Number of respectable Persons in the Wharff ——— as they pass'd the Castle she paid a Salute by another discharge of Cannon, which was genteely return'd; and the Captain of the Castle joining the Gentlemen on board, she proceeded into the Bay ——— An Elegant Entertainment was ordered by Mr. Hancock, and the company having spent the Day in the most agreeable Scenes of Social Pleasure, which is ever diffusive in such a circle of warm Friends of Liberty, in the Evening they return'd to Town. —— At Landing, the cannon on board were again discharg'd as a Mark of respect to the Town; and a numerous crowd of Spectators, with three hearty cheers, shouted a Welcome to the Gentlemen on shore —— The Brig is just 92 tons burthen, is esteemed a prime Sailor and in every respect does honor to the builder.

BOSTON Sept. 4, 1769. Advertisement.

Whereas I have full evidence that Henry Hulton, Charles Paxton, William Burch, and John Robinson, Esquires, have frequently and lately treated the character of all true North-Americans in a manner that is not to be endured, by privately and publickly representing them as Traitors and Rebels, and in general combination to revolt from Great-Britain. And whereas the said Henry, Charles, William and John, without the least provocation or color have Represented me by name as inimical to the rights of the Crown, and disaffected to his Majesty, to whom I Annually, swear and am determined at all events to bear true and faithful allegiance, for all which general, as well as personal abuse and insults, satisfaction has been personally demanded, due warning given, but no sufficient answers obtained. These are therefore humbly to desire the Lords Commissioners of his Majesty's Treasury, his principle Secretaries of State, Particularly my lord of Hillsborough, the Board of Trade, and all the other who it may concern, and who may condescend to read this, to pay no wind of regard to any of the abusive misrepresentations of me on my country, this may be transmitted by the said Henry, Charles, Will, and John, or their confederates, for they are no more worthy of credit than those of Sir Francis Bernard, Nettleham Bart. or any of his cabal, which cabal may be well known from the papers in the House of Commons, and every great Office in England.

James Otis.

BOSTON Sept. 11. Copy of a letter from Mr. Otis to his Council.

Gentlemen,

Besides the action of defamation against Sir Francis Bernard of Nettleham, Bart. I had it in contemplation to pursue the same method against Hulton, Paxton, Burch, and Robinson, for the many unprovoked and unparalleled falsehoods they have uttered, written and published of me; but on more mature deliberation desire that one step toward a process of that kind may be taken, at least for the present, 1. For that I have ever had a general aversion to actions of this kind. Every man's character is good or bad: If good, such action will not make it better: If bad, no such action can mend it. 2. On a more careful perusal of the papers and publications in my power, and duly considering the character of the above Five, I cannot in my conscience think either their tongues or their pens any slander. 3. On the contrary, I have ever had the pleasure to find, that in full proportion to the malice and distraction of those and the rest of the cabal, my reputation has been more firmly established in the opinion of those with whom I wish to stand well at home and abroad. 4. Should I recover even so high damage at law, I know nothing to restrain them from paying them out of the public Chest, which money extorted as it is, I desire not to touch. 5. It is absolutely impossible that I should take a penny from a man in this way, after an Acknowledgement of his error. The cabal therefore are at liberty, id they please to remonstrate, memorial and lease-make against me forever: and I can devise no other chastisement for their impudence, nor get any other satisfaction for their insolence than what action of defamation will give me, I shall rest as easy as possible.

Your's James Otis.

BOSTON Sept. 11. Early on Tuesday Evening a Disturbance arose at the British Coffee-House in this Town between James Otis, Esq; and John Robinson, Esq; the latter demanding satifaction for certain Expressions in a Publication signed by Mr. Otis in the Boston Gazette on Monday last, and 'tis supposed tho' no Cause was expressed. —— After a Proposal on the Part of

Mr. Otis to decide this Controversy by Themselves, abroad, or in a separate Room, the former was refused, but the latter found to be consented to by Mr. Robinson, but very unexpectedly to Mr. Otis, and while he was following Mr. Robinson in the presence of the Publick Company in the Coffee-Room, suddenly turned and attempted to take him by the Nose; but failing in the attemt, he immediately struck at him with a Cane, against Mr. Otis defended himself, and returned the compliment. A close Engagement then ensued, and Mr. Otis having disarmed his antagonist, several Persons in the Room prevented Mr. Otis from having fair play, some of which held him, while the others struck him with canes Cutlasses and other Weapons, and a cry was, kill him! kill him! ⸺ A Young Gentleman, Mr. John Gridley. passing by the Room, and seeing Mr. Otis treated in so ungentleman like and Barbarous a Manner and without a Friend near him, press'd in, and endeavouring to interpose, was also attacked in that Manner, Mr. Otis was, by as many as could come near him, and after a resolute and manly Defence of himself, was at length overpowered, as Mr. Otis had been by Numbers. ⸺ By this time several others had got into the Room, whereupon Mr. Robinson and those who were with him, retired through the back Door of the Coffee-House. Mr. Otis and Gridley were carried of much wounded. and it is tho't had not the People come in to their Assistance the Consequence of this ungenerous Assault wold have been fatal. ⸺ The Company in the Room when Otis was first attacked consisted chiefly of the Officers of the Army, Navy and the Revenue; and it is allowed without Contradiction that both Mr. Otis and Gridley acquainted themselves with a Resolution becoming Gentlemen of Honor.

BOSTON Sept. 11. To Messiers Mein & Flemming, To guard against misrepresentation, I think it necessary to publish the following relation of what passed between James Otis, jun. Esq; and myself, and I am to desire you, to give it a place in your paper. I am Gentleman Your's
John Robinson.

Being at the Board Friday morning, the first

of September inst. about half after ten o'clock, I was acquainted, that Mr. James Otis, jun. had called in the morning, and desired to speak with Mr. Hulton and myself; and had left word, that if it was not convenient for us to call at his House, he would come to us. Mr. Hulton came to the board soon after, when Green the Messenger was directed to acquaint Mr. Otis, that Mr. Hulton and myself were at the Board-Room, where we were ready to see him. About 11 o'clock we were told that Mr. Otis was at the street door. Mr. Reeve the Secretary, at our desire, asked Mr. Otis to walk into the room, which he refused. Mr. Hulton, Mr. Reeve and myself then went to the door, when I accosted Mr. Otis and Samuel Adams who was with him thus. ―――― Your Servant Gentlemen; pray what your business with us? ―――― Mr. Otis answered that he wanted a free conversation with us: I replied, it is necessary that we should first know upon what business. Will not you walk into the room Gentlemen? He answered that his business was of such a nature, that it could not be transacted in our Houses; and he could not mention it until he met us: and he would bring a friend with him. I then asked him, whether his business was official? He answered, he did not understand what I meant by Official; I replied does it relate to us as Commissioners? He said, it related to his character, he wanted a free conversation with us on the subject, and that he was to meet Mr. Burch at the Coffee-House the next morning at seven o'clock. I answered, that as I live in the country, I did not know whether I could attend at that time and Mr. Hulton said the same in respect to himself. Mr. Otis then said, any time will do. We answered we would see him at a convenient opportunity, and parted. ―――― Although I had not promised to meet Mr. Otis at any particular time, I came to a determination, to accompany Mr. Burch the next morning at seven o'clock, rather that he should be alone: but having come about four miles, and having a few interruptions on the road, I was a few minutes late, so that I met Mr. Burch coming from the Coffee-House, and without knowing what passed between him and Otis, I proceeded to the Coffee-House, accompanied by Mr. Reeve intending to give Mr. Otis the opportunity of speaking to me if he thought proper. —— Mr. Otis was there in the back room, and finding that I was in the Coffee-House he immediately came to me, and accosted me civilly, asking me the same time, if I would walk into another room, and drink a dish of coffee with me, —— to which I asserted, as I had just before called for coffee, and proposed that Mr. Reeve should accompany us, supposing that Mr. Adams was with him. He answered, That he had no objection to Mr. Reeve, and would send for his friend; but observed, we might be either single or double. Upon my signifying that it was agreeable to me to be alone with him, we went into a room together when he helped me to a dish of coffee, and the following conversation ensued.

Mr. Otis. "I am informed that I have been represented to government by your Board, as a rebel and traitor, and I have two or three questions to put to you, that I think as a gentleman, I have a right to an answer, or at least to ask: The first is, whether your Board of Commissioners, Gentlemen, in any other manner, ever represented me in that light, in any of their Memorials or letter to the Treasury."

Mr. Robinson. "Before you can expect an answer, you should show your authority; —— I mean just how you came by such Information."

Mr. Otis. "I refer myself to the Board's Memorials to the Treasury, copies of which are lately come over here."

Mr. Robinson. "Your question is improper to be put to me singly as whatever I did with the rest of the board, I ought not to speak of, without consent of the other members, However, I can see no impropriety, in telling you that I do not remember your name being mentioned in any of the memorials which the board sent to the Treasury, and I cannot speak of the Correspondence of the individuals."

Mr. Otis. "The second question I have to ask you is, whether the copies of the questions I have ask you is, whether the copies of the memorials and letters obtained from the clerk of the House of Commons, and sent by Mr. Bollan to this town, as the memorials and letters of your board, are true copies transcripts?"

Mr. Robinson. "I never saw the copies you mention."

Mr. Otis "Then you certainly cannot answer that Question."

Mr. Robinson. "Surely as a Lawyer Mr. Otis, you must be sensible of the impropriety of putting these questions to us singly. I think Mr. Burch did right not to answer them; and I do not know but I have been wrong; however, what passes between us as Gentlemen, is, I suppose, to go no further."

Mr. Otis. "I shall nor make no unfair use of it."

Mr. Robinson. "Why did you not apply to us as a Board, as your business is altogether official?"

Mr. Otis. "I did not chuse that method of application, as it might be said that I obstructed you in the execution of your duty."

Mr. Robinson. "Pray what could you do that could bear that construction?"

Mr. Otis. "We might have had some altercation which might have been construed an insult upon you as a Board, which I was determined to avoid ——— I have been used very badly Mr. Robinson. I have been represented home as a traitor, and a Rebel for a long time. It is not about nine years since, that Bernard first began to write against me, and I am determined to vindicate my Character."

Mr. Robinson. "That is your own business Mr. Otis, ——— you and I have always been in different boxes, ———and though we might disagree in politics it is no reason that we should think ill of one another as men, ——— and I never had a bad opinion as you as a Man."

Mr. Otis. "That is right, why we should think ill of one another as men, you acted for the best according to your opinion, and I according to mine. I take the annual oath of allegiance to my King, and resolve to clear my character."

Mr. Robinson. "That is your own business, ———

I have nothing to do with it, ——— but if you think that I have done you any injury, I am ready to give you the satisfaction you have the right to expect from a Gentleman."

Mr. Otis. "I have one further question to put to you, ——— That old fellow Harrison the collector has represented me to your Board, as disaffected, and I shall be glad if you will let me know to what office at home you send his representation, for that I may obtain a copy of it."

Mr. Robinson. "This is a matter I do not chuse to answer."

Mr. Otis. "I have been used ill, and I am determined to have justice."

Mr. Robinson. "If I have done you injury, you will find me ready at all times to give you the satisfaction you have the right to expect as a Gentleman."

This is the substance that passed between us, though perhaps not exactly in the same words, which I the same day committed to writing. The matter thus rested until Monday, when Mr, Otis's publication appeared in the Boston Gazette, and Country Journal, signed by himself upon which I shall make no further comment, than that they must be viewed by the impartial world, as very injurious to my character and derogatory to my reputation; and considering his scurrilous treatment of me in particular, a few men, I presume would be able to command themselves upon so trying an occasion. On the evening the next day, Tuesday I went to the Coffee-House between the hours of 7 and 8, and seeing Mr. Otis without a sword, I went into the back room, where I laid mine aside, and immediately returned into the public room. ——— I then addressed myself to Mr. Otis, in these words or to this effect. ——— Some days ago you wanted free conversation with me, now I want a free conversation with you: He immediately stood up in a rage and said he was ready to answer me in any manner; I replied have a little patience; and let me ask you whether I did not repeatedly tell you when we met the other day, that if I had done you some injury, I was ready to give you anytime the satisfaction you had a right to expect from from a Gentleman. ——— How therefore could you publish the account in Edes and Gill's paper of Yesterday's? It was proposed by some persons, (his friend I supposed,) that we should go into a room. I said, that I had been in a room with him once already; and perceived that he frequently menaced me with his stick, I took him or at least attempted to take him by the Nose.

——— What follows is known to the company, to whom I appeal for the truth. All I can further say, is, that I verily believe, that no man besides myself, struck Mr. Otis, nor even offered him the least unfair play, (of which ample proof may be produced if necessary) though I am informed that more than one person, besides my antagonist, attacked me.

If this should be thought by some, that in any part of this transaction. I am not altogether to be justified, yet to men who have nice sentiments of honour, I shall not be thought an high offender; and I hope everyone will have so much candour as to make a just allowance for the fallacies of human nature, which cannot easily bear such gross provocations and indignities,

——— I even flatter myself that Mr. Otis in his cooler hours, will allow that this treatment of me, was such as could "not be endured" by a Gentleman.   John Robinson.

Boston Sept. 18. Messieures Edes and Gill. "Mr. Robinson Commissioner, must have a very good opinion of his Memory, or he could never have adventured to publish in Green and Russell's Gazette and Mein & Fleming's Chronicle, what he calls a Conversation that had passed between us. I shall however take the liberty to correct some of his many errors, and will leave the Public to determine whether the man who could write of this Country and Individuals as it appears by copies of Letters jus published he has done, or myself, deserves the greatest share of Credit? Mr. Robinson says, "He," Otis, "answered he did not understand what I meant by the Term official." This should have been, "he asked me what I meant by the Term official. And the Answer should have been I know not." R. "I did not know whether I could attend at that Time." Hulton indeed hesitated; had like to have promised the same, but finally evaded it, and I have not heard from him since, tho' he assured me in general terms that he would give me an Opportunity of a free Conversation with him. R. "I had no promised to meet Mr. Otis at any particular Time." False! R. "I proposed that Mr. Reeve should accompanied us, supposing Mr. Adams was with him." Otis. Of this I never before heard; nor do I now believe one Word of it, It is probable Mr. Adams should be with me, what occasion for "calling" or "sending for him." R. Absurd and inconsistent! In Truth Mr. Adams left me before Mr. Adams left me before Mr. Robinson came, one Mr. Burch choosing to be alone with me. What passed between Mr. Burch and me I shall not now relate. It may in time appear, tho' I choose he should follow the example of his Brother Robinson, and first publish his Edition of the Dialogue, never agreed to be kept secret," especially as that Gentleman expressed himself somewhat impertinently at the British-Coffee-House on Tuesday Evening se'nnight, of which more hereafter. R. "he". Otis"answered he had no objection to Mr. Reeve, and would send for that Friend, if present, as Mr. R. had just before asserted? R. I observed we might be single or double." a very sage Observation indeed! Not a single "Iota" of truth however is there to support the assertion. Yet had any proposal of the kind been made in substance, tho' in terms, and answer would have been the same. R."I can see no impropriety in telling you that I do not remember your Name being mentioned in any of the Memorials the Board sent to the Treasury, &c. and I cannot speak of the Correspondence of Individuals," Just the reverse of this is the Truth. He declared that in his private Correspondence he had never mentioned my Name: At the same Time he absolutely refused to answer any questions in relation to what had been "officially done by the Board," or by him as a "Commissioner" Truth is ever uniform. But behold the Inconsistency of the Man! In one Breath he says my "question was improper to be to be put to him singly; as whatever he did with the rest of the Board he ought not to speak of without the other Members;" Yet in the breath he says, "However I can see Impropriety." In What? Why "in telling," what had he had just before said was improper to tell; namely, that he did "not remember my being mentioned in any of their memorials." But besides this Inconsistency, why should he then deny, as he declares he did, to give me any Answer relating to Mr. Harrison's Report, which I know the Board have transmitted. If as Mr. R. "What passed between us was agreed should go no further," how come he attempted to publish it? It may be depended on, not from any Compact, but from a sense of honor, that "I shall make neither an unfair or fair Use of it." I shall only state Facts, That I ever said "he" Robinson "acted for the best," is without the least Color or Truth. I ever thought, and now think he has in all respects acted and now acts directly the reverse. R. "Scurrilous Treatment!" What does the man mean by Scurrilous Treatment? I should be glad of an "official" Definition of these Terms from the Commissioners. They have presumed to call all Colonist Traitors or Rebels, and I only said in effect that if no other Satisfaction could be obtained for such gross abuse, a natural Right would result to every Colonist of giving them such Chastisement as is due to the meanest and most insolent Offenders. And the Position I retract not. R. "Few Men I presume would be able to command themselves on so trying an Occasion" I believe so. Very trying indeed! On the one Side to be called Rebels and Traitors. On the other to be asked a few civil Questions. Very Trying indeed! But on which side of the Occasion most Trying? R. "I then addressed myself to Mr. Otis, in these Words or to that effect &c." I was not addressed in those Words, not to that effect. "he," Otis "Stood up in a rage." Nothing is further from the Truth than the Information that I was in a Rage. R. "he," Otis "said he was ready to answer me in any Manner." True in Substance, but not in Terms. Not a Word did I hear of "publication in Edes & Gill," nor "from a Friend of going into another room." This was my own Proposal, after having first offered to go abroad with him. The former was refused. The latter I thought was consented to, but why neither was complied with. I leave the Publick to Judge, from the known Circumstances of the Affair. I have since transiently heard that as Mr. R. went towards the Bar one missing the Word instead of "bruise him first and then fight him," solemnly gave out, "Kill him first and fight him afterwards." R. "I said I had been in a room with him already." What then? R. Why "perceiving" what was imperceptible, "that he frequently Menaced me with a Stick." Everything is a menace with the Commissioners; yet when I made the Proposal I felt not the least Emotion, and if not carelessly leaning on my Cane, sure I am I had not then lifted it up. R. "To Men of nice Sentiments of Honor!" George Cornnell's Letter, his own Letters, and his conduct here and in Rhode-Island, have fully evidence the Delicacy of his Sentiments! R. "Such cannot easily bear such gross Provocation and Indignities!" Pray what have I borne? What has this Town and Province borne? And I may say a whole Continent borne? from him and the cabal? Can any Thing be more abusive intolerable than the Conduct, and particularly the foul Misrepresentation of a N. American Commissioner? in short, I ask Mr. Robinson but three Questions at our first Interview at the British Coffee-House. 1. "If he in his private Correspondence had ever represented me in a disadvantage or light?" Answered "I never did." 2. "Sir. did you ever so represent me jointly or severally in your Capacity as a Commissioner?" Answered, "Refused." 3. "Sir, do you avow the Copies sent here by Mr. Bollan as authentic?" Answered, "I never saw those Copies." Little or nothing alse passed between us; And as two out of three of my Questions were not answered, and the other but in general Terms, there was nothing further to be said. I remember nothing. I believe nothing of Mr. Robinson's offering me the Satisfaction of a Gentleman. By this I suppose he would insinuate he gave me a Challenge. Nothing could be further from his Thoughts. Why should he challenge a Man asking a few decent Questions in Order to clear his Character from vile and villainous Aspersions? On the whole. I must say Robinson's Performance is from first to last a gross Misrepresentation of what passed between us, and I think I have proved as much from his Inconsistencies. James Otis.

BOSTON Sept. 25. The following are Depositions of Two Gentlemen of undoubted Reputation.

On Tuesday the 5th Instant being in a Shop almost opposite the British Coffee-House. I heard on a sudden a sudden unusual Noise there, which, made me curious enough to go see what was the matter. When I entered the Coffee-room I perceiv'd two Gentlemen fighting with each other the rest of the Company round them. I perceived several people rush upon Mr. Otis. But in particular when Mr. Otis made a trip (as they call it) at Mr. Robinson, which I believe would have brought him to the ground if he had not been supported by many people, who held him up. A young Gentleman (who I hear was Mr. Gridley) seeing the ungentleman behaviour of the Company went up (as I suppose) to have fair play shown: when immediately several people with sticks struck at Mr. Gridley in particular, and then (if I don't mistake) he was turned out of the Coffee-room Door along with Mr. Otis. Mr. Gridley in a short Time made his Appearance the second Time with his Arm (if I don't mistake) tied up, and his Face very much disfigured with Blood, who said they were all a Pack of cowardly Rascals to take such an Advantage of a single Man, and told them altho' one of his Arms was disabled, he would fight any cowardly Rascal of them all: when he left the Coffee-room the second Time I heard several Gentlemen say he deserv's what he got and much more, for making himself so busy; but in particular I heard John Mein say, that he was very gland if Mr. Otis had got as much more: but said he was sorry for Mr. Gridley, as he believed he was an honest fellow. I heard him say to some other Man he lost his Wine about it, but should pay it with the greatest Pleasure. upon the whole, as I was a Stander-by. In my opinion there was foul

Play shewn to Mr. Otis. Boston Sept. 21, 1769.
Thomas Brett.

The above named Thomas Brett, late of Cork in the kingdom of Ireland, Merchant, made oath to the above affidavit, taken to perpetuate the remembrance of the Thing, before.

Richard Dana, Justice of the Peace and the Quorum.

Sam. Pemberton Justice of the Peace.

I Mungo Mackay, of lawful Age testify as say, That on the Evening of Tuesday the 5th of Sept. instant, between seven and eight o'Clock, being in the Street near the Front-Door of the Coffee House in Boston, hearing an unusual Noise in the Coffee-House, I went in and saw a Crowd of people in the middle of which I perceived a Man hustled back by the Crowd towards the Door in the Entry, but soon saw the same Man advance towards the middle of the room, with his Arms up, as though he was striking at some Person, which person I then knew not, but afterwards heard his name was Robinson. The Person who was hustled by the Crowd was bare-headed and I observed a Number of Sticks at least three over his Head, and Blood running; and as I approached nearer I found it to be James Otis Esq; I saw two Officers of the Navy talking together, one of whom said "You have come too late to see your Friend Otis have a good Drubbing." to which he replied. "I am very glad to it, he deserves it," I saw William Burnet Brown in the Room with a Whip in his Hand, who came up to Capt. Bradford whom was looking for Mr. Otis's Hat and Wig, and asked him in a scornful Manner what he looked at him for, it appeared to me that he had a desire to pick a Quarrel with Capt. Bradford. I further declare that after the confusion was over, I looked around and observed that the Company in the room was almost all Officers of Army and Navy. Boston Sept. 21, 1769.

Mungo Mackay.

Richard Dana, Justice of the Peace of the Quorum.

Sam. Pemberton Justice of the Peace.

BOSTON Oct. 9. Last Thursday Evening the Hon. John Robinson, Esq; one of the Commissioners of his Majesty's Custom, was married to miss Nancy Boutineau, second daughter of James Botineau, Esq; of this Town.

BOSTON Oct. 9. Messiurs Mein and Fleming, In consequence of my intentions heretofore signified in your paper, application was made to many gentlemen to give their depositions of what happened in the British Coffee-House, on the 5th ult. between Mr. Otis and myself, but three only of those who were present during the whole transaction, have been so obliging as to comply with my request.

I am informed that the law does not compel any person to give in his testimony in cases of this kind. I therefore only thus openly express any whishes that the rest of the Gentlemen will at their leisure prepare their affidavits of what passed on that occasion, and furnish me therewith, sworn to before one of the justices of the peace, to be published with those already taken. ——— They are particularly desired to declare whether they saw any person or persons strike Mr. Otis, "hustle or pull him." or offer him the least unfair play. It is not for my own vindication that I am solicitous of obtaining these depositions, (my own conduct being I flatter myself all ready sufficiently justified in the opinion of all good men.) but that a true impartial account of the affair may be laid before the public, as the best answer to the many misrepresentations that have been industriously circulated. I am Gentlemen, Your's &c. Boston October 5th 1769.

John Robinson.

BOSTON Oct. 9. Extract of a Letter from New-York, Oct. 5.

"Yesterday was exhibited, to the great Terror of evil doers, three Men, who have for some time past made the practice of giving information to the Custom house Offices against goods Illegaly imported; ——— Their punishment was being put on a Cart, after being well tarr'd from Head to Foot and covered with Feathers, and then rid thro' every street in the city, surrounded by some thousands of People; they were greatly terrified and very penitent.

BOSTON Oct. 30. We are desired to publish the following paragraphs of a Law of this Province, now in force. viz.

Be it enacted That if any Persons being more than Three in Number, and being armed all or either of them with sticks, clubs, or any kind of Weapons, or disguised with Vizards (so called) or painted or discoloured Faces, or being in any Manner Disguised, shall assemble together having Imagery or Pageantry with them as a public Shew, in any of the Streets or lanes of the Town of Boston, or any other Town within this Province, or if any Person or Persons being of or belonging to any Company, having any Kind of Imagery or Pageantry for a Public Shew, shall by menaces or otherwise exact, require, demand, or asked, any Money or other Things of Value from any of the Inhabitants or other Persons in the Streets, Lanes, and Houses of any Town within the Province, every Person being of or assembled with such Company, shall for each Offence forfeit and pay the sum of Forty Shillings or suffer Imprisonment not exceeding one Month; or if Offender shall be a Negro Servant he may be whipped not exceeding ten Stripes, at the Discretion of the Justice before whom the Trial shall be.

And be it further enacted, That if any Persons to the Number of Three, or more, between Sun-setting and Sun-Rising, being assembled together in any of the Streets or Lanes, of any Town within this Province, shall have any Imagery or Pageantry for Public Shew, altho' none of the Company so assembled shall be armed or disguised, or exact, demand, or ask any Money or other Things of Value, every Person being of such Company shall forfeit and pay the sum of Forty Shillings, or suffer Imprisonment not exceeding one Month; or of Offender shall be a Negro Servant in lieu of the Imprisonment, he may be whipped not exceeding ten Stripes at the discretion of the Justice before whom the Trial should be.

BOSTON Oct. 30. Last Wednesday evening a very melancholy Occurrence happened in this Town, as Mr. Jonathan Lowder, Post Rider from this Town to Hartford, with Mr. Hide, each of them on Horseback, were riding through a narrow Lane leading from Pond-Lane into Summer Street, just below from the New South-Meeting-House, when Mr. Hide discovered a Truckman endeavouring to clear his Truck that was entangled with a Cart, and passed on the side of them, expecting Mr. Lowder to follow; but the Truckman pulling his Horse's Head over that way Mr. Lowder endeavoured to pass on the other Side; when one of the Shafts struck his Horse, who suddenly starting, threw him off, and it is supposed he fell with his Head against one of the Wheels which went over his right Shoulder, and down his Side. Mr. Hide immediately returning, carried him into a House, and Surgeons were sent for: He had his Sense till they came, but died in about an Hour ——— He was decently interred last Saturday Afternoon. The Accident happened on the Birth-day of Mr. Lowder, having completed 55 Years.

He returned the beginning of the Week from Philadelphia, having been employed by Mr. Hancock to attend him on his Tour thither. He was well known and respected in many Places, where he has been employed to do Business.

BOSTON Oct. 30. Last Saturday afternoon, as Mr. John Mein, Publisher of the Boston Chronicle was returning from his shop in Kingstreet some Gentlemen then upon Charge, who thought themselves ill treated in a late Publication of his, to Occasion to "catechize' him with which, after a few words had passed between them; he drew a Pistol out of his Pocket, and threatened to fire if they did not stand off; but that was far from intimidating them, that they followed close up in order to seize him, and he apprehending some danger to himself from the resentment of the People who began to collect together pretty fast, precipitately retreated to the main Guard, which was near, with Pistol in his Hand, where, as soon as he entered the Door he discharged it at random among those who closely followed him (tho' without doing other damage than wounding the Sleeve of the Coat of a Grenadier who was upon Guard) and the immediately took shelter in the house under the protection

of the Military Conservators of the Place. ——
Application was soon after mad to Mr. Justice
Dana and a Warrant issued for apprehending him
in order to answer for the atrocious Offences;
but tho' search was made in the Guard House and
other Places, by the proper civil Officers to
whom the Warrant was committed, they have not
yet been able to serve it upon him.

The same afternoon, a person who lately belonged to the Sloop Liberty, and came around to
this Place in the Sloop Success from Rhode-
Island, and soon after his arrival informed of
her having a Cask or two of Wine on board, which
occasioned the Vessel's being seized, was discovered and pursued, but took shelter in a House
where he secreted himself till the beginning of
the Evening, when thinking the Coast clear he
ventured out, but the Avenue to the House being
strictly watched the whole of the time, he was
immediately seized upon by the Populace, and
soon placed in a Cart, his Jacket and Shirt
taken off, and his naked Skin well tarr'd and
feather'd: they obliged him to hold a large
Glass Lanthorn in his Hand that People might see
the doleful Condition he was in, and to deter
others from such infamous practices. —— He
was then carted from the Town-house thro the
main Street up to Liberty Tree, amidst a vast
concourse of People, where he was made to swear
never to be guilty of the like Crime for the
future; but in they going thither, as they passed Mein and Fleming's Printing Office a Gun was
fired from thence and two others snap'd at them
just as they got by upon which some of the Company rushed into the Office in order to secure
the Offender, but they had fled; however they
bro't off three Guns, two of them well charg'd
as Evidence against them whenever they can be
taken: —— The Impudent Conduct of those in
the Printing Office (for what reason we know
not, as no injury seemed designed them) did not
interrupt the Carting the feather'd informer
thro' the principal Streets in Town for about
three Hours, when he was brought back to King-
Street, and after renewing his Obligation of
behaving better for the time to come, and asking

Pardon for his past Offences, he was dismissed without further Damage, after Having his Cloaths returned him again; and then all peaceably dispersed about Nine o'clock.

A few days since died a very valuable Negro belonging to Capt. Jacobson: His Death was occasioned by Mortificasion from several stabs with a Bayonet given him by two Soldiers a short time before, without the least Provication from the Fellow. ——— Enquiry has been made, the Soldiers who assaulted him have not yet been discovered.

BOSTON Nov. 2. Monday last, his Honour the Lieutenant Governor, issued a proclamation, for discovering and bringing to justice, all the persons concerned in the tarring, feathering, &c. of supposed informer.

BOSTON Nov. 6. Last Thursday Afternoon a young Woman from the Country was decoyed into one of the Barracks in Town, and most shamefully abused by some of the Soldiers there; ——— The person that enticed her thither, with promises of disposing of all of her marketing there (who also belonged to the Country) was afterwards taken by the Populace and several times dunk'd in the water at one of the Docks in Town; but luckily for him he made his escape from them sooner than was intended: ——— however, we hear, that after he had crossed the Ferry to Charlestown, on his return home, the People there being informed of the base Part he had been acting, took him and placed him in a Cart, and after tarring and feathering him (the present popular Punishment for modern Delinquents) they carried him about Town for two or three Hours, as a Spectacle of Contempt and a warning to others from Practicing such vile Artifices for the Delusion and ruin of the virtuous and innocent: He was then dismissed, and permitted to proceed to the Town where he belonged, for them to act with as they should think proper.

BOSTON Nov. 10. We hear that John Mein is appointed by the honorable Commissioners Stationer of the board. It is somewhat curious to observe, how industrious these honorable gentlemen have been, ever since they arrived, to

integrate themselves with the Americans ———
Every person that has rendered himself odious, in the fight of all the true lovers of their country, and been despised to the last degree, has become a favorite with them. ——— the present may be considered as a stinking instance of this ——— A person who, by his impertinence grossly abused a false publication, became obnoxious to, and hated by the inhabitants both in town and country, is, for this very reason, immediately provided for by them, as far as they were able. Administration at home could never carry on government upon such principals: and we doubt not, they will disapprove and resent such unaccountable conduct in their servants abroad. It has been all along said. that this Mein was encourage if not assisted, in his abusive reflections by the well beloved Commissioners.

We hear that John Mein went to England last week in the hope Schooner Capt. Dawson.

BOSTON Nov. 13. We hear that a Soldier was handsomely drub'd on Monday last, by one of the young persons who Mr. Draper tells us carried about some Pageantry, for attempting to stop them as they pass'd by the Main Guard, which is still posted at the Door of the State House.

BOSTON Nov. 20. Last Wednesday Evening, a woman in the prime of Life, in a House close to Oliver's Dock, being intoxicated with Liquor, fell into the Fire; and in a most shocking Manner was burnt to Death. It is but a few Months since a Woman in the same house, intoxicated with Liquor, fell down Stairs and broke her neck.

BOSTON Nov. 27. Extract from the North-Briton September 30, 1769.

"Has not the Honor of Knighthood been conferred upon the Traitor to his Country, that Disgrace to all good Government, Sir, Francis Bernard, Gov. of Massachusetts-Bay, who had had a principal Hand in alienating the Affections of the Colonist from their Mother Country, and who, by his Ignorance, his Obstinacy, and his Cruelty, has excited such a Flame in America, as though it may be allowed, can never be extinguished."

BOSTON Dec. 11. From the Essex Gazette of November 28, 1769.

These are to desire the Youth of this Land to beware of lying in Bed and sleeping with a certain filty Vagrant, who, by all accounts, has destroyed the health, it not the reputation, of a number of hopeful young Men, (sometime since in the Country of Hampshire, and most lately in the County of Essex, where he has been strolling about for these 7 or 8 months last past) in communicating to them venereal disease, which he attempts, unnatural and detestable practices while they are deep in their sleep, so that he may impart the destructive Venom before which they are enough awake to make proper resistance.

He calls himself Dr. John Jones, says he has owned Land, and lived at Westfield, Granville, &c. pretends to be a Preacher, and have been a settled minister ——— sometimes wears a black calamanco gown, and ministerial band ——— A blue serge cloak, with a black cloth Cape to it ——— a black strait bodied coat ——— and sometimes a plain Gown, lined with a red Baize ——— of late grey Wig, and a great number of Rings on his fingers. He has a Blemish in one of his Eyes, and a Gash in his Head, which he says he received in the Time of War, from the Indian's Tomahawk, at the Westward; Pretends he is craz'd at Times, occasioned, as he says, by a young Woman dying in Love for him. He makes and sings off a hand, songs of various subjects; and many are so imprudent as to give him Money for his doggrel stuff. It is said he had a good deal of Money given him for singing at the Concord Court, and the last Court at Newbury-Port. He was at Salem at the time of the sitting of the Superior Court the present month.

BOSTON Dec. 11. A list of the names of those who audaciously continue to counteract the United Sentiments of the Body of Merchants throughout North America: by importing British Goods contrary to the Agreement. John Bernard, lower end of King Street. James McMasters, of Treat's Wharf. Patrick McMasters, opposite Sign of the Lamb. James Mein, opposite the White Horse, and Book Store in King Street. Ann and Elizabeth

Cummings, Shop-Keepers, opposite the old Brick Meeting House. and Henry Barnes, Trader in the Town of Marlborough.

Have, and do still continue to import Goods from London, contrary to the Agreement of the Merchants. ——— They have been requested to Store their Goods upon the Same Terms as the rest of the Importers have done, but absolutely refuse, by conducting in this Manner.

It must evidently appear that they have preferred their own little private Advantage to the Welfare of America: It is therefore highly proper that the Public should know who they are, that have at this critical Time, sordidly detached themselves from the Public Interest; and as they will be deemed Enemies of their Country by all who are well wishers to it; so those who afford them their Countenance, or give them their Custom, must expect to be considered in the same disagreeable Light.

BOSTON Dec. 21. on the 3d of this inst. between 1 and 2 o'Clock on the Lord's day morning, one Patrick Freeman, a soldier of the 29th regiment, broke into a house of Capt. James Brett, at the north end, and was heard by a woman who lived in part of the same, who immediately rose out of bed, put on a loose gown, and entered the room; the first sight that presented was this soldier with a lighted candle looking in a desk drawer, upon which she immediately seized him by the collar, and he then put out the light, but she notwithstanding kept fast hold till he by some means twisted himself out of her hands, and fell headlong into the shop; By this time her daughter came to the assistance & catched him by the leg, while the former got him again by the collar; and then another daughter came to them and took him by the club of his hair and bro't his head to the ground, while the other held him by the feet on the shop window, then crying out for help, the man soon came to their assistance, bound him & delivered him to the watch who carried him to goal ——— There were one or two others with him but they ran off, and sundry things were found in his pocket which he had taken out of the desk. ———

It is said that this is said to be a fellow who bro't a man and woman into a theft with him at Halifax, when he turn'd King's evidence and had them both Hanged.

BOSTON Dec. 25. A letter from a Gentleman at New-York, says "That the Merchants there are very uneasy for fear the Merchants in Boston will not stand to the Non-Importation Agreement, if the Acts are not repealed this Session of Parliament: they say they should not be any way uneasy about it, if the Merchants of Boston would act with the same Spirit as they do in New-York and not suffer a single Man to import Goods, which is actually the case there; They think the People here are not in earnest, or they would not suffer so many Importations contrary to Agreement, but do now lie in Public Stores, and the Keys are in the Hands of the Committee; they say Persons who has raised reports that they have a back Door to the Public Stores are enemies to the Country, and report Falsehoods."

BOSTON Dec. 25. From Providence Dec. 16. Came to Town, Capt. Foster Williams, late Master of the Brig John, belonging to Boston. ——— He informs, as we are requested to publish, that he sailed from thence for Surinam the 21st of January last, and proceeded on his passage as far as lat. 34 and half, long. 60. where he met with a violent gale of wind, which so disabled his Vessel that she became water logg'd and unfit to proceed to any part, her deck being level with the surface of the water. ——— About eight days after the Sloop _____, Abijah Smith, of Martha's Vineyard, Master, bound from this Port to the West-Indies, hove in sight, and came within two rods of the wreck; the unhappy sufferers endeavoured to throw Ropes on board the Sloop. as they say no preparations making for their relief. After taking view of their distress, and most inhumanly refusing to take up the crew (7 in number) the Sloop proceeded on her passage, notwithstanding the pleading cries and lamentations of the distressed Seamen. In this situation the wreck remained till the first of March, at which time none but the Captain remained alive, when he was providentially taken up by the Duncanon Packet, Capt. Edwards, bound from Carolina to Falmouth.

A great Numbers of Prisoners are now in our Goal in this This Town for Theft Ect; It has been remarked that the great Severity used in the Southern Provinces in punishing Criminals, is a Means of driving many to this Place, where from the Lenity of our Laws and Tenderness of a jury, they expect a light Punishment, At New-York for a small Theft the petty Criminal is carted thro' the principal Streets of the City, so that he or she may be reviewed & known, and the Lashes given not at one Post, but at each Corner, and as the Crime rises, the Punishment increases.

We hear from Portsmouth that Last Friday the unfortunate Ruth Blay was executed there, pursuant to her Sentence, she behaved in a penitent Manner, but denied the Crime laid on her charge, that of murdering her infant Child. Before she suffered the Pain of Death, she sign'd a Declaration and Confession, in which among other things says; ——— "And now for the truth of what I am going to say, I appear, and I call Heaven and Earth to Witness, that, though I was with Child I had never a single thought of murdering the Infant, which makes me ever shudder to think that it is possible any Mother could be guilty of such Cruelty ——— and therefore I made preparations for his Birth, and could now produce Cloaths and Women in whose keeping they are; but alass it is too late; and on that unhappy Day when I was delivered, I know it had not been eight Months from when I was with Child, therefore had no thought of being delivered at that Time; But an unhappy Fall which I then received, brought on the Birth Instantly.

We hear from Charlton, that, about the 13th of November last the Son of Jacob Davis of that Place, four Years of Age, was bit in the throat by a Mad-Dog; the wound soon healed, and no appearance of Maniaism till about thirty Days atter, when, at the Full of Moon, the Child being at he Grandfather's Deacon Thomas Davis of Oxford, it was seized with a Nancia reaching, and an aversion to any Food the Day following the Symptoms increased, a wildness in the Eyes with irregular Gestures, inconsistent Talks, Risibility and Anxiety; then following in a few Hours the Hydrophobia or aversion to water or any Liquid, with Ferosity in his Countenance, Canine Actions, swelling in the Face, and a large Discharge of Saliva or Frothing at the Mouth, with frequent Convulsive Actions; and next Forenoon his Death closed the Scene. ——— After his Death his Body swelled and livid spots appeared upon his Stomach.

  Boston Dec. 28. We hear that a single Person has had spun within Six Months in this Town, by Children (chiefly) that have been learned to Spin during that Space, Thirty-six Thousand six Hundred and eighty Skiens of fine worsted Yarn, which will make about Seven thousand three Hundred and twenty Yards of fine Women's Apparels, which it is hoped will soon be weaved, dyed and dressed in the province Factory House in Boston.

1770

BOSTON Jan. 8. As the number of Dogs have run mad in several Parts of the Country, it is necessary the inhabitants should know the Symptoms of the Disorder, that they may destroy their Dogs are as follows, "When they are going to run mad, they appear dejected, shun Company and hide themselves; they will not bark, but seem to murmur, and are averse to Food and Water; they will fly upon strangers, but retain some Regard for their masters; their Ears and Tails hang down, and they walk along as if they were sleeping; other Dogs will shun them. This is the first Degree of the Disease, and though the bite is then bad, it is not at the worst. Afterwards they begin to pant, hang out their Tongues, froth at the Mouth, and gape. Sometimes they seem dull, and half asleep, sometimes they will run, but not directly forward, and soon cease to know their Masters, A bite at this Time is extremely dangerious."

BOSTON Jan. 8. The Committee of Merchants in this Town having by last Night's Post received a Letter from the Committee of Merchants of New-York, whereby it is suggested that I the Subscriber, with others, having Imported Goods from Great Britain contrary to the Agreement of the Merchants which I accorded. This is once for All to certify whom it may concern, That I have not in any single Instance, directly or indirectly diverted from said Agreement; and I now publickly defy all Mankind to prove the Contrary; And I am determined to co-operate with the Merchants, and others, in every legal and laudable Measure, for the redress of all Grievances under which this Province and Continent have so long laboured. Boston January 4, 1770.
John Hancock.

BOSTON Jan. 11. At the Court of Common Pleas

now sitting in Boston for the County of Suffolk, is to come on an Action of Trespass, wherein James Otis, Esq; is Plaintiff, and John Robinson, Esq; Defendent. The sum demanded in Damages is said to be 3000 Pounds Ster. His Majesty's Writ of Original Summons on this Occasion is very elegantly engross'd on the best-gilt Paper. The above Writ was serv'd according to the Laws of this Province, not by holding to bail; but by leaving a transcript engross'd in the same hands and Paper at the Defendant's House.

BOSTON Jan. 15. On Thursday last one Johnstone stood in the Pillory here one Hour, and was to have received 30 Lashes at the Whipping Post, pursuant to his Sentence, for attempting a Rape on a Girl at Dorchester about 10 Years of Age; but he was so severely handled by the Populace that he latter part of his Sentence was obliged to be postponed.

BOSTON Jan. 22. The Committee of Inspection of this Town having sent Information to the Committee at Marblehead, That a Chest of Tea and a case of Goods belonging to Mr. John Spawhawk, has been seen going out of the Fortification, and that a Marblehead Carriage was ready to receive them: Upon which Enquiry was made in said Town and the Truckman found out to be one Thomas Butman: The Committee wrote him, That he was imposed upon, and that he would lose his Employment if he did not see the said Chest and Case safe returned to the Store from whence he took them: It seems he went to Marblehead the back way, and put the Goods in his Barn at Ten o'Clock at Night, and the Letter was delivered him about 3 in the Morning: and on Receipt of which he set out, and very prudently put off for Boston, with the Tea and the Case, and on the 11th Instant delivered them to Mr. Joseph Jackson, from whence he received them.

BOSTON Jan. 29. Messiers Fleets. It is confidently reported the two Shopkeeping Women in this Town, being near Dock Square and Bromfield's Lane, in their greedy pursuit of filty Gain, have been frequently seen Winging and Driving away to some of the infamous importers for Goods, and that their Husbands cannot or

will not restrain them from such disgraceful practices: As I hold them who purchases of, equally guilty with those that Import, would not the worthy Committee of Inspection do well to make enquiry concerning this unsavory Report, and if solemn Promises not be offered in this sort any more, that they then publish in next Monday's Papers the Names of these Persons, together with the situations of their Shops, that so the good People of the Town and Country may decline buying and selling, and every friendly intercourse with such Wives, and such Husbands.
A Friend of the Country.

P. S. It is hoped a good look out will be kept in Town and Country, that so the ruin of a whole Continent may be prevented, by the evil practices either of shameless Men and more shameless Women.

BOSTON Jan. 29. By the Lieutenant Governor. To the People assembled at Ferneuil-Hall.

I should be culpable if I should any longer omit to signify to you my Sentiments upon your Proceedings. Your assembling together for the Purpose for which you propose to be assembled, cannot be justified by any authority or Colour of Law. Your going from House to House and making Demands of the Delivery of Property, must strike the People with Terror from your great Numbers (even if it be admitted that it is not done in an tumultuous Manner) and if of very dangerous Tendency.

Such of you as Persons of Character, Reputation and Property, expose yourselves to the Consequence of irregular Actions, of any of your Numbers who have been assembled together, altho' you may not approve of them, and altho' it may be out of your Power to restrain them.

Therefore as the Representatives of his Majesty, who is the Father of his People, I must from a tender Regard to your Interest caution you: And as cleated with Authority derived from his Majesty, I must enjoin and require you, without Delay, to separate and disperse, and to forbear all such unlawful Assemblies for the future, as you would avoid Evils to which you may otherwise expose yourselves and your Country.

Boston 23d Jan. 1770. T. Hutchinson.

BOSTON Feb. 12. The following Agreement has lately been come into by upwards of 300 Mistresses of Families in this Town; in which Number of Ladies of the highest Rank and Influence that could be waited upon in so short a Time, are included.

Boston, January 31, 1770.

AT a Time when our invaluable Rights and privileges are attacked in an unconstitutional and most alarming Manner, and as we find we are reproached for not being so ready as could be desired, to lend out our Assistance, we think it our duty perfectly to concur with the true Friends of Liberty, in all the measures they have taken to save this abused Country from ruin and Slavery" And particularly, we join with the very respectable Body of Merchants and other Inhabitants of this Town, who met in Faneuil-Hall the 23d of this Instant, in their Resolution, totally to abstain from the use of Tea: and as the greatest Part of the Revenue arising by Virtue of the late Acts, is produced from Duty paid upon Tea, which Revenue is wholly expended to Support the American Board of the Commissioners: We the Subscribers do strictly engage that we will totally abstain from the Use of that Article (sickness excepted) not only in our respective Families: but that we will absolutely refuse it, if it should be offered to us upon any Occasion whatsoever. This Agreement we cheerfully come into, as we believe the very distressed Situation of our Country requires it, as we do hereby oblige ourselves religiously to observe it, till the late Revenue Acts are repealed.

BOSTON Feb. 26. By the last Advises from London, we learn, That the Non-Importation Agreement of the Merchants in America begins to be so severely felt by the Manufactures, as to render very necessary for Parliament to do something for the relief, that if we continue to be united and firmly to adhere in the salutary Measures we may be sure of success. the Ministry begin to see that they have been deceived by the fallacious representation of some interested tools on this side of the Water, they no longer believe that the opposition in America is a petty dying Faction, that instead of the colonies being irresolute and divided, they are more firmly united than ever, and that they can neither be intimidated nor amused. ⸺ in short that the Ministry had hitherto built much upon accomplishing their Scheme for raising a Revenue in America from the diffusion of the colonies: That they now found themselves mistaken, & that Sir Francis Bernard never will or can have any connection with us, or be able either to serve or hurt us.

New Toast

The Patriotic Ladies of Virginia, who have nobly distinguished themselves by appearing in the Manufactures of America and may those of the Massachusetts-Bay be laudably ambitious of not being out-done even by Virginians.

BOSTON Feb. 26. Last Thursday Morning about 10 o'Clock some Boys and Children set up a Large wooden Head, with a Board faced with paper, on which was painted the figures of four of the Importers, who had entered into, and violated the Merchants agreement, in the middle of the street before Theophilus Lillie's door, who was one of them. Soon after it was set up, Ebenezer Richardson, the famous Informer, came by, and endeavoured to persuade a countryman to overturn it with his waggon; which he refusing, he applied to a Charcoal Man to drive his Cart against it; but he said he had no business with it, and would not concern himself about it. Richardson (as the Boys say) pressed him to it, saying he was a magistrate in the town, and would bear him out in it: The Man still denying to meddle therewith, Richardson laid hold of the horse and oxen and endeavoured to shove them upon the pole which supported the pageantry: the cart however passed without disturbing it. Richirdson then left the place and came towards his own house at about 50 or 60 paces distant, and meeting with Messirs Edward Proctor, Thomas Knox, Capt. Riordon and Skillings, faced them in a very impudent manner, & Cry'd out perjury! perjury! often repeating it as he passed them.

The Gentlemen halted in the street, till he was getting within his door, and asked him what he meant by perjury? He said, I don't mean you Mr. Proctor, but looking spitefully at Mr. Knox said damn you, perjury, villains!

Mr. Knox retorted the abuse; on which Richardson said, by eternal God, I will make it too hot for some of you before night! The Boys on hearing the words began to gather round, and called him Informer on which both he and his wife went out talked to them in a very provoking manner, flourishing their arms, and advancing out into the street, with high threatening; and with squeeling and noise they usually made on such occasions. This farce soon made a notable diversion in favor of Mr. Lillie, Mr. Richardson and Lady having drawn the whole attention of themselves. The boys at length began to throw light rubbish of one kind or another, as it to drive them back in the house; this the woman often returned, till the matter became more earnest. They then retreated into the house, and speedily Richardson opened the door, and snapp'd a gun presented on the people indiscriminately. This raised them so much that they pelted the house, and broke some of the windows. In a few Minutes after this, Richardson fired out of one of the windows among the people and wounded Mr. Sammy Gore, son of Captain John Gore, thro' both thighs and two fingers on his right hand, besides which, drove (one would think) a moderrate charge into the breast and abdomen of Christopher Snider, a boy about 11 years of age, who lived with Madam Apthorp. The child fell, but was taken up carried into a neighbouring house, where all the surgeons within call were assembled & speedily determined the wound mortal, as they indeed proved about 9 o'clock that evening. The people on hearing the report of the gun, seeing one wounded and another as they thought killed got into the new brick meeting and rang the bell, on which they soon had company enough to beset the house front and rear; by the latter of which they entered and notwithstanding the menaces of Richardson & his faithful aider and abettor George Wilmot seized on both, and wrenched a gun from the latter, heavily charged with powder and cram'd with 179 goose and buck shot.

"Tis said that some person went into Richardson before he fired and dessuaded him from it, but the event shewed he was not to be diverted from his design. The criminals were first carried before Justice Ruddock, who was pleased to send them to Faneuil-Hall, under a sufficient guard, where three other magistrates, Richard Dana, Edmond Quincy, and Samuel Pemberton, Esqrs; with Ruddock took their examination before at least a thousand people, and committed them. The numberless affronts and abuses both these persons had heaped on the Inhabitants, exasperated, them to such pitch, that had not gentlemen of influence interposed, they would never had reached the prison; but to the satisfaction of every good Man, they are now in safe custody, where we leave them, to observe, that soon after the Child's decease, his body was opened by Doct. Warren and others, and in it we found 11 shots or slugs, about the bigness of large peas, one which pierced his breast about an inch and a half above the midriff, and clear thro' the right lobe of the lung lodged in his back. This, three of the Surgeons deposed before the Jury of Inquest, was the cause of his death: and which they brought in their verdict, wilful murder by said Richardson. The right hand of the boy was also cruelly torn, whence it seem to have been across his breast, and to have deadened the force of the shot, which might otherwise have pierced the stomach.

Doct. Warren likewise cut two slugs out of young Mr. Gore's thighs, but pronounced him in no danger of death, tho' in all probability he will lose the use of his right fore finger, by the wound received there: much important to a youth of his dexterity in drawing and painting.

BOSTON Feb. 26. Mess'rs Fleets. The general sympathy and concern for the murder of the Lad by the base infamous Richirdson, on the 22d inst. will be a sufficient reason for you to notifying the Public that he will be buried from his Father's house in Frog Lane, opposite the

Liberty-Tree this Afternoon; when all the Friends of Liberty may have an opportunity of paying their last respects to the remains of this little hero and first Martyr to the noble cause ——— whose manly spirit (after this accident happened) appear'd in his discreet answers to the Doctor, his thanks to the Clergymen who prayed with him, & firmesss of mind he shewed when he first saw his parents, and while he underwent the greatest distress of bodily pain & with such he met the king of Terror. These things, together with several heroic pieces found in his pocket, particularly Wolf's Summit of Human Glory, gives reason to think he had a martial Genius, and would have made a clever man.

A Mourner.

It is said that the Funeral of the young Victim, This afternoon, at 6 o'Clock, will be attended by a numerous a Train as was ever known here. ——— It is hoped none will in the procession but the Friends of Liberty, and then undoubtedly all will be hearty Mourners.

There is a tide in the affairs of men,
Which taken at the flood leads on to fortune
Omitted, all the voyage of their life
On such a full sea we are now afloat ———
And we must take the current when it serves,
Or lose our venture. ———

BOSTON March 2. Lieutenant Governor Hutchinson, by particular Instructions from England had prorogue the Great and General Court, or Assembly till the 13th Instant, then to meet at Harvard College.

BOSTON March 5. One day last week a Soldier who has long passed for the bully of the 29th Regiment bought two baskets of Charcoal from a Stoughton Man and in payment offered him a Pistereen in lieu of a Shilling Sterl. which the man refused and insted on his Money or the return of the Coal. The Soldier denied to do either, on which the charcoal man said he would take it out of his Hide, rather than trouble himself much about it. To which the Bully very readily agreed, and was laid sprawling at every pass, till quite tired of the diversion, he professed his satisfaction, took his fellow combatant to an ale house, and amicably settled the dispute.

Not quite so fortunate were two or three Don Quixote adventurers, who fell upon a young Man walking quietly near the lower end of Kingstreet and stopping him in his way, informed him with very opprobrious language, on which after a very short parley he laid both sprawling, and went about his business. Two or three more such encounters having happened lately. "Tis said many of the 29th Regiment, have armed themselves with blugeon of about two feet long a round handle, and the body of a club three square. With such weapons as these, swords and cutlasses, on Friday inst. about 11 o'clock they made a formal attack on the Ropewalk of Mr. James Gray; one of them appearing first & complaining that some of their people had affronted him, & declared he would have satisfaction. The workmen not much attending to him, he grew very abusive, and challenged any one in the ropewalk to turn out and fight him; one of the hands step'd out to him very speedily tript up his heels and took his sword from him. He then went from them, and soon returned with 8 or 9 more, armed as aforesaid asking very haughtily, why he had been used in that manner? The answer probably not pleasing to the Gentleman soldiers, (as it seems they affect to stile themselves) they fell upon the ropemakers, who being accidentally well provided for the reception, made it necessary for the whole body to march in quest of auxiliaries. Recruited to the number of 30 or 40, they again visited the ropewalk, and challenged any or all of the workmen to come out anf fight them. This offer was readily enbraced & notwithstanding the soldiers were three to one, prepared on purpose, they were beat off, many of them much bruised and 2 or 3 of the workmen slightly wounded.

Mr. Justice Hill came up as this last riotous multitude advanced, told them he was in Commission of the Peace, and commanded them to go to their Barracks. In this execise of his Duty he was struck at by one of them with a club, which he had in reached him, that it might have been fatal, and so daring was this fellow, that in the Magistrate's presence, he knocked down a labourer, dragged him about, and beat and abused him much in despite of the Justice's utmost interposition.

No less audacious was the behaviour of a tall Negro Drummer, to whom Justice Hill particularly spoke, ordering him home, but he intent on wounding, or probably killing the inhabitants, headed the party sword in hand; but had his sword beat from his hold, which however being chained to his body he carried with him, He is said to be much wounded.

The gallant party assaulted many single persons in the street, as they returned from battle, but did no considerable damage as we learn.

Between 5 and 6 the same evening; a large body of them collected again, and were in full march for the field of battle; when Mr. John Gray, owner of the walks, met them, and diverted their intentions for the evening. But on Saturday, about half after 4, three stout grenadiers, armed with blugeons as above described came into the bottom of the walks, and finding three young men spinning together unarm'd accosted them in these most impudent words, "You damn'd dogs, don't you deserve to be kill'd." The lads not answering, Mr. James Young came up and spoke boldly, on which a grenadier aimed a blow at his head, but Mr. Young fended it off with his arms; he then turned from Young and made a pass at Mr. Achibald M'Neil. jun. which he avoided, otherwise believes it might have killed him. During this bluster one of Mr. W. Calef's journeymen went into the tan house, got two batts, and giving one to his comrade, soon cleared the walks of the soldiers.

BOSTON March 5. Missieurs Edes and Gill, Northampton, Feb. 21. Please inform the following and you'll oblige the Subscriber.

On The 5th of January last we were at Boston, and purchased a Quantities of Goods of Mr. William Jackson, and it is now reported in this Part of the Country to our no small Disadvantage, that we have been trading with one of the Importers: We therefore take this method to

inform the Public that we are very cautious with whom we traded before we made enquiries; and before we traded with Mr. Jackson, we were informed by several of the principal Merchants that he had come into the Non-Importation Agreement, and was then in good standing with the Committee: We hope this will be sufficient to satisfy the Public, and justify the Subscribers
Northampton, Feb. 21.
Robert Breck, John Shepard.
[The Committee of Merchants and the Public might think the foregoing a sufficient Validation of the Gentlmen who have subscrib'd as if they had mention'd the Names of the principal Merchants from whom they say they had their information. It is a Pleasure to us however to find the Effect of the Non-Importation Agreement extend to the most distant Part of the Province.]

BOSTON March 12. On Monday evening the 5th current a few Minutes after nine o'clock four youths, named Edward Archbald, William Merchant, Francis Archbald & John Leech, jun. came about Cornhill together, and separating at Dr. Loring's corner, the two former were passing the narrow alley leading to Murray's barracks, in which was a soldier brandishing a broad sword of an uncommon size against the walls, out of which he struck fire plentifully. A mean looking Irishman armed with a large cudgel bore him company.

Edward Archbald admonished Mr. Merchant to take care of the sword, on which the soldier turned round and struck Archbald on the arm, then pushed at Merchant and pierced thro' his cloaths inside the area close to the arm-pit and grazed the skin. Merchant then struck the soldier with a short stick he had and the Irishman ran to the barracks and bro't with him two soldiers, one armed with a pair of tongs and the other with a shovel: he with the tongs pursued Archbald back thro' the alley, collar'd and laid him over the head with the tongs. The noise bro't people together, and John Hicks a young lad, coming up, knock'd the soldier down, but let him get up again; and more lads, coming up, drove them back to the barracks, where the boys stood some time as it were to keep them in. In less than a minute 10 or 12 of them came out with drawn cutlasses, clubs and bayonets, and set upon the unarmed boys and young folks, who stood them a little while, but finding the inequality of their equipment dispersed.

On hearing the noise, one Samuel Atwood, came up to see what was the matter, and entering the alley from Dock-Square, heard the latter part of the combat, and when the boys had dispersed he met the 10 or 12 soldiers aforesaid rushing down the alley towards the square, and asked them if they intended to murder people? They answered yes by God, root and branch! With that one of them struck Mr. Atwood with a club, which was repeated by another, and being unarmed he turned to go off, and received a wound on the left shoulder which reached the bone and gave him much pain.

Retreating a few steps, Mr. Atwood meet two officers and said, gentlemen, what is the matter? They answered, you'll see by and by. Immediately after, those heroes appeared in the square, asking where the Boogers? Where the cowards? But notwithstanding their fierceness to naked men one of them advanced toward a youth who had a split of raw stave in his hand, and said damn them here is one of them; but the young man seeing a person near him with a drawn sword and a good cane ready to support him held up his stave in defiance, and they quietly passed by him up the little alley by Mr. Sillby to Kingstreet, where they attacked single and unarmed persons till they raised much clamor, and then turned down cornhill street, insulting all they met in like manner, and pursuing some to their very doors. Thirty or forty persons mostly lads, being by this means gathered in Kingstreet, Capt. Preston, with a file of men with charge bayonets, came from the main guard to the commissioners house, the soldiers pushing their bayonets, crying, make way! They took place by the custom house, and continued to push to keep people off, pricked some in several places: on which they were clamorous, and, it is said, threw snow balls. On this, the Captain commanded them to fire, and more snow balls coming, he again said, damn you, fire, be the consequence what it will! One soldier then fired and a townsman with a cudgel struck him over the hands with such force that he dropt his firelock; and rushing forward aimed a blow at the Captain's head, which gras'd his hat and fell pretty heavy upon his arm: However, the soldiers continued the fire, successively, till 7 or 8, ar some say 11 guns were discharged.

By this fatal manuvre, three men were laid dead on the spot, and two more struggling for life; but what shewed a degree of cruelty unknown to British troops, at least since the house of Hanover has directed their operations was an attempt to fire upon or push with their bayonets the persons who undertook to remove the slain and wounded! Hoe the author of the almost entire subversion of British faith, British Liberty, Justice, Humanity, and mutual affection of all and all, can bear to read this tale, let others imagine!

Mr. Benjamin Leigh, now undertaker in the Delf manufactury, came up, and after some conversation with Captain Preston, relative to his conduct in this affair, advised him to draw off his men, with which he complied.

The dead are Samuel Gray, killed on the spot, the ball entering his head and beating off a large portion of his skull.

A Mulatto man, Crispus Attucks, who was born in Framingham, but lately belonged to New-Providence and was here in order to go to North-Carolina, also killed instantly; two balls entering his breast, one of them in special goring the right lobe of the lungs, and a great part of the liver most horridly.

Mr. James Caldwell mate of Capt. Morton's vessel in like manner killed by two ball entering the breast.

Mr. Samuel Maverick, a promising youth of 17 years of age, son of the widow Maverick, and an apprentice to Mr. Greenwood, jioner, mortally wounded, a ball went through his belly, and was cut out at his back: He died the next Morning.

A lad Christopher Monk about 17 years of age, and apprentice to Mr. Walker, shipwright; was wounded, a ball entered his back about 4 inches above the left kidney, near the spine, and was cut out of the breast on the same side; apprehended he will die.

A lad John Clark, about 17 years of age whose parents live at Medford, an apprentice to Capt. Howard of this town; wounded, a ball entering just above his groin and came out at his hip, on the opposite side, Apprehended he will die.

Mr. Edward Payne, of this town, merchant, standing at his entry-door, received a ball in his arm which shattered some of the bones.

Mr. John Green, taylor coming up Laverett's Lane, received a ball just under the hip, and lodged in the under part of his thigh, which was was extracted.

Mr. Robert Patterson, a seafaring man, who was the person that his trousers shot through in Richarson's affair, wounded; a ball went through his right arm.

Mr. Patrick Carr, about 30 years of age, who work'd with Mr. Field, Leather Breecher-maker in Queen street, wounded, a ball enter'd near his hip and went out his side.

A lad named Davis Parker, an apprentice to Mr. Eddy the wheelwright, wounded, a ball entered in his thigh.

An apprehension of a settled plan for a general if not universal massacre, for such barbarous outrages, in conjunction with their former attacks and continued menaces, justly alarmed the people: ──── The bells were set ringing, & great numbers assembled, while some were taking care of the dead and wounded, others were in consultation what to do in these dreadful circumstances: The 29th regiment were under arms and drew upon Kingstreet. His honor the Lieutenant Governor came immediately to the Town-House, and there met some of his Majesty's Council and a number of the civil magistrates. His Honor requested they would let matter subside for that night, promising to do all in his power that justice should be done, and the law have its course, a pretty plain intimation that heretofore there had been complaints of a contrary procedure! The regiment being then under arms, the inhabitants insisting that they should be ordered to their barracks before they would seperate; which being done, the people returned to their dwellings by one o'clock. At three Capt. Preston was committed, and in the forenoon ensuing the soldiers who fired were also imprisoned. —— Capt. Preston strongly denied his giving order for the party to fire.

    Tuesday morning at eleven the Inhabitants met at Fafeuil-Hall and after some very pertinent speeches on the occasion of their assembling they chose a committee of 15 respectable gentlemen to wait upon Lieutenant Governor in council to request of him to issue orders for the immediate removal of the troops. The message were in these words.

    That it is the unanimous opinion of this meeting that the inhabitants and soldiery can no longer live together in safety: that nothing can rationally be expected to restore the peace of town and province blood and carnage, but the immediate removal of the troops; and that we therefore most fervently pray his honor that his power and influence may be exerted for their instant removal.

    His honor's reply was,
Gentleman, I am extremely sorry for the unhappy differences between the inhabitants and the troops, and especially for the action of the last evening. I have exerted myself upon that occasion that a due enquiring may be made, that the law may have its course. I have in council consulted with the Commanding officers of the two regiments which are in town. They have their orders from the General at New-York. It is not in my power to counter command these orders. The Council have desired that the two regiments may be removed to the Castle. From the particular concern which the 29th regiment has had in your differences, Col. Dalrymple who is commanding officer of the troops has signified that the

regiment shall without delay be placed in the barracks at the Castle until he can send to the General and receive his further orders; concerning both the regiments, and that the main guard shall be removed, and the 14th regiment so dispersed and lain under such restraint that all occasion of future disturbances may be prevented.

The foregoing reply having been read and fully considered ——— the question was put, wether the report be satisfied? Passed in the negative almost unanimous, (1 dissented.)

It was then moved and voted that John Hancock Esq; Mr. Samuel Adams, Mr. William Mileneux, William Phillips, Esq; Dr. Joseph Warren, Joshua Hensaw, Esq; and Samuel Pemborton, Esq; be a committee to wait on his honor the Lieutenant Governor & inform him that it is the unanimous opinion of this meeting that the reply made to a vote of the inhabitants presented his honor in the morning is by no means satisfactory, and that nothing less will satisfy then a total immediate removal of the troops.

The committee having waited upon the Lieut. Governor agreeable to the following vote of Council received from his Honor.

His Honor the Lieut. Governor laid before the Board a vote of the town of Boston, passed this afternoon, and then addressed the Board as follow.

Gentlemen of the Council, I lay before you a vote the town of Boston which I have just now received from them, and I now ask your advice what you judge necessary to be done upon it.

The Council thereupon expressed themselves to be unanimously of opinion that it was absolutely necessary for his Majesty's service, the good order of the town and the peace of the province that the troops shou'd be immediately removed out of the town of Boston, and thereupon advised his Honor to communicate this advice of the Council to Col. Dalrymple, and to pray that he would order the troops down to Castle William. The committee also informed the town that Col. Dalrymple after having seen the vote of Council said to the committee, that he now gave his word of honor that he would begin his preparation in the morning, and there should be no unnecessary delay until the whole of the two regiments were removed to the Castle.

A committee was also appointed to take information of the transaction of Monday night, who proceeded with great diligence and collected so much light as well satisfied the meeting, which was adjourned in the afternoon to Dr. Sewell's meeting-house, that the people apprehensions were but too well grounded. Soon after the second committee had reported the grand committee returned the second time and Mr. Hancock, their chairman, read their report as above, which was received with a clap of universal applause. The meeting was dissolved; and a number of the inhabitants appearing to watch the center of the town and the prison, the rest quietly to their respective habitations.

Out of many very daring instances of the soldiers behaviour on Monday night, their stopping Messiers, Joseph Ayers, Edward Crafts and John Alden, in the street, and threatening their lives is selected, the number being to large to be any was particular at present. These gentlemen from the south part of the town were moving towards the town-house, when two corporals with about 20 soldiers passed them, with muskets and fixed bayonets, then halted, wheeled about and surrounded them, calling them a pack of damn'd rascals and saying for three coppers they would blow their brains out; at the same time giving orders for one half of the soldiers to cock their flintlocks and the other to make ready. Messier's Ayers &c. told them they had nothing to say to them but had other business: On this corporal Eustice struck Messier's Alden and Crafts with his bayonet and bruised them much, but attempting to push Mr. Crafts with his bayonet was prevented by the corporal, who ordered the soldiers to march off.

A military watch has been kept every night at the town-house and prison, in which many of the most respected gentlemen of the town have appeared as common soldiers, & night after night have given their attendance. This promises a revival of the military spirit which had too much subsided under the administration of the Governor who flattered the British Ministry that Boston ladies would plunge both themselves and posterity into perdition rather then deny themselves a cup of tea.

Thursday two companies of the 29th went to the Castle, others went the next day & the remaining are to go today; and the 14th will likewise be sent with all possible dispatch, as Col. Dalrymple assured the committee, who can get no rest unless they can at all times certify the people that all diligence is using to free them from the society of such dangerous inmates. The neighbouring towns have shewn such a generous and brotherly disposition towards us that we want words to express our gratitude and esteem for their regard.

It is strongly suspected, from several Circumstances, that one or more of the guns were discharged from a window in a room over the custom-house, improved by the commissioners, in the tragical affair of last Monday evening; several persons have been taken up and examined relative thereto.

BOSTON March 12. Last Thursday, agreeable to the general request of the Inhabitants, and by the consent of Parents and others, were followed to their Graves in succession, the bodies of Mess'rs Samuel Gray, Samuel Maverick, James Coldwell, and Crispus Attucks, the unhappy victims who fell in the bloody massacre the Monday evening preceding! ——— On this occasion most of the shops in town were shut, all the bells were ordered to toll a solemn Peal as were also those in the neighbouring Towns of Charlestown & Roxbury.

The Procession began to move between the hours of 4 & 5 in the afternoon: two unfortunate Sufferers, viz. James Coldwell and Crispus Attucks who were strangers, borne from Faneuil-Hall, attended by a numerous train of Persons of all ranks; and the other two, viz. Mr. Samuel Gray from the house of Mr. Benjamin Gray (his Brother) on the North side of the Exchange, & Mr. Samuel Maverick from the house of his distressed

Mother Mary Maverick, in Union Street, each following by their respective Relations & Friends The several Hearses forming a junction in King-street, the Theatre of the inhumane Tragedy! proceeded from thence thro Main-street, lengthened by an immense concourse of People, so numerous as to be obliged to follow in ranks of six, and brought up by a long train of carriages belonging to the principal Gentry of the Town. The Bodies were deposited in one vault in the middle Burying ground: The aggravated circumstances of their Death, the distressed and sorrow visible in every Countenances together with the peculiar solemnity with which the whole funeral was conducted, surpass description.

The Town in this instance, not only eye the particular hand of Providence, but resent with Gratitude, the generous Sympathy with which the adjoining Towns, as well as the Province in general, seem to have been affected, by this melancholy Catastrophe.

BOSTON March 19. Last Wednesday Night died Patrick Carr, one of the Persons wounded by the firing of the Soldiers in the tragical Affair of Monday Evening the 5th instant. His funeral was attended on Saturday Afternoon by a great number of People, and his remains buried in the same Grave of the other four Persons mentioned in our last Paper.

BOSTON March 26. Not only John Robinson has left us abruptly, but we hear others of the commissioners have been secretly conveying away from their Houses their Goods and Effects —— It is indeed notorious that they and the infamous Bernard were the means of introducing those Troops into the Town, that have most wantonly shed Blood of its Inhabitants; that dark Circumstances are turning up, respecting the Conduct of themselves and their inferiors: But whatever their guilty Fears may have suggested, this is certain, that no kind of insult has been offered any by their Persons, or the least interruption given them in the Execution of their Office.

BOSTON April 2. It will perhaps be surprizing to the People in the Neighbouring Provinces to be told, that there is not above one seller of Tea in the Town of Boston who has not signed an Agreement not to dispose of any more of that Article; until the late Revenue Acts are repealed.

BOSTON April 9. Last Friday Ebenezer Richardson was brought into the Superior Court in order for his Trial, having been indicted by the Grand Jury for the cruel murder of the unfortunate young Snider, on the 22d of February, but the trial was postpon'd.

BOSTON April 9. Ran-away from his Master John Langdon, the 20th of this Instant February, an Indented Servant Lad of 14 years of Age, named Ebenezer Blancher. He had on when he went away a Frock and Trousers, over a dark striped Homespun Jacket and Breeches, a striped cotton and linen Shirt, Shoes almost worn out, a Pair of Brass figured Buckles, this Country made. He is a smart ready boy, and will tell a good plausible Story. Whoever will take him up and bring him to his Master, shall be rewarded for his Troubles.

All Masters of Vessels and others, are warned against carrying off, concealing or entertaining the said boy, as they would avoid the utmost Penalty of the Law, in that case made and provided.

Boston April 16. On the 11th Instant his honor the Lieutenant Governor sent the following Message to the Honorable House of Representatives. The platforms at Castle-Williams are in many Parts of them very defective, and the neglect of them will Occasion much greater Expense that if constant Attention is given in order to their being kept in repair. Repairs are likewise necessary in some parts of the Works. The Commissioners do not think themselves authorized to engage in these necessary Repairs, until they shall be a sum of Money in the Treasury appropriated to that purpose. It depends upon you to make these Provisions as his Majesty's Service and the Safety of the Province.

Council-Chamber, Cambridge, April 11, 1770.

Just Published, and to be Sold by Paul Revere, Opposite Dr. Clark's at the North-End, and by the printers hereof, a Copper-Plate Print, containing View of Part of the Town of Boston in New-England and the British Ships of War landing their Troops in the Year 1768. Dedicated to the Earl of Hillsborough.

BOSTON April 23. At the Superior Court sitting here last Friday, Ebenezer Richardson and George Wilmot were tried for the Murder of one Christopher Snider, a Lad of about 11 Years of Age, who was assembled with a number of other Boys, on the 22d of February last, before the shop of Theophilus Lillie, by means of an exhibition there, and the said Richardson was found guilty of the charge, viz. of firing a loaded Gun among them by means whereof said Christopher was killed: Wilmot was acquitted.

In the present Term of the said Court, one George White was convicted of Burglary, in breaking into the Province House and Stealing, for which he was sentenced to be branded in the Forehead with the letter B and to pay cost; he was also convicted upon two other indictments against him for Stealing of each of which he has been sentenced to be whipt 20 Stripes, and pay treble Damages & Cost.

At the same Court Patrick Freeman a Soldier, was convicted of burglary, and admitted to his Clergy accordingly burnt in the Hand. Richard Smith was also convicted of breaking into the Province House with the said White, and sentenced to be branded upon the forehead with the letter B and pay cost; he was also convicted upon six indictments against him for Stealing, on each of which he was sentenced to be whipt 20 stripes and pay treble Damages and Cost.

At the same Court one John Newington Clark and Charles Lee were convicted of Stealing, and each of them sentenced to be whipt 20 Stripes, and pay treble Damages and Costs; and the said White, Smith, Clark, and Lee, having nothing wherewith to pay said treble Damages, they were ordered to be sold upon an Indictment for six Years, upon another for four, and upon another for two Years, an so in proportion to the Value of the Goods Stollen for paying said Damages. And Stephen Bedge was convicted upon indictment against him for second theft, and sentenced to be set upon the Gallows with a Rope around his Neck, to be whipt 20 Stripes and pay Cost.

BOSTON April 23. On Tuesday last the House of Representatives, by a Majority of 70 Of 74 votes made choice of John Hancock, Esq; to be speaker pro Tempore, for the present Session and during the bodily Indisposition of Thomas Cushing, Esq; and having presented him to the Lieutenant Governor for his Approbation, His Honor was plaesed to send to the House the following Message.

Gentlemen of the House of Representatives, You having signified to me by reason of sickness and that you have made choice of John Hancock, Esq; to be pro Tempore, for the present Session and during the Indisposition of the said Thomas Cushing, Esq; and having presented him to me for my Approbation, pursuant to the Directions of the Royal Explanatory Charter:

By Virtue of Authority given me by the Explanatory Charter, I disapprove of the Choice you have made.

Council-Chamber, Cambridge 17th April 1770.
T. Hutchinson.

The following message was read, and then the House was adjourned till next Morning for Ten o'Clock.

We hear on Wednesday last the House of Representatives made Choice of James Warren, Esq; Member for Plymouth, Speaker, pro Tempore, who his Honor the Lieutenant Governor was pleased to approve of.

BOSTON April 23. On Friday Morning last, came on before the Superior Court. The Trial of Ebenezer Richardson, and George Wilmot, for the Murder of Christopher Snider, on the 22d of February last. —— The Trial lasted till near Midnight, when the Jury withdrew, and the Court was adjourned till next Morning at seven o'Clock; and gave their Verdict, Richardson Guilty, and Wilmot not Guilty.

BOSTON May 7. The Goods lately imported from London contrary to Agreement are reshipping with all possible Dispatch on board the Lyndia Capt. Scott, who will sail in two or three days.

At the Meeting of the body of Trade and others in Faneuil-Hall on Saturday last, a Letter was sent by one of the Importers, offering to set up two Ships in Town if his Goods might be admitted to be Sold; but the publick spririted Tradesmen rejected it with contempt, alledging that they chose rather to be out of Business than have it at the Expence of Risque of the Liberty of their Country.

BOSTON May 14. At the Meeting of the Freeholders and other Inhabitants of the Town of Boston, duly qualified and legally warned in public Town Meeting assembled at Faneuil-Hall, on Tuesday the 8th Day of May, Anno Domini, 1770.

The Hon. James Otis, Esq; having by advice of his Physicians, retired into the Country for his Recovery of his Health.

That the Thanks of the Town be given the Hon. James Otis, Esq; for the great and important Service which as a Representative in General Assembly through a Course of Years He has rendered to this Town and Province; particularly for his undaunted Exertion in the common Cause of the Colonies, from the beginning of the present glorious Struggle for the Rights of the British Constitution. At the same Time the Town cannot express their ardent Wishes for the Recovery of his Health, and the Continuance of the Public Service that must long be remembered with Gratitude, and distinguished his Name among the Patriots of America.

Voted, That the Gentlemen the Selectmen be a Committee to transmit to the Hon. James Otis, Esq; an attested Copy of the above vote.

Attest. William Cooper, Town Clerk.

BOSTON May 21. Last Friday Evening one Richards employed as a Tide-Waiter in the customs being suspected of having given information of a parcel of Sugar bro't here in a Vessel from Connecticut, which was seized that Day, was taken by a number of Persons, who after tarring and Feathering him agreeable to the modern mode of punishing Informers, carried him thro' all the principal Streets in Town for about three hours, and then dismissed him.

BOSTON May 28. On Tuesday and Wednesday last

four companies of Militia trained at Salem: Their behaviour proved that Men may be discipliner without becoming Regulars, when they have officers of Spirit, Capacity and Assiduity to instruct them.

Monday Night last some Villain or Villains enter'd the Dwelling House, supposed by the cellar Door, of Mr. Joseph Bradford, in Union Street, and carried off a Number of Articles; and returned the Way they enter'd, a Piece of Handkerchief being found in the Cellar-Stairs.

BOSTON June 4. We hear from Cambridge, That last Wednesday Afternoon Mrs. Fissenden, Wife of Nathaniel Fissenden of that Town, was unhappily killed by the following Accident, viz. A number of Persons had been shooting at Marks, and after they had done, went to the House of Mr. Philip Beamis, Father to the unfortunate deceas'd, and put their Guns against the House, when a Lad of about 23 Years old, took one of the Guns not knowing it to be loaded, and snap'd it at a Girl in order to frighten her, when the Gun went off; but it missing the Girl, the Ball went in Mrs. Fissenden's and lodged in her Head, and killed her instantly. Mrs. Fissenden had her infant about nine Months old in her lap, which providently was unhurt. She is the only Daughter of Mr. Beamis and it is remarkable the Gun which she was kill'd belong'd to her Husband in particularly refused to be comforted.

BOSTON June 4. The bold and generous spirit of freedom increases every day among us, as was abundantly evident in the conduct of the people on Friday evening, who went to the store, supposed lodging, and shop of McMasters, the noted Importer, and informed them, it was the mind of the inhabitants that they might clear the Town of their persons and properties by six o'clock Monday evening, as they would avoid the Consequence of the public resentment; since which, they have agreed to shut up their Store and Shop, get proposal digested in writing, signed by them, and come personally into the Meeting on Thursday next, being the Term Adjournment, and take the minds of the Body upon their case, and thus it rests for the present. —— However, the refference of the matter to the whole body will answer two good purposes, viz. give them a full hearing and meanwhile of clearing the town of thesselves and their stuff.

BOSTON June 11. Last Thursday Afternoon being the Adjournment of the Meeting of the Trade, there was a very general Attendance, probably on account of the promissed appearance of the imfamous McMasters, and the proposal of Nathaniel Rogers, for the readmission to the favour and friendship of his fellow citizen. The McMasters agreeable to the usual generosity of their conduct, left the trade to make what reflection they pleased upon good faith; and it is thought are conveying themselves, and property out of town privately.

We are informed that the imfamous Importer Barnes of Marlboro, has the Audacity to continue his Importing to this Time; & that his Goods have been constantly, but privately, conveyed to him thro' Assistance of a few sly Tories who inside in this Metropolis; but by their great Mortification a Waggon was discovered last Thursday Night between 10 & 11 o'Clock, near the Fortification, going off with a Number of Packages for said Barnes; the Committee of Inspectionat that part of the Town being soon apprized of it, made inquiries of the Waggoner whose Property they were, and from whence they were taken, he being struck with a violent Panick at this unexpected Discovery, very readily informed them, and promised to return them immediately to the Place he took them from, which happened to be at the North Part of the Town; Number of People collected as the Waggon passed the Street, and followed it, suspecting that some of the execrable Plant Bohea was concealed in some of the Packages; and arriving at the Place, a strict Examination ensued, and the Goods were all found to be contraband, though none of the Poison was among them: The shopkepper refused to receive them, and the waggoner likewise refused to carry them to Marlboro; so the Committee rather than they should perish in the Stretts condescended to let the Waggoner put them into the public Store for the present.

This being done about 12 o'Clock, the Spectators who were supposed to be upward of a thousand, gave 3 Cheers, and retired peaceably to their respective Habitations.

BOSTON Jume 11. Extracr of a letter from Philadelphia May 24.

Our Sons of Liberty make up almost the whole of the People, and are determined to support the Non-Importation Agreement ——— and very sorry that any goods were shipped to Boston &c. but are well satisfied with the conduct of the Bostoneans respecting the last importations: However, they seem to think that the goods which cannot be reshipped should be burnt, or sent somewhere out of British America. We are governed much by the principal, that no stranger by importing shall take the advantage of our selfdenial in trade, but as our merchants have nobly sacrificed their business for the public good, they shall not be deprived of the first run of business, as they would, had either full stores ready to be vended on the first news of repeal.

We are highly offended at Rhode-Island ——— 'Tis a pity there is not virtue enough in that place to support their honor, at least modesty enough to forbear the attempt to Frustrate the united endeavours of all the Colonies of the Continent to support their liberties. 'Tis expected here that Boston, New-York &c. will all unite in expressing their resentment against Rhode-Island as we have done.

I have only to add that there is no danger of our Merchants taking the lead in violation of the agreement, nor will they attempt to support it alone.

BOSTON June 25. Last Tuesday afternoon, between two and three o'Clock one of the McMasters, the noted Importers, contrary to the Agreement of the Merchants and to whom it was lately intimated that it was the Minds of the Inhabitants in general that they should depart the Town with their Persons and Properties, as they would avoid the consequences of public resentment, was taken at the South Part of the Town and put in a Cart with some tar in a Barrel and a bag of Feathers; but on his being carted some time on his way to Kingstreet we hear it was said he was to undergo the indignity of the Modern Punishment; when the Cart drew near the Town-House he appeared to be greatly frightened which the humanity of the People present imagining might produce a fainting Fit, he was therefore permitted to go into a Gentleman's House for a short time, properly attended, in order to recover himself; where he soon after solemnly promised that if he might be spared from being Tarred and Feathered, he would immediately leave the Town and never come into it again, which being agreed in, upon condition that he should be carried out in the Cart, he readily consented, and a Chair being placed therein in lieu of the Tar Barrel, he was then carted out of Town as far as Roxbury Line, and having swore that he would abide by his Promise, he was dismissed without receiving any Damage, and his numerous Attendants peaceably returned again.

――― Search was made for one other McMasters but he could not be found. ――― A third who went to Marblehead, was ordered out of Town; from whence he went to Salem, where he could get no lodging, and a Signal being given, he was obliged to quit that Town also.

Boston June 26. A committee of the Town of Marblehead having applied to the late General Court setting forth, That there has been lost at Sea, since January, 1768, belonging to the Town, 24 Sail of Fishing and Merchant Vessels, in which 170 Men and Boys have perished, whereby 70 Women are left Widows, with 150 Fatherless Children, and many Parents deprived of the earnings of their Sons which was their chief support; and that many Families since these unfortunate Shipwrecks have had scarce any other Subsistence than what has come from the Bounty of their charitable Friends and Neighbours, &c. praying for a brief; and the Council and House of Representatives having desired the lieutenant-Governor to issue a Brief; His Honor accordingly issued one last week.

BOSTON July 2. At a Meeting of the Merchants and others in Trade on Monday a Letter received by Express from the Merchants at New-York was read; The Subject Matter of the Letter was maturely considered and debated; and it was thereupon Resolved to adhere to the Non-Importation Agreement, without the least Diversion until the Revenue Act imposing a Duty on Tea, &c. was totally repealed: And the Trade further voted, That the standing Committee should immediately inform the Merchants of New-York of this their Resolution; and the Express returned on Tuesday last.

BOSTON July 2. On Thursday morning last Ebenezer Cutler. of Oxford came to Boston, and pulling out some quantity of Money, began discourse with the several Persons concerning buying Tea, and in special insulted one of the Committee of Inspection of land-carriages at the south end, repeatedly declaring he would buy Tea, or what he pleased, and of whom he pleased, without regard to any honorable committee-men, or any other men. In the afternoon he returned to the south end, where he began the farce, and boastingly shewed a bag of Tea, containing about a dozen pounds, on which the Committee Man aforesaid grew a little more serious with him, and told him he thought the offence he offered him as an individual, deserved resentment, but when thro' him, he meant to insult the Community, he looked upon himself in honor obliged to inform the people of his behaviour. Considerable passed on this head, when he agreed to deliver the Tea into the custody of a friend, till the trade should be open, and he departed for that time. About 4 o'clock on Friday morning, two waggons were heard driving hastily out of town, which being detected in Little Cambridge, on examination, were found laden with goods imported (or he says) by Theophilus Lillie, contrary to the Merchants agreement. Mr. Cutler, tho' he seemed very obstreperous at the first consent to return to Town with the Goods; and puy them under the care of the Committee of Inspection there to be stored till a general Importation should take place. Mr. Lillie's concern in these Goods in very apparent, he having hired a Chaise at

Charlestown to go to Oxford the same day, and we hear that the inhabitants of that place have testified their great displeasure at the man who hired the horse and carriage to a perfidious imported.

BOSTON July 9. It is said, that upon the arrival of Capt. Gardner in London, with the authentic Account sent from this Town of the late Massacre, the Orders which had been issued for getting ready a number of Men of War and troops, which were preparing to sail in consequence of the Misrepresentation of some Persons who carried home the first Account of that tragical Affair, were immediately countermanded.

The Freeholder and other inhabitants of this Town are to meet at Faneuil-Hall to-morrow, at Nine o'Clock in the morning, in order that certain Letters received by Capt. Gardner, in answer to those sent by him to our Friends in England, relative to the horrid Massacre of the 5th of March last, may be laid before the Town, so that such steps may be taken as shall be judged necessary, to counteract the Design of those inveterate Enemies among us, who, there is reason to think, are still continuing their Misrepresentations, and using their Endeavours to increase the present unhappy Misunderstanding between Great Britain and the Colonies.

BOSTON July 12. Last Friday Night Some of the Prisoners, in the Goal in this Town, set Fire to the Partition of the Room in which they were confined, in order to make their Escape: but being timely discovered by some other Prisoners in the Apartment above them, who alarmed the Watch, was soon extinguished, and the Persons concerned therein secured in the Dungeon.

BOSTON July 17. Of Friday last, one Aaron Hartshorn went into a cistern, at the South end of this town, in order to clean it, but instantly expired; Two others who went to his Assistance like to have shared the same fate, their breath being stopped as soon as they were down, and it was with difficulty they were drawn up alive.

BOSTON July 30. There was a meeting of the Trade on Tuesday last, at Faneuil-Hall, as were known to take into Consideration the Report relative to the Defection of New-York, and what Measures were necessary to be pursued for re-shipping the goods which had been stored as being imported contrary to the Merchants Agreement.

On Thursday the house of Representatives Unanimously came into Resolution, there being upwards of Seventy Members present, to abide by their Resolution of the late Session, viz. "That it is by no means expedient to proceed to Business while the General Assembly is thus constrain'd to hold the Sessions out the Town House in Boston. " and on the same Day appointed a Committee to prepare a Message to his Honor the Lieut. Governor, acquainting him with this Determination.

BOSTON July 30. Paul Revere take this Method of his most sincere Thanks to the Gentlemen and Ladies who have employed him in the care of their Teeth , he would now inform them and all others, who are unfortunate as to lose their Teeth by accident or otherways, that he still continues the Business of a Dentist, and flatters himself that from the Experience he has had these Two Years, (in which time he has fixt some Hundred Teeth) that he can fix them as well as any Surgeon-Dentist who ever came from London, he fixes them in such a Manner that they are not only an Ornament but real Use Speaking and Eating: He cleanses the Teeth and will wait on any Gentleman or Lady at their Lodgings, he may be spoke with at his Shop opposite Dr. Clark's at the North-End, where the Gold and Silver-smith's Business is carried on in all Branches.

BOSTON Aug. 9. A very melancholy Occurance happened Yesterday at Lynn: Two young Men and several young Women all of the Denomination of Quakers, going off in a Canoe to a Schooner that lay from Shore, in which they were going on a Party of Pleasure, being along side the Schooner, one of the Men jump'd on board, and two of the Women, in a hurry to get on board also, got hold of the side of the Schooner, which made the Canoe heel down, whereupon the other Women got upon the opposite side to prevent its oversetting, this occasioned the Canoe to go off from the Schooner, the two Women let go of their hold, fell into the water, and sunk; the Canoe however overset on the other side, but the Man left therein got on her Bottom, catched hold of the five Women by their Hands and held them, the Tide carrying them down near a mile: The Man that got on board the Schooner, who was Brother to one of the Women that sunk, dove after them, who both catch'd hold of him, but finding he could not save them, disengaged himself and came up almost spent: There was but 1 Man on board the Schooner when the Canoe came off from the shore, he seeing the Persons floating with the Tide, got a Rope and swam after them, fastened one end of the Rope to the Canoe, and taking the other end between his teeth, got to Shore, and towed them in, almost spent. The Names of the young Women drowned were Basset and Wood: The body of the former has since been taken up.

The People on Shore who were of the same Company, had no boat to go off to their Assistance.

BOSTON Aug. 10. Last Tuesday two men, belonging to the Fowey man of war, being in the ship's boat then lying at the Wheelwright's wharf, having some differences together, blows ensued, and one struck the other with such force that he fell overboard, and was taken up dead. The Jury gave the opinion that the blow was the occasion of his death. The survivor was taken up and committed to goal.

BOSTON Aug. 11. The Freeholders and other inhabitants of this town were notified, yesterday to meet at Faneuil-Hall on Monday next; some of the inhabitants having set forth in a petition, that the passage-way leading from the north part of Faneuil-Hall market into Ann street and Union street, is so narrow as oftentimes to obstruct the passing of carts, trucks, and other carriages, thereby endangering the lives and limbs of the inhabitants, and is a public nuisance, and praying that said Passageway may be widened and enlarged.

BOSTON Aug. 13. On Wednesday last his Majesty's Court of General Session of the Peace held here for the County of Suffolk, a Person was indicted for willfully and presumptuously firing a hand Gun in the Main Street, whereby a Horse then tacked in a Chaise took Fright and three People, then in the same Chaise thereby put in great Hazard of their Lives; was upon conviction sentenc'd to pay fine of Ten Shillings to the King, suffer 30 Days close Imprisonment, give bond and for his good behaviour for twelve Months: and as a Number of Gentlemen have determin'd to put a stop to such Misdemeanours for the future by prosecuting the offenders to the utmost extent of the Law. 'Tis hoped this Instant will be a sufficient Warning to these who are frequently guilty of such breaches of the Law, by firing Guns, and various other kinds of Fireworks within the Streets and Lanes of this Town, and particularly on the Neck leading to Roxbury, to the great Hazard and Annoyance of His Majesty's good Subjects.

BOSTON Aug. 30. A Letter from a Gentleman in London to his friend in New-York, dated June 5th, says, "The People of England now curse Governor Bernard, as bitterly as those in America. Bernard was drove out of the Smirma-Coffe-House, not many days since by General Oglethorpe, who told him he was a dirty faction scoundrel, who smelt cursed strong of the hangman; that he had better leave the room, as unworthy to mix with Gentlemen of Character, but that he would give him the satisfaction of following him to the door, had he any thing to reply. The Governor left the house like a guilty coward."

A Letter sent to London from Boston March 28, mentions the transactions of the 5th of that month, and adds, that every friend of Government is now left to the mercy of the mob, headed by a people without property or principle, and who will stick at no Villainy to gain their ends, which appears to be nothing less than to shake off entirely the British government.

The news-mongers in Boston dare publish nothing relative to the late proceedings, by which means the people are kept entirely in the dark; and as most letters are opened which come from Boston by these Sons of Liberty, few people dare to write their sentiments, or even give a true account of the late operations, for fear of being maltreated by the mob.

BOSTON Sept. 8. Yesterday Captain Preston and the soldiers imprisoned here, for the massacre on the 5th of March last, were arraigned, and all pleaded not Guilty; and, we hear, the tryal is put off to an adjournment on Oct. next.

BOSTON Sept. 10. A few weeks since the operation for a Hare Lip was performed to great perfection on a young Man in Milton near Brush-Hill; and a Child in Boston had received as much Benefit from the Operation as the Case would admit of, by Mr. Hall, Surgeon to the 14th Regiment. —— The impression of these unhappy Sights are apt to make a married Woman, should be an indictment to have the defect in Nature rectified early in the Life, as these numerous Instances of the Mother's Affection having impressed her Offspring with the like Deformity.

BOSTON Sept. 10. His Honor Lieut. Governor having received his Majesty's Orders to withdraw from his Majesty's Castle William the Garrison in the Pay of the Province, and his Majesty's having been pleased further to order that the Castle should be garrisoned by his Majesty's Regular Troops, on Monday the 10th Instant the Garrison in Pay of the Province wereby his honor's Order withdrawn and the Custody and Government of the said were, by his Honor committed to Lieutenant-Colonel Dalrymple and garrisoned by a Detachment of the Regular Forces under their Command accordingly.

BOSTON Sept. 17. Messieurs Edes and Gill, The disgraceful manner in which our countrymen have lately been turned out of Castle William, and the arbitrary method in which this province has been disposed of that fortress has justly alarmed every one who regard either the honor or safety of this country. As to the man who has been chiefly active in the business here, I leave him to his own concience (if he has any). —— But I believe that has long ago been committed to the keeping of Lord Hillsborough. —— The people of this country from the first settlement of it, have ever been loyal subjects, and upon all occasions have proved their readiness to pay all constitutional obedience to their rightful King; and it may be said with truth, that the present generation, notwithstanding, the treacherous assertions of interested calumniators, have as clearly proved their affection to his present Majesty, as any of his subjects in any part of his dominions.

They exerted themselves in the late war much beyond their abilities, and greatly to the detriment of their landed estates, which in many parts of the country have lost one third of their value, by the great acquisition of uncultivated lands to the crown of England. For the truth of which, I appeal to the landholders in general thro' the province. Nevertheless we patiently submit in every hardship which we think conductive to the safety of our country, or the honor of our Sovereign. And altho' we find the debt incurred by our great exertions, is by an adversary basely and cruelly turned into an engine to destroy our Rights, we yet do not repent of having nobly contributed to the success of his Majesty's arms in the late glorious war, and are still ready to do every thing in our power to defend his person, and our happy constitution.

These our sentiments being well known to every one who takes the trouble of making a careful enquiry into the state of this country, we cannot but apprehend that something dangerous to our constitution, or to our sovereign is intended, when we are not look'd upon as fit to be trusted with the possession of a fortress that was erected by our Fathers for their defence against the enemies of Great Britain and this Country, and which has for those purposes been kept and supported at the expence of the province ever since ——— Whatever may be expected by these who are watching to betray their King and enslave his subjects, they may be assured, that the people of this country will never tamely suffer the loss of their Rights which their ancestors so dearly purchased; that spirit which led our Forefathers to encounter the unavoidable hardships attending them in this then howling wilderness: that bravery which supported them in the numberless battles which they fought with the savage natives, who aimed at their destruction, will, if every other method fails, be found in an eminent device to be now lodged in the breast of their descendents, the present possessors of their honorable acquisitions.

I have not time to be particular, but I would advise all who have any concern in managing the affairs of the country, to search the history of it from its first settlement; and if blest with common sense, they may very easily determine what must be the consequence of an attempt to enslave us.   Hurraclius.

BOSTON Sept. 24. Tuesday arrived here the ship Britania, Capt. Daverson, from London; He had almost loaded his Vessel in London when Capt. Scott arrived there with returned Goods from this Place, but immediately took out all such Articles he had on board which were not allowed of by the Non-Importation Agreement here, except of a few which were at the bottom, his owners at the same time advertised in the following Manner.

Whereas there may probably be on board the Britania, William Deverson, Master, bound for Boston, in New-England, sundry Articles prohibited by the Committee of Merchants of that Port to be imported. It is therefore thought necessary to give this public Information, that any Gentleman who may have shipped such goods on board the abovenamed Vessel may have them taken out immediately applying to Champion & Dickason no. 17, Bishopsgate Street within.

BOSTON Sept. 29. By Capt. Cook, who arrived here last Thursday evening in four days from Halifax, we learn, that it was reported there, that all the troops now in that place, consisting of two regiments and part of a third, has orders to be in readiness to embark for Boston. And that Commodore Hood, and the Romney man of war, was shortly to sail from thence to this place.

Yesterday his Majesty's armed schooner St. John arrived here from Halifax. It in said schooner came fourteen men belonging to the royal train of artillery.

Monday afternoon, a company of youth, selected from several companies of the militia of the town, to the number of about thirty mustered on the Common with flintlocks, under the direction of a serjeant of the Major's company, as I am told, and went through the various exercises to the general satisfaction of the spectators of various denominations, except some little trifling errors, as splitting a gun barrel, by having two or three charges in it, which happily did no other mischief; indeed, by mistake, one of the front rank fired an iron remmer out of his gun, but providentially this also did no damage. Soon after which they quietly returned to their respective homes.

About nine o'clock, in the evening the same day, a number of Negro Grenadiers, gathered up in the Common, and from thence, under commanders (flushed with military spirit) took upon them to patrol several streets in the town, with a drum beating, fifes playing and other music, until some of the inhabitants, fearing the ill consequences from such unlawful assemblies, broke the drum and quietly dispersed them, ordering them to go peaceably home to their masters. This may serve to caution masters against allowing their servants to much liberty, in the execution of preconcerted schemes, which may be attended with consequences fatal to the inhabitants.

BOSTON Oct. 1. At a meeting of Merchants at Philadelphia, on the 12th September, applied by letter, signed by 14 of them, to the Merchants Committee there, desiring that the sentiments of the Subscribers to the Non-Importation Agreement might be taken, whether said agreement should be continued or dissolved, so far as to open the importation of Goods from Great Britain as usual, tea and such other articles as are or may be subject to Duties for the purpose of raising a Revenue in America excepted; in consequence of which desire a general Meeting of the Subscribers was accordingly called for that purpose. —— And by a letter from a Gentleman at Philadelphia, dated 22d September, we are informed, that at a very numerous Meeting of the Merchants on the 21st, it was determined to import Goods agreeable to the Resolution of New-York, with the Exception of Tea; but that Goods would not be permitted to be delivered in imported before the 15th of January 1771.

BOSTON Oct. 2. An Admonition to those who play in seducing the Affections of the Fair, and then deserting them.

No Man ought certainly to make his Pretensions to a Lady, till he is fully convinced her Person, her Temper, and her Fortune, are perfectly agreeable to his circumstances and Way of Thinking; for, without such previous Knowledge he undertakes at Random the most important Affair of Life; and then no Wonder if he involves himself in Difficulties and Uneasiness.

Love, whatever some may think of it, is not a Passion to be Sported with: Nor is Affection of a Lady to be attempted, till a Man is assured his own is fixed on a lasting Principle. All imaginable Caution is necessary and advisable beforehand; but after his Profession of Regard, his Services and Solicitations, have won the Heart, and made him dear to her, Reason, Honour, Justice, all oblige him to make good his engagements, and to be careful of his Peace. Then there is no retreating; nor can any Thing but her Loss of Virtue, justify his leaving her. And whether he has promised her Marriage, or not, make very little Difference; for surely, if he has her Affection, and gained them, upon a reasonable Supposition, that he intended making her his Wife, the Contract, in the sight of Heaven, is of equal Force. He, who basely imposes on the honest Heart of an unsuspecting Girl, and after winning her Affection and esteem, by soft and prevailing Rhetoric of Courtship, can ungenerously leave her to sorrow and Complaining, is more detestable than a common Robber, in the same Proportion as of Private Treachery is more villaimous than open Force, and Money, is less Concerned than Happiness.

BOSTON Oct. 15. We hear at the Superior Court held at Taunton last Week, one Elisha Buff of

Rehoboth was convicted of assaulting a young Woman of that Town, and attempting to ravish her, and was sentenced to be set in the Gallows for a Space of an Hour, with a Rope about his Neck and the other end cast over the Gallows, to be whipt 20 Stripes under the Gallows, to suffer 3 Months Imprisonment, and to be bound for his good Behaviour for seven Years.

BOSTON Oct. 15. Last Week at a Meeting of the Merchants in this Town at the British Coffee-House, it was unanimously Voted to alter the Non-Importation Agreement, and to open the importation of Goods from Great Britain, except Tea, and such other Articles as are, or may be subject to Duties for the Purpose of raising a Revenue in America.

BOSTON Oct. 25. Last Saturday Morning a most violent Storm came on, the Wind at about N. N. E. attended with Rain and Hail: The Tide rose about Noon to such a height that it overflowed most of the Wharves in this Town the Water came up into Kingstreet as far an Admiral Vernon's Head Tavern, as also into Dock Square, about the Draw-Bridge, and into the Streets at the South and North Part of the Town, that were nearest to the Sea-side, so that it ran not only into the Cellars, but into the Shops and rooms of the Dwelling-Houses, obliging several Families to retire up into Chambers: Many Stores on the Wharves were almost filled with Water, whereby great quantities of Sugar, Salt, Lime &c. were destroyed: Several large Stores removed by the Violence of the Wind and Waves: Vast Quantities of Fire Wood, Timber, Staves, Shingles and other Lumber, were washed off the Wharves, and carried down the Harbour: A Number of the Vessels were forced from their Anchors, and drove ashore on Dorchester-Neck and Braintree Bay: Capt. Dunn in a Ship from Glascow, last from Newbury-Port, being at anchor in Nantasket Road parted her Cables, and was obliged to cut away the Masts, and drove at Braintree Flats, Capt. Bennet in a Ship bound for Africa, was the only Vessel in Nantasket that rode out the Gale without Damage.

BOSTON Oct. 29. The Superior Court of Judicature, Court of Assize and General Goal Delivery, met at the Court-House in this Town Tuesday last, according to adjournment, and on Wednesday Morning began the Trial of Captain Preston which was continued each Day till Saturday Afternoon when the Court adjourned to this Morning at 8 o'Clock to proceed with the said Trial: The Jury (which consist of Inhabitants both Town and Country has not been permitted to seperate during all this Time.

BOSTON Nov. 5. The Trial of Captain Preston mentioned in our last, who was indicted for the Murder of Mr. Gray, Mavarick, and others, on the Evening of the 5th of March last was continued till Monday Afternoon when the Jury went out, and the next Morning brought in their Verdict. "Not Guilty," and Capt. Preston was then dismissed.

BOSTON Nov. 5. On Friday last one John Russel formerly coachman to Mr. Hancock of this Town, was accidentally run over by a loaded cart, which he was driving. This put an end to his life in a few minutes.

BOSTON Nov. 19. The Superior Court at Salem the last Week a Mullatto man, named George, was indicted for riotously and tumultuously assembling, with divers other Persons at Gloucester the 23d of March last, in the Night of that Day, and breaking and entering the house of Jeffe Savill, and forcibly pulling him out of his Chamber by the Hair of his Head and dragging him sometimes by the Hair and sometimes by his Heels, from his Dwelling-House to a Place near four Miles distant, stripping him almost naked, placing him in a Cart, and carrying him through the Streets in the cold, and then besmearing him with Tar, beating and wounding and otherwise evil entreating him, &c. and that upon Trial the said George was found Guilty by the Verdict of the Jury, and sentenced by the Court, to be set upon the Gallows with a Rope about his Neck, and the other end over the Gallows for the Space of one Hour, to be whipped 39 Stripes opon the bare back under the Gallows, to suffer 2 Years Imprisonment, and at the Experation thereof to give Security for his good Behaviour for the Term of 7 Years in the sum of 100 pounds with two sufficient Sureties in 50 pounds each, and to pay Cost of Prosecution, standing committed until sentence be performed. We are informed the other Offenders who were all disguised at the Time of the Riot, are not yet taken.

BOSTON Nov. 26. It is said that the late Verdict of the Jury on Favor of Captain Preston, arose from a doubt whether he gave Orders to Fire; and the Soldiers who are to be Tryed this Week expect to obtain a Verdict in their Favor, by bringing full Evidence that in firing they obey'd the Orders of their Captain —— But whether such Orders will be sufficient to clear them, is said to the Matter of Speculation among some of the learned in the Law. However there may be a short and easy Method of clearing them all, by proving that the Inhabitants were the Agressors, or which is the same thing, objecting to Evidence to prove that they were not.
—— The Noted Richardson who was convicted of Murder in March Term remain yet unhang'd —— Christopher Monk who still survives the Wounds which he receiv'd in the horrible Massacre of the 5th of March, lives to see that the Death of his Fellow Sufferers is not yet reveng'd, and the poor innocent young Snider is quite forgot! —— What say the Law of God? "Who Sheddeth Man's Blood, by Man shall his Blood be shed." —— "The Murderers shall flee the Pit," and who dare slay him? —— Some indeed begin to doubt whether there Murder on the Evening of the 5th of March, and whether the dogs greedily licking human Blood in King Street, as had been said, is any Thing more than a Dream. But others will have it, that it calls for Vengeance, and the righteous Heaven will avenge it, sooner or later —— He that formed the Eye, shall he not see!

BOSTON Nov. 26. Friday last was tried at his Majesty's Superior Court of Judicature, &c. now sitting here, one John King, a mariner, belonging to his Majesty's ship Fowey, for the murder of a sailor belonging to the said ship, in a skirmish on board a boat at Wheelwright's Wharf. The Jury brought him in guilty of Manslaughter only; and the prisoner was immediately branded in court fot the same, and dismissed.

BOSTON Nov. 29. Tuesday the Trial of the Soldiers for the Massacre of the fifth of March last, came before the Superior Court of Judicature, &c. and it is not yet finish.

BOSTON Dec. 29. On Wednesday last ended the trial of the Soldiers, for the Murder of Samuel Gray, Patrick Carr, James Caldwell, Samuel Maverick, and Crispus Attucks, on the Evening of the 5th of March, after being continued nine days, successively, Sunday excepted. The Jury went out about two o'clock in the afternoon, and in about two hours after brought in their verdict; seven were found not Guilty, the other two (Montgomery & Kilroy) were convicted of Manslaughter only, and are to be branded in the hand. Thus ended this long expected and important trial!

BOSTON Dec. 17. To the Printer of the Boston Gazette.

That the trial of the soldiers concerned in the carnage on the memorable 5th of March, was the most solemn trial that ever was held in this country, was pronounced from the bench. To see eight prisoners bro't to the bar together, charged with the murder of five persons at one time, was certainly, as was then observ'd, affecting: But whoever recollects the tragedy of that fatal evening, will I believe readily owe that the scene then was much more affecting —— There is something pleasing and solemn when one enters into a court of law —— Pleasing, as there we expect to see the scale held with an aqual hand to find matters deliberately and and calmly weighed and decided, and justice administered without any respect to persons or parties, and from no other motive but sacred regard to truth —— And it is Solemn as it brings to our minds the tribunal of God himself! before whose judgement sent the scriptures assured us all must appear: And I have often tho't that no one will receive a greater share of rewards at the decisive day, than he who has approved himself a faithful upright judge.

Witnesses who are bro't into Court of justice, while their veracity is not impeached, stand equal in the eyes of the judge; unless he happens to be acquainted with the different characters, which is not presum'd ——— The jury who are taken from the vicinity, are suppos'd to know the credibility of the witnesses: In the late Trials the witnesses were most if not all of them either inhabitants of this town or transients persons residing in it, and the jurors were all from the country: Therefore it is not likely that they were acquainted with the characters of all the witnesses; and it is more than probable that in so great a number of witnesses there were different characters, that is, that some of them were more, others less creditable. If then the judge, whose province it is to attend to the law, and who, not knowing the characters of the witnesses, presume that they are all good, and give equal credit to them, it is the duty of the jurors who are sovereign in regard to facts, to determine in their own minds the credibility of those who are sworn to relate the fact: And this in a trial for murder requires great care and attention. I would just observe here, that in the last trial there were no less than eighty-two witnesses for the jury to examine and compare, which was an arduous task indeed! And I will venture further to observe, that some of these witnesses who swore very positively were not so credible as others, and the testimony of one of them in particular, which was very precisely related and very peremptory, might have been invalidated in every part of it. I shall not at present suggest what I take to be the reason why it was not done. These matters will not doubt their place in the history of the present times in some future day, when the faithful recorder it is to be hoped will, to use the language of our Courts justice, relate the truth, the whole truth, and nothing but the truth.

It is enough for the jury to receive the law from the bench: They may determine this for themselves; but of facts they are ever the uncontroulable judges. They ought therefore to receive the facts from the mouths of the witnesses themselves and implicitly from no other:

Unless the jury particularly attend to this, they may be in danger of being misled by persons who would be far from doing it with design: For instance, if one should swear that a being forwarn'd against it levell'd his gun and killed B: and afterward it should be forgot, that the witness also swore that A immediately advanc'd and push'd his bayonet at c, which pass'd between his waistcoat and his skin; if this I say should be forgot, and should be overlook'd by the jury when they are together, perhaps instead of bringing it in murder according to the rules of the law laid down by the bench, they would bring it in Manslaughter ——— I do not here affirm that this has ever been a fact: I mention it as what may hereafter be a fact, and to show the necessity of a jury's relying upon facts as they receive them from the Witnesses themselves and from the alone.

The furor brevis which we have heard much of, the fury of the blood which the benignity of the law allows for upon sudden provocation, is suppos'd to be of short duration ——— the Shooting a man dead upon the spot, must have stopp'd the current in the breast of him who shot him, if he had not been upon killing ——— an attempt to stab a second person immediately after, infers a total want of remorse at the shedding of human blood; and such a temper of mind afterwards discovers the rancorous malice before, especially if it be proved that the same man had declared that he would never miss an opportunity of firing upon people, and that he had long'd for an opportunity so to do: If this does not imply malice at first, I do not see but he might have gone on stabbing people in his furor brevis, till he had kill'd an hundred; and after all, it might have been adjudg'd in indulgence to the human passion, excuseable homicide.

The law of benignity makes allowances for the human passions: but the law is just; and makes this allowance upon the principle of justice: It gives no indulgence to malice and recour against any individual, much less against a community of the human specie ——— He who threatens or thirst for blood of the community is an enemy to the publick; and hostis humani gere generis, the enemy of mankind consummates the villain. I will not take upon myself to say that either of those characters belong to any of the late prisoners ——— There are two remaining yet in goal, convicted of manslaughter, and waiting for their judgement of the court. With regard to one of these namely, Kilroi, it was sworn that about a week or a fortnight before (the 5th of March, which must be before the affray at the ropewalks, that happening on the 2d) he said he would never miss an opportunity of firing upon the inhabitants, and that he had wanted such an opportunity ever since he had been in the country ——— It is said that these might be words spoken in jest, or without any intention, when they were spoken, on acting to their true import meaning: But the witness said he repeated the words several times: and that after he had told him he was a very great fool for saying so, he again declared he would never miss an opportunity. ——— It appears that the witness himself, as anyone might, tho't him to be earnest, and rebuked him for saying so; and in truth, none but a madman, or one whose heart was desperately wicked, would repeatedly, especially after such wholesome reproof, have persisted in such a threat; It discovered, to honor the expression of a very polite and humane gentheman, upon late occasion, a malignity beyond what might have been expected from a Barbarian.

It was also sworn, that this Kilroi was with a party of soldiers in the affray at the ropewalks a few evenings before the 5th of March —— and that they had clubs and cutlasses ——— That Kilroi was of the party of soldiers that fired in Kingstreet ——— That as the party came round before they form'd, Kilroi struck a witness, upon his arm ——— and after firing began, Kilroi struck at the same witness, tho' he had hear'd nothing said, nor seen any thing done to provoke the soldiers ——— Another witness declared, that he saw Kilroi there, that he knew him well before, and was positive it was he —— —— that he heard the word fire, twice, upon which he said to the soldiers, damn you, don't fire, and Kilroi fired at once, and killed Gray, who had no weapon, and his arms were folded in his bosom —— Gray fell at the feet of this witness, and immediately Kilroi pushed his bayonet at the witness, which passed through all his clothes, and came out at his surtout behind, and was obliged to turn round to quite the weapon —— the witness suppos'd he designed to kill them both —— How long is this furer brevis, this short hurricane of passion to last in the breast of a soldier, when called, not by the civil magistrate, but by his military officer, under a pretence of protecting a Centinel, and suppressing a Riot? who had taken with him weapons, not properly of defence, but of death, and was calm enough in the impetuosity of anger, to load his gun, and perhaps with design, to level it, for it killed one of the very men with whom he had a quarrel but a few evenings before: He had now a fair opportunity, which he had wished for, and resolved never to miss, of firing upon the inhabitants. It was said upon the word he uttered, that if all the unjustifiable words that had been spoken by the inhabitants of this town, were to be bro't in judgement against them, they would have much to answer for.

Those who believe the letters Governor Bernard, the Commissioners of the customs, and some of the others who I could name, and will name in proper time, may think so. I dare say, if Bernard could have proved one overt-act of rebellion or treason, after the many things he pretended had been said, and he or his tools could have had any influence, the words if prov'd, would have been adjudg'd to have been said in sober earnest, and would have shown the malignancy of the heart.

This Kilroi's bayonet was prov'd to be the next morning bloody five inches from the point, it was said to be possible that this might be occasion'd by the bayonet's falling into the human blood, which ran plentifully in the street, for one of their bayonets was seen to fall. It is possible, I own; but much more likely that this bayonet was stabbed into the head of poor Gray after he was shot, and that this may account for it being bloody five inches from the point ——— Such an instance of savage barbarity there undoubtedly was. ——— It was sworn before the Magistrate who first examined into the cruel tragedy, though the witness who then swore it, being out of this province, could not be produced in Court upon this trial. It is not to be wonder'd at that any material witness was out of the way when it is consider's that the trial did not come on till the second term, and nine months after the facts were committed, I shall continue the subject at my leisure.

December 11, Vindex.

BOSTON Dec. 17. At the superior Court holden in this Town on Wednesday last, came on the Trial of Edward Manwaring, Esq; an Officer of Customs, Mr. John Munro, Notary Public, Hammond Green and Thomas Greenwood, who had been charged with firing Guns out of the Customs House on the evening of the 5th of March, and indicted by the Grand Jury for the Murder of those Persons that were killed at that Time, and for which Manwaring, &c. were imprisoned. ——— The Evidence against them being not credited, the council for the Crown gave up the Cause, and the Jury acquited the Prisoners without going from their Seats.

1771

BOSTON Jan. 11. At the Court of Common pleas sitting in Boston for the County of Suffolks, is to come an action of trespass, wherein James Otis, Esq; is plaintiff against John Robinson Esq; Defendant. The sum demanded in damages is said to be 3000 Pounds sterling, his Majesty's writ was serv'd according to the laws of this province. not by holding to bail, but by leaving a transcript engross'd in the same hand and paper at the defendant's house.

BOSTON Jan. 17. Seamen are wanted for his majesty's ship Boston, now in the Harbour; for two days past, they have been beating up for men, and we hear, have enlisted ten or twelve, and pressed five or six more.

BOSTON Jan. 21. They still continue to beat for seamen in this town, a place of rondezvous is appointed at the sign of General Wolfe, Dock Square.

We are informed, that on Friday last a man, said to be in liquor, receiving the King's money for those who were beating up for seamen; and then refused to enlist, was endeavoured to trifle with the officers of the man of war, whom he knocked down, but was afterwards taken by a proper officer and carried on board one of his Majesty's ships.

BOSTON Jan. 21. On Thursday last Commodore Gambier used a proclamation, for the encouragement of seamen to enter into His Majesty's service, offering the Royal bounty of 31s. Sterling, for such as chuse to enter on board any of the King's ships in the harbour. Able-bodied landmen will be expected, and a bounty of 30c, sterling to be given each.

BOSTON Jan 21. Ten Dollars Reward. Whereas on the Evening of the 19th of this Instant a Horse and Chaise belonging to the Subscriber, standing at the King's Arm Tavern on Boston Neck, was taken from thence and kept all Night, and the Horse badly used, and on the Sabbath Morning was left in the common. I hereby promise afterward a Ten Dollar to anyone who will discover the real Person or Persons that took said Horse and Chaise, that he or they may be brought to Jistice. January 21, 1771.   John Hancock.

BOSTON Jan. 24. A correspondent has sent us the following.

An odd and sad accident lately happened to a Gentleman, who has a considerable post in the ----, This Gentleman had the misfortune to fall deeply in love with another man's wife ——— she was averse to his importunities for a long while, at length, tired of them ——— she informed the husband ——— he advised her to make an appointment with the Gentleman ——— this she does. the wife is put out of the way ——— the Husband equipped in the wife's cap, &c. at the appointed goes to bed ——— the Gentleman gets in at the window, and fastly makes his way into the room where his supposed mistress lay — he undresses for bed where, behold, just as he was entering, madam with the cap on, gave a whistle, when three or four sturdy rouges bursted out from a neighbourhood closet, seized my Gentleman, who met with an irreparable loss, and is now under the care of a skillful Surgeon.

BOSTON Jan. 24. Last Monday evening, we are informed, an affray happened between some officers of his Majesty's ships in this harbour, and the watchmen of the town, in which we are told, the former were aggressors, and that the latter have recovered damages.

BOSTON Jan. 28. On Friday Evening, the 18th Instant an Assembly was first opened at Concert Hall for the Winter Session. It is said a large Number of the principal Gentlemen of the town who had been of very different Sentiments in the late party disputes are Subscribers, and that the Assembly was proposed, in order to restore Peace, Harmony and the Blessing of socila Life.

BOSTON Feb. 18. Messieurs Fleets, I find in your paper of the 25th of December 1769, under the Province head, a relation of the misfortune of Captain John Foster Williams, late Master of the brig John, belonging to Boston, in which he has called my humanity in question in not endeavouring to take himself and people off the wreck. I desire you to publish the following account of the true state of that transaction, that the publick may be determine whether I was so void of humanity towards my fellow creatures in distress as Captain Williams have endeavoured to make me.

On the 7th of February 1769, being in lat. 34, 30. long. 62, 20. I spied a double decked Vessel to windward of me dismasted, and supposed had been a Brig: She was full of water, and had a small jurymast forward with a small sail set on it, by the help of which she ran down on me as I was a lying under my trysail, wind blowing hard at Sout-West; at 2 o'clock in the afternoon she came up so near me as to speak to them to lay their vessel by the leeward of me and I would endeavour to help them, which I did all in my power; I endeavoured notwithstanding the hazzards of the attempt to keep so nigh them as to heave ropes on board the wreck, but could not; and the wind being so high and turbulent sea that no boat could live. I immediately put my sloop under such sail as I could bear, in order to keep them company; at 5 o'clock I ran within call of the wreck and told them I would bie by them till morning, and if the wind abated I would take off; they made me some reply but the wind continued to blow hard I could not understand them. I accordingly stood alternately to the northward & southward all night. If possible to be in sight of them the next morning. As soon as it was light and the wind abating I made more sail and stood to the northward, I being at mast head myself to look out for the wreck but could see nothing of them; at 10 o'clock tacked to the southward; the wind being at the west, stood by the wind till 12 o'clock and could see nothing of the wreck, notwithstanding I kept a man aloft to look out; I then concluded that they must either have run before the wind all night or that the vessel had washed to pieces by the violence of the sea. I then stood my course for the West Indies. If the wreck I say was Captain Williams, he being in such distress might think that I ought to have run a greater Hazzard of my own life than I did, but he might have remembered that mankind in general in their distresses circumstances, let people do as much as they may, are apt to think they could do much more than they have power to do in order to relieve them.

However, this I can say I can aquit myself to God and my fellow low-creatures, in doing my duty in endeavouring to relieve Captain Williams and his people from the situation I found them in upon the wreck. Abijah Smith.

The Public may think it strange that the above account has not been published before now; but when Captain Williams made his public declaration I was gone on a voyage to sea; As soon as I came home I wrote this account, and left a copy with a friend to convey to a printing-office, but thro' mischance it failed, having no opportunity to publish it till now. A. S.

BOSTON Feb. 18. To be sold at the Heart and Crown in Cornhill. A Short Narrative of the horrid Massacre in Boston, perpetuated in the Evening of the 5th of March 1770. by soldiers of the 29th Regiment; which with the 14th Regiment were then Quartered there: with some Observations on the State of Things; prior to that Catastrophe. To which is added an Appendix containing the several Depositions referred to in the preceding Narritives.

At the same Place may be had, the trial of the eight Soldiers of the 29th Regiment for the above massecre.

BOSTON Feb. 25. On Friday last two Woman belonging to the 14th Regiment were crossing the ice at the South End of the Town, they both fell through, and altho' they were soon taken out by the Assistance of the Town's People, yet one of them, Susannah Mills, was so chil'd with the cold, that she expir'd immediately; the other is like to do well.

BOSTON Feb. 25. From the Essex Gazette, Mr. Hall the following lately came to hand, which you are desired to publish in your patriotic Gazette

To all the free-born Sons of America. I have long beheld with detestation the many injuries and insults you have received from tyrannical ministers, and their infamous tools (the genuine offspring of my antient enemies, and the Popish Stuarts whom I subdued) continue your exertions in the glorious cause of Liberty,and banish all foreign superfluities especially the destructive Tea from which the greatest revenue is drawn from you; and if your enemies continue their oppressions, I will soon point out a way for relief, a way in which you may relieve yourselves, and put it out of the power of any vile Bute, Hillsborough, Bernard, or any other Tyrants, ever to oppose you.

In the mean time, I am with perculiar affection, your assured friend,   Oliver Cromwell.

BOSTON March 4. The late Cold Weather has prevented the Posts performing their Stages regularly: —— The Southern Post, which usually went from hence with the Mail on Monday afternoon, being detained by Ice at Seabrook, Narraganset and Newport Ferries, not arrived in Season, staid till last Thursday before he set out again, and it is not expected to return before the beginning of next Week.

BOSTON March 7. French Aspesions to English Liberty.

The boasted liberty of the English is, in reality, only an imaginary liberty, and has a very near affinity with that of Venice amidst the carnival revelries.

A cartman in England conceits a point of liberty that he can call any well-dressed man a French son-of-a-bitch, without being punished for it.

A soldier who has been clasped in Newgate for robbery and manslaughter, seeing one of his comrades in the street going by, called to him through the gates of the prison, asking him what news? Why, answered the other there is a rebellion broke out in Scotland. God preserve us, cries the fettered soldier, should those rascals get the upper hand farewell the Liberty of old England.

The English upon the French as a mob of slaves; a Frenchman however at the foot of the throne, is more free than the English who dispise and insults him.

The spirit of liberty is quite independent of the form of government it is the delicious fruit of philosophy. The real philosopher is satisfied in all moderate governments; he knows that there is not, that there cannot be any so well constituted, as to be totally free from fault or inconveniences.

BOSTON. March 11. Last Friday Morning came on before his Majesty's Superior Court of Judicature &c. now sitting for the County of Suffolk, the trial of Charles Bourgatte (commonly called the French Boy) for wilful and corrupt Perjury, set forth the Substance of his Testimony at the last Capital Trial of Edward Manwaring, Esq; (his Master) John Monro, &c. for the supposed Murder of Crispus Attucks, on the 5th of March last, and concluded with an allegation that the whole was false and malicious, and corrupt Perjury. The accusation of the above mentioned Persons, was grounded upon a pretended firing out of the Custom House Windows that Evening, flatly and wickedly sworn to by the said Bourgatte.

At his Arraignment the prisoner pleaded not guilty, but when set at the Bar for Trial, he signed his Desire to retract Plea, and throw himself upon the mercy of the Court: The whole Bench however, apprehending. As it was a cause of popular Expectation that the Verdict of the Jury might be most satisfying to all Parties, thought fit to hold him to his first plea: accordingly a Jury of Twelve was impaneled and sworn, who, upon, full evidence of the fact from the Testimony of divers Witnesses of undoubted Credit corroborated by the voluntary Confession of the Prisoner returned their Verdict, without going from their Seats, Guilty.

The Boy in Excuse for himself urged nothing, but that he was advised to it by a Man who treated him well, and promised him he should not suffer for it.

BOSTON March 11. Tuesday last was the Anniversary of the never to be forgotten 5th of March 1770, when Messirs, Gray, Maverick, Coldwell, Carr & Attucks, were inhumanely murdered by a Party of Soldiers of the 29th Regiment in King-street ——— The Bells of several Congregational Meeting-Houses were tolled from Twelve at Noon till one: ——— In the Evening there was a very striking Exhibition at the Dwelling House of Paul Revere, fronting the old North Square: At one of the Chamber Windows was the appearance of the Ghost of the unfortunate young snider, with one of his fingers in the Wound, endeavouring to stop the Blood insuing therefrom: Near him his Friends weeping: And at a small distance a monumental Obelisk, with his Bust in front: On the front of the Pedestal were names of those killed on the 5th of March: Underneath the Lines:
Snider's pale Ghost fresh bleeding stands,
And Vengeance for his Death demands.

In the next Window were represented the Soldiers drawn up, firing at the People assembled before them ——— The Dead on the Ground ——— and the Wounded falling, with the blood running in Streams from their Wounds: Over which was wrote Foul-Play. In the third Window was the figure of a Woman representing America, sitting on the Stump of a Tree, with a Staff in her Hand, and the Cap of Liberty on the Top thereof, one Foot on the Head of a Grenadier lying prostrate grasping the Serpent ——— Her finger pointing to the Tragedy.

The whole was so well executed that the Spectators, whose Numbers amounted to several Thousands, were struck with solemn Silence, and their Countenance were covered with melancholy Gloom. At Nine o'Clock in the Evening the Bells tolled a doleful Peal until Ten; when the exhibition was withdrawn, and the People retired to their respective Habitations.

BOSTON March 18. On Thursday last were published his Majesty's Commission, appointing the Hon. Thomas Hutchinson Esq; Governor and Commander in Chief; and the Hon. Andrew Oliver, Esq; Lieutenant Governor of this Province. The

Particulars of the Parade upon this Occasion, for want of certain Intelligence, we are obli'd for the present to omit.

We hear that the Episcopal Clergy of the Town have already waited on his Excellency the Governor with a congratulatory Address upon his Appointment to the Government of the Province.

This Day, it is said, the Merchants of this Metropolis, are to present an Address to the Governor in consequence of which, If the Address be conceived in proper Terms of deep Repentance for their having in Times past presum'd to hold their Meetings without leave from the Chair, and their promising to pay proper Deference to Authority for the future, in this Regard: Its expected they will be indulged with the Liberty of meeting once in every Year for the Purpose of Trade; provided nevertheless, that the Board of Commissioners either preside or otherwise prescribe the Substance, Scope and end of said Meetings, will be declared as on the late occasion, "Unlawful and Tumultuous."

MARCH 25. At the superior Court now holden in Boston one Charles Bourgatte, a French Boy, who was a swift Witness against Manwaring and others last Winter, was convicted of Perjury, and last Wednesday sentenced to be set in the Pillory for the space of one Hour be whipt 25 stripes, and pay Cost.

BOSTON April 1. Massachusetts Bay. By the Governor, A Proclamation.

Whereas His Majesty's Pleasure has been Signified to me by the Right Honorable the Earl of Hillsborough, one of his Majesty's principal Secretaries of State, that I should exert my utmost Endeavours to give Efficacy and Dispatch to a Plan of Augmentation of the King's Troops by assisting His Majesty's Officers in raising Recruits within this Province; and whereas His Excellency Lieutenant-General Gage, Commander in Chief of His Majesty's Land Forces on the Continent of North-America, has requested me to issue my Orders to the Magistrates, Constibles and others of His Majesty's Civil Officers to be assisting to any Recruiting Parties and their Recruits, in providing them with quarters,

Carriages and otherwise, as they shall be occasioned;

And it being of the utmost Importance to his Majesty's Subjects at this Time, when we are in the most imminent Danger of a War with Spain, that His Majesty's most gracious Intention for their Protection and Defence should have its full Effects :

I have therefore fit, with the Advice of His Majesty's Council to issue this Proclamation requiring all civil Officers within the Province to be aiding and assisting to any Recruiting Parties for the purpose aforesaid, and to their Recruits, and in all Respect to conform to the Directions of an Act of Parliament, entitled, "An Act to amend and render more effectually in His Majesty's Dominions in America, an Act past in the present Session of Parliament, Intitled, an Act for punishing Mutiny and Desertion, and for the better Payments of the Army and their Quarters."* as they would avoid the Penalties imposed by the said Act for the neglect. And I recommend to all His Majesty's good subjects to endeavour, in their respective Stations and Capacities, to promote and forward His Majesty's most gracious Purpose for their Protection and Defence, as aforesaid.

Given at the Council-Chamber in Boston, the Twenty-Eight Day of March, 1771, in the eleventh Year of the Reign of our Sovereign Lord George the Third, by the Grace of God of Great-Britain, France and Ireland, King, Defender of the faith, &c. By his Excellency's Command,
Thomas Flecker , Secr'y.   T. Hutchson.
God Save the King.

* This Act, which as appears by the printed Act in the Province Temporary Laws, Page 335, would have expired in 1768, has been continued by several subsequent Acts, and is now in force.

BOSTON April 4. Whereas the Great and General Court or Assembly of this Province meet at Harvard-College in Cambridge, according to Proclamation, The Representatives being assembled in the Chapel, appointed a Committee to wait upon His Excellency, and acquaint him that upward of Forty Members were in the College Chapel and that they were earnestly desired his Excellency would be pleased to remove the General Assembly to its ancient and legal Place the Town-House in Boston.

To which Message his Excellency was pleased to send to the House the following answer.

Gentlemen of the House of Representatives.
As soon as you had opportunity for it, you appointed a Committee to present to me a verbal Message, requesting me to remove the Court to its ancient and legal Seat in the town of Boston.

Immediately after I sent, for you to the Council Chamber and there recommended to both Houses to propose upon and give Dispatch to such public Business as, in the common course of our Affairs, lay before them. I do not know how I could more fully have signified to you that I declined complying with your Request. But as this was not satisfactory and you have sent me a second Massage, I must tell you in the most explicit terms that I cannot remove the Court to Boston.

I have done my endeavours that all the Obstructions to the Court's sitting in Boston might be removed, but I have failed.

In my endeavours, One of the Obstructions is your denying, in effect, the Right reserved by the Crown to convene the Court in such Places as the Governor thinks proper. If every other impediment was out of the way, which you continue to urge that by Law the Court must be held in Boston, I may ask his Majesty's leave to carry you there. I should give up to the House of Representatives a Right which would have restrained in the Crown if no notice had been taken of it in the Charter. I could, even then, have had no plea, If I had been called to answer. except my ignorance of the Constitution, but now it is expressly reserved I should be wholly without excuse.

I am sensible there is Business of Great Importance lying before the Court, but I am less concerned whether you proceed to act upon it, because it is but a short time before I shall be obliged by Charter to meet a new Assembly; therefore if you decline proceeding I shall,

without delay put an end to the Session.
     Cambridge 5th April 1777.   T. Hutchinson.
  BOSTON April 4. Yesterday his Excellency Thomas Hutchinson, Esq; lately appointed Governor of this Province, on an invitation from the Corporation of Havard-College, was pleased to visit that ancient seat of Learning.
  His Excellency with his Honour Lieutenant-General and the Honorouble his Majesty's Council, in their Carriages, attended by the sheriff of the County of Suffolk, and a detachment of the Troops of Guard, went from the Province House in this Town in procession and were received at the County Line by the Sheriff of the Sheriff of the County of Middlesex, and the principal Gentlemen of Cambridge in their Carriages. At the steps of Havard-Hall, his excellency was received and congratulated by the President, Fellows, Professors, Tutors in their Habits ——— In the Philosophy Chamber he was met and welcomed by the honorable and Reverend overseers.
  BOSTON April 15. On Wednesday last Mr. Jacob Edes of this Town, bought a Sheep from a Countryman at Market, who said he killed it the Day before; but after he had paid him for the same and carried it home, it was perceived to be much mangled in several Places, and the Neck and part of a Shoulder cut off, which made some of the Family suspect that the Sheep had been bit by a mad Dog; whereupon Mr. Edes went in search of the Man he bought the Meat of, whom he chance to find, and acquainted him with the suspicions: The Countryman at first denied knowing any thing of the matter, but upon Mr. Edes threatening him with Prosecution for an Imposition, he at last confessed the Sheep had been bit. The Countryman returned Mr. Edes his Money, and in the presence of several People threw the Sheep into the Mill Pond.
  BOSTON April 15. Extract of a letter from a Gentleman of Considerable Note in London, dated Feb. 24, !771.
  "I hope the ill Treatment you have had from the Ministry is drawing to a perion. There are, I believe heartily sick of the Affair, and so

hard pressed by the Opposition, as to be willing to lessen the Number of your Enemies, and of the objection to your Management. I am so well persuaded, that North-America will, within a Hundred Years, be the Seat of Commerce, Liberty, and Power, and the refuge of the Friends to Liberty, and the Protestants Religion; that were not I so far advanced in Life, I would come over to you, with my Family."

BOSTON April 25. It is observed by a wag, that lawyers never put an end to a cause, they only prune it, in order that it may foread into more branches.

In the famous law suit between the Duke of Portland and Sir James Lowther, that now engages so much of the talk of the public, it began with one suit, which is now happily multiplied to 300: for there have been that number of ejectments served at six guineas a head. All the fur cats in England have been engaged on one side or the other; they have drawn up for these two Years past, with their briefs and quills, terrible as any army, with banners; both parties have been fleeced to their mutual satisfaction; and now when the cause is just going to be decided, the council on both sides concur (from a love of justice) in carrying it to the legislature, to make a new law before it can be decided; and when by the grace of Westminster-Hall, and the harmony of both houses, it may probably remain as much perplexed, and as fresh a case as at the beginning.

BOSTON May 5. His Excellency the Governor, by Advice of the Council, has been pleased to give the keeper of the Powder Magazine, several instructions relating thereto: One which is in the Words, "You are not to suffer any private powder to be delivered, or received, but between Sun to sun except upon my special Orders therefore.

We hear from Plymouth, that one Turner, who has been committed to goal for abusing his wife, cut her Throat, half thro' his Wind-Pipe, and was found wallowing in his Blood some time after almost expiring; a Surgeon was called, but is dubious whether he will survive the wound.

BOSTON May 6. Messirs Edes and Gill. In the

year 1769 the House of Representatives, of this Province remonstrated to Governor Bernard then in the Chair, against the indignity of sitting in general assembly surrounded with armed troops and with cannon pointed at their very door. The governor, instead of vindicating the honor of that legislative body of which himself was a part, meanly condescended to disclaim any authority over the Troops within the province, over which his Majesty had appointed him Governor & Commander in Chief, and remov'd the assembly to Cambridge: This the House protested against as a new grievance, but concluded the business of the session; after which the assembly was prorogu'd to a very distant day to meet in Boston. The Governor soon embark'd for London, and left Mr. Hutchinson to fill the Chair, who further prorogu'd the assembly to meet at Harvard-College; alleging in his speech to both houses, that he was otherwise instructed. The House again remonstrated against the holding the assembly out of its ancient and established seat, arbitrarily, to the manifest inconvenience and the injury of the province. Since which another assembly has been called at Harvard-College and there continued by three several prorogations, till a dissolution in the course took place; and now again writs are issued for the calling of a new assembly to meet the same place. The most charitable construction that I could ever put upon this conduct was, that Lord Hillsborough knowing that the Troops were posted in Boston, and expressing they would remain there, though it best that an assembly so tenacious of their honor, should be held in another place, and accordingly instructed his honor; who perhaps from the character given of him by Bernard, he was well assured, would always be subservient to the honor of the minister. But might his Honor who was "born and educated among us" have improved a lucky incident which occur'd namely, the unexpected removal of the troops from Boston, and acquainted his lordship that the objection to the setting of the assembly there was then at an end. It would have been natural for a gentleman dispos'd to oblige his

native country, that have taken such an opportunity: and presuming that it could not have been displeasing to a wise and prudent ministry, to have even of his own accord, prorogued the assembly to its most convenient place.
This might have been rather expected, of his honor's friends have told us, that he was uttering a verse to an appointment as chief governor if therefore he could have imagined that such a measure would have been given offence to the minister, the evil would have been more than balanced in the mind of his Honor, by its having saved the province in a point which he well knew the two houses of assembly and by far the majority of the people judged to be essential. Besides which as his honor has at last been prevail'd upon accent of a commission for his Majesty appointing him governor and commander in chief, it would have afforded some ground of hope that liniment measures would have been pursued, on his part, and that the change of men would have been happy to the province.

 May 3d, 1771,   Your's T. Q.

 BOSTON May 13. We hear that Mr. William Sanford Hutchinson, youngest Son to his Excellency the Governor, will be appointed Clerk of inferior Court of Common PLea and of General Sessions of the Peace for the County of Suffolks.

 At a Meeting of Freeholders and other inhabitants at Faneuil-Hall, on Tuesday last, there were 410 Votes, for Representatives, the ensuing Year, when the following Gentlemen were elected; Mr. James Otis, Esq; 399 Votes. Thomas Cushing, Esq; 410 Votes. Mr. Samuel Adams, 403 Votes. The Hon. John Hancock. Esq; 410 Votes.

 BOSTON May 17, The Freeholders & other Inhabitants of the Town are notified, that the May Meeting stands adjourned to this Afternoon 3 o'Clock, when the consideration of Salary and Grants will come on, and such Sum Voted to be raised by the Tax upon Polls and Estates, and may be tho't sufficient for the relief of the poor, & defraying other necessary Charges arizing within the Town the year ensuing.

 Tuesday last the Body of a Man was washed

ashore at the Bottom of the Common, which, by being so much destroyed, was thought to have been in the water several Months. The Jury of Inquest judged it was a Seafaring Man, and probably drowned in attempting to swim from a Man of War.

BOSTON June 3. In the House of Representatives May 29, 1771.

Ordered that Mr. Otis, Mr. Adams, Mr. Hancock, Captain Tayer, and Mr. Ingersool, be a committee to wait on his Excellency the Governor with the following message. Thomas Chushing, Speaker.

May it please your Excellency,

The Great and General Court Assembly being again convened at Harvard-College by vertue of his Majesty's writ, under your hand and seal, the House of Representatives think it their duty before they proceed to the public business humbly to lay their remonstrances before your Excellency.

By the Charter of the Province, the Governor for the time being is invested with full power of convening, adjourning, Proroguing and Dissolving the Assembly, yet it is a power in trust, and the House conceive that your excellency is indispensably obliged to exercise it for the public good of the Province, for which end alone you are intrusted with it.

It had been found by experience that the Town of Boston is the only convenient place for the holding of General Assembly; accordingly the Province has been at great expence in erecting and supporting a suitable building for that said purpose; and the Assembly has been usually convened and held there, from the time of the settlement of the Country, excepting at times when, by reason of contagious sickness, the lives of the members have been endangered.

The House cannot conceive of the good purpose that can be served by the holding the assembly at present in this place: On contrary, it must unavoidably be attended with great, inconveniences and real injuries not only in the members themselves, but also to others whose Business necessarily call for their attendance here. These are so your Excellency, that it is needless at this time to mention them.

The holding the Assembly out of the Town of Boston through the whole of last year, so strongly and justly remonstrated against to your Excellency by both Houses, was considered as a grievance by the people in general in the Province, and while it is continued, it will have a tendency to prevent a restoration of that harmony between the several branches of the Assembly, which is so earnestly to be desired by all good men.

The House therefore cannot but persuade themselves, that upon these considerations, your Excellency will, for the sake of promoting his Majesty's service, and the good of the Province exercise the power fully vested in you by the charter and adjourn or prorogue this Assembly to its ancient, usual and inly convenient place the Town-House in Boston.

The Next day his Excellency the Governor sent the House the following Message in answer to the above.

Gentlemen of the House of Representatives, You may depend upon my representing to his Majesty, by the first vessel, the inconveniencies which you mention, in your Message of yesterday to attend your sitting in any other place than the Town of Boston. I am restrained from holding the Court there without his Majesty's expressed leave: I hope before another Session to obtain this leave: I will endeavour that every obsticle may be removed, and upon this, and every other occasion, to convince you that I am desirous not merely of preserving to you the enjoyment of your just Rights and Privileges, but of procuring every Convenience so far as shall consist with my duty to the King.

Cambridge 30th May 1771.   T. Hutchinson.

BOSTON June 6. Tuesday last being the anniversary of the birthday of our most gracious Sovereign when he entered to the 34th Year of his Age, the Hon. His Majesty's Council, and the Hon. House of Representatives, sitting at Cambridge, adjourned to Captain Steadman's public House, where, with a Number of other Gentlemen they joined in expressing their joy by drinking His Majesty's health, and other loyal and constitutional Toasts.

In this Town the Batteries were fired at 12 o'Clock, also the Cannon of the Train of Artillery under Captain Paddock, the Company being mustered on the occasion, and marched to King Street, where they performed many military Maneuvers with such Order and Regularity as gave Pleasure to a large Number of Spectators. ——— At one o'Clock the Guns at Castle William, and on board his Majesty's Ships in the Harbour were fired.

In The Afternoon, His Excellency the Governor gave an elegant Entertainment at the British Coffee House to the Officers of his Majesty's Navy, Army, and Custom: At drinking the King, after Dinner the Ships fired a Feu de Joi.

In the Evening, the Honourable Commodore Gambier gave a Ball at Concert-Hall, where were present a great number of Gentlemen and Ladies.

There was an Appearance of the greatest Demonstration of Loyalty and Joy, among People of all Denominations, on this Anniversary.

BOSTON June 27. Last Friday Afternoon we had a Storm of Thunder and Lightning. The Blaze-Castle, Captain Smith of Bristol, laying at the Wharf of John Hancock, Esq; was struck with Lightning. It first took the Main-topmast, and shivered it to pieces, then gouged the Main-Mast in several Places almost down to the Deck, when it is most probable the Lightning divided Part taking the Steerage (where were ten Persons, who were all knocked down and stunned, but happily soon recovered) and Part down the Companion, where it broke a Glass Window, and did some other trifling Damage, and then enter'd into the Cabin, (where also three Persons were sitting who received no hurt) and melted the Gilding and Painting in several Places, and then it is thought it returned to the Companion. Notwithstanding there were thirteen souls on board, through divine Goodness, none receiv'd much Hurt.

BOSTON July 1. Tuesday last a Man from Philadelphia pretending to mighty Feats at wrestling, and bidding Defiance to any Man in Town or

Country, one Mr. Hersey, of Highham, excepted the Challenge, and soon gave him a fair fall to the Diversion of a large Circle and to no small mortification of the dougty Champion.

From Swanzey we hear that on Monday se'nnight a Farmer of that Town committed a young Horse in the care of a Negro Boy, who imprudently tied the Halter round his legs, when the Horse taking a Start, ran away with the boy, and dragging him over rough Roads quick deprived him of his Life in a few Minutes.

Last Friday in striking the Top-gallant Yards on board the Martin Sloop of War at the Sun-Set, a Man fell from the Round-Top into the Water, and it is tho't in the fall he struck against the side of the Vessel, as he was not seen to rise again.

BOSTON July 8. We hear that Mr. Edward Hutchinson of Connecticut, one of the Governors's Cozens, is appointed a Clerk of the Inferior Court for that Province.

Insurance Office 1771, These are to notify the Merchants, and all others in Trade, That there is opened by the Subscribers in king-Street, adjoining the Sign of Admiral Vernon in Boston, An Office of Insurance, in which all ships and other Vessels, goods, Wares and Merchandize, to and from any Part beyond the Sea, may be insured at a very reasonable Premium. And as Underwriters are Gentlemen of undoubted credit and Reputation, he flatters himself that he shall give general Satisfaction to all such Persons as shall have Business down in his Office where Attendance will be given.   Joseph Turell.

BOSTON July 15. Last Tuesday Evening, a number of people besset a house of ill-fame, near Oliver's dock, known by the name of Whitehall, and broke several windows, &c. which has been the means of treating a number of disorderly persons, who live therein.

BOSTON July 15. Wednesday the Select-Men of the Town visited the Public Schools, at whose invitation His Excellency the Governor, His Honor the Lieutenant Governor, several of his Majesty's Council, and a Number of other principal Gentlemen, with some of the Rev. Ministers attended, who all expressed great Satisfaction in the good order and Proficiency of the Youth in the respective Schools which did Honor to their several Instructors.

BOSTON July 29. We hear from Albany that another expedition, like the formerly carried on against Noble-Town, is proceeding against Bennington, More of the Salubrious effects of the Extensive wisdom ond goodness of a righteous administration, who first instructed Governor Wentworth, to grant these lands for speedy settlement; then turned right about, and countenanced monopolizing grandees of New-York in tearing the industrious farmers to pieces! How long, O Lord, shall the land mourn such incessant violence and cruel oppression!

Last thursday Morning came on the Court of Common Pleas, a Cause between James Otis, Esq; Plaintiff and John Robinson Esq; Defendent, in an Action of Trespass; and after a full and impartial Hearing, which continued till Friday Afternoon, the Jury next Morning brought in a Verdict on favor of the Plaintiff for two Thousand Pounds Sterling Damages, and Cost.

BOSTON Aug. 1. Mr. Otis laid his action at 3000 Pounds and has appealed from the Judgement.

BOSTON Aug. 5. On Tuesday last come here, before the Court of Common Pleas, the cause between Owen Richard, plaintiff, and Benjamin Jones, defendelt, for assaulting, tarring, &. Thursday the Jury brought in their verdict in favor of the defendent.

It is said, that a certain Governor is Hooted at by the boys in the streets of a chief city of his new government.

BOSTON Aug. 5. Province OF Massachusetts-Bay. Pursuant to an Act of the Great and General Court made and passed in the Eleventh Year of His Majesty's Reign; entitled, an Act for enquiring into the rateable Estates of this Province:

The Inhabitants of the Town of Boston are hereby notified, to give in to the Assessors of said Town, according to the Tenor of said Act, agreeable to the following Lists, viz. The Number of all the Male Poles of sixteen Years old and upward whether at home or abroad, distinguishing such, as are exempt from Rates; and of all rateble Estate, both real and personal; particularly Dwelling Houses and Shops under the same Roof, and adjoining to them, Shops separated from them, Still-Houses, Tan-Houses, ware-Houses, Slaughter-Houses, Pot and Pearl Ash Works, Superficial Feet of Wharf, Grist Mills, Saw-Mills, Iron works and Furnaces, and all other Buildings, and their annual Worth, and other Real Estate with the annual Worth; and of all Indians, Negro or Molatto Servants for Life, from fourteen to forty Years of Age, and the Number of tons of Vessels of every Kind, upwards of ten Tons Burton, to be given in Carpenter Tonnage, whether at Home or Abroad of their own Property, paid for or not, also including those in the Hands by Factorage; Money at Interest, which any Person has more than he or she pays Interest for; and also of all Horses and Mares of three Years old and upward. Oxen of four years old and upward, Cows of three years old and upward, Goats, Sheep, and Swine on year old; The Number of acres of Pasture, and the Number of Cows the same will keep, with the after-feed of the whole Farm; The Number of Barrels of Cyder that can be made upon the Farm in one year with another, the number of Acres of Tillage Land, Bushels of Grain and Corn, including all Sorts the same will produce by the Year; The Number of Acres of Salt-Marsh, with the Tons of Hay produced therefrom by the Year, The Number of Acres of English and upland and fresh Meadow mowing Land, with the Tons of Hay of each sort produced therefrom by the Year.

The Time limited by said Act is from the twentieth of September following. —— And every person not necessarily out of the Province in that Time, refusing or neglecting to give into the Assessors in writing, and on Oath; as required, a true Account of his or her Rateable Estate, agreeable to the true intent of this Act, shall be doomed by the Assessors according to their best Skill and Judgement, and also for Offence shall forfeit and pay the Sum of Fifty Pounds.

The Assessors propose to open their Office at their Chamber at the East End of Faneuil-Hall Market, on Monday the Twelfth Instant, where due Attendance will be given from Day to Day, to the Twentieth Day of September following, for the Purpose aforesaid, in Compliance with said Act. Assessors Office, August 1, 1771.

BOSTON Aug. 12. Last Thursday Afternoon David Murray, a Shoemaker belonging to this Town, was found dead on the Beach near the Neck, and some Marks of Violence appearing on several Parts of his Body, and the Jury of Inquest being of opinion that his Death was occasioned by some Violent Blow, one Wilson, a Tobacconist, who wad been with him in a Boat to the Castle, and came off with him from thence the Evening before, was taken up and examined, and telling many contrary Stories relating to the Affair he was the next Day committed to Goal on a strong suspicion of being the Means of the untimely end.

BOSTON Aug. 12. A Caution to Women not to meddle with Powder. The Week before last a Woman at Newbury went to strike Fire with Powder and Tow, and not knowing the Effect of Powder, it burnt her Eyebrows and Eyelids, and besmear'd her Face all over, so that she has been under the care of two Doctors ever since, but is likely to do well.

BOSTON Aug. 21. There is arrived in this town this day to be seen at the House of Widow Bignall, the next door to the King's Head Tavern, a little above Mr. Hancock's wharf. A Maiden Dwarf, who is fifty three years old, and of but twenty-two inches in stature. It was by the councel of some Gentlemen, that she came to pay a visit to this place, and she is willing to exhibit herself as a shew to such Gentlemen and Ladies as are desirous to gratify their curiosity, for one shilling lawful money for each person.

BOSTON Aug. 26. On Tuesday four men three of whom we hear were petty Officers, belonging to the Swan sloop of war, lately arrived from England, were whipped from ship to ship for desertion. We are told they are to receive 500 lashes each, 100 to be administered to each man weekly, for five weeks.

The following Paragraph is taken from a London Paper of June 1. ——— The revived hostilities between the Bostoneans and Governor Hutchinson, are, it is said, likely to be attended with very disagreeable consequence, for tho' insurrections beyond a certain limit, can never safely be trifled with, yet woe to the man that attempts to govern a free born people by the sword.

BOSTON Aug. 26. On Tuesday last a Number of respectable Merchants of this Town waited on Commodore Cambier with the following Address.

To the Honorable James Gambier, Esquire, Commodore and late Commander in Chief of His Majesty's Ships stationed at Boston.

Sir, We the Subscribers, Merchants of this Metropolis, do now wait upon you with our hearty Thanks for the Care and Attention you have shewn to the Trade on general of this Place during your short Command of the Fleet on this station, and for the ready Assistance you have afforded to some of us in Cases where our Property has been in imminent Danger.

Although the stationing of the Fleet in this Port in a Time of Peace, must be attended with ill Consequences to our Commerce; yet the Order and Decorum that has been maintained, and the Prudence and Discretion which has been exercised, particularly in the Part of the Service which bears the hardest upon Trade, the impressing of Seamen, has greatly abated the Evil we dreaded.

Justice obliges us to make these Acknowledgements to a Commander who has distinguished himself as an Officer and a Gentleman, and inspires us with the warmest Whishes for our Prosperity and Happiness. Boston in New-England, 16th August 1777.

To which Address, he was pleased to reply.

Gentlemen. I return my hearty thanks for this obliging Mark of your Regard and Esteem.

In the faithful Discharge of my Duty, during my short Command of His Majesty's Squadron in North-America, I have attentively had in view the Commercial interest of this Metropolis, and the Preservation of Order and Harmony. Accept,

Gentlemen, my warmest and most cordial Whishes for your Prosperity and Happiness, which upon every Occasion I shall be glad to promote.

BOSTON Aug. 29. It is reported a few days since that the Murderer Richardson's pardon came with Capt. Jarvis; but some people think that it arrived some months ago, and could not be applied, because he was not condemned, and that some other means end to be found out, whereby he may escape Justice and the laws of God, nature and the land be eluded.

BOSTON Sept. 1. Last Friday se'nnight, one Samuel Fellows, late Commander of an armed vessel for the protection of trade, &c. received ten stripes at the public whipping-post at Falmouth, in Casco-Bay for stealing ⸺ This is the same person, who, a year or two ago rescued a prisoner from the civil authority at Cape anne after firing a few bullets among the people. ⸺ He has since, with a number of others, broke out of goal at Falmouth, and a reward of 4o Shillings is offered by William Tyng, Esq; the sheriff of that County, for apprehending him.

BOSTON Sept. 1. On Saturday last one John Sennet of Wenham in the Province of New-Hampshire, was committed to his Majesty's goal in this town for the Unnatural crime of Beastiality, which he committed to same day on Boston Common in the Face of the Sun, in it's Meridian Lustre, and in the sight of several People. "Tis reported he was in Liquor at the time of committing the detestable Act. We hear he has a Wife and Children. The owner of the Beast had her immediately put to Death.

BOSTON Sept. 9. A guinea Reward, Will be given by the Subscriber, to any one who shall inform him of the Person or Persons that on Thursday last, cut and hacked one of the trees opposite his House in Long Acres.

As said Row of Trees were planted and cultivated at a considerable Expence, it is hoped all Persons will do their Endeavour to discontinue such Practice.   Adino Paddock.

BOSTON Sept. 16. At the Court held here the 9th Instant, John Willson was tried for the murder of David Murray, who was found dead on the

Neck, mantioned in the Paper of the 12th of August last: The Jury brought in their Verdict. Not Guilty.

On Tuesday last a fellow was tried and found Guilty of breaking into the Office of Joseph Goldthwait, Esq; and stealing a considerable Sum of Money, and sundry other Articles: He was sentenced to receive 20 stripes, and pay 500 Pounds Damages, and Cost: but having nothing to pay, he was sentenced to serve 20 Years; —— Next Day he received 20 stripes at the Public Whipping Post.

BOSTON Sept. 23. To the Ladies. William Warden Wig-Maker, in King-Street Boston, respectfully informs the Ladies, That he has invented a Hair-Roll upon an entire new Construction: The Roll in common use weigh from seven to ten Ounces, whereas those he makes do not exceed three —— The Advantage of a light Roll over the heavy one are so obvious that it would be affrontive to the Understanding to point them out.

Also He colours Hair on the Head from a Red or any other disagreeable colours to a dark brown or black, so nigh Nature that the most scrutinizing Eye cannot perceive the Difference.

—— From some Casualty or other it frequently happens that the Hair or some Part of the Head is different from the rest: This he also changes, and makes all the Hair properly uniform.

BOSTON Oct. 17. We hear last Saturday night the Admiral's ship lying in the Harbour, by some accident took fire in the store room, which consumed a quantity of Oakum, but being soon discovered, the fire was happily extinguished.

BOSTON Oct. 21. We hear that Captain Preston, who was lately justified by the law of his country, for killing some rioters, on the 5th of March 1770, has had a still further compensation from his sovereign, for his service. It is said, that the King ever willing to reward those who best promotes the interest of the crown, has conferred on the Captain 500 pounds sterling, to recruit him in what he expended, and also a pension of 200 pounds per annum. "Vengeance is mine saith the Lord, I will repay."

BOSTON Oct. 21. From Bingley's Journal of June

29, 1771. to the Earl of Hillsborough.

My Lord. Could experience teach you wisdom, or time remove the very unjust resentment you have conceived against his Majesty's most loyal, and most deserving subjects, of Massachusetts-Bay, you would not have given fresh cause of discontent in that province. The people however unsatisfied were silent. When then, my Lord, did you repeat that odious grievance of removing the Assembly from the ancient, most convenient, and most desirable place of session, to one entirely reversed? is there any good end of government, that can possibly be answered by a measure totally nugatory, but in subjecting the Assembly to much inconvenience, and in gratifying your pique and that of Governor Bernard, against the people of Boston, whom neither your threats could awe, nor your arts could seduce from boldly asserting their rights? Does so pitiful gratification of it, become the rank, or the place for your fill?

But my Lord, this measure is not only irritating and impolitic, but illegal. The Assembly has fully proved in such, and all the art and sophistry of your Government, could not evade the force of their argument. It is true, indeed, not only this, but every act of your administration give full proof, that to act comformable to law was never in your inclination, or intention. In a mind not totally unprincipled, the signal services of that province would have outweighed their late opposition to the unsurpations of Government. Their gallant storm and Capture of Louisbourg, in the year 1745; their maning Admiral Saunder's fleet, so as to effectuate those operations, to which we owe the important reduction of Quebec and the conquest of Canada; their defence of his Majesty's garrison at Annapolis, and of all Nova Scotia, in the war preceding the last; with many eminent instances of their zeal and ability to serve his Majesty and this country, are buried in oblivion; while every opposition of Government, however justified by the clearest principles of the constitution, is noted down, and marked for vengeance. This is the method your Lordship takes of securing their future services to the crown, and their attachment to the House of Hanover. The success will certainly be adequate to the means. But even, if the present generation had no defects to plead, the rights for which they are contending against your usurpation, for parliament is only instrumental, are less then they would have merited through the unexampled hardships their ancestors endured in conquering the savage country.

Your Lordship must have seen the detail of their suffering in the history of your very obsequious Governor Mr. Hutchinson. He indeed has betrayed those liberties, which he has taught us were so dearly purchased, for the pitiful ambition of being a Governor, under such a Minister as your Lordship. He may now judge, whether there are sweets in power and gratified ambition to sooth the anguish of recollecting, that he has betrayed his country, and ruined his character forever. The perfidy too, of Mr. Oliver, has its reward. To do justice, it is not your Lordship's fault, if a single eminent malefactor in America remains undignified and unrewarded. The account of Mr. Oliver's promotion is worthy the attention of the public. It will shew to what a consummate degree corruption has arrived, under your Lordship's American Administration.

Mr. Oliver was Secretary to the Council, when the late memorable military massacre was perpetrated in Boston. To take off the horror of this bloody business, it was the object of Administration, and of its creatures to make it suspicious that an insurrection was intended by the people. The Secretary, therefore, framed some minutes of Council, in which he prevented to their purpose what one of the Members had said, and having secretly sworn to the truth of them, he, in concert with the present guiltless Governor, dispatched them, by no less a personage than a Commissioner of the Custons to Lord Hillsborough. —— My Lord, was it with this happy mixture of perjury and baseness, that you appeased the resentment our righteous Sovereign manifested for the barbarous murder of so many of his Majesty's subjects? When an account of these minutes and affidavit returned, for the sending them had been profoundly secret, the Council unanimously resolved, and separately made oath, that what was there minuted, did not pass Council. Mr. Oliver stood recorded on the Council books as to perjured traitor, and can it be believed? he was immediately appointed his Majesty's Lieutenant Governor of the Province!

It is obvious, my Lord, and you have no doubt considered, that, in the hands of such men, government cannot fail of being respectable, and be loved among the people. That such a temper in America may eventually, be desirable, will appear in your Lordship from the fillowing anecdote; a little more than a century past, when Charles the Second was driven from the throne, the Colony of Virginia sent over him a refuge, and proclaimed him king before his restoration in this country. The revolution of empires are in the hands of God. and we may hope that the present pious Court will never experience the misfortunes that overwhelmed that of Charles the First, but, say Lord, what has happened may happen again, and, in the most distant apprehension of such calamity, it cannot but administer great consolation to your Lordship, that by your singular management the deposed Monarch would be secure of finding a most cordial reception in America.   Junius Americanus.

BOSTON Oct. 23. In Council, His Excellency the Governor laid before the Board, a Paper published by Messieurs Edes and Gill, On Monday the 21st Instant, entitled, the Boston Gazette, and Country Journal, in which they have printed a Letter, under the Signature of Junius Americanus, directed to the Earl of Hillsborough, said to be taken from Bigley's Journal of the 25th of June 1771, expressly asserting, that the late Secretary Oliver, the present Lieutenant Governor, stood recorded in the Council books as a purjured traitor: And desire their advice thereof:

"Whereupon Resolved, that the Assertion afore said, printed in said Paper, is false, groundless and malicious.

A true Copy from the minutes of Council. Tho's Flucker, Secr'y."

BOSTON Oct. 24. For the Massachusetts Spy, Mr. Thomas, please to publish in your paper the following paragraph from the Boston Gazette, and the structure that follows.

"It has been currently reported form the arrival of Capt. Hall from London, that the governor of this province has received a fresh order from Lord Hillsborough peremptorily to insist upon a former instruction, requiring him not to give his effect to any Tax bill, and some say, any bill at all, until the Commissioners of the Custom are exempted from paying a certain proportion for the support of this Government."

It is impossible for 20 Englishmen to read the above paragraph and indignation to sleep; vengeance is justly due to any man or set of men, by whose means a people are enslaved.

Unless the representatives of a people exempt a set of villains, who are plundering us, under pretence of law, from paying their proportion of the public tax, the whole machine of Government must stand still !!! Forbid it heavens that we should submit such insult. ——— This is one of the blessed effects of being governed by a pensioner, who has no check. The King of Great Britain cannot get rid of his dependence upon the people there, if he refuse his assent to carry any bill brought in by his Parliament at home. they have the right to deny him any support, and shall the King himself be subject to this controul, and Governor Hutchinson not !!! if the King himself cannot get quit of his check of his power, he has certainly no legal right to free any of his representatives from it, at the moment that he or they attempt to render themselves independent of the people, that moment their authority ceases, they themselves break the compact with the people, and from that momemt the people become animated from their jurisdiction, and have a constitutional right to form their government anew. It is dissolved in all intents and purposes, for no government can subsist without laws, no law can be made without the consent of the King, or his representatives, that consent is denied to the repectable people, when they barely submit to dishonourable Terms, treasonable to their own safety which I hope in God never will take place. Rather let the present system of government tumble into ruin, even though it should crush every tyrant to death.   Mucius Scaevola.

BOSTON Oct. 28. Last Friday being the Anniversary of his Majesty's Accession to the throne, when he entered the twelfth year of his Reign: The Guns at the Batteries in Town, and those at the Castle William and on board the Men of War in the Harbour were fired on the occasion.

BOSTON Oct. 28. As the instructions of Youth into Harvard-College before they are properly acquainted with the Latin and Greek Language, operates much to their Disadvantage in the in the Course of their Education: —— Notice is hereby given, That Candidates for admission will for the future, be examined in any part of the following Books, —— The greek Testament, Virgil's Aeneid, Cicero's select Orations. It is also expected that they be well acquainted with Latin prosody.

Samuel Locke in the name of the President and Tutors,   Harvard-College, October 10, 1771.

BOSTON Nov. 4. We are informed by several Gentlemen of Character lately arrive from London, that the present administration that three out of four feel for America; and that could it be decided by the people, we should soon have our privileges restored, and the present tyrannical Ministers rewarded according to the works.

BOSTON Nov. 11. Last Thursday Evening, pretty late, two young Women, Tayloresses, coming home across King street, the foremost carrying a Lanthorn, was stopped by a Man of War's Man, who tried to wrest the light from her with one hand while he seized her by the neck with the other. She struck him in the face with the hand that was at liberty, which he returned with his fist upon her ear, till he knock'd her down on the pavement; the other young woman then attack'd him with her layet board, and at length reaching a blow to his head bro't him in his turn to the ground; the young Women having made an outcry betime in the engagement, and people gathering round, the Hero march'd off, leaving the one he first engaged much hurt.

BOSTON Nov. 4. For the Massachusetts Spy.

If it is true, that the exceptional clause in the last proclamation, was not proposed by Mr. Hutchinson, but by one of the council, yet it stands, and is nevertheless exceptionable, and must reflect dishonour somewhere, even though it were immediately inserted.

It is not denied even by Mr. Hutchinson's friends, that the other part of the proclamation was drafted by him: We may consider him then as triumphing over us as Slaves, or persons who have no privileges; and though he well knew it would be a piece of treachery, to lead us to the throne of grace, with thanksgiving for the preservation of privileges, which, by his means, in part, we have been deprived of: yet he thought fit with the advice of six out of twenty eight of his council, (if he by his craft, could make it their act) to insert it.

We have need of the wisdom of serpents, who are concerned with such rulers: to be considered by them as fools, in irritating; for fools they must think us. If they can imagine that we can complain of loss of liberty in one breath, and with the next solemnly thank God for the preservation of it. What account can be given for such conduct, consistent with common honesty, mankind must judge.

It would give me pain to harbour one thought, that the six members, who it is said voted for the insertion of that impious paragraph intended thereby to curry favour with the Ministry; I cannot indulge such a thought besides there is no danger that this people will ever receive a council appointed by the King himself: And certainly it is unlikely that if the representatives of this people should once adopt such a sentiment of them, that these men should ever again be re-chosen into the Council. Mr. Hutchinson may think we are easy, because we long waited for a redress of grievances; but our patience is nearly exhausted. It cannot be that we shall bear much longer, to have our money forced from us.

An Englishman should never part with a penny unless by his consent, or the consent of his agent of representatives, especially as the monney thus forced from us, is to hire a man to Tyrannize over us, when his Master calls our Governor. This seems to be Mr. Hutchinson's situation; therefore I cannot but view him as a usurper and absolutely deny his jurisdiction over this people; and am of opinion, that any act of assembly consented by him, in his pretended capacity of Governor, is ipso facto, null and void, and consequently, not binding upon us. A ruler, independent on the people, is a monster in government; and such a one is Mr. Hutchinson; and such would George the third be, if he should be rendered independent on the people of Great Britain. A Massachusetts Governor, the King by compact, with the people may nominate and appoint, but not pay; for his support, he must stipulate with the people, and until he does, he is no legal Governor; without this, if he undertakes to rule he is a Usurper.

It is high time my countrymen, that this matter was inquired into for we have no constitutional Governor, it is time we had one. If the pretended Governor or Lieutenant Governor, by being independent of us for their support, we rendered incapable of completing acts of Government, it is time I say, that we have a lawful one preside, or that the pretended Governors, were dismissed and punished as Usurpers, and that the council, according to charter, should take upon themselves the government of this province.   Mucius Scaevola.

BOSTON Nov. 18. We hear that at Council held in Council chamber last Saturday, a piece signed Mucius Scaevola, published in the Massachusetts Spy of Nov. 14th, printed by Isaiah Thomas, was taken into consideration, when it was unanimously Ordered, That the Attorney General be directed to prosecute the publisher thereof.

It is said the Piece referred to above (from its Nature and Tendency) is the most daring Production ever published in America.

BOSTON Nov. 20. Mr. Thomas, I have just received the following paper, by the hands of a deputy sheriff, which I am asked to lay before the public for their contemplation. I know not the design of it, nor why it is sent to me rather than to any body else. Your publishing it, therefore, in your paper will oblige your humble servant,   J. Greenleaf.

"Province of Massachusetts-Bay.
To Joseph Greenleaf of Boston, in said province, You are required to appear before the Governor and Council at the Council-Chamber in Boston, on Tuesday the tenth day of December next, at ten on the clock in the forenoon, then and there to be examine touching a certain paper called the Massachusetts Spy, published the fourteenth day of November, 1771, whereof you are not to fail at your peril, Dated at Boston, the 16th day of November 1771. By order of the Governor with the advice of Council.
                       Thomas Flucker, Secry."

BOSTON Nov. 22. On Friday last in the afternoon his Excellency the Governor laid before the Council for the advice thereon, a paper in the Massachusetts Spy of Thursday, signed, Micius Scaevola, said to contain divers seditious expressions, &c. The Council after debating till sun down, adjourned till the next day, when they met again and sent for the printer, who in answer to the summons, told the messenger he was busy in his office and should not attend: Upon which it is said a motion was made for his commitment to prison for contempt, but did not obtain --- Whether through the abundant lenity of the honorable board, or from the having no legal authority in the case, had not yet transpired to us. The final result was their unanimous advice to the Governor to order the King's Attorney to prosecute the Printer at common Law.

Boston Nov. 28. A correspondent has furnished us with the following droll occurrence, viz. "Not long since, on one of our harmonious nights, when the gentry of either sex visit our Concert House, one of the black musicians left the place before all the company had retired, and proceeded home, but his Master's door was shut, and he took up his abode in the barn for the night, other than be exposed to the night air; he had wrapped himself up in the hay and was preparing for sleep, when he was amused with the appearance and discourse of an amorous pair, who not knowing the musician was there, come from the Concert (which was near by) to taste those joys, those stolen pleasures, which Hyman had forbid unless by him conferred. It seems this couple were a single gentleman, and a married lady, the latter had a white satin pettycoat, which she took off, and carefully laid by until their pastime should be finished. They had just prepared to receive each other in mutual embrace, when unluckily for the lady she uttered these words, "O my dear, I wish I could have that tune played all night." "What tune my jewel?" returned the amorous swain. "Why bobbing Joan." answered the lady.

The musician unnoticed had been very intent upon their behaviour all this time, and having his violin by him, immediately rose up and played the before mentioned tune to the no small astonishment of the gentleman and lady; who presipitously retired, the latter leaving the white satin pettycoat behind her and the gentleman the covering of his nakedness.

BOSTON Dec. 2. From the Massachusets Spy of Thursdat last.

Mr. Thomas, I was not a little surprized when I heard that Mr. Hutchinson had laid before the honorable board, the piece published in your paper on the 14th current, under the signature of Mucius Scaevola, and that the King's Attorney was ordered to prosecute the publisher, and that a private Gentleman of this town should be cited for interrogated relative to said publication. Until now never heard that it was unlawful, barely to ask, and to desire assistance of our fellow citizens, in this important inquiry, whether the person in the chair is a lawful and constitutional Governor, yea or not. If an Officer arrest me in the street, I have a right to know from him whether he be in fact a lawful officer, if he refuses to satisfy me in this point, I have a right to resist him unless it appears from the notoriety of his practices, that he is an officer, and has been commonly submitted to a free people; and this is all that Mucius intended if the offensive publication.

Indeed I have said "An Englishman should never part with a penny, but by consent, or the consent of his agent &c." This certainly must be a harmless proposition, the truth of which is known by intuition, I assign a reason why we should nor consent, viz. because "Money forced from us," meaning by the Revenue Act, is appropriated, in part at least, "to hire a man to tyrannize over us, whom his master calls our Governor." This idea was suggested in a ministerial paragraph, in a late London paper in which it is intimidated, that the sole reason, why the Ministry undertake to pay our Governor, &c. is because the pay or hire has always operated as a bribe, and that when they are hired by the people over who they preside, they, having such a check, always favour the interest of the people. That the Ministry whom I have called his, that is Mr. Hutchinson's master, doth apply the Money, forced from us by the Revenue Acts, to this purpose, is very evident, and we have no reason to think that he can have any other intention than that mentioned in the said London paragraph. We also know, Mr. Hutchinson has refused his assent to a bill for his Support. This shews his total independence on us. The paper that gives offence, says, "This seems to be Mr. Hutchinson's situation, therefore (i. e. because he is independent) I cannot but view him as Usurper, &c." this I proposed as a matter to be enquired into, and, the rule by which we are to try this opinion in the Charter, wherein this people reserve to themselves the privilege of paying Governors, this appears from hence, they compliment the King with the privilege of nominating and appointing only. This is paying Governors lie with the people, even by compact, appears by the perpetual instructions which have been given to Governors to apply to the people for their wages or Hire. Indeed I have the strong conclusion, which I suppose naturally followed the premises, viz. "until he does," that it "stipulates with the people," for his support he is no legal Governor. If the premises of reasoning, and false, Mr. Hutchinson must be acknowledgement a constitutional Governor. I have not pretended to determine this matter, but refer it wholly to his Majesty's Council, upon whose shoulders the Government must rest, if it should appear to be true, that the ministers has mistaken the Charter rule in the appointment of a Massachusetts Governor. There is nothing in all this, that has a tendency to disturb lawful and constitutional authority; I appeal to my countrymen, whose peace, freedom and happiness I esteem as my chief Joy.

Mucius Scaevola.

BOSTON Dec. 4. Extract from the Massachusetts Gazette, Nov. 28.

The indecent treatment of his Majesty's Governor, pressing him to comply with the measures contrary to his instructions, and making his substance to depend upon that complyance: This has occasioned his Majesty to render him more Independent, by taking the Payment of his Governor upon himself. What now is the remedy to warm Patriots propose in this Exigence, is it to cease from opposition, and humbly supplicate his Majesty to restore our former privilege. No it is to deny the Governor's Authority, and and stile him a Usurper, although they know he has his Majesty's Commission to produce. It is not long that our wise Patriots thought proper to deny the Parliament of England has any authority over us, since we are not represented in it. ——— Thar we substituted by a Charter from the Crown, and owed Subjection to none but our Royal Master King George: Now it seems we dispute his authority, and will not suffer him to appoint a Governor that is not dependent upon the people for his subsistence. And yet there are no people in the Province more ready to boast of this Loyalty than these Patriots. But inconsistency is not their only foible. Whether the present Opposition will end in the entire subversion of our Charter, and the increase of the Naval and Military force among us, is what, although I do not pretend to foresee, yet I confess I greatly fear. ——— Such are blessed fruits of what some People call Patriotism.

But for the sake of my fellow Citizens and Countrymen, I will point out a few of the many evils that will unavoidably arise if the insolent opposition proposed in the Massachusetts Spy of Nov. 14, should meet with success. Supposing them what is there impudently affirmed, that the Governor is a Usurper; the consequence will be, that all his Administration since his appointment must be null and void. All officers and commissioners derived from him invalid, The council themselves, the validity of whose choice depended on his approbation, must be desolved. Every deed sale under such administration can be of no force, and the seller who has received his purchase money for a Farm or House may re-enter at pleasure, as no deed could be properly authenticated for want of legal Magistrate, &c.

BOSTON Dec. 12. A Girl about 4 Years of Age, was found dead Yesterday Morning in one of the Tenements in Boarded-Alley so called. A Jury of Inquest was summoned, who brought in their verdict, died of excessive Drinking. It appears that a Woman in the Tenement the Evening before had brought a Pitcher with rum therein, and while she went to get a Candle, it's supposed the Child being thirsty, took the Pitcher and drank a great part of the Liquor, which stuperfied it till it died.

BOSTON Dec. 16. At a Council held at the Council Chamber in Boston Tuesday December 10th, 1771. His Excellency having acquainted the board at their Meeting, that Joseph Greenleaf, Esq; a Justice of the Peace for the County of Plymouth was generally reputed to be concerned with Isaiah Thomas, in printing and publishing a News Paper, called the Massachusetts Spy, and the said Joseph Greenleaf having thereupon been summoned to attend the Board on the third Day in order for his examination touching the same, and not attending according to summons, it was therefore unanimously advised, that the said Joseph Greenleaf be dismissed from the Office of Justice of the Peace; which advice was approved of and consented to, by his Excellency: and the said Joseph Greenleaf is dismissed from said office accordingly. A true Copy from the minutes of Council.   Tho's Flucker, Secr'y.

BOSTON Dec. 19. Last Tuesday se'nnight died suddenly at Stoneham, Mrs. Abigail Richardson, mother of the noted Esquire Richardson, now under conviction of murder, and whose habitation is now, as it has long been, in Suffolk County goal ———— She has turned out a true prophetess, having often declared, that she should never live to see this ———— famous fellow hanged.

BOSTON Dec. 23. Messieurs Edes & Gill. Please to put the following, and you'll oblige your constant Reader.

The Printers, who are Friends to Liberty and their Country, we desire you to publish the following.

To The People of America.

As it is the highest point of wisdom in all nations and civil societies, to provide, not only for present peace and safety, but for future contingencies, and to guard against every political evil that human foresight can conceive possible to happen; and as times of tranquility when the state is free from convulsions, are the most proper to deliberate on and settle the important and fundamental laws of government, to draw the critical lines of a happy civil constitution, and determine all those delicate points ———— This Day seems to be pointed by Providence for the Sons of America to take this momentous concern into their serious and most deliberate consideration ———— For if the present destructive system of politicks in Great-Britain is pursued much longer, it is evident to every discerning mind, that her fall and final ruin is inevitable. ———— The waste of public money ———— standing armies ———— the luxury and wickedness that prevails among the great ———— are presages of Britain's fall! And as when Rome fell, Britain, who was then one of the dependent colonies, was obliged to set up a government on her own, to prevent her falling with the sinking empire; so the Americans, if

Britain falls, will be oblig'd to set up a government of their own independent of any other people.

Therefore it is of the highest moment to the security and future welfare of the Americans, that a system of civil policy should now be written (to be ready for them whenever necessity shall oblige them to set up government of their own) that will establish the union, and connect the interest of the United Provinces, in such a manner as to lay a sure foundation for a righteous government, built upon those solid principals of virtue, justice, liberty and sound policy, as will make it lasting as time ——— and produce all those blessings that exalt a people & make them at once glorious and happy.

We ardently wish, and pray, that the union between Great-Britain and America, may never be dissolved ——— that we may live in harmony with the parent state to the end of the world: — We study to promote her welfare, and even aim to exalt her true felicity and real glory. It is our duty thus to do, and what Heaven has made our duty, we consider as ever connected with our happiness. To break off our connection with the parent country, before the law of self-preservation absolutely obliges us, is a thought we never harbour in our breasts. The reigning principle which animates the Americans, is love to Great-Britain: This passion warms our hearts, and kindles an ardour for her happiness united with and inseparable from our own ——— Yet the dictates of reason, and the experience of all nations and ages of the world, teach us to provide for our security; for the worst that can happen ——— that we never may be surprized with an evil unthought of ——— thrown into circumstances unprovided for, nor involved in difficulties against which we made no provisions. And for this purpose, we should weigh every thing in the scale of reason, tried by the test of experience collected in all the ages, and handed down in the history of mankind. This teaches us, that mighty kingdoms have fallen; and empires that once reached the summit of

human greatness, power and glory no more ——
This, teaches us that Great-Britain is in a
perilous situation, and gives us a melancholy
presage of her final ruin! —— At the same
time, admonishes us to be eagle eyed to discern
and even studious to guard against the remotest
danger —— to stand fortified, and compleatly
provided for all the vicissitudes and revolutions of time.

The Subscriber, has begun to write a system
of government, and civil policy for the united
Provinces in America which will be published as
soon as it is compleated. He proposes not only
to take a view of the political system in other
nations, and all former states that have flourished in the world, as well as consult the political writers of the present and past ages,
but likewise collect the sentiments of all gentlemen that he has the opportunity to consult,
who are distinguished for knowledge in government and political transactions. Therefore he
request of all gentlemen who are dispos'd to
offer their sentiments upon this very interesting subject, that they will favour him therewith; and send them (free from charge) to Messieurs Edes and Gill, Printers in Boston.

I cannot forbear congratulating my countrymen
that notwithstanding all the machinations and
united efforts of our enemies on both sides of
the atlantic, liberty is yet alive —— she
has suffered a small eclipse, but will soon appear with more than her former splendor. It is
clear to every penetrating eye that view all the
wheels of state, that every injury done to America, although it may spread a dim aspect at
first, will vanish like a transient vapour and
establish liberty on a finer foundation. ——
Fleets, armies, taxes, and impositions of every
kind, are a weight thrown into our scale, and
will finally operate in favour of freedom, if
wisdom guides the sons of America.

Let us my countrymen, ever keep in mind the
vast importance and infinate worth of freedom
—— and while we exert our utmost endeavours,
to preserve it, servently employ the assistance
of Him that makes us free —— Round the throne

of liberty, religion, truth, virtue and honor, always thrive. ——— Where she reigns, every thing is found that exalts a nation, enobles and blesses mankind.

Not only for a concern for the welfare of our own country, but love of Great-Britain should animate us; for nothing can preserve her from slavery and ruin; but the freedom of America. If the colonies are enslaved, it is impossible for Britain to be free; their slavery would inevitable prove her destruction. Therefore, we have every weighty and powerful incitement that can animate good men in a good cause. Every consideration that touches the springs of action in noble souls, urges us to the most vigorous and unremitted exertions! Our own happiness, the welfare of the present country, and unborn generations, are the great, the glorious object we have in view! ——— Let these awaken all the passion and touch every spring of mind! To the grand Point, let all our views centre, and all the wisdom of America be collected ———To this according to the will of Heaven, let us dedicate the powers of our minds, and the future moments of our time ——— Then we may hope the great Governor of the Universe will look down with gracious approbation, while we contend for the freedom which He has taught man to love, and crown our ardent efforts with glorious success! ——— Under His propitious smiles, here may freedom reign until the last hour cuts the thread of time, and the world expires!

America Solom.

1772

BOSTON Jan. 2. The Southern Post was last Week detained four days at Seabrook ferry, whereby the Mail of last Saturday did not arrive until Tuesday: The Post set out again Yesterday and is not expected to return until the latter End of next Week.

Ther has been a Stoppage of the Hartford Post, he arrived last Evening, and set out again this Day.

BOSTON Jan. 6. We hear that his Majesty's writ of superficy as was on Tuesday last served of Joseph Greenleaf, Esq; late Justice of the Peace for the County of Plymouth, requiring him to surcease all further proceedings in that office.

BOSTON Jan. 13. Missieurs Ededs and Gill. Sir, The enclosed I received some time since, and as it is explanatory of the conduct of the author, and may be published in your next paper. I have not ask'd leave for the freedom with the writer, but hope he will excuse it. I am, sir, your humble Servant.   A. Z.

Dear Sir,
As you are desirous of having an account of the late transaction of the Governor and Council relating to me, and my conduct respecting the same, I shall gratify you by giving you a short detail, that you may be able to judge, not of their unpoliteness but their cruelty towards me. I now consider myself as a magistrate, or public person, and as such I have a right to expect to be treated: but was disappointed.

It may not be amiss to give you an account of the whole proceedings. ——— On the 15th of November last I received a polite message from the Governor and Council, by Mr. Baker, desiring my attendance at the Council Chamber, this I have no fault to find: The distress of my Family, on account of a sick child, who died that day, was such that I could not possibly attend, and I excused myself in the most polite manner I was capable of. A few days after came a citation conceiv'd in the terms following viz.

"Province of Massachusetts-Bay
To John Greenleaf of Boston, in said province, You are required to appear before the Governor and Council at the Council Chamber in Boston, on Tuesday the 10th Day of December next, at Ten of the Clock in the forenoon, than and there to be examined touching a certain Paper called the Massachusetts Spy published the 14th Day of November, 1771. Whereof you are not to fail at your Peril. Dated at Boston the 16th day of November 1771. By the order of the Governor with the Advise of Council.   Tho' Flucker Secr'y."

This proceeding alarmed me, as I judged it wholly Illegal, for I could have no idea of the legality of erecting a court of Inquisition in a free country, and could find no form for such a citation in the province law books: My duty to my country therefore forbad my paying any obedience to it, especially as it might hereafter be used as a president.

I should be very unwilling to be thought a despiser of the laws of my country. I religiously submit to them all. "not only for wrath, but for conscience sake." I have not such a mistaken notion of liberty, as to think it consists in a freedom from obligation either to the laws of nature or the laws of the land: But the freedom I now contend for, is a right of resistance, or rather withholding my obedience, when unlawfully commanded.

Had the governor and council certified to me, in a legal manner, that a complaint had been made exhibited against me for any thing done, or said by me in the capacity of a magistrate, contrary to my duty, or injurious to the subject, I should have held myself in duty bound to have obeyed these summons, to answer such impeachments. Here, I acknowledge the jurisdictions, and would with cheerfulness have obeyed; but this was not the case; the citation sent me, was, in my judgement, more suitable, to be sent to a Porter; and considering myself as a magistrate, the dignity of the office forbad me taking any notice of it: I have not been influenced by whim or caprice, my design was an act in character, and whether I have so done, you must judge.

By this time Sir, I suppose you are anxious to know the determination of the governor and council, upon my refusal to attend; you would scarce believe me, should I attempt to satisfy you in my own language; I shall therefore give it to you from the minutes of council.

"At a Council held at the Council Chamber in Boston, Tuesday December 10, 1771. His Excellency having acquainted the Board at their last Meeting, that Joseph Greenleaf, Esq; a Justice of the Peace for the county of Plymouth, was generally reputed to be concerned with Isaiah Thomas, in printing and publishing a News-Paper, called the Massachusetts Spy, and the said Joseph Greenleaf having thereupon been summoned touching the same, and not attending according to summons, it was thereupon Unanimously advised, that the said Joseph Greenleaf be dismissed from the Office of a Justice of the peace, which advice was approved of, and consented in, by his Excellency; and the said Joseph Greenleaf is dismissed from the said Office accordingly. A tru Copy from the Minutes of Council.
   Tho. Flucker Secr'y."

When you have read and thoroughly digested this, from Dal. c. 3d. By him we learn that when a justice is dismissed from his office, it must be either "express'd by writ under the great seal, or by implication by making a new commission, and leaving out the former justices names. but until notice, or publishing the new commission, the act of former Justices are good and in Law."

I have no remarks to make here and am willing you should judge by a bare comparison, whether I have been righteously dealt with in the late proceedings. I have heard of no writ under the great seal to make void my commission, and the commission for the peace here, being different in form from those granted in England, I cannot be dismissed by implication. The commission there runs thus, "George the third, by the grace of God, &c. to A,B,C,D, &c. greeting. "Known ye that we have assigned you, jointly and severely, and every one of you our justices to keep our peace in the county of,&c." One commission answers for every justice in a county there, here every justice has a separate commission, there, upon the accession of a King, the commission is made out anew, and if Mr. Justice A is omitted in the new commission, and Mr. Justice B inserted in his place, which may be done for certain reasons, and after legal notice thereof, Mr. Justice A has no further jurisdiction, yet this cannot take place till after a fair hearing and a legal conviction for a real crime.

The reason why a Justice may not be set aside, but for male administration, is founded in common justice; it should also be remembered that a Justice doth not hold his commission durante bone placite, nor quam diu se bone gesserit, and therefore, in justice, cannot be deprived of it, unless he makes a misuse of it: But if a Justice of the Peace may be dismissed from his office, because he refuses to be examined about a common News-Paper, by any Court, by one legally empowered to summon and examine him, if he may be dismissed, because he is "supposed by people in general" to be concerned with a Printer, or any other person, that the governor has conceived a dislike to, we are in a pitiable case. This is holding a commission durante ma ─────────,upon such terms no honest man would care to accept of one; besides what would be the consequence of such deprivation to the public? I have given you this hasty account of the matter for you to present perusal, I may give you hereafter some more digested remarks.

This affair, as it concerns myself, gives me no uneasiness, for by leaving the County where I had jurisdiction, I voluntarily relinguished it, yet according to Dalton I still have jurisdiction when I please to take my seat on the bench at the Court Sessions in the County of Plymouth.

I am, Sir, your most humble Servant,
                    Joseph Greenleaf.
   P. S. A secret had leaked out, it is said, it was my duty as a Magistrate to have prevented the publication of the Piece signed Mucius Scaevola! But I have no such connection with Mr. Thomas or any other Printer, as gives me a right to restrain him or them in any pubilcations, though, I must confess, that if I had power to restrain the Press, I should have no inclination to hinder Mucius, iven Chomus; or Impavidus, from laying their sentiments before the public.
   BOSTON Jan. 28. On Friday Evening the 18th Instant an assembly was first opened at Cocert-Hall for the Winter Session. It is said a large Number of the principal Gentlemen of the Town who have been at very different Sentiments in the late party disputes are Subscribers, and that the Assembly was proposed, in order to restore Peace, Harmony and the Blessing of social Life.
   BOSTON Feb. 3. To the Free Electors of the Massachusetts-Bay, Friends and Brethren in our common Cause.
   The strongest apprehension that our present Representatives will not be allowed any further opportunity to act in public induces me to be thus early in the Address to you with respect to a future Election.
   As the character of the British Ministry, and the conduct of him, who the King has appointed our commander in chief, fully evince with what property I, last year, recommended you the choice of Veterans in the cause of Liberty; so the frequent prorogations of our General Assembly demonstrates with what judiciousness you gave your votes, at that time.
   The generosity of our right to act in the Election of the Representative Body gives an easy opportunity to the British Ministry of knowing the general sentiments of this people. For instance ——— The uniformity of our conduct in chusing men honorably conspicuous for not recinding, but rather confirming a Vote of Rights uncontrouble by the British Parliament, to a

full declaration of our intentions to maintain such rights. And this seems at length to be as well comprehended at St. Jame's as at the Province-House. I am very solicitous to have this channel of communicating our sentiments to the British ministry enlarged; and think the practice of Instructing our Representatives, is observed in every town, would effectually answer that purpose. I must instance again —— if the future Members should be instructed either to protest strongly against, or uttering to refuse allegiance to a Governor paid otherways than by their own free act, it would cut off all pretence that that is the sentiment of only a few gloomy politicians. I first declare such an instrument to be my dealing which, after the most mature considerations of every thing which has been published by the friends of the Chair, in its present independence upon us for its support; and that I recommend to you to carry that into effect. Not too vain, however of my own judgement, I with earnest sincerity advise you to use the discretest precaution. You will find some few in every town who do not express honor at the present change in the system of government Converse with such; and beg them, as in alms, that they would favor you with Reasons of their patient acquiescence. If you gain them, or if you have any previous questions for the more full satisfaction of your own minds, send the whole to some press. I think I may promise you free access to every one in Boston; and I know I may promise you a friend who, at present imagines himself able to give you the most satisfactory answer.

We have many fine patriotic writers, But, as there are various modes of reasoning upon the same point, perhaps one little versed in law or history may have a consciousness in his manner, different from theirs, and better suited in general capacity. This consideration, and that of its being the duty of every individual to contribute in a public cause, I plead as apology for what follows.

All mankind are equally free by nature, but, upon stanch, all society will find their natural freedom lessened; some by brutal force, others by voluntary compact. I count myself among the latter; for though I dislike the compact of our ancestors yet while I consent to remain in this territory, I am bound by it. I dislike it, because I find the governor of this province is to be nominated by another voice than that of this people, whom he is to govern, and who cannot remove him by the quiet method of a vote, tho' he should prove a diabolical tyrant. I dislike it also, because therein the King of Great-Britain has such a negative upon our legislation, that posterity have not a certainty of recovering, in the quiet method of a new act, any thing lost by some unguarded one of their fore-fathers. Now I beg to know what our compact leaves us to boast of, except that, the governor's interest being involved in our own, we can make him retain a fellow-feeling for us. Change the situation of his interest and what claim have we upon his feeling? Let his nomination and revenue come from the Popery and the Pope's instructions will doubtless be his sole rule of conduct!!!

With this train of thought, and the most natural servant whishes for your happiness, I leave you for the present. An Elector, 1772.

P. S. Having called myself a subject of voluntary compact, I shall hereafter show wherein I think my self also in common with you unvoluntary subjects of brutal force.

BOSTON Feb. 4. Messieurs Edes & Gill. If you think the following worthy a Place in your valuable Paper, you may possibly oblige some Persons, who at all time have a claim to Compassion, I mean the sick; and certainly your constant reader, and most humble Servant, Humanus.

Another considerable quantity of Snow falling, enough to give us the prospect of sledding and also playing (as it is called) again; bring to mind a scene I witness to about three weeks past; which I would recommend to the serious consideration of all lovers of slay-frolicks. I was called to watch with a sick friend, who lived in one of the main streets of the town, his disorder, which was a fever, had affected his brain. I soon found it to be sleigh-bells and persons hurraing, hallowing, bellowing, screaming, lashes of horses, &c. all which together made a most horrid discord. When I first found what the noise proceeded from, I was aware that it might affect my friend; and accordingly with two other persons, who watched with me, went to his bed side: We soon found that our precaution was well taken, for as the noise drew nearer to the house his wildness increased, and when it was opposite to it, he was in agony; insomuch, that it was with difficulty, that three persons kept him in his bed.

This was a case three times that night. My friend did not enjoy one moment's interval of reason after that time, and died the next day!

Since the above instance, the ingenuity of some of those noctural slay-frolickers, have added the drum and conc-shell or pope-horn, to their own natural, noisy abilities; which I dare say this auditors think enough in all conscience without addition.

BOSTON Feb. 7. Messieurs Fleets, Please insert the following Paragraph in your next Monday's Paper.

There are many Prisoners for debt in the Goal of this County, who have experienced a long and tedious Confinement, their affairs being so situated as to deprive them of any relief from the present Act of insolvency, and others who have Advantage, after delivering their whole Effects to one single Creditor, are left to the mercy of every other, and may, if induced by an uncharitable Deposition (which too often imbibes in Mankind) be confined from time to time without the least Allowances for their Subsistence and Families distress'd to the greatest degree, and thereby forever disenable from sirmounting their Misfortune. It is therefore hoped from the known humanity of the Legislative Body of this Province, that they will at the next General meeting take these unhappy distress'd People's situation into their Consideration and afford them the necessary relief.

BOSTON Feb. 24. To the free Electors of the Massachusetts-bay. Friends and Brethren in common cause.

The manner in which the Printer of the Massachusetts Spy, and Joseph Greenleaf, Esq; reported to be concerned with him in Business, has been treated, should not tend to discourage you or me from endeavouring to bring about a strict and proper scrutiny into the Question whether we have at present any true constitutinal Governor. I do not find that the Famous piece signed Mucius SCaevola, has given offence as denying the Jurisdiction of him, who now claims the Chair, but as tending to excite improper Modes of Redress. I believe you are blind to such a Tendency; I profess myself to be. Nor can I attribute that Blindness entirely to the want of consular Spectacles, while the State of the Province so manifestly contradicts the scare-crow Consequence which were prophesied upon that innocent Publication. Mucius, unlike me, would not put off the important Enquiry to a distant Day, but apply'd to a constitutinal Power actually in Being. His Application was as regular as mine is; and, if our Opinion of the eventual Efficacy had not been different, we should doubtless have both fought Redress in the same Channel. But, instead of looking up to his Majesty's Council, I address the Free Electors of the Massachusetts-Bay. Upon Prudence and Resolution, My Friends and Brethren, place my whole Dependence. I hope again, once more at least, to see your Veterans embodied. and more formidable than ever from the Armour of your Instructions.   An Elector, 1772.

BOSTON 24. The paper in the Massachusetts Spy of the 14th of November last, signed Mucius Scaevola, was laid before the last Grand Jury, and we hear a bill was prepared by the King's Attorney agreeable to an order of the Governor and Council. But the good Men of the County returned Ignoramus thereon, not being able to find upon their Oath that it was false, &c.

Query, Whether this is a Proof that seven-eights of the people of the Province detest the writings of our "pretended Patriots," as we have lately been told in the Massachusetts Gazette.

BOSTON March 2. An ancient register, which

may be depended on gives the following very mortifying instance of the brevity of human life. of one hundred persons who were born at the same time.

At the end of 6 years there remained only 64,
At the end of 16 years there remained only 46,
At the end of 26 years there remained only 26,
At the end of 36 years there remained omly 16,
At the end of 46 years there remained only 10,
At the end of 56 years there remained only 6,
At the end of 66 years there remained only 3,
At the end of 76 years there remained only 1.

BOSTON March 5. It is said, a certain pompositous Gentleman of the Robes, upon hearing a supported part of a contents of the paper delivered by the Grand Jury to the Court, that expressed their great grief of surprize that Richardson should lie so long in goal at the expence of this county and the delay of justice, said more like an honest Teague than a Lawyer, "If I was the judges, I'd send them all to goal! Strange and new doctrine this, even from a friend to government, that a Grand Jury of inquest for the county ought to be sent to goal, for scrupulously adhering to their oath, whose virtue and fortitude rises Superior to distinction of persons. ——— Does he find any such rigid doctrines registered, even in the goodly Star Chamber codes; however such an intrepid partizan and doubtless merits some notice to the gods.

BOSTON March 9. By the governor a proclamation for Public Fast. From a Sense of our indispensable Duty to seek from the Blessing of Heaven upon all our Affairs:

I have thought fit to appoint, and I do, with the Advice of His Majesty's Council, appoint Thursday the Second of April next, to be a Day of Fasting and Prayer throughout the Province, recommending to Ministers and People of the several Denominations of Christians in their respective Assemblies, Religiously to observe the same, by offering up fervent Prayers and Supplications to Almighty God, mercifully to forgive our Sins; and notwithstanding our past Ingratitudes, to continue to give us those distinguishing Favours which of his unmerited Bounty we enjoy; and to bestow upon us those further Mercies, spriritual and temperal, which are most fit and proper for us: ―――― Particularly, that it may please him long to preserve the Life and Health of our Sovereign Lord the King ―――― to bless and prosper the several Branches of his Illustious Family ―――― to direct and succeed His Majesty's Council for the promoting the Welfare and Prosperity of his Subjects throughout all Parts of his Dominions ―――― to afford the divine Conduct and Blessing to the Administration of Government in this Province ―――― to continue our Health ―――― to prosper our Husbandry, Merchandizing and Fishery ―――― to grant the Holy Religion which we profess may have a powerful Influence upon the Tempers and Dispositions of Men of every Degree and Order among us, and that the Kingdom of our blessed Saviour maybe enlarged and spread through the World.

And all servile Labour and Recreation are forbidden on the said Day.

Given at the Council Chamber, in Boston the fourth Day of March, 1772, in the twelfth Year of the Reign of the Sovereign Lord George the Third by the Grace of God, of Great-Britain, France and Ireland, King, Defender of the Faith &c. T. Hutchinson.

By his Excellency's Command,
Tho's Flecker Secr'y.

BOSTON March 9. Last Monday the Man, who was committed to goal some time ago, on suspicion & Crime of Beastiality, was tried at his Majesty's Superior Court, now sitting here, and found Guilty of the Attempt.

The same Day one William Stoody was also tried and found guilty of breaking open the Store of Mr. John Short, (which he accomplished by means of false Keys) and stealing sundry goods.

BOSTON March 16. On Tuesday last, in the afternoon, his Majesty's Suprior Court finished business.

John Sennet, for attempting sodomy with a Mare, was sentenced to set on the gallows an Hour with a halter round his neck. and whipped thirty stripes under it.

Elizabeth Smith for a second conviction of theft, was sentenced to sit on the gallows one hour with a halter round her neck and to be whipped twenty stripes under it, and she being unable to pay the value of the goods stolen, will be sold for a term of years.

William Stoody for house breaking and theft, to be branded on the forehead with the letter B, and pay cost &c.

BOSTON March 16. The infamous murderer Ebenezer Richardson was on Tuesday last dismissed by his Majesty's Justices of the Superior Court, from his confinement in goal, for the murder of that innocent youth Snider recognizing without sureties in the sum of five hundred pounds, for his appearance when the court shall call upon him to plead his Majesty's pardon!! O tempora! O mares! May he not adapt the language of Cain and say, whoever meeteth me will slay me! This affair was transacted in presence of a very few people all the inhabitants being assembled at Faneuil-Hall, it being their annual Town meeting. The Murderer fled with precipitation and crossed the ferry before the inhabitants were informed of it. Tell this in Britain, publish it in Ireland, and may America remember it for ever.

BOSTON March 19. Last Friday morning early, was found in a rope-yard, expiring, one Matthew Haines, a sea-faring man, who lately came from New-York. It fully appears to the jury of Inquest who sat on the body, that he was frequently in liquor, and the preceding day was much intoxicated therewith; and they as also the Doctor who was called, apprehended that he got into the rope-yard, and lying on the ground, and it being exceeding cold, and he in liquor, by that means came to his death.

BOSTON April 6. We hear Sir Francis Bernard, Bart. was lately taken with a light paralytick Disorder at Lincoln in England, and by advice of his Physician was gone to Bath to drink the Waters, and that if he did not recover his health, intended with his Lady to go to Italy on the South of France in the Summer.

BOSTON April 6. Last Wednesday in the forenoon, a Female Infant was found in a Well near Archmuty's-Lane: Upon a Jury of Inquest being summoned, it was found to have a blow on the head, and the Throat cut from ear to ear even to the Back Neck Bone; Who the cruel Murderer was is not yet discovered, The Child was supposed to have been in the Well some Time, and it was killed soon after birth.

BOSTON April 9. Yesterday the Great and General Court met at Cambridge, and we hear they will be adjourned to Boston.

It is said by some, that the Parliament of Great-Britain will do nothing at present for America for the repeal of the Tea Act.

BOSTON April 13. Extract of a Letter from London, Jan. 18. 1772.

"I was in hopes I should have had the pleasure of communicating something that might be agreeable to you. But the conduct, particularly of the Court Commissioners at Boston, had baffled the exertion of the few friends you have left here. I believe, never a country, since the world began, so injured by its own children. I will only tell you, that the representations, and reconsiderations of your Town-Born Child has done more real hurt to New-England, than you can easily imagine. This may depend upon as sacred truth."

We are told in the Drapers's Paper, that Sir Francis Bernard, Bart. was lately taken a Light paralytic disorder, but, light as it was, one related to him writes, "that it had incapacitated him for business of any kind." The account from others is, that it was not likely he would recover his former state of health. 'Tis supposed this shock took rise from a mind overwhelmed with anxious, desponding, tormenting ideas in reflecting on his folly in having lost the first seat of government in the Massachusetts province, by being a faithful, however abandoned, tool of these, who, having no more use to make of him, have left him to shift for himself as well as he can. A speaking instance to ministerial tools and dependents; it is a striking specimen of what may be expected will be the fate of those, who can bring themselves to act without honor, reason, or conscience; that they may recommend themselves to tyrants, who when they have no further ends to serve them, will lay them aside as no longer worthy of their notice, whatever contempt they may meet with from others. Dependence upon state ministers is attended with so much uncertainty, that 'tis strange a man of ordinary understanding should venture his reputation, his character, or so much of the gratification of his Ambition or avarice upon so precarious a bottom.

BOSTON April 16. The friends and intimates of Thomas Hutchinson have been pleased to declare in private conversation, that there are a few writers and enemies to the present Administration, and a superior part of the province join in sentiments with his Excellency: If this has afforded any consolation to his Excellency and encouraged his "transmitting in a regular manner, all applications" to his ministerial master, he may alter his opinion as soon as he pleases, and rest assured, that every sincere lover of his country despises his sentiments and actions, which are contemplated in the eyes of all honest men.

We hear from Cambridge that the Hon. House of Representatives having made an alteration in the Superior Court's time of sitting, voted that this act should be published in all the Boston news-papers, which was sent to the upper House for their assent, but was returned non-concured with this amendment, that it be Published in Draper's and all the Monday's news-papers, [by which the "dirty Spy" would be excluded] upon this the house unanimously agreed to adhere to the former vote.

It is the nature of these, under the influence of instructions from an abandoned minister, to be greedy of the opportunity to shew their malice against the Liberty of the Free Press; but be it known, "Undaunted by Tyrants we'll Die or be Free."

BOSTON April 23. Whereas for several days past, during my absence from town, there has been propagated many false, malicious and wicked

stories of me, and having with unrelenting cruelty bore hard upon, threatened, and otherways ill-treated Capt. Lewis Turner, whose late unhappy death it seems is laid to my charge.
——— It is therefore incumbent upon me, in order to remove this strange and unaccountable prejudice that now prevails, to lay a state of my dealings with him, and treatment of him before the public. I have had a very long uninterrupted friendly intimacy with him, ——— and as a physician attended him and his family upward of 24 years. ——— In December of 1758 I furnished him with my first account to the amount of 53 pounds, 6 shillings and 8d. which had been then standing upwards of ten years; for which he gave his note, payable at a short period, with interest 'till paid. Since which for 13 years attendance of his family he stands indebted upon my books 42 pounds 14 shillings 6d. having never received of him a single shilling in part of either note or account, although I have paid him severeral large sums for the purchase of real estate, of which he owed a part, which came by his wife, without stopping even what had been so long due. ——— Having for a year past retired from business into the country, when I came into town from time to time, I naturally applyed to such as were in debt, and among others, to my old friend Turner in my usual friendly manner, but having put me off many times with a laugh, ——— I shall pay you one of these days, some time last fall I left the aforesaid note with an attorney, who upon writing a letter to Capt. Turner he waited on him, and made him acquainted with his absolute incapacity, and low-circumstances, which being communicated to me by my attorney, I took no further notice of it, nor was he sued or threatened to be sued; ——— but as sometimes I Casually met him on the street, I might, as I believe I did ask him in my usual friendly manner if he could not do something towards the notes; he always answered me in the negative: His gratitude induced him it seems to express his uneasiness and inability to his brother-in-law Mr. Inches, who about three weeks ago,

communicated to me, and wondered I should press the poor & withal telling me he owed two persons, who pressed him very hard for their money, but the poor man had nothing to pay only wild lands of little value: To which I replied, I would take 10 shillings in the pound. —— The last time I saw Mr. Turner was in the street towards New-Boston, and taking him by the hand we talked upon many mixt matters; he discovered an uneasiness of mind to me, but wished I would see Mr. Dublois, I told him I would, but went out of town that day and could not. In short I was very easy respecting my debt when I knew his circumstances; yet I tho't it was but reasonable, as my debt was of long standing, I should share some of the part with the other creditors; but never after had thought of suing or any other way distressing him; and have no reason to believe by his behaviour to me, as I never to my knowledge uttered to him an unfriendly expression. Therefore I rest satisfied every canded person will, from this representation, believe that I have rather acted, not only a patient and friendly, but kind sympathizing part; and do most sincerely, commiserate his numerous unhappy, distressed children, and the loss of their only parent. April 22, 1772.

J. Sprague.

BOSTON May 7. We hear that the duties on Tea, paid into the revenue chest have arisen solely for the Colony of Massachusetts-Bay. A great sign that all the Colonies are presently acquiescent in the acts of trade, except the factious Bostonians!

It is said that the several ships which from time to time have sneaked out of this harbour, are gone to cruize on the southern governments, to prevent their trading, like freemen with people against whom the laws of their country have not prohibited there commerce.

Last Friday morning a new born male baby was found in a pond at Lynn, with several stones tied round his body; we hear the jury of Inquest agreed that it was willfully murdered by one Sarah Goldtwalt, the mother of the infant, who wa thereupon committed to Essex goal.

Another newborn was taken up last Saturday floating in the Charles-River, supposed to have been lately thrown in there by it unnatural mother.

BOSTON May 14. Mr. Thomas, It is reported that many people in town are greatly disturbed, at the unnatural behaviours of a certain young gentleman of high Tory family, towards his wife: A most amiable and well educated young lady, the eldest daughter of a worthy and patriotic gentleman of this town, whose family the young gentleman has lately I hear prohibited his wife from visiting; which brutish act, I am credibly informed had had such an effect upon her delicate mind, that has occasioned her with floods of tears to express herself as being equally the unhappiest of all women, whether she does or does not visit he most tender parents.

BOSTON May 11. On Wednesday last the freeholders and other inhabitants of this Town met at Faneuil-Hall, for the choice of Representatives. ——— The number of Votes was 723. Hon. Thomas Cushing, Esq; had 699 Votes. Hon. John Hancock, Esq; 699. Mr. Samuel Adams, 505. William Philips Esq; 668. Mr. Henderson Inches 197. Whereupon the first four Gentleman were declared elected.

"We are told there is a great exultation among the Tories for the shake they pretend to have given Mr. Adam's Interest in the last Election; But whoever will go over the matter attentively will easily perceive that inordinate thirsts for triumph alone could inspire such a behaviour. For may years past Mr. Adams has been losing ground in the affection of a certain set of people, and at length has become so intolerably odious to them that at all adventures they resolved to attack this year, concluding that should he retain his seat in the general court he might urge some enquiries, that most passionately whishes to be passed in silence; and all the essays which have hitherto been made to answer them, have only served to injure the cause they were intended to support. To accomplish this important enterprize, they set up against him a gentleman not unpopular, nor gennerally supported unfriendly to the constitution of this country.

The opposition to Mr. Adams was supported by the whole power of the court, even to the lowest clerk and waiters in the Custom-House, who took off so many votes as to leave him about the number he used to have when none was Attempted. Hence instead of his friends receiving any mortification, they have reason to felicitate themselves on the appearance of such a laudable majority in his favour, when so well concerned and warmly pressed a measure was conducted against him with little success.

BOSTON May 18. Last Wednesday John Sennet, for Beaststality, and Beth Smith, for the second time of Thieving, were set upon the Gallows, and received the Discipline of whipping, they were severely pelted by the Populace.

Among the Crowd a Fellow was discovered with a number of Handkerchiefs, offering them to sale under the Gallows, which were suspected to be stolen; he was taken up and proved to be one John Bryan, but called himself John Baker: he had received the Complement of the Post but a few Days before for making to free with anothers Property, was discharged from the Goal on Tuesday last. He pretended when taken, to be fainting, whereupon he was put upon a Board and brought along the Streets, on Men's shoulders, and committed again.

Same day a Negro Fellow of Mr. Hugh Tarbet's fell into a Kettle of boiling hot Tar which soon put an End to his Life ——— his body became so offensive that they were obliged immediately to bury him.

BOSTON May 25. At the meeting of the freeholders and other inhabitants of Boston, Hon. John Hancock, Esq; presented the town with a new and finely constructed engine for the extinguishing of fires, which was expected as a fresh mark of his regard to its safety and welfare, and the thanks of the town were unanimously returned him.

BOSTON May 25. A very fine Female Negro Child of good Breed, very handsom and healthy, Three months old, to be given away, or put with consideration to a good place. Enquire Thomas

Oliver, Esq; of Cambridge.

BOSTON June 15. We have advice from Rhode-Island, that on Tuesday last, as his Majesty's armed schooner Gaspee, commanded by Lieutenant Duddingston, with about 16 or 17 men, was going up to Providence River, she ran ashore at high water at a place about seven miles below the town; and that about two o'clock the next morning a number of men, (some of the depositions of the schooners people say only about fifty, others, perhaps more frightened than the rest, makes them 150) came along side her in five or six boats; upon the first notice whereof the commander instantly got out of bed and came upon deck with his pistol and sword, and fired the pistol at the boats, which was returned by the discharge of another from them, when the ball went through his wrist, as his hand was hanging down by his side, and lodged into his groin; the people in the boats immediately took possession of the vessel, without any further damage, (except a slight wound which one of the sailors received by a stick) and bound and held the crew, and after dressing the Captains wounds as well as they could, put them all on shore, they then set fire to the schooner, which, with all her stores, &c. were entirely consumed.

We are told that the Captain of the schooner, after he was wounded and secured, desired that his money and papers might be delivered him, the former was complied with, but the latter, with every thing else he had on board, were destroyed: ——— It is said he is in a fair way of recovery.

The Governor of Rhode-Island has issued a proclamation, offering a reward of one hundred pounds sterling, for the discovery of the persons concerned in this affair.

BOSTON June 15. At the Council held at the Council Chamber Cambridge June 13th 1772.

His Excellency acquaints the Board that he was restrained from removing the General Court to Boston whilst the Assembly continued to dispute the authority by which was directed to cause it to be held in any place except Boston: And laid before them the signification of his Majesty's principle Secretaries of State, together with his Speech to the Houses, and the several messages which had passed between him and them the present session, and required the advice and opinion of the Council upon their oath, as councellors, whether consistent with this signification of his Majesty's pleasure to him he may now remove the Court to Boston: The Council thereupon gave their opinion and advised unanimously, in the affirmative.

A true Copy. Attest.   Tho. Flucker, Secr.
His Excellency then directed the Secretary to acquaint both Houses respectively, that it was his pleasure the Great and General Court be adjourned to Tuesday next, then to meet at the Court House in Boston, which was done accordingly.

BOSTON June 20. The Provisions made for the supports of the Governor of the province is fifteen hundred pounds sterling, to be paid annually out of the American revenue. This is one of the regulations produced by the power assumed by the British Parliament to Tax the Americans, which Bernard told us "would appear disagreeable only from their novelty:" But if it be admitted by the two Houses of Assembly, or even passed over in silence by either of them, it will inevitably prove the destruction of our civil constitution. ——— It is an intolarable grievance for another state, because she imagines herself to be the most powerful, to take our money on any pretence whatsoever, without our leave; but to apply it for the purpose of setting up an absolute tyranny over us, must excite the highest indignation in the breast of a people, who we hope in God, will never consent to be enslaved. We have reason to expect that the Justice of the Superior Court will be rendered thus independent of the people, and it may be added, thus independent upon British Administration, and subject to their direction and controul. ——— "The general settlement of the American province," as Bernard expressed it, is hastening faster than ever to a complexion; and into what a state of infamy and misery, the colonies will then be brought, may easily be seen by the eye of a common observer. The Arch-Traitor recommended "a respectful submission," but this is neither our interest nor our Duty. If ever a manly rational, steady and persevering opposition was necessary, now is the time. The Governor of New-York in the matter of an independent support has been open and unrelieved with the Assembly there, without the necessity of being repeatedly solicited to come to an explanation; but we cannot help pitying our brethren and fellow-subjects in that Province, if their Representatives are unattentive to this attack. A ruler independent of the people both for his being and support, is a monster in any free Government. A power without a check is tyranny every where.

BOSTON June 25. From the New-Hampshire Gazette, to the printer of the Massachusetts Spy.

Being at Boston on the King's birthday, I observed with great pleasure the improvements made in the military art, by the militia of that city; The troop of guards, the train of artillery, grenadiers, and regiment, all made a shinning figure; and did honour not only to Boston and the Massachusetts-Bay, but to North-America ——— As the military art is so essentially necessary to the security and happiness of this country, I cannot but lament that a matter of vast importance, is so little attendedto in this and many provinces. Gentlemen of fortune and influence cannot do a more important service to their country, than by promoting the military art. If this is neglected we shall be exposed to every invader; but if our men are properly disciplined and equipped, we may bid defiance to all nations on the earth, and maintain our standard against the united kingdoms of Europe.

BOSTON July 6. It's reported, that a few Days ago at Rhode-Island, two Tide-Waiters belonging to his Majesty's Customs, being put on board a Vessel just arrived in the Night, some Persons unknowed striped the Waiters, then rubbed their

Bodies over with Oil and Tar and Lampblack, and carried them on board an empty vessel that lay nigh the other, put them in the Hold under lock, and left them until Morning.

BOSTON July 6. The Stage-Coach between New-York and Boston, Which for the first time set out this Day from Mr. Fowler's Tavern, (formerly kept by Mr. Stout) at Fresh Water, in New-York, will continue to go course between Boston and New-York, so as to be at each of those Places once a fortnight, coming in on Saturday Evening and setting out to return, by way of Hartford, on Monday Morning.

The Price to Passengers, will be 4d. New-York or 3d. lawful per mile, and baggage at a reasonable rate. Gentlemen and Ladies who chose to encourage this useful new, and expensive undertaking, may depend upon good Usage, and that the Coach will always put up at Houses on the road where the best Entertainment is provided.

The Stage Coach next Trip arrive at New-York and Boston, on Saturday the 11th of July, and will set out from thence to Hartford on Monday the 13th meeting at Hartford on Wednesday the 15th, where, after staying a week, they will set out again on Wednesday the 23d for New-York and Boston where they will arrive on Saturday the 25th and set out to return the 27th &c.

If on Trial the Subscribers find Encouragement, they will perform the Stage once a Week, only altering the Day setting out from New-York and Boston to Thursday instead of Monday Morning.   Jonathan and Nicholas Brown.

BOSTON July 13. Two English Seamen arrived last week in a vessel at Nantucket from Havanna, where we learn they had been imprisoned 6 or 7 years; one of them came to Town this week, and informs, That he was taken on the Spanish main, and carried Prisoner to Havanna for being concerned in illicit Trade, (as it is phrased by those who do not choose to resent the Behaviour of the Dons) During which imprisonment he suffered many Hardships and at length growing old and infirm was released. He says, there were 46 stout able-bodied English Seamen imprisoned at the Havanna when he left.

BOSTON July 13. Tuesday last in the forenoon His Excellency's Company of Cadets, in their Uniforms commanded by Col. Hancock, paraded in King-Street, and marched to the Common, where they went through the various Military Exercises and Evolutions, to the pleasure and Satisfaction of a great Number of Spectators; they afterwards marched thro' the main Street to their Parade, where they made exceeding regular Fires. A Elegant entertainment was given to the Company at Bunch of Grapes Tavern by their Colonel.

In the afternoon the Company of the Train of Artillery, the Company of Grenadiers in their uniforms, and the Company of Militia, belonging to the Boston Regiment, under the Command of Col. Erving, mustered on the Common for military Exercises, which they performed in separate Companies in a Manner superior to any heretofore done.

Towards the close of the Afternoon Major Paddock's Company of the Train, after going through many Evolutions, performed something that was new to most People here, viz. a mock Fight, with their Field-Pieces and Small Arms. The range of ground was extensive, and the Company in Divisions having to march round Hills, in Valleys, &c. engaged the attention of a vast Concourse of People, who were greatly diverted by the marching, Firing, and various Modes of Attack; but as we are not sufficiently acquainted with the Phrases of Military Performances, must be saying anything further than that those who are esteemed good Judges, gave their Opinion that the whole was conducted in a regular martial Manner.

BOSTON July 14. Yesterday the Governor sent the following Message to the House, viz.

"Gentlemen of the house of Representatives, I think it incumbent on me to put you in a mind of the ruinous state of the province house, I imagine it must cost double the sum to repair it the next year as will be sufficient at Present, and it is most probable that I shall not be able to keep my family there another winter.

It would be more agreeable to my inclination

to reside wholly at my house in the country, and it is for the convenience of the inhabitants of the Town of Boston, and other persons who occasionally come there and have public business to transact, that I spend so much of my time in Boston. When the house provided for the Governor is not in a tenantable repair, I think there can be no exception if I change the place of my residence."

To which the house this day returned the following Answer. viz. "May it please your Excellency, In Answer to your message of yesterday, this house beg leave to observe, That they are not unapprized that the province house is out of repair, and that expence might be saved, by making such repairs as are necessary as soon as may be. But that building was procured for the residence of a Governor, whose whole support was to be provided for by the grants and acts of the General Assembly. according to the tenor of the charter: And it is the opinion of the House, that it was never expected by any Assembly of this province, that it would be appropriated for the residence of any Governor for whose support adequate provisions should be made another way. Upon this consideration we cannot think it our duty to make any repairs at this time.

Your Excellency may be assured that this House is far from being influenced by any personal disrespect: Should the time come which we hope for, when your Excellency shall think yourself at Liberty to accept of your whole support from this government, according to ancient and invariable usage, we doubt not but you will find the Representation of this People ready to provide for your Excellency, a house not barely accountable, but elegant. In the mean time, as your Excellency receives from his Majesty, a certain and adequate support, we cannot have the least apprehension, that you will make any town in your province the place of your residence, but where it will be most conductive to his Majesty's service and the good and welfare of the people.

BOSTON July 27. Last Saturday Capt. Smith

arrived here in a large Schooner from Halifax, having on board two Companies of the 64th Regiment which, with their Baggage, were immedeately landed at Castle William —— The Remainder of them are shortly expected.

Since our last the 14th Regiment, which was quartered at the Castle soon after the Massacre in King Street on the Evening of the 5th of March 1770, embarked on board the Transports lately arrived from New-York, and are daily expected to sail, but upon what particulars Service they are destined, still remains a secret to Us who are not in the Cabinet, Junta or the Caucus.

BOSTON Aug. 3. Last Wednesday several gentlemen went out in a boat to catch Mackerel, and had sailed a little way beyond the light-house, when unluckily the boom knocked Mr. Joseph Howe a tinman over board as he was stooping to haul in his line; the sea running very high and the wind blowing fresh, by the time they could wear the boat, he was at a great distance from them, and must have been drowned had they not has a small canoe alongside and by that means saved him; he had sunk twice before they could go to his assistance and was sinking a third time when they reached him. They carried him ashore at the light-house, and by the means used he greatly recovered in five or six hours.

BOSTON Aug. 6. We hear that on Saturday evening se'nnight a seaman, struck and otherwise abused a woman at the north end, so that she died the Saturday following, it is said he had made his escape.

Query. Would it not be better for the British Ministry to employ his Majesty's ships, who are now poking into every river, creek, &c. distressing the trade of the colonies, to defend protect the subjects of Great Britain from the tyrannical grips of the Spainiards who are every day seizing some of them?

BOSTON Aug. 10. Messieurs Edes and Gill, In the account of the Salary, Perquisites of Office, Pillage, Pilfering, and Plunder of the detestable Bernard, is mentioned a Sum he received of Mr. Story, as part of the profits of his Office. —— In humble Imitation of such wicked Practice, it is reported publickly, that the governor, benevolent, and pious Mr. Hutchinson has determined upon certain Proposition of every Office of Profit, in his own Gift, or given by his Influence or Instructions, to be paid such of his disabled and idle Relations, ar are unable or unwilling to earn their own Bread. "Self Interest, when extended too, fat, become Rapine." —— Perhaps in some future Paper may be exhibited to the Public, an Account of the Salary, Perquisites, &c. of Mr. Hutchinson, singular to the Nettleham Baronet.

            Detector.

 BOSTON Aug. 12. On Monday last, Mr. William Boxley, Clerk of the St. John armed schooner, was attempting to step on board a boat at Wheelwright's wharf, being near-sighted, he unluckily fell overboard, and notwithstanding he had no speedy assistance was drowned.

 BOSTON aug. 14. Lieut. Doddington, late commander of the Gaspee armed schooner, which was lately destroyed in Providence River, and himself much wounded in the groin, was removed on the 18th ult. by Capt. Lingee from Benton's Neck on board his ship, upon account of a report among the marines, who were a shore to guard him, that the inhabitants of Newport intended to raise a mob and take him out of Mr. Benton's house and murder him; and notwithstanding Mr. Benton told them there was not the least danger and would pledge himself and all he had for Mr. Duddington's safety, yet, to keep up the farcical fear, and to bring a further odium upon Lord Hillsborough's loyal colony of Rhode-Island, they persisted in carrying him on board the Beaver.

 BOSTON Aug. 25. Last Friday Afternoon a melancholy Accident happened at Charlestown, Mr. Jabez Whittemore and wife of that Town, returning home in a Chaise from attending Lecture, and were cross-met by a man in a Sulkey, who driving very furiously overset Mr. Wittemore's Chaise, whereby Mrs. Wittemore was instantly killed, and Mr. Wittemore so greatly bruised, that we hear it is at present uncertain whether he will recover. The Fellow was committed to Charlestown Goal the same Evening.

BOSTON Aug. 27. Last Sabbath Day towards Evening a Gentlewomen, sat by a Window fronting the Street, eating Bread and Milk. ——— A bold Fellow observing her, waited for her finishing, in hopes of seizing the Porringer and Spoon, which were both Silver. He succeeded in the latter, for as she put the Spoon on the Table, (which was handy and by the Window,) he reached his hand in, while the person stooped to give the cat what was left in the Porringer, and carried it off. Had not the cat been by, and she had put the Porringer and Spoon on the Table, he would very probably have stole them both. There was no Man in the house, the Woman cry'd stop Thief, in which Chorus he loudly join'd and escaped.

BOSTON Aug. 27. For the Massachusetts Spy. Mr. Thomas, It is whispered that the judges of the Supreme Court are also become pensioners of the Ministry. I wish it may be true, for in such a case there can be no question of the design of the Court; Mr. Hutchinson himself allowing that the Executive and Judiciary powers, being freed from the constraint of known established laws, is despotism. In this case even the Lawmakers have no more check upon them than on the manderins of China.   Simon Zelotes.

BOSTON Aug. 31. Yesterday Morning a very valuable Negro Servant belonging to James Gardner, Truckman, in attempting to take up some meat which was hung down a well in order to keep it cool, was so overcome with the Vapor arising therefrom, that he fell senseless to the bottom and expired before assistance could be got to take him out again.

BOSTON Sept. 2. Saturday last a Woman buying turnips out of a cart discovered a silver watch, which the countryman being ignorant of, the town Cryer was employed to cry the same; soon after the owner appeared, and received it, generously satisfied the person that found it. It is supposed the thief was apprehensive of being detected, and conveyed it among the turnips to avoid the theift's being proved upon him.

BOSTON Sept. 10. Saturday night last the people near the Head of Griffin's Wharf were disturbed by the groaning of a person in distress, and it was some time before they discovered from whence the groans proceeded, at length it was found to be from a shop improved by Mr. Homans, Tailor, and Mr. Williams, Cordwainer, upon opening the door, they saw the feet of a man that had got down the chimney to the grate, but his body was so jamm'd that he could not move himself, a rope was let down from the top whereby he was pulled down; upon being asked what his design was, he replied that he was very hungry and intended to get into the shop for bread and cheese: He was committed to goal, and afterwards examined before a Magistrate; he said his name was John Parks, and came from Montreal, and that he fell into the chimney as he was walking by the shop. By the description it was not improbable that he is one of those that broke Salem Goal, by the name of Samuel White.

BOSTON Sept. 14. At his Majesty's Honourable Superior Court of Judicature, Court of Assize and General Goal Delivery, held at Boston in and for the County of Suffolk, of the Massachusetts Bay in New England. August Term 1772.

Be it remembered, that this same term in a case here depending, wherein James Otis of said Boston is Applicant and original plaintiff against John Robinson, late of said Boston, Esq; that said John Robinson, Esq; by James Boutineau, Esq; his father-in-Law and Attorney, comes into Court and on his behalf and in the name of the said John Robinson, Esq; who is now in Parts beyond the sea, to wit, in the Kingdom of Great-Britain, being thereunto fully empowered as by his letters of Attorney on file in the case may appear, freely confesses that in the assault committed by him the said John Robinson, Esq; on him the said James Otis, in presumptuously attempting to take him the said James Otis by the nose, was the first assault, which occasioned and brought on all the consequent insults, wounds and other injuries whereof the said James Otis in his Declaration more particularly complained: He the said John Robinson,

Esq; was greatly in fault, is very sorry for his conduct and behaviour that night towards the said James Otis, and ask the pardon of the said James Otis.
James Boutineau, Attorney of John Robinson, Esq;
   Done in court and ordered, that the paper be filed among the records of the Court.
                Att. Samuel Winthrop, Clerk.
  A True Copy as on file, Examined, S. Winthrop.
  Whereupon the said James Otis, being personally present here in court, duly reflecting that he had ever been as ready to give, as to ask on demand gentleman's like satisfaction for an insult real or supposed, at the same time being fully conscious, and, as apprehended, able abundantly to prove, that he then publicly offered that kind of satisfaction to the said first assault, as on the part of behalf of the said John Robinson, Esq; by his Attorney James Boutineau, Esq; in above confessed —— And said James Otis having ever entertained a most consummate contempt of seeking a purse or a Pecuniary reparation for personal insult, if any other more gentle-like could be obtained, by the consent of the parties, and that consistently with the laws of his country: Accept of the above submission here in court, in full for assaults, insults, injuries and damages above complained if the declaration of the said James Otis, and confessed as above. And upon the same submission, so far as the said John Robinson, Esq; was concerned in the assault, insults and injuries above-mentioned and confessed, as he thinks a gentleman and Christian ought in such a case on such submission, freely forgive the said John Robinson, Esq; and by these present remiseth, releaseth and dischargeth him the said John Robinson, Esq; from all actions, suits, and demands, by reason of, or occasioned by the premises; and also, all rights and cause of claim in the declaration specified.
  Furthermore the said James Otis knowing full the right well that by operation of law Hereupon, he also of course releseth and dischargeth the alleged and supported confederates of the said John Robinson, for all demands supports be

on the premises against any of the said alleged and supposed Confederates.

At the same time the said James Otis if his own free will and mere motion thinks fit to give it under his hand, to remain on record in favour of said John Robinson, Esq; as the said James Otis has often privately and publicly, in the hearing of his friends and others, and even in the Court of Common Pleas declared, as he now does in this honourable court, that he looks on the said John Robinson, Esq; to be infinitely less to blame in this (for both parties in the suit) very unhappy affair than those, who the said James Otis, were he inclined to give himself the trouble, thinks, and is persuaded, he could fully prove actually and most insidiously as well as maliciously incited the said John Robinson, Esq; to so very unworthy an action.

Provided the said John Robinson, Esq; by the said James Bautineau, Esq; his said attorney, the common cost of court, amounting to thirteen pounds ten shillings and eight pence, with thirty pounds cost, for the use of Samuel Fitch, John Adams, Esq; and Sampson Saltes Brower, Council retained by the said Otis, in the case, and very diligently attended the business for three years; also the doctors bills amounting to seven pounds, 12 shillings, the sum of one pond eight shillings for taking affidavits out of court, amounting to the sum of hundred and twenty pounds ten shillings and eight pence, lawful money, but not a farthing for the use of said James Otis, he having (as before observed) a most through contempt for pecuniary recompence when a better can be obtained.

James Otis.

N. B. The sum mentioned above as agreed upon, viz. one hundred and twelve pounds ten shillings and eight pence, was paid in court; ant it is ordered by the court that this paper filed in the said case among the records of the Superior Court.

Att. Samuel Winthrop, Clerk. A true copy on file, Examined, per Samuel Winthrop Clerk.

BOSTON Sept. 24. It is confidently reported in town, that Lord Hillsborough is no more

Secretary of State for the American Department, and, that the Earl of Dartmouth, is appointed in his room. This intelligence came from a Gentleman, who arrived here, on Tuesday evenimg from England, who had a letter from a friend in London, while the vessel on which he was aboard lay at Gravesend.

BOSTON Sept. 28. To Mr. Thomas Hutchison, Esq;
Sir,
We have been waiting for a redress of the grievances, which no freeman ought to endure for the moment, and which necessarily subject our lives, liberty and prosperities to the caprice of the worst and vilest of our species; and instead of receiving the least encouragement, that our humble petitions and just remonstrances have met with a favourable regard, we are alarmed with certain advice that the last hand is put to the destruction of our free constitution, in the rendering the supreme arbiters our lives and fortunes the absolute dependents of our avowed enemy. The first inflict of the human mind therefore impels us to advertize you, that unless prevented by an immediate recession from the measures which have so nearly completed our ruin, we shall look upon ourselves obliged to recur for relief to that law, which need none of the glosses and convenient accommodations of corrupt mercenaries, to prepare it for execution. The continued seizures of our properties and conversion of them to the support of our despoilers, the imposition of the edicts of the servant of a foreign state to the absolute controul of our whole legislature, and the enforcement of these by a military power, and the wrestling out of our hands the sole fortress of our province, and committing it to the custody of our murderers, the manifest partiality shew to those murderers in the trial they underwent for the bloody act, to the infamous Richardson on the one hand, and the hardly comparably Pierpoint on the other. Those examples, Sir, we esteem quite sufficient to blacken the annuals of the present century, and are at length come to a determination to be no longer passive to the ruin of one individual after another,

singled out to grace the thriumphs of despotism. But in case we must perish, to fall in company with the glorious satisfaction of involving our destroyers in the common ruin.

We request you to lay this paper before your council in preference to the trifling essay in the Spy, that they as well as yourself may know the minds of the people.

BOSTON Oct. 1. For the Massachusetts Spy, to Mr. Hutchinson.

Sir.

When any branch of the administration by their foremost manifest that they mean to establish an Interest distinct from, and opposite to that of the people, their government becomes a Tyranny, for which Charles lost his Head. You have been told over and again that you were in pursuit of such scheme; and now what was even reasonably supported being positively confined, Do you not fear the people will deal with you in a manner suitable to the merits of your general conduct, and no longer questionable Intentions? It is acknowledged that the twentieth part of what has been directed to you under different, addresses to a real constitutional father of the people might with great propriety be called seditious; it is therefore plain that your circumstances alone can warrant treatment, which your confederate Bernard, considered as an attempt to overthrow the very being of government, and this people seem frankly to acknowledge that how matters now stand, they would be far from repining at a very material charge.

It might be wise of you to consider whether this so much desired Reform and better flow spontaneously from the parties who consider tyrants as less tolerable in civil society than the most ferocious beast of prey, and themselves more highly criminal in suffering the former to ravage their country than the latter.

Clericus.

BOSTON Oct. 5. Last Friday Evening four or five young Lads at the South part of the Town, having got together about 4 lbs. of Gun-Powder, which they were making up serpents and other Fire-works, it was thro' the carelessness or

Impudence of one of them set on fire and blew up, by which means three of the Boys were much burnt, one of them in such a Manner, that his Life is tho't to be in great danger.

BOSTON Oct. 8. One Celeb Darling and Samuel Alby were indicted for attempting to set fire to a dwelling-house, confessing the Fact they were sentenced to be set on the Gallows with a Rope about their Necks for the space of an Hour. ──── That said Darling and Alby were also indicted for breaking into the same House, and stealing from thence; which Fact they likewise confessed, and were sentenced therefore to be branded upon the Forehead with the letter S, and pay Damages and Cost.

BOSTON Oct. 12. We hear from Cambridge, That on Tuesday last at the training there, the Companies of Artillery (with Field-pieces) and Militia, commanded by Captain Gardner and Lieut. Tacker performed a mock Battle under inspection of the Honorable Major-General Brattle, The Companies divided, one detachment went off some Distance and entrenched themselves: upon which the remainder marched to besiege them: An Engagement then began, and was carried on in a very regular Manner by Marching, Counter-marching, Retreating, Ambushing, and Attacking, with Cannon and Small Arms, until the Assailants took the Entrenchment and setting fire to the works blew it up. The performance was well-pleasing to a great Number of Spectators.

At the above training a young Man, named Richardson, belonging to the Artillery Company, having a Number of Cartriges, &c. in his pocket, they by some means took fire, which hurt him in so terrible a Manner that his Life is despaired of.

BOSTON Oct. 19. Upon Application made to me by three of the Proprietors of Boston Pier or Long Wharf in Boston, to call a Meeting of the Proprietors of the said Pier. The said Proprietors are accordingly hereby notified to meet at the British Coffee-House in Kingstreet on Tuesday the 3d Day of November next at 10 o'Clock A. M. then and there to choose a Moderator; to consider and determine on enforcing the Payment of several Assessments for defraying the Expences incurred for building a new Head and for the repair of the Wharf; also to make any other assessment for the same purpose if they shall think proper; to agree upon a Method for securing those who shall advance Money therefor; and generally to transact any business relating to the Interest of the Proprietors which may properly come before the said Meeting.

Job Price, Proprietors Clerk. 15 Oct. 1772.

BOSTON Oct. 29. A commission of Oyer and Terminator this day passed the great seal, authorizing and empowering the Governors of New-York and Connecticut, and others named therein, to try any person or persons That may be taken in consequence of the proclamation issued apprehending any that were concerned in plundering and burning the Gaspee schooner.

BOSTON NOv. 2. To the people of America.

He that hath an Heart to obey the Calls of duty and Honour, let him now obey. ———

My Countrymen, years ago I assured you from good authority, that the British Parliament was determined to subject you to her taxation and controul; and, that your petitions for redress of grievances, would all prove ineffectual, as your subjection and slavery was the fixed plan ——— The event, has confirmed the truth of my assertion. Your slavery, my brethren, is sealed in the British counsels; despotism is systematically pursued, one link after another is added to the chain, by bribing and pensioning men of office; and tyranny, like time of death, is creeping on unperceiv'd, [by too many].

We are every day robbed by state plundering, court of admiralty, commissioners, custom house collectors &c. in the most flagrant violation of our liberty, and the right of mankind ——— Would we suffer ourselves thus to be robbed by the people of France, or Spain? Why then do we suffer robbery from the people of Britain? The former have as just a claim to our interest as the latter, and why robbers from one nation should have more indulgence than from another, no man can conceive?

So long my countrymen, as the people of Britain

claim a right to take any of our interest from us without concent, or to interfere in our government, we cannot be safe —— and as they do claim and insist on exercising a power of taking our money, and interfering in our government. We must Now strike a home blow or sit down under the yoke of Tyranny.

The people in every town must immediately instruck their Representatives, to send a remonstrate to the King of Great-Britain, and assure him, that they will (unless their liberties are immediately restored whole and entire) form an independent commonwealth, after the example of the Dutch provinces —— And to secure our seaports, offer free trade to all nations —— This is the only method that affords any prospect of success; and this, will undoubtedly preserve our Freedom.

Should any one province begin the Example, the other provinces will immediately follow; and the people of Britain must comply with our demands, or sink under the united force of all their enemies the French and the Spaniards. —— This is the plan that wisdom and providence point out to preserve our rights, and this alone —— Also, by these means we may bring the people of Britain to reason, and thereby preserve them from slavery and destruction —— Every consideration that animates a free and noble mind, urges our putting the plan above-mentioned, into immediate execution —— It is practicable, safe, and easy, and if not pursued, slavery will be our inevitable portion.

My brethren, our present situation is very dangerous, but not desperate; let us now unite like one band of brothers in the noblest cause, look to Heaven for assistance, and He who made us free, will crown our labours with success.

                                        An American.

BOSTON Nov. 4. Mr. Robert Davis of Andover, as he was bringing a load of Cyder to this town three or four weeks ago, fell from the tongue of the cart, and came with his head to the ground in so dangerous a position as that a wheel of the cart took off one of his ears close to the head. After he twicked it off and threw it away.

BOSTON Nov. 5. At the adjournment on Monday afternoon. The committee appointed to present a petition to his Excellency the Governor of this province, reported, and laid before the town the following reply, which his Excellency had been pleased to deliver them in writing.

Gentlemen,
"The Royal Charter reserves the Governor full power and authority from time to time, as he judges necessary to adjourn, prorogue and dissolve the General Assembly.

In the exercise of the power, both as or time and place, I have always been governed by a regard to his Majesty's service and in the interest of the province.

It did not appear to me necessary for those purposes that an assembly should meet at the time to which it now stands prorogued, and, before I was informed of your address, I had determined to prorogue it to a further time.

The reason which you have advances have not altered my opinion.

It notwithstanding in compliance with your petition. I should alter my determination and meet the assembly, contrary to my own judgement at such time as you judge necessary, I should in effect yield to you the excercise of that part of the Prerogative, and should be unable to justify any conduct to the King.

There would, moreover, be danger of encouraging the inhabitants of the other towns in the province to assemble, from time to time, in order to consider of the necessity or expedience of a session of the General Assembly, or to debate and transact other matters which the law that authorized towns to assemble does not make the business of town Meeting.

        T. Hutchingson."
"Province House, Nov. 2. 1772. To the inhabitants of the town of Boston, in the town meeting assembled at Faneuil-Hall."

The reply, having been read several times and duly considered; it was moved and the question accordingly put, whether the same by the satisfactory to the town, which passed in the negative, nem, con, and thereupon,

Resolved, as the opinion of the Inhabitants of this town, that they have, ever had, and ought to have, a right to petition the King or his Representative, for the redress of such grievances as they feel, or so preventing of such as they have reason to apprehend, and to communicate their sentiments to other towns.

It was moved, that a committee of correspondence be appointed, to consist of twenty-one persons, to state the rights of the colonist and of this province in particular, as men, as christians, and as to further to communicate and publish the same to several towns in this province, and to the world, as the sense of this town, with the infringements and violations thereof, that have been, or from time to time may be, made. Also, requesting of each town, a free communication of their sentiments on this subject. And the Question being accordingly put, passed in the affirmative. nem. con.

A committee of twenty-one persons were appointed for the purpose aforesaid of which the Honorable James Otis, Esq; is Chairman; and they were desired to report to town as soon as may be.   Attest. William Cooper, Town Clerk.

BOSTON Nov. 12. Whereas Elizabeth the wife of me the subscriber hath clandestinely taken many things from me, and hath absented herself from me sundry times, and is now absent, and hath run me in debt; to prevent further trouble, I hereby forwarn all not to trust her on my account, and declare I will not pay any debts of her contracting after the date hereof.

October 27, 1772. George Cheesman.

BOSTON Nov. 19. The following is an account of the horrid murder, committed by the crew of a Pirate schooner, in our bay, last Sunday morning, as near as can be collected from the various reports. Last Saturday evening, sailed from this port for Chatham, Cape-Cod a schooner Nikerson, master, who having been on a fishing voyage, came here and discharged, a top-sail schooner bearing down hard upon them, which at length fired and brought them too, a number of men, from the top-sail schooner then came on board Capt. Nikerson, in one boat, and examined him, whither he was bound, what he had on board, &c. They then returned to the schooner, but soon after came on board again with more assistance in three or four boats, armed with guns and cutlasses, one Nikerson, a passenger on board (and a relation of the captain's) when he perceived their coming, flung himself by a rope over the stern, (thinking their intent was to press some of them) and there continued during the bloody scene; and soon as they came on board, after lashing the helm, and setting the sails, they killed captain Nikerson and two other men, and of whom was the captain's brother, and the other his brother-in-law named Newcomb, and threw them overboard, they then all the hands belonging on board, except Nikerson, who had flung himself over the stern, as before mentioned, and a boy named Kent; It is said, Nikerson heard one of the pirates say 'let us kill the boy, another make answer, No, it is not known, however, the boy is missing. After perpetrating the inhuman deed, they plundered the vessel, knocked out the head of a barrel of rum and drank and wasted a great part of it, and taking a considerable sum of money went off with their booty. When they dropped astern of the schooner, they came so near Nikerson, (the only one supposed to be saved) that he could have set his feet in their heads, but it providentially happened they never perceived him. Some time after they were gone, Nikerson, who could not have survived much longer in the condition he was in, came on board, and made sail for Cape-Cod and about 10 o'clock the same morning, saw a sail, which proved to be Capt. Doane, from Cape-Cod bound for Boston, and hanging out a signal of distress, Capt. Doane with some of his people came on board, and assisted him getting into port. The persons who were murdered, were all married men, and left three disconsolable widows.

Yesterday the Lively sloop of war sailed in quest of the pirates.

BOSTON Nov. 23. From the Public Advertiser dated Sept. 23, 1772. (London)

Please acquaint the Public the Address lately presented to the Earl of Hillsboruogh by a pretended Committee of American Merchants, was a most infamous and clandestine Proceeding; that those few who carried it up to his Lordship did it in a secret and shameful Manner; the most considerable and respected merchants trading to America who neither consulted in it, or made acquainted with the measure; that those who signed and presented the Address are very fearful of having their Names made known, that they are a set of prostituted Tools of Despotism & Contract Hunters; that they may be made to appear as much the moment they are particularly and personally pointed out; that the principal Merchants trading to that country have the most contemptible Opinion of Lord Hillsborough's Abilities, and detest his anti-commerce and despotic Principles.

I am astonished that the American Merchants do not justify themselves, by publicly declaring that they and their correspondents hold directly opposite Sentiments; for however the Merchants in America be divided in their interest, or Modes of proceeding with respect to laws of Revenue, they all agree to execrating and deriding the name of Hillsborough, and the system of his Politics.

I Hope those insolent and prostituted Tools, who have thus daringly insulted the whole body by stiling themselves a Committee of the American Merchants, may be dragged to the bar of the Public. Their insignificacy conceals them, or their Deeds should long since have been brought into light.   Atticus.

BOSTON Dec. 4. One John Thorp a Blacksmith, was taken up at New-York for the supposed Murder of his Wife, and committed. He acknowledged that while he was sitting at Dinner with his Wife, a Quarrel happened between them, and that she having snatched a knife from his Hand and cut his finger ——— he threw another knife at her, when she in a fit, (he supposed) fell down, and in the fall received the fatal Wound.

The Wound deeply penetrated the Brain, and much fractured the Skull: The Woman then lived, without any sign of sensibility till next morning, and then died.

This tragical event, whereby a Number of helpless infants are exposed to the world, deprived at once of both parental supports, affords a melancholy Proof of the dangerous Effects of ungoverned Passion ——— and consequently of all practices whereby the Powers of that Reason which is given us to govern and direct them, may be suspended or impaired.

BOSTON Dec. 5. Last Wednesday night seven prisoners broke out of the goal in this town, viz. John Daly, Robt. Anderson, John Clark, Tho' Williams and John Hopkins, all Irishmen, committed for theft; John Parks, and Englishman charge with an intention of Theft. and Polidore a negro, servant to Benjamin House of Scituate, committed for deserting his master's servive.

All the prisoners immediately after they got out of goal, broke into the dwelling-house of Mr. William Jackson, and carried off some wearing apparel and other things: ——— The next morning John Parks was apprehended, and several of the articles belonging to Mr. Jackson found upon him.

BOSTON Dec. 14. It is currently reported, the two regiments are ordered from New-York to Rhode Island, to support the trial of persons there suspected, or rather informed against, for being concerned in the burning of the Gaspee armed schooner. The Governor and Lieut. Governor of this province, two of the appointed judges, will shortly set out for Newport. The lively ship of war is also to sail, on board of which the Admiral, another of the Judges, is to hoist a flag. Other say, that these devoted persons are to be taken agreeable to the late Act of Parliament, and sent for trial to London! ——— Can anyone hear of troops and ships of war posting from one part of the continent to the other. ——— Governors, Admirals and Custom Officers parading from colony to colony, subjecting the inhabitants to trial, without any Juries, on matters done within the body of a country, or which is worse, if possible, transporting them beyond the seas, and think himself secured in the enjoyment of his natural and constitutional rights!

BOSTON Dec. 17. Yesterday was held at the courthouse in Queen Street, a special Court of Vice-Admiralty under the Royal Commission for the trial of piracies, murder, &c. committed upon the high seas, when Ansell Nickerson, was arranged for the murder of Captain Thomas Nikerson, (&c. as mentioned in this and other papers) and pleaded "Not Guilty." The Court adjourned to Wednesday the second day of June next, when we hear his trial convene.

BOSTON Dec. 24. We hear from Bridgewater that several hundred Persons of different Ages are now sick with the Measles in that Town, and many of them dangerously ill.

BOSTON Dec. 28. Last Wednesday night about 12 o'Clock a Fire broke out in a barn at the South Part of the Town belonging to the Widow May, which was soon consumed together with a waggon load of Hogs, and a quantity of hay; the fire communicated to a large Dwelling-House tenanted by Mr. Ebenezer Sever, and belonging to Samuel Welles, Esq; which almost entirely burnt the back Part but the Vigilance of the people the fire was prevented doing any further Damages. It is supposed the Fire was occasioned by carrying a Candle or a lit Pipe in the barn.

BOSTON Dec. 29. Extract of a letter from a gentleman of character in England to his friend in Boston.

"Our tyrants on Administration are greatly exasperated with the late maneuvers of the brave Rhode Islanders, as a regard to the rights of the subjects and the principles of justice never marked the measure of the present wretched conductors of the wheels of government, you will not be alarmed when I tell you that they have determined to vacate the charter of that colony, to effect this purpose, which in their own apprehension will be attended with some difficulty: Admiral Montagu is ordered, with the small crafts which are with him, to line the harbour of Rhode Island, with positive orders to apprehend the persons concerned in the enterprise above mentioned. Awed by this great commander and his gallant squadron, these bitter pills are to be crammed down their throats; but the friends of the true British freedom are not without hope that the stomach of that heroic colony will reject the noose prepared for them; be united or dear suffering brethren, be steady and success awaits you; freedom, gracious freedom, will be purchased. We believe the ancient British spirit of independence which once bless this Island, has improved by transplantations, and preserve its vigor in the breast of America; cherish it my dear friends! And by receiving yourselves save this small remnant of the virtuous in Britain."

BOSTON Dec. 31. We have the following advice from Newport Dated Dec. 21. 1772.

"We hear a letter to our governor, from Admiral Montagu, was read at the General Assembly held at Providence, last week; In which letter the Admiral we are told requested his Honour the Governor, that Capt. Keeler of his Majesty's ship Mercury now in this harbour, might be permitted to come on shore, without being insulted and protected from arrests, &c. Now it is certain that Capt. Keeler has often been ashore in this town and other parts of the colony, and we never heard of his having received the least imaginable insults: But as for his being protected from arrests, we are humbly of opinion, that neither Capt. Keeler nor his Excellency Admiral Montagu himself, has any more right of protection from arrest, than any other the least or poorest of his Majesty's subjects. —— For the truth of which opinion, we are not afraid to appeal to the People of Great-Britain; though we don't chuse to be transported thither for trial."

Quary, Whether Capt. Keeler will publicly declare that one single attempt was ever made to insult him in this town?

1773

BOSTON Jan. 9. From Newport Jan. 4. The Hon. Daniel Horsmander, Esq; Chief Justice of the province of New-York, his lady and the honourable Frederick Smyth, Rsq; Chief Justice of New-Jersey, arrived here last Thursday, in the sloop Lydia, Capt. Frebody from New-York: And Saturday evening the honourable Peter Oliver, Esq; Chief Justice of the Massachusetts-Bay and the Hon. Robert Auchmity, Esq; Judge of the court of Vice-Admiralty throughout New-England, came to town by land: These four gentlemen are appointed, by the King to join his Honour the Governor of this Colony, in making enquiry into the circumstances of plundering and burning of his Majesty's schooner Gaspee, on the 10th of June last.

We hear Lord Darthmouth, Secretary of State for the American department, in a letter concerning the Gaspee schooner, has assured his honor our Governor, that his Majesty is determined to punish, in the severest manner, any of his Servants who shall obstruck the legal Trade, or in any wise insult & abuse any of his subjects of this Colony; so that it is hop'd there will be no more unnecessary firing on and terrifying the poor, honest, industrious workmen, and others who bring the necessaries of life to this market, nor any more of knocking down boatsmen throwing their wood overboard and cutting down the best wood and timber on private Gentlemen's estates; of which almost numberless have been the complaint within some eighteen months past; though, in practice to the present Commander here, we can say have heard of scarce any against them.

This Harbour, here is now guarded by the Mercury of 24 Guns, the Arethusa of 36, The LIzard of 28, the Swan of 20, and the Halifax schooner,

Capt. Crispin.

BOSTON Jan. 11. Messieurs Printers Edes and Gill,

At the time when great things concerning our nation and America, are under consideration, and every man speaks and acts freely, I will also shew my opinion, since the disputes began between Britain and America. I have read with great attention, Locke, Sidney, and the rest of the inspired patriots and politicians of the last age, and find that they all maintain the principle of liberty and condemning arbitrary power, as it is against the laws of God and nature. Thus for they. I find also that the great men of this age are the same opinion with those of the last.

My own opinion is this, that no people on earth have a right to make laws for the Americans but themselves. It is as evident as anything in the world, that the people of this Country have as just a right to make laws for the people of Britain, as they have to make laws for me. It is certain if one people can make laws for the other, the law makers are masters and the other are slaves; and therefore I am astonished that any person of common understanding should say that the people of Britain have any authority over the Americans; for it is nothing less then to say we are subjects to subjects, and servants to Briton.

Truth and common sense will at last prevail, and if the Britons continue their endeavours much longer to subject us to their governors, and taxations, we shall become a separate state ——— This is as certain as any event that has not already come to pass; for the people from every quarter of the world are coming to this country, of all riches, arts and science, soldiers and seamen, and in a short time the Americans will be too strong for any nation in the world.

I am glad to hear that the people are meeting in the towns to declare their minds upon important matters in dispute, it is most certainly a very mild measure, and all who neglect it at this time will deserve slavery with all its horrors, but hope none will, and trust they will do it in every town of any consequence throughout America, this is the most likely method ever yet devised to establish our rights and restore peace and harmony, for if the people of Britain see that we are united and determined they will give up there vain pretention, and then a foundation will be laid for the peace and prosperity of the nation.

I always desire the happiness of the King and the people of Great Britain, and I am very sure that a perfect freedom of the country is the surest was to promote their happiness; therefore shall always pray for it, and give it in charge to my children and grand children to preserve the right of America sacred as their life.

May the Father of mercies and of liberty, inspire all that fear him to defend those rights which he has generously given them.

Age & Experience.

BOSTON Jan. 18. On Monday the 21st of last Month the following Accident happened at Scarborough, at the House of Mr. William Hummun, of that town, viz. as John Stone, Paul Thompson, and John Waterhouse was about to assist him in butchering a large hog; Waterhouse with an Ax went into the pen and struck the Hog on the Head; Thompson enter'd with a knife in order to stick the Hog, but the stroke with the Ax not being effectual, the Hog rose, ran between Thompson's legs and brought him against the corner of the Pen, where in order to secure himself, he placed his Arm and Hand in which he held the knife, over the side of the Pen; Stone unfortunately came to the Place and reached over to seize the Hog by the Brussels received the Knife into his Bowels; He has left a poor Widow, and seven Children.

BOSTON Jan. 18. To the Public. It is proposed that all the proceedings of the Preservation of Rights of America, be collected and published in a Volume; that posterity may know what their Ancestors have done in the cause of Freedom — It is expected that the Inhabitants of every Town however small, will at this Time publish their sentiments to the World, that their Names with those who have already published be recorded in the Catalogue of Fame, and handed down to future ages.

BOSTON Jan. 28. Wednesday last Admiral Montagu returned to Boston from Newport. ——— On the Road we are told, he was met by two farmers, with loaded carts, and were ordered to give way for the Admiral's carriage: One of them complied, but the other refusing, his Excellency threatened him in high terms, and proceeded to brandish his cane. The honest farmer resolutely asserted his right, and raising the butt of his whip, stood on his defensive. This was accompanied with gestures that rendered any explanation of his intention unnecessary; when the Admiral thought proper not to contest the matter further, prudently lowered his cane, gave way to the cart, and pursued his Journey. ——— He was very particular in his enquiries, at the next Inn, after the farmer's name perhaps with a design agreeable to the mordern mode; to indict him for high treason.

Providence Gazette.

BOSTON Jan. 29. Last Saturday a large Sley, containing a number of gentlemen, drawn by four Horses, in returning to town from a small excursion into the country, met, just at the entrance of the town, a noted market woman, known by the name of Betty Whittemore, riding in a chair; the horses in the sley were drove with great violence, and being near the chair before it could be seen, there was no time for either to turn out of the way; accordingly the horses and sley came with such violence as to throw Betty a considerable way fron the carriage, broke her chair to pieces, and killed her horse (which she valued very highly) dead on the spot: The driver of the sley was considerably hurt, and his horses all fell to the ground by the violence of the shock.

BOSTON Feb. 1. Last Thursday afternoon, died at the North End, after a few Days illness, Mrs. Christian Bell, Wife of James Bell, of this Town, Cordwainer, who is a native of Scotland; it being notorious to Number of People that this Woman had for several Years past very undeservidly suffered frequent and cruel abuse from her said Husband; a suspiciom immediately arose after her Death; that she had been murdered by him, in consequence of which a Warrant was issued on Friday, by Mr. Justice Gardner, ans the said James Bell was apprehended, and after an Examination had before the Justice, was on the Evening of that day committed to Goal. On Saturday a Coroner's Inquest was summoned, who after carefully examining the witnesses, and critically inspecting the Body, with assistance of Messieurs Dansworth, Reed and Fudger Physicians of the Town, upon their Oaths declared, that the said Christian Bell came to her Death in consequence of repeated Blows on her Body, given by her said Husband, James Bell; more particularly by one blow or blows upon her Head, just over the right Eye, which she received from him, on and since the Evening of the 16th ult.

BOSTON Feb. 2. Among the many acts of generosity in Mr. Thomas Bradshaw, while secretary of the treasury, it ought to be remembered with gratitude that he procur'd for his private clerk Martyn Leake (who is also clerk in the treasury) the sum of two hundred pounds sterling a year of the public money for the said clerk's being, as he is called, agent at the treasury for the Boston commissioners! And that upwards of a thousand pounds sterling has already been faithfully expended in that very useful and necessary appointment —— Whether any future minister will think proper to cause the said treasury clerk to disgorge that sum of the public money, or whether, deeming it a notorious misapplication, it will be thought more just and proper to require the Boston Commissioners to replace the money out of their own pockets, in a matter that is yet uncertain. An agent however for the Boston Commissioners is here understood to be a person at the treasury ready upon all occasions, secretly to convey intelligence to Boston of the movements of the Lords in all the matters concerning the Board, and to conceal from, or gloss over their Lordships, every matter and things he finds corrupt, partial, or reprehensible in the Board! to be ready upon all occasions to support, as far as it is able, at the treasury, such persons as shall be recommended to him by the Board, and to impede, censure and defame all others which the Board, shall signify their emity to! ——— also, in a private manner to send hither to the Board, copies of all letters, and papers that go hence from such officers as are here persecuted and distressed by the most infamous men that ever disgraced a Royal commission, knaves that are already grown rich in the spoils of the very business they were employed to manage and improve!

BOSTON Feb. 15. On Friday last the Honorable House of Representatives sent the following Message to the Governor.

May it Please your Excellency,
Your Message of the 4th Instant informs this House, that his Majesty has been pleased to order that Salaries shall be allowed to the Justices of the Superior Court of the Province.

We conceive that no Judge who has a due Regard to Justice, or even to his own Character, would chuse to be placed under an undue Byass as they must be under, in the opinion of the House by accepting of and becoming dependent for their Salaries upon the Crown.

Had not his Majesty been misinformed with the Respect to the Constitution and Appointment of our Judges by those who advised to this Measure, we are persuaded he would never have passed such an order; as he was pleased to declare upon him accession to the Throne, that he looked upon the Independence and Uprightness of the Judges as essential to the impartial Administration of Justice, as one of the best Securities of the Rights and Liberties of his Subjects, and as most conductive to the Honor of the Crown.

Your Excellency's Precaution to prevent all Claims from this Province for any service, for which the Justices may also be entitled to a Salary from the King, is comparatively of very small Consideration to us.

When we consider the many attempts that have been made, Effectually to render null and void those clauses in our Charter, upon which the Freedom of our Constitution depends, we should be lost to all public feeling should we not manifest a just Resentment. We are more convinced, that it has been the design of Administration, totally to subject the Constitution, and introduce an arbitrary Government into the Privince: And we cannot wonder that the Apprehensions of this People are Thoroughly awakened.

We wait with impatience to know, and hope your Excellency will very soon be able to assure us, that the Justices will utterly refuse ever to accept of Support in a manner so justly obnoxious to the disinterested and judicious Part of the good People of this Province: being repugnant to the Charter, and utterly inconsistent with the safety of the Rights, Liberty and Prosperities of the People.

There were 91 Members present when the message was brought into the House, and it passed by a Majority of it.

"If the Governor has signed the Grant of the General Assembly to the Judges of the Superior Court, as it is said he has, what will it avail? as long as the degree is gone forth that they shall receive the Grants of the Crown for their Support at present or in the future, whenever they please? Let us have an answer to this."

BOSTON Feb. 22. Tuesday last the House of Representatives sent the following Message to his Excellency the Governor.

May it please your Excellency,
The House of Representatives think it of the last Importance to wait on your Excellency, and pray that you would be pleased to inform whether pour Excellency can now satisfy the House that the Justices of the Superior Court have refused or will refuse to accept of this support from the Crown. A Matter which appears to have filled the Minds of the good People of this Province with great Anxiety; and a determination of which in the affirmation will tend to promote his Majesty's Service and the Peace and Happiness of the People.

His Excellency's Answer.
Gentlemen of the House of Representatives. I

most certainly am not able to inform you that the Justices of the Superior Court, have refused or will refuse to accept the support from the Crown, All that I thought necessary for me to do before I gave my Assent to the Grants, which you have made, was the taking proper caution to prevent their being entitled to a Salary prom the Province after a Salary from the Crown should hereafter be received.

Council Chamber. 16 Feb. 1773. T. Hutchinson.

BOSTON March 1. On Friday the 19th his Excellency the Governor was pleased to send the following Message to the honorable House of Representatives.

Gentlemen of the House of Representatives, The Province House is in such a ruinous State then when I recommended to you to make provisions for the repair at the last Session of the General Court.

The present inconveniencies which I submit to by having continued to reside in it, I hope will have some weight with you, but the dishonour which must reflect upon the Province from its appearing to be unfit for any Person to dwell in, I hope will have a much greater weight with you and induce you to provide for its thorough repair.

I am well assured that his Majesty does not expect from me that any part of my support should be applied to repairs of this House, and I have reason to think that if you shall continue in your refusal, which I hope you will not, provisions will be made for the decent residence of the Governor; and I do not thus repeatedly press you to make this provision for the sake of my own future convenience, but from a real regard to the honor and interest of the Province.

Council Chamber, 19 Feb. 1773. T. Hutchinson.

Thursday last the following Message was presented to his Excellency the Governor, (in answer to his Message to the House of the 19th ult.) by Capt. Derby, Col. Bower, Col. Thexter, Col. Tharter, and Capt. Morse, viz.

May it please your Excellency, The House have with great Attention considered your Excellency's Message of the nineteenth Instant, and beg leave to say, that they are not unacquainted with the present State of the province House, and are sensible that it might be repaired at a less expense now than in the future.

The Governor of the Province when this Building was purchased by the Government for his Residence, was constitutionally dependent upon the free Grants of the Representatives of the People for his Support; but as the connection between the Governor and the People in this respect, is now the great Grief of the inhabitants of this Province so materially altered, the House conceive that they are not only bound by the Honor of Justice, but that they cannot, consistent with the Duty they own their Constituents, proceed to make the repairs which your Excellency desires at this Time.

The House are so far from being influenced by any the least personal Disrespect, that they Leave to assure your Excellency, if the Time was to come, as they wish it soon may, when your Excellency shall think best to receive your whole support from this this Province, it would give them great Pleasure to provide your Excellency a convenient and elegant House, such as should be honorable to the Province, and suitable to the Dignity of the chief Magistrate of the Province.

BOSTON March 1. Last Thursday on Josiah Wellington sold at the Market, to a Woman a measly Hog —— These are to warn the said Josiah, That he come and make Reparation for the Offence, otherwise he will be prosecuted without further notice.

Last Thursday came on at the Superior Court, the Trial of James Bell, cordwainer, for the Murder of his Wife: The Jury brought in a verdict Manslaughter, when he plead the Benefit of the Clergy, and was accordingly burnt in the Hand on Saturday, then discharged.

BOSTON March 9. Friday being the anniversary of the 5th of March, when, agreeable to a vote of the town a meeting was called, at which the committee appointed last last year for that purpose, reported that they had engaged Dr. Benjamin Church, to deliver an Oration, on the dangerous tendency of standing armies being placed in free and populous cities, and to perpetuate the memory of the horrid massacre perpetuated on the evening of 5th March, 1770.

The Oration was accordingly delivered at the Old South meeting , where the people crowded in such numbers, that it was with difficulty the Orator reached the pulpit, which was covered with a black cloth: The Orator took up about half an hour, and was received with universal applause: And his fellow citizens unanimously voted him this thanks, and requested a copy of his oration from the press.

At Night a select number of the friends of constitutional liberty, met at Mrs. Chapman's in King-Street and exhibited on the balcony a lanthorn of transparent paintings, having in the front a lively representation of the bloody massacre which was perpetrated near that spot on the 5th of March 1770, over their heads was inscribed the fatal effects of a standing army being posted in a free city. On the right, America sitting in a mournful posture, looking down on the spectators, with this label, Behold my Sons. On the left, a Monument, sacred to the memory of Messrs. Samuel gray, Samuel Maverick, James Caldwell, Patrick Carr, and Crispus Attucks, Who were barbarously murdered by a party of the 29th regiment on the 5th of March 1770.

At a quarter after nine, the time of the evening when the bloody deed was acted, the Paintings were taken in, and most of the bells in town tolled till ten.

BOSTON March 18. Mr. Thomas please insert the following.

A Plan to perpetuate the Union between Great-Britain and America to the latest Period of time.

It is just observation, That the most simple proposition, are hard to be rendered more intelligible by any explanation; this remark is applicable to the present dispute between Great-Britain and America; altho' the truth is obvious to common sense, yet there have been volumes written on the subject. A few words may make the matter clear to every mind. The Law of Nature, the Charter and the British Parliament all declare that the Colonist are free men; —— It is self evident truth, that their total subjection to a parliament independent of them, destroys every idea of freedom and property, and it is equally certain that no line can be drawn between the supreme authority of the Parliament and the total subjection of the Colonist, the consequence is, The Colonist are independent of the British Parliament. —— This truth is so clear it must blaze upon every mind. —— The great question now is, How shall the union between Great-Britain and America be preserved? The answer id easy Common interest is that bound of union; the people of each country must treat the other in such a manner as to make it their interest to preserve the connection. The people of both countries are united in the King, who is at the head of the empire, and interest (the only cement of political bodies) must preserve union between them and their head.

When the King wants assistance of his American subjects, he must apply to their House of Commons for grants, in the same way he now does to his Parliament in Britain. The Colonies finding themselves treated like free men by the King. and fellow sibjects in Britain, and their rights established upon a firm foundation, they will be animated to contribute the utmost in their power to promote the honour of the crown and the Support of the Kingdom. And as the Colonies increase in wealth and numbers, so will their assistance to the present state increase until Britain flows with the riches of America —— and by union and harmony between the two countries, founded on freedom and common interest, the British empire may continue firmly united and flourish to the latest ages.

BOSTON March 29. " Last Friday about 3 o'clock in the afternoon, a Fire broke out in the Custom House; but by the timely Assistance of the inhabitants of the Town, a stop was put to its progress before it had done much damage. It is generally tho't the Fire's not happening at Night have prevented much lying and falsehoods. If we may judge from the Representation sent home upon other occasions, it would not argue the want of Candor to suppose, that the Commissioners, or some of their Tools, would have made a formidable story of it, and influenced the Money to Ministry to believe it was done on purpose; either in testimony or Resentment against the Custom-House Officers, or with a View to a mobbish scramble for the Revenue Money, which is so wantonly taken from the Colonies, and worse than thrown away. Perhaps some certain Persons might have repaired to the Castle for fear of their Lives, and more Regiments wrote for to keep the rebellous Town of Boston in good order."

BOSTON March 31. Agreeable to the late law for the regulating vendues, the Selectmen on Saturday last appointed me to officiate as one of the Vendue Masters, for this town: I would now, through your paper, offer my services to the public, promising the utmost fidelity and care, in executing any business intrusted in me, as an Auctioneer, in the sale of houses, lands, shipping, merchandise, household furniture, &c. my employers may depend on my exerting myself for their Interest. I have for the present opened a vendue Office at my store in Cornhill, where goods of any kind will be gracefully received in for sale.   William Greenleaf.

N. B. I have a large and valuable assortment of goods to be sold at private sale, on such terms as must please the purchasers.

BOSTON April 1. Extract of a letter from a Gentleman of eminence in Rhode Island Government, to a Gentleman in this Town, that is dated March 18, 1773.

"I have just been looking over the Papers, and am charmed with the behaviour of the Town of Boston, and the House of Representatives and Council of your Province: If I was not chained down by Interest Connections and every Thing to this Colony, I should think myself very happy in living in Boston. ——— I hope the Spirit which spreads throughout your Province so gloriously will extend throughout the Colonies, and secure our most invaluable Liberties.

BOSTON April 5. Yesterday afternoon, about five o'clock. a fire broke out in a building belonging to Alexander Edwards, cabinet-maker, at the north part of the town, which was almost wholly in flames as soon as discovered, and the same in a very short time consumed, together whith his work shop, several stores, barns, sheds, &c. and a large quantity of mahogany and other stock, with a number of articles of Furniture which was furnished for sale, the fire likewise communicated to the Sandemanian meeting house, that was near adjoining which was also entirely destroyed, and it is owing to the alertness of the inhabitants, and the constant supply of the engines with water from the millpond, that many other wooden buildings, which were in imminent danger, were prevented sharing the same fate ——— The engine from the Charlestown, esteemed the best in America, with a number of people from that town, with the usual activity, came over very expeditiously to assist at the fire, and were very serviceable. Mr. Edward's loss is said to be very great.

BOSTON April 17. An action of trespass was brought by Richard Hardwick, Mariner, late belonging to the Brig Skywood, against Robert Keeler, Esq; commander of his Majesty's ship Mercury, for assaulting and imprisoning him fourteen days on board the said brig, on her arrival from the West-Indies, in September last. ——— The Court assessed twenty-five pounds damages for the plaintiff, with costs.

BOSTON April 20. We hear from Porthmouth, that last Friday se'nnight, a melancholy affair happened at the Globe Tavern, on the plains of the town, viz. Mr. Joseph King, who kept the said tavern being in his garden ay work; Mr. Joseph Moulton, jun. a deputy sheriff attempted to take him for a sum of about 40 dollars. King observing Moulton coming towards him, and suspecting his design, ran to a tree where he had left a gun: When Moulton came near him to keep at a distance for he would not be taken by him:

However when he had got within about 10 Feet of King, he fired a full charge of goose shot in his face. Moulton was taken up by a person who saw King shoot. It was thought he would soon expire, but he was alive last Friday, tho' there was little hopes for him. The Doctors think both his eyes and part of his nose, with 5 or 6 teeth are shot away, and the whole of his face and head in a terrible condiction. About a dozen shot have been extracted from his head already. ——— By this unhappy affair two families are in deplorable circumstances ——— A reward of 20 dollars is offered by the high sheriff for apprehending the said King, who immediately absconded.

BOSTON April 26. Last Friday we had another Specimen of Insolence of Office, When R. Parker, by with a writ of assistance presumed to break open several Ware Houses on the Long-Wharf, on Pretence that he had information of Contraband Goods being lodged there, which was not the case, we say on pretence, for its only for a dirty fellow to be induced to tell such to an Officer, that there is seizable Goods in any store, and they will immediately be broken open and exposed; may it be said Mr. Searcher boasted that he had a Right to make as free with our bed Chambers ——— Thus we see what a monster in this writ of assistance, is intrusted in the keeping of the petty Officers of the Navy as well as the Custom House, and the wisdom of those provinces, who have not suffered such a monster or monsters to prowl their streets for prey. ——— As most of the Men of War had lately sail'd for Halifax, it is thought this wanton and affrontive behaviour was with design to excite the Opposition in the trade, and for the pretence for the return of those Guarde Costas.

BOSTON April 29. We have information that Ebenezer Richardson, the murderer, who have lived, since he was let out of goal, at or near Stoneham, has been sent to Boston, by his friends the Board of Commissioners, with Intelligence that they had received a commission for him, in one of the late Ships from London, appointing him to some command at the Southward.

BOSTON May 3. Yesterday arrived the Gaspee Brig from Halifax, being a Vessel lately Commission'd in the Room of the one of the same Name, said to have been burnt at Providence some time since.

BOSTON May 10. The week before last an Indian came to town from St. Francois by way of Kennebeck, with a Frenchman for his Interpreter, and on Tuesday last he attended his Excellency the Governor, and the Honourable Council at Cambridge. We are informed that 5 Chiefs of the Aresaguntacook Indians, of which the Indians of St. Francois are a part, left Canada the latter end of summer, and that when they came to the height of the land four of them, were taken with the measles and determined to proceed no further, but desired the fifth with the Interpreter to go on.

We hear the purpose of the message was to obtain satisfaction for the death of several Indians alleged to have been killed at different times in the woods by the English, and to seek security in some way or other against such actions in the future; but they had rather have satisfaction in money than by punishment of the guilty persons, if they should be discovered. We are not informed what answer had been given.

BOSTON May 10. On Wednesday last the freeholders and other inhabitants met and chose the Hon. John Hancock, the Hon. Tho. Cushing, Wm. Philips and Samuel Adams, Esq; their representatives, and afterwards recommended to their consideration the late plan proposed by the colony of Virginia, and the divers other weighty matters for the redress of grievances, securing their liberties &c. &c.

BOSTON May 10. The Hon. John Hancock, Esq; appointed by the General Court one of the Commissioners for the setting the Line between this Province and New-York, set out on his journey for the same place on Friday for that purpose.

BOSTON May. 24. Some time last week Ebenezer Richardson Esq; who lately had such a fortunate and surprising Escape from the Gallows for the Murder of young Snyder: through the extraordinary clemency of our pious and great Monarch, set out for the city of Philadelphia, being appointed an Officer in the Customs, for his notable Exertions in behalf of the Government.

BOSTON May 24. By a Vessel from Baltimore we learn, that a few days before she sailed 2 informers were taken up in the Afternoon, and after being Tarr'd and Feather'd, were carted about the Town till Night, and then ordered to depart the Place in 24 Hours. ——— The next Day it was reported they had returned, upon which diligent Search was made after them, but they could not be found; and 'twas supposed they had set out for Boston, as the Receptacle for the Preference of such Vagrants, where, no Doubt, from the pacific Disposition of the Inhabitants, and the encouragement given here to such Persons, they will find an Asylum both of Profit and Security.

BOSTON May 27. Several accidents happened yesterday in this town, the son of Mr. Hammund at the North End, being in Common-Street a horse ran over him and bruised him so that his life is dispared of.

A lad named Smith, fired a gun yesterday, the piece split and tore it in his leg so terribly a manner that it was obliged immediately to be cut off.

BOSTON May 31. Saturday last at Noon, a fire broke out on board the fine large Store-Ship (which has been laying in this Harbour for several Months past commanded by Captain Walker, having stores for the Navy) which soon communicated to the Masts, Rigging & Turpentine on Deck, and before assistance came her upper works were almost wholly in a Blaze; that little or no attempt was made to extinguish it: The Boats from the Men of War with some of the Town towed the Ship over to Noodle's Island, where, after scuttling her she was left to burn to the Water's edge ——— The fire, it is said, was occasioned by some Coals falling from the hearth of the Cabouse on the Deck, which had been pay'd over with Turpentine, and spread with such Rapidity that nothing could be taken out her.

The Captain, with his Wife and two Children, who usually kept on board, likewise a Boy (the other People belonging to her being ashore) were obliged to be taken out of the Cabin Windows, with out being able to save the least Thing but what they had on: —— A Report prevailing at the Time of the Fire, that a large quantity of Powder was on board, put the inhabitants in general into a great Consternation, for fear of the Consequences that might arise from an Explosion thereof; but being afterwards assured that none was in her, they became perfectly easy and the Hills and Wharfs were much covered with Spectators to view so uncommon a Sight. Some of the Stores in the Hold, such as Cordage, Cables and Anchors, which were under Water before the Fire could reach them will be saves.

BOSTON June 10. Yesterday some copies of the letters returned from England, were laid before the Hon. Common House of Assembly, and in the afternoon the copies were compared with the originals; The galleries were opened, and a great concourse of people attended to hear the contents, who were filled with abhorrence of the measures proposed to ruin the constitution of this unhappy province.

It is said another budget of the letters are returned in one of the last ships from England.

The Letters read in the Common assembly yesterday, was signed by Messrs. Hutchinson, Oliver and Paxton, names which will be but seldom blessed by posterity, and which the present generation are as much disaffected to, as they are to that of the notorious Bernard.

BOSTON June 11. Thursday se'nnight his Excellency the Governor was pleased to send the following message to the House of Representatives,

"Gentlemen of the House of Representatives, I Am informed that certain private letters said to have been wrote by me to a gentleman in England lately deceased, were yesterday laid before your House, and that you have come into a resolution or Vote that they tend to subvert the constitution.

I have never wrote any public or private letter with such intentions, and am not conscious of any letter which can have such effect.

Before you take any further proceedings, I must desire that a transcript of the proceedings of yesterday be laid before me, and that I may be informed to what letters they refer, in order to my considering what steps are proper for me to take up on the occasion." T. Hutchinson.

To which the House on Saturday returned the following Answer.

May It please your Excellency,
"In answer to your message of the third of June, the House of Representatives have resolved, that the date of certain letters now before them, referred to in the message, together with a transcript of the proceedings thereof as requested by your Excellency, be laid before you.

And as your Excellency has been pleased in your message to say, that you have never wrote any public of private letters, with an intention to subvert the constitution, it is the desire of the house, that your Excellency would be pleased to order, that copies be laid before us of such letters as your Excellency has written on those dates, relating to the public affairs of this Province, together with such other letters as your Excellency should think proper.

BOSTON June 14. Wednesday last his Excellency was pleased to send the following message to the honourable House of Representatives, viz.

Gentlemen of the House of Representatives.
By your committee you have laid before me the dates of six original letters with my signature to them, which have been brought in you house and read, together with other letters from several other persons. You have also laid before me an extract from the Journal of the proceedings, by which it appears you are of opinion, that the tendency and design of the letters thus read was to overthrow the constitution of this government and introduce arbitrary power into the province.

I find by the dates of the letters with my signatures that, if genuine, they must be private letters wrote to a gentleman in London, since deceased; that all, except the last, were wrote months before I came to the chair; that they were wrote not only with the confidence which is always implied in a friendly correspondence by private letters, but that they are expressly confidential; notwithstanding which they contain nothing more respecting the constitution of the colonies in general than what is continued in my speech to the Assembly. and what I have published in more extensive manner to the world; and there is no one passage in them which was ever intended to reflect, or which, as I am well assured the gentleman to whom they were wrote, ever understood to respect the particular constitution of this government as derived from the charter.

I am at a loss for what, purpose you desire the copies of any letters the original of which you have in your hands. If it is with a view to make them public, the originals are more proper for that purpose than the copies. I think it would be very improper and out of character in me to lay my private letters before you at your request. My public ones, I restrain'd from laying before you without express leave from his Majesty. This much I can assure you, that it has not been the tendency and design of them to subvert the constitution of this government, but rather to preserve it intire, and I have reason to think they have not been altogether ineffectual to that purpose.

Council Chamber 9th June, 1773.   T. Hutchinson.

BOSTON June 14. Messieurs Printers,
The day, the important Day; is come —— of Old by our prohetic Ancestor's foretold.

The repeated insults and oppression which the Americans have suffered for a number of years have at last opened their eyes to see their danger, likewise their remedy. Any people who have the means of redress in their own hands will by oppression, be taught to make use of them; this is the case with the Americans; experience has taught them their strength, and importance among the Nations, and wisdom has now led them to adopt a Plan of Union which will complete the freedom, and set them above the reach of Oppression. The lurking Foes to America, who have been nourished in her bosom, and at the same Time been aiming at her Ruin, will soon appear in open Day and meet with due Contempt —— Things are moving with rapid Proggress to complete the Triumph of Freedom in America the hand of Providence is evidently working out Political Salvation; the whole face of Affairs is every day visible altering in our favor —— our wicked Enemies are daily taken in their Craftiness, our Friends increase, our Patriots grow firmer and wax stronger by repeated Exertion, —— every appearance is favourable and promises the consummation of American Liberty and Happiness.

BOSTON June 14. Last Saturday se'nnight as Mr. Coolidge of Watertown, was passing over the Charles-River in one of the Ferry-Boats, wherein was a Horse, who just as they arrived at the Ways, by some means fell into the after Part of the Boat on Mr. Coolidge and broke his leg in a most terrible manner.

BOSTON June 24. On Monday last his Excellency sent the following Message to the Hon. House of Representatives, Viz.

"Gentlemen of the House of Representatives. I Perceive, with concern for the honour and reputation of the province, that you have passed and caused to be published, a number of votes resolve, in which you have an unparalleled and most injurious manner determined the intentions and designs of the Governor and Lieutenant Governor, in certain private letters, wrote several years since, the originals of which, as alleged, have by some means or other come into your possessions.

While I was the subject of the debate occasioned by these letters, I do not think it advisable to give you any interruption. Now that you have come to your determination, I must remind you that you are near to the close of the fourth week of your session, and that you have done little or none of the usual business of the court.

To prevent all unnecessary burthen upon your constituents, by too long a session, I must desire you to give dispatch to such matters as lie before you or are proper to be acted upon by you."

Province House, 21st June, 1773.
                                    T. Hutchinson.
The House appointed a committee to take the above into consideration.

Tuesday last the Governor sent the following Message to the hon. House of Representatives, viz.

"Gentlemen of the House of Representatives, I Desire that as soon as may be, you will cause to be laid before me any attested copy of the Votes of Resolve, which have passed your House, and have been made public, and to which I referred to in my Massage of Yesterday.

"Province House, 22 June 1773."
                                    T. Hutchinson"

Yesterday the House of Representatives, passed a humble Petition and Remonstrance against the conduct of his Excellency Thomas Hutchinson, Esq; Governor, and the Honourable Andrew Oliver, Esq; Lieut. Governor of this province, praying that his Majesty would be graciously pleased to Remove them from their posts in the government. Present ninety one members, eighty for, and eleven against, the petition.

BOSTON July 12. Tho. Hutchinson in the first of his printed letters dated June 8, 1768. evidently designed to procure an armed force to put the revenue laws in execution: For after giving an account of the opposition made to the Crown Officers, and artfully insinuating that it was done under the influence of "Mr. Hancock, a representative from Boston," he tells his correspondent that the Commissioners were "destitute of protection" ―― Then he endeavoured to shew the inactivity of the government, by asserting contrary to notorious truth, that "no notice was taken of the extravagance of the mob by any authority except the Governor." ―― "calling it a brush or small disturbance." ―― Next he goes on to speak of the "resentment" that must be shown by the Nation at this inactivity and connivance of the government here. He falsely represent the town of Boston, as countenancing the riot, and concludes, "it is not possible that this anachy should last always,"

It is not plainly held in the letter, that the province was in an disorder'd state; that the government so far from inclining to suppress the disorders, conniv'd at and countenanced them; that in consequence hereof the officers of the crown were "oblig'd to quit the place of their residence," and seek protection "on board am King's ship" ——— that without other aid than what this government would or could afford it was impossible that the King's authority should be supported ——— that this must be resented in England; and when Hallowell should arrive there, who went fraught with letters from him and the board of commissioners and others, and to whom Mr. Hutchinson refers "for a more full account" of his opinion, it would be taken and should effectually put an end to this "anarchy!"

In about two months from the date of this letter Hallowell arrived in London: and soon after orders were given by the Lords of the Admiralty for providing transports to bring the 64th and 65th regiment from Ireland to this Place, of which Capt. Smith who then had the command of the ships in the harbour had due notice and appears by his printed letter dated Boston the 26th of October; and in November following a part of these Transports arriv'd here. Yet it is impossible this letter could, in point of time, have the least influence towards the sending of the troops.

BOSTON July 13. Last Thursday his Majesty's 64th Regiment was reviewed by the Hon. Lieut. Col. Leslie at Castle William, in presence of his Excellency Governor Hutchinson, Admiral Montague, and a number of the Gentlemen of distinction from this town.

BOSTON July 29. The following Petition was presented to the Governor, Council and House of Assembly, during the last session in the General Court. &c.

To his Excellency Thomas Hutchinson, Esq: Governor of said province; to the Honourable his Majesty's Council and honourable House of Representatives in General Court assembled, June, a. d. 1773.

The Petition of us the subscribers, in behalf of all those who by divine permission are held a state of Slavery, within the bowels of a free country.

Humbly sheweth,

"That your petitioners apprehended, they have in common with other men, a natural right to be free, and without molestation, to enjoy such property, as they may acquire by their industry or by any other means not detrimental to their fellow men; and that no person can have any just claim to their services unless by the laws of the land that have forfeited them, or by voluntary compact become servants; neither of which in our case; but we were dragged by the cruel hand of power, some of us from the dearest connections, and others stolen from the bosoms of tender parents and brought hither to be enslaved.

Thus are we deprived of every thing that has a tendency to make life even tolerable. The endearing ties of husband, wife, parent, child and friend, we are generally strangers to: And when ever any of those connections are formed among us, pleasures embittered by the cruel consideration of our slavery. By our deplorable situation we are rendered incapable of Shewing our obedience to the supreme governor of the Universe, by conforming ourselves to the duties, which naturally grows out of such relation. How can a slave perform the duties of husband and parent, wife and child? We are often under the necessity of obeying man, not only in omission of, but frequently in opposition to the laws of God. So inimical is slavery to religion! As we are hindered by our situation from the observance of the law of God, so we cannot reap equal benefit from the laws of the land with other subjects.

We are informed, there is no law in this province, whereby our masters can claim our service; mere custom is the tyrant that keeps us in bondage, and deprives us of the use of the law, which he, who happens to have white skin, is entitled to. We are not insensible, that if we should be liberated, and allowed by law to demand pay for our past services, our masters and their families would by that means be greatly damnified, if not ruined: But we claim no rigid Justice: Yet as we are honestly entitled to some compensation for all our toil and suffering; we would therefore, in addition to our prayers, that all of us, excepting such as are now infirm through age, or otherwise unable to support themselves, may be liberated and made free men of this community, and be entitled to all the privileges and immunities of its free and natural born subjects; further humbly ask, that your Excellency and Honours would be pleased to give grant to us some part of the unimproved land, belonging to the province, for a settlement, that each of us may there quietly sit under his own fig-tree, & enjoy the fruit of his own labour.

This scheme we apprehend, will remove all rational objections to our freedom; and promises so much good to our oppressed petitioners, as well as future advantages to the province, that we cannot but hope, that your Excellency & Honours will give it due weight and consideration; and that you will accordingly cause an act of the legislative to be passed, enabling all slaves thro'-out the province to demand and obtain their freedom from their masters and Mistresses; and at the same time prohibit any being sent out of the province, previous to the said Act's taking place.

But if your Excellency and Honours cannot in wisdom adopt this plan of relief for us, we humbly and earnestly request, that you would release us from bondage, by causing us to be transported to out native country within a short time; or by such other way or means as your Excellency and Honours shall seem good and wise upon the whole. And your petitioners, as in duty bound shall ever pray."

BOSTON July 29. Yesterday a special court of Admiralty, for the trial of piracies, murder, &c. on the high seas, was convened here, for the trial of Capt. Nikerson, for the murder of three men and a boy, on board a vessel in our bay in November last. The day was taken up in examining part of the evidence: The Court adjourned to this day, nine o'clock when they again met and proceeded on the trial.

BOSTON Aug. 2. On Friday last the Honorable Reverend Corporation of Havard College, having agreeable to the charter procured the presence of the Honorable and Reverend Overseers, by their advice and consent proceeded in the choice of a treasurer in the room of the Honorable Thomas Hubbard, Esq; deceased, who for about twenty years discharged that trust with uncommon attention and fidelity, greatly to the advantage of the College; and unanimously made choice of the Honorable John Hancock, Esq; to succeed in that office: which election was the same day confirmed by the Overseers.

BOSTON Aug. 5. A letter from London by the last ship says, That the petition of the House of Representatives of this province for the redress of the intolerable grievances, occasioned by the Governor and the Judges of the Superior Court being made dependent on the crown for support, have been presented to the King, but that the fate of them is dubious; his Majesty having been informed that it did not express the sense of the good people of the province, and that it was carried in the House by an artifice of a few of the Members.

BOSTON Aug. 9. On Wednesday the 28th of last Month came before a special Court of Admiralty in this Town, the Trial of Ansell Nickerson for piracy and Robbery on the High seas; the Examination of the Witnesses for the Crown and the prisoner held till Friday night, when the Court adjourned till Tuesday following at ten o'Clock, when Samuel Fitch, Esq; advocate-General, after reexamining several of the Witnesses for the King, applied the Evidence on the Crown Side; the Afternoon and the next Day were taken up by John Adams and Josiah Quincy, jr. Esqs; Council for the Prisoner in his Defence: and on Thursday Afternoon the Advocate General closed the Cause. The Court told the prisoner if he had any further to say in his Behalf, he would have the Opportunity the next Day; and adjourned to ten the next Morning. ——— The Court then meeting, proceeded to ask the prisoner if he had any thing further to offer the Court, in addition to what his Council had already said: Upon which the Prisoner express'd his wishes that certain Witnesses (who he apprehended would testify in his Favour) had been present; and concluded in saying that "If I lose my Life. I am innocent of the Crime laid to my charge."

The Court then gave Orders that all Persons depart except the Register; and having considered of the Evidence &c. for about 2 Hours and a half, the Prisoner was again called in, when the President, after a solemn Pause, told the Prisoner, "The Court have considered of your Evidence offered to them sufficient to support the Charges alleged against you in the Information answered, therefore adjudge you Not Guilty.

Motion was then made by the Prisoner's Council that he might be discharged, and the Advocate-General not objecting it was granted: The Prisoner being informed of it, respectfully bowed to the Court and said, —— "I thank the honorable Court —— and God for my delivery!"

The Court was then adjourned without Day.

Thus ended a Trial, for the most surprizing Event, which has happened in this, and perhaps any other age of the World.

BOSTON Aug. 9. A Number of Jersey indented Servants, a quantity of extraordinary good cordage, and Jersey knit Hose, to dispose of on board the Sloop London Expedition, Nicholas Chevalier, Master, from the Island of Jersey, laying at Tudor's Wharf.

Enquire of Philip Laurens, on board the said Sloop, or at Mrs. Bennett's opposite Deacon Tudor's at the North-End.

BOSTON Aug. 23. Extract of a Letter from London, May26, 1773.

"I take the first Opportunity of acquainting you that the East-India Company has obtained Leave, by Act of Parliament, to export their Teas from England Duty Free, and in a short Time, perhaps a Month a Cargo will be sent to Boston (subject to the Duty payable in America) to be sold in that Place on their account; and they mean to keep America so well supplied, that the Trade to Holland for the Article must be greatly affected."

BOSTON Sept. 2. Last Monday the Militia in this town had their second training for the present year; the company of Cadets, under the command of Colonel Hancock, mustered in the forenoon, and fully convinced numerous spectators, among whom were real judges of military exercises, that they were justly deserving of the reputable character they had acquired in the knowledge of that Art. —— The company of Artillery under the command of Major Paddock, and the company of the Grenadiers under the command of Lieutenant Pierce, made a very fine appearance, and did themselves honour in the characters of soldiers; and other militia companies in general performed their exercise with exactness that could not be expected from companies who have so little experience.

An unfortunate accident happened on Monday last, an the Artillery company was firing their field-pieces, a young lad named Milton, living with Mr. Tayer, house-wright, near the South Battery, ran before the mouth of one of the canon the instant it was fired, and the wad of which struck him in the head and wounded him in such a terrible manner that he died the next morning.

It is said there will be some appointments of a Governor, in one of the New-England governments at least very shortly.

BOSTON Sept. 6. Last Week one Joseph Attwood, was taken up at Portsmouth and brought to this Town; and after an examination before a Magistrate, was committed to Goal, on suspicion of being concerned with Levi Ames, who was apprehended a few Days before, in robbing the House of Mr. Martin Bicker of about 60 Pounds. —— said Ames confessed of the Fact and produced about 30 Pounds of the Cash; And also informed on Attwood, who he said was concerned with him, had hid some Plate at the Bottom of the Common; which upon searching was found, and proved to be the Takard, Spoons, &c. stolen from the rev. Mr. Jonas Clark of Lexington, the 2d of May Last. —— There was found upon said Attwood when taken, five Johannas, seven Dollars, and some small Silver, hid in his pocket, provided for that purpose, under the Crotch of his Breeches.

BOSTON Sept. 13. At the Superior Court of Judicature, Court of Assize and General Delivery held at the Court-House of this Town, on Monday last one Joseph Attwood was tried for Burglary, by breaking into the House of Mr. Martin Bicker as mentioned in our last, when the Jury brought in their Verdict Guilty in Fact; ―――― Guilty of the Theft, but not in Burglary. ―――― The next Day Levi Ames was also tried for the same Crime, when the Jury brought in their Verdict, ―――― Guilty. And on Friday Afternoon Sentence of Death was pronounced upon he agreeable to a late Law of this Province for the Crime of Burglary. Thursday the 14th of October next, is the day appointed for his Execution.

It evidently appeared that Ames entered the House and stole the Money, while Attwood watched in the Street ―――― Attwood was admitted as an evidence against him.

Attwood was sentenced to receive 20 stripes at the Publick Whipping Post, to pay Cost and treble Damages; but he signifying to the Court that he had nothing to discharge that sum, he was order'd to be at Mr. Bickers Disposal for ten Years.

BOSTON Sept. 17. To the Printers in the Land of Liberty are desired to publish the following.

The very important dispute between Britain and America, has for a long time employed the pens of the statemen in both countries, but no plan of union is yet agreed on between them, the dispute still continues, and every thing floats in uncertainty. As I long contemplated the subject with fixed attention, I beg leave to offer a proposal to my countrymen, viz. That a congress of American states be assembled as soon as possible, draw up a bill of Rights and publish it to the world; choose as Ambassador to reside at the British court, to act for the united colonies; appoint where congress shall annually meet, and how it may be summoned upon extraordinary occasions, what farther steps are necessary to be taken, &c.

The expence of an annual congress would be

very trifling, and the advantages would undoubtedly be great; in this way wisdom of the continent might upon all important occasions be collected, and operate for the interest of the whole people. Nor may any one imagine this plan, if carried into execution, will injure Great-Britain; for it will be the most likely way to bring the two countries to a right understanding, and settle matters in dispute advantageously for both. So sensible are the people of America that they are in possession of a fine country and other superior advantages, their rapid increase and growing importance, it cannot be thought they will ever give up their claim to equal liberty with any other people on earth; but rather, as they find their power perpetually increasing, look for a greater perfection in just liberty and government that other nations, or even Britain enjoy. As the colonies are blessed with the richest treasures of nature, Art will never be idle for want of stores to work upon; and they being instructed by the experience, the wisdom, and even errors, of all ages and countries, will undoubtedly rise superior to them all in the scale of human dignity, and give the world new and bright example of every thing which can add luster to humanity. No People that ever trod the stage of the world have had so glorious a prospect as now rises before the Americans ⎯⎯⎯ There is nothing good, or great, but their wisdom may acquire; and to what heights they will arrive in the progress of time no one can conceive. ⎯⎯⎯ That Great Britain should continue to insult and alienate, the growing millions who inhabit the country, on who she greatly depends, and on whose alliance in future time her existence as a nation may be suspended, is perhaps as glaring an instance of human folly as ever disgraced politicians, or put common sense to the blush.

                 Observation.

 BOSTON Sept. 20. In Capt. Calef, from London came passengers Capt. Hillhouse and Lady, Mr. Aleing; also Phillis, the extraordinary poetical Genius, Negro Servant to Mr. John Wheatly, of this Town.

BOSTON Oct. 7. We hear that a sloop belonging to Scituate, and fron Kennebeck to Boston, loaded with lumber, was stranded on Hampton beech last Saturday morning, when two men and a woman took to the boat, but were all lost. Two other men and a woman are missing. So that four men and two women have, by this melancholy accident lost their lives. Two men, staying on board the wreck were saved.

BOSTON Oct. 13. Last Saturday towards evening, a duel was fought on Noddle's Island, with pistols, between Capt. Maltby, of the Glasgow man of war, and Mr, Finney, late lieutenant of Marines on board the same ship, when the later received a ball through his neck, but it is thought will not prove mortal.

Extract of a letter from London, Aug. 4. The East-India Company has come to a resolution to send 900 chest of Tea to Philadelphia, and the like quantity to New-York and Boston, and their intention I understand is to have warehouses, and sell by public sale four times a year, as they do here.

Capt. Cook was offered part of that for Philadelphia, but refused it. ——— I suppose they will charter ships to take it in, as here are enough that would be glad of the freight. ——— What will the consequence when it arrives on our side the water I know not; but suppose but if it is landed, you will hardly let it be sold.

BOSTON Oct. 18. Mssrs. printers, A Merchant of this Town informed a Friend of mine, that some Days ago he had an Order by water from his Correspondent in Philadelphia to buy and send him a Number of Chests of Tea, on Arrival of the first East-India Cargo; but by the last Post he had a countermand of said order, with Instructions to make the best he could of any Tea he might have purchased on Consequence of it, as it would inevitably be destroyed if an Ounce of it was known brought into that City.

A notable Evidence this of the Spirit of our Philadelphia brethren, and you may venture to assure them, Messr's Printers, that they will find no Importer's Factors, or any other self interested wretches here at this Day, hardy enough to make a new Experiment on the Temper of the People. X. Y.

It is said that the merchantile spirit which so notably distinguishes the Father, bids fair to eternize the name of his excellency's children, their known principles having incited the East-India Company to pitch upon them as Consignees of the Axes and Scalping knives by them to the Port of Boston.

It is the current Talk of the Town that Richard Clarke, Benjamin Faneuil Esq; and two young Messieurs Hutchinsons, are appointed to receive the Tea allowed to be exported for this Place. This new Scheme of Administration, lately said to be so friendly to the Colonies, is at once so threatening to the trade, and so well calculated to establish & increase the detested Tribute, that an attempt to meddle with the pernicious Drug, would render men much more respected than they are as obnoxious as were the Commissioners of the Stamp-Act in 1765.

Should the Tea shipping for Boston be returned to England, as it undoubtedly will, if the people do not insist of copying the resolutions of Philadelphia and New-York to destroy it, Lord North will meet with a rebuff, which will put his utmost firmness to a trial. It will be inpossible for his Lordship after having exerted all his cunning in flattering the East-India Company to withstand their peremptory command of a trial repeal of the Tea Act.

A correspondent has hinted, that it would be highly improper to return those great Cargoes of Tea that are expected, without sending the important Gentlemen whose existence depends on it, to give the Premier the reason of such conduct.

The only objection to reshipping the Tea is, that in such case our excellent Governor and Superior Judges will inevitably fall back into a dependence on the Populace for their support.

BOSTON Oct. 25. Last Thursday was Executed pursuant to his sentence Levi Ames. ——— His Confession and Dying Words may be had at the shop opposite the new Court-House.

We learn that the late intention of the East

India Company of sending Bohea Tea to the Colonies, has created so much uneasiness and Opposition among the Merchants and others, trading in America, that it was uncertain whether any would be shipp'd hither on their Accounts or not.

BOSTON Nov. 1. It is positively asserted, said to be from good authority, that the barracks would be built on the foundation for barracks, laid at Fort Hill, before July next. [Fort Hill is an Eminence that would command most of the town.]

BOSTON Nov. 4. Mr. Thomas, one purpose, that whereas the peace of this community is inevitably destroyed, if the unconstitutional commissioners, &c. which some years past have been intruded upon us, get leave to remain any longer here; That the selectmen who are the fathers of the Town, assemble and go in body to them, respectively declaring their apprehension, that the people are not safe while they reside among them, and setting a time for their departure. And in case they do not comply with the proposal, for the whole body of the people to rise and expel them, as infected and dangerous Persons.   X. Y.

BOSTON Nov. 8. On Friday last there was a very full Meeting of the freeholders and other Inhabitants of this Town in Faneuil-Hall agreeable to the Notification issued to the Selectmen; When Hon. John Hancock, Esq; was chosen Moderator, and the Town after due Deliberation, came into the following Resolution viz.

Whereas it appears by an Act of the British Parliament passed in the last Session, that the Eas India Company of London are by the said Act allowed to export their Tea into America, in such Quantities as the Lord of the Treasury shall Judge proper: And some Persons with an evil intent to amuse the People, and others through inattention to the true Design of the Act, have so constructed the same, as that the Tribute of three Pence on every Pound of Tea is not to be exacted by the detestable Task Masters here. Upon the due Consideration thereof, Resolved, That the sense of this Town cannot be better expressed, upon this occasion, that in the words of certain judicious Resolves lately entered by our worthy Brethren the Citizens of Philadelphia.

At the same Time the Town passes the following Resolves, viz.

Whereas the Merchants of this Continent did enter into an agreement to with hold the Importation of Teas until the Duty laid thereon should be repealed; which Agreement, we are uniformed, has been punctually observed by the respectable Merchants in the Southern Colonies; while by reason of the peculiar Circumstances attending the Trade of this Place, some Quantities, thought very small on proportion to what had been usual before said agreement, have been imported by some of the Merchants here: And whereas it now appears probable to this Town, that the British Administration have taken encouragement even from such small Importations, to grant Licences to the East India Company as aforesaid: therefore Resolved, That it is the Determination of the Town by all means in their Power, to prevent the Sale of Teas exported by the East India Company: And as the Merchants here have generally opposed this Measure, it is the just Expectation of the Inhabitants of this Town, that no one of them will, on any pretence whatsoever, import any Tea that shall be liable to pay the Duty, from this time until the Act imposing the same shall be repealed.

And then the Town adjourned till three o'Clock in the Afternoon.

At three o'Clock there was again a very full Assembly; and the Committee reported to the Town that they had waited on Richard Clarke, Esq; & Son, and Benjamin Faneuil, Esq; said to be Factors of the East India Company, and communicated to them the Resolve of the Town, whereby they were requested immediately to resign their appointments. And that said Gentlemen informed the Committee that as Messieurs Thomas and Elisha Hutchinson (who were also reported to be Factors of the said Company) were at Milton, nor expected in Town till Saturday Evening, and as they chose to consult them, they could not

returned an answer to the Town till Monday Morning.
   Then another Committee was chosen, viz. Mr. Samuel Adams, Mr. William Molineaux, and Dr. Joseph Warren, to acquaint Messieurs, Clarke and Faneuil, that as they were not joint Factors for the East India Company with the Hutchinsons it was supposed they could determine for themselves, and therefore it was the expectation of the Town that they return an immediate answer to the message, and this Committee reported to the Town that an answer might be expected in half an hour.
   A Motion was then made that a Committee be appointed to repair to Milton, and acquaint Messieurs, Thomas and Elisha Hutchinson with the request of the Town, that they immediately resign their appointment; and John Hancock, esq; Mr. John Pitts, Mr. Samuel Adams, Mr. Samuel Abbot, Dr. Joseph Warren, Mr. William Powell, and Nathanial Appleton, were appointed a Committee for that purpose.
   A Letter was brought into the Hall signed by Richard Clarke & Son, and Benjamin Faneuil for himself and Joshua Winslow, and directed to the Moderator to be communicated to the Town, viz.
                    Boston November 5th 1773.
   Sir,
It is impossible for us to comply with the request of the Town signified to us this Day by their committee as we know know not what Terms the Tea. If any Part of it should be sent to our care, will come on, and what obligation either of a moral pecuniary Nature we may be under to fulfil the Trust that may be devolved of us. When we are acquainted with the circumstances, we shall be better qualified to give a definite Answer to the Request of the Town.
   We are sir, your most obedient servants.
Richard Clarke and Son, Benj. Faneuil, jun. for self, and Joshua Winslow Esq.
   Given to John Hancock, Esq; Moderator of the Town Meeting at Faneuil-Hall.
   This Letter was read, and unanimously voted to be not satisfactory to the Town and then the Metting was adjourned until next Day at Eleven o'Clock to receive the Report of the Committee

appointed to wait on the Hutchinsons.

The Town met by adjournment on Saturday (the Meeting still continued very full) and the Committee reported that they had seen Thomas Hutchinson only, (his brother being neither in Milton or Boston) and that the Town might expect an answer from him immediately.

The following Letter was sent in, to the Moderator, signed Thos' Hutchinson: which was read and unanimously voted to be an unsatisfactory answer, viz.

"Sir,
I know nothing relative to the Tea refered to in the request or Vote of the Town, except that one of my Friends has signified by Letter that Part of it he had Reason to believe would be consigned to me and my brother jointly. But upon what terms he could not then say. Under these Circumstances, I can give no other Answer to the Town at present, than that if the Tea should arrive, and we should be appointed Factors, we shall then be sufficiently informed to answer the Request of the Town.

I am for my Brother and Self, sir your humble Servant.   Thos. Hutchinson jun."

Honourable John Hancock, Esq; Moderator of a Town Meeting now assembled at Faneuil-Hall.

It was then voted that the Letter signed by Richard Clarke and Son, Benj. Fanneuil for self and Joshua Winslow, and also the Letters signed Tho. Hutchinson, which had been read were daringly Affrontive to the Town! and the meeting was immediately Dissolved.

BOSTON Nov. 8. Messieurs Edes & Gill.
It has been reported that a Company of Soldiers belonging to the Castle were seen marching armed towards the Town last Saturday a little before Sunset, about four Miles off; and it is strongly suspected that they came into town in separate Gangs. It is certain that several of them have been seen in different Parts of the Metropolis, brandishing their naked weapons, and otherwise behaving in a most insolent Manner. ——— This is sufficient to raise the apprehension of the Inhabitants.
                                        Determinatus.

BOSTON Nov. 22. Wednesday Evening a number of People assembled before the House of Richard Clarke, Esq; one of the Tea Commissioners and huzzared, upon which a Musket was fired from his House among the Populace, which so enraged them that they broke his windows, &c.

One of the Sons of Richard Clarke, a Tea Factor, having some Time since been in Bargain with Benjamin Jepson for a quantity of Oil, came in on Friday last to Mr. Jepson: But Mr. Jepson like a true Friend of his Country told Mr. Clarke with indignation that he could not have any Thing further to say to him, as he had given the Town so much trouble and Danger, he would not let him have it for twice what he offered. A noble Example this of Uniformity in public and private Conduct. These Persons having beem unanimously voted public Enemies in Case they persist in the Resolution to dispose of the East India Company's Teas.

BOSTON Nov. 29. Last Saturday arrived Capt. Clark, in a Brig from London, which he left the latter End of August. ——— and Yesterday Morning Capt. Hall, in the Ship Dartmouth, came to Anchor near the Castle, in about 8 Weeks from the same Place, and early this Morning came up into the Harbour; on board of whom it is said are 114 Chests of the much talk'd of East India Company's Tea, expected arrival of which pernicious Articles had for some Time past put all these northern Colonies in very great Ferment: ——— And this Morning the following Notification was posted up in all Parts of the Town, viz.

Friends! Brethren! Countrymen!
That worst Plague the detestable Tea shipped for this Port by the East India Company, is now arrived in the Harbour, the Hour of Destruction or manly Opposition to the Machination of Tyranny stares you in the Face; every Friend to this Country, to himself, and posterity, is now called upon to meet at Faneuil-Hall, at Nine o'Clock this Day, (at which Time Bells will ring) to make a united and successful Resistance to this last, worst and most destructive Measure of Administration. Boston Nov. 29 1773.

BOSTON Dec. 6. At a Meeting of the People of

Boston, and the neighbouring Towns at Faneuil-Hall, in said Boston, on Monday the 29th of November 1773 Nine o'Clock A. M. and continued by adjournment to the next Day; for the purpose of consulting, advising and determining upon the most proper and effectual Method to prevent the detestable Tea sent out of the East India Company, Part of which being just arrived in this Harbour:

In order to proceed with due Regularity, it was moved that a Moderator be chosen, and Jonathan Williams, Esq; was then chosen Moderator of the Meeting.

A Motion was made that as the Town of Boston had determined at a late meeting legally assembled that they wou'd to the utmost of their Power prevent the landing of the Tea, the Question be put, whether this Body are absolutely determined that the Tea now arrived in Capt. Hall be returned to the Place from whence it came at all events, And the Question being accordingly put. It passed in the affirmitive. Nem. Con.

It appearing that the Hall could not contain the People assembled, it was Voted, that the meeting be immediately adjourned to the Old South Meeting-House, Leave having been obtained for this purpose.

The People met at the Old South according to Adjournment.

A Motion was made, and the Question put, viz. Whether it is the firm Resolution of the Body that the Tea shall not only be sent back, but that no Duty shall be paid thereon; & pass'd in the Affirmative. Nem. Con.

It was moved, that in order to give Time to the Consignees to consider and deliberate, before they sent in their proposals to this Body, as they had given Reason to expect would have been done at the opening of the Meeting, there might be an adjournment to Three o'Clock, and the Meeting accordingly for that purpose ad-, journed.

Three o'clock, P. M. according to adjournment A Motion was made, whether the Tea now arrived in Capt. Hall's Ship shall be sent back in the same Bottom ——— Pass'd in the Affirmative Nem. Con.

Mr. Rotch the Owner of the Vessel being present, informed the Body that he should enter his Protest against the Proceedings.

It was then moved and voted Nem. Con. That Mr. Rotch be directed not to enter the Tea; and that the doing of it would be at his Peril.

Also Voted, that Capt. Hall the Master of the Ship, be informed that at his Peril he is not to suffer any of the Tea brought by him, to be landed.

A Motion was made. That in Order for the Security of Captain Hall's Ship and Cargo, a Watch may be appointed ——— and it was Voted that a Watch be accordingly appointed to consist of 25 Men.

Capt. Edward Proctor was appointed by the Body to be the Capt. of the Watch for this Night, and names were given in to the Moderator, of the Townsmen who were Volunteers on the Occasion.

It having been observed to the Body that Governor Hutchinson had required the Justices of the Peace in this Town to meet and use their endeavours to surpress any Routs or Riots, &c. of the People that might happen. ——— It was Moved and the Question put ——— Whether it be not the Sense of the Meeting, that the Governor's Conduct herein carries a design'd Reflection upon the People here met; and is solely calculated to serve the Views of Administration ——— Passed in the Affirmative Nem. Con.

The People being informed by Col Hancock, that Mr. Copley, son-in-Law to Mr. Clarke, Sen. had acquainted him that the Tea Consignees did not receive their Letters from London till last Evening, and were so dispersed, that they could not have a joint Meeting early enough to make their Proposals at that Time intended; and therefore were desirous of a future Space for that Purpose.

The Meeting out of the great Tenderness to those Persons, and from a strong Desire to bring this matter to a conclusion notwithstanding the time they had hitherto expended upon them to no purpose, were proclaimed upon to adjourn to the next Morning Nine o'Clock.

Tuesday Morning Nine o'Clock, met according to Adjournment.

The long expected Proposals were at length brought into the Meeting, and not directed to the Moderator, but to John Scullay, Esq; one of the Selectmen —— It was however voted that the same should be read, and they are as Follows, viz.

Monday Nov. 29th 1773.

Sir,

We are sorry that we could not return to the Town, satisfactory answers to their two late Messages to us respecting the Teas; we beg Leave to acquaint the Gentlemen Selectmen that we have since received our Orders from the Honorable East India Company.

We still retain a Disposition to do all in our Power to give Satisfaction to the Town, but as we understood from you and the other Gentlemen at Messr. Clarke's Interview with you last Saturday, that this can be effected by nothing less than our sending back the Teas, we beg Leave to say, that this is utterly out of our Power to do, but we do now declare to you our Readiness to Store the Teas until we shall have the Opportunity of writing to our Constituents and shall receive their further Orders respecting them; and we do most sincerely with that of the Town considering the unexpected Difficulties devolved upon us will be satisfied with what we now offer.

We are, Sir, Your most humble Servants.
Tho. & Elisha Hutchinson, Benja. Faneuil, jun. for self and Joshua Winslow, Rsq; and Richard Clarke & Sons.

John Sculley Esq;

Mr. Sheriff Greenleay come into the Meeting and begg'd Leave of the Moderator that a Letter he had received from the Governor, requiring him to read a Proclamation to the People here assembled might be read; and accordingly read.

Whereupon it was moved, that the Question be put, whether the Sheriff should be permitted to read the Proclamation —— which passed in the Affirmative, Nem. Con.

The Proclamation is the following, viz.
Massachusetts-Bay, by the Governor.
To Jonathan Williams, Esq; acting Moderator of the Assembly of People in the Town of Boston, and to the People so assembled:

Whereas printed Notifications were on Monday the 29th Instant posted in divers Places in this Town of Boston and published in the News-Papers of the Day calling upon the People to assemble together for certain unlawful Purposes in such Notification mentioned: And whereas great Numbers of People belonging to the Town of Boston, and divers others belonging to several other Towns in the Province, did assemble in the said Town of Boston, on the said Day, and did then and there proceed to chose a Moderator, and to consult, debate and resolve upon Ways and Means for carrying such unlawful Purposes into Excecution; openly violating, defying and setting at nought the good and wholesome Laws of the Province and the Constitution of Government under which they live: And whereas the People thus assembled did vote or agree to adjourn or continue their Meeting to this the 30th Instant, and great Numbers of them are again met or assembled together for the like purpose in the said Town of Boston.

In Faithfulness to my Trust and as His Majesty's Representative within the Province I am bound to hear Testimony against this Violation of the Laws and the warn exhort and Require you and each of you thus unlawfully assembled forthwith to disperse and sucrease all futher unlawful Proceedings at your utmost Peril.

Given under my Hand at Milton in the Province aforesaid the 30th Day of November 1773 and in the fourteenth Year of his Majesty's Reign. By His Excellency's Command, Tho's Flecker, Secr'y

T. Hutchinson.

And the same being read to the Sheriff there was immediately after, a loud and very general Hiss.

A Motion was then made, and the Question put, whether the Assembly would disperse and suspend all further Proceedings, according to the Governor's Requirement ──── It pass'd in the

Negative Nem. Con.

A Proposal of Mr. Copley was made, that in case he could prevail with the Mssrs. Clarkes to come into this Meeting the Question might now be put, whether they should be treated with civility while in the Meeting, though they might be a different Sentiment with this Body; and their Persons be safe until their Return to the Place from whench they should come ——— And the Question being accordingly put, passed in the Affirmative, Nem. Con.

Another Motion of Mr. Copley's was put whether two Hours shall be given him, which also passed in the Affirmative.

Adjourn'd to Two o'Clock P. M.

Two o'Clock met according to Adjournment. A Motion was made and passed, that Mr. Rotch and Capt. Hall be desired to give their Attendance, the Question was put, Whether it is the firm Resolution of this Body, that the Tea brought by Capt. Hall shall be returned by Mr. Rotch to England in the Bottom in which it came; and whether they accordingly now require the same, which passed in the Affirmative, Nem. Con.

Mr. Rotch then informed the Meeting that he should protest against the whole proceedings on Yesterday, but that tho' the returning of the Tea is an involuntary Act in him, he yet considered himself as under a Necessity to do it, and shall therefore comply with the Requirement of this Body.

Capt. Hall being present was forbid to aid or assist in unloading the Tea at his Peril, and ordered that if he continued Master of the Vessel, he carry the same back to London; who reply'd he should comply with these Requirements.

Upon Motion, Resolved, that John Rowe, Esq; owner of Part of Capt. Bruce's Ship expected with Tea, and also Mr. Timmins, Factor for Capt. Coffin's Brig desired to attend.

Mr. Ezekiel Chrever was appointed Captain of the Watch for the Night, and a sufficient Number of Volunteers gave their Nanes for that Service.

Voted, That the Captain of the Watch also be

desired to make out a List of the watch for the next Night, and so each Captain of the watch for the following Nights until the Vessels leave the Harbour.

Upon Motion made, Voted, that in case it should happen that the Watch should be in any Ways molested in the Night while on Duty, They give Alarm to the Inhabitants by the tolling of the Bells. ——— and that if anything happens in the Day Time, the Alarm by ringing the Bells.

Voted, That six Persons be appointed to be in Readiness to give due Notice in the Country Towns when they shall be required so to do, upon any important Occasion. And six Persons were accordingly chosen for that Purpose.

John Rowe, Esq; attended, and was informed that Mr. Rotch had engaged that his Vessel should carry back the Tea she bro't in the same Bottom, & that it was the Expectation of this Body that he does the same by the Tea expected in Capt. Bruce; whereupon he reply'd that the Ship was under care of the said Master, but that he would use his utmost Endeavours, that it should go back as required by this Body, and that he would give immediate Advice of the Arrival of said Ship.

Voted, That it is the Sense of this Body that Capt. Bruce shall on his Arrival strictly conform to the Votes passed respecting Capt. Hall's Vessel, as tho' they had been all passed in reference to Capt. Bruce's Ship.

Mr. Timmins appeared and informed the Capt, Cossin's Brig expected with Tea was owned in Nantucket, he gave his Word of Honor that no Tea should be landed while she was under his care, and touched by any one until the Owner's Arrived.

It was then Voted, That what Mr. Rowe and Mr. Timmins had offered was satisfactory to the Body.

Mr. Copley returned and acquainted the Body the following; as he had been obliged to go to the Castle, he hoped that if he had exceeded the Time allowed him they would consider the Difficulty of a passage by Water at this Season as his Apology: He then further acquainted the

Body, that he has seen all the Consignees, and tho' he had convinced them that they might attend the Meeting with safety, and had used his utmost endeavours to prevail upon them to give Satisfaction to the Body; they acquainted him, that believing nothing would be satisfactory short of shipping the Tea, which was out of their Power, they thought it best not to appear, but would renew their proposal of storing the Tea, and submitting to the same to the inspection of the Committee and that they could go no further without incurring their own Ruin; but as they had not been active in introducing the Teas, they should do nothing to obstruct the People in their Procedure with the same.

It was then moved, and the question put whether the return made by Mr. Copley from the Consignees be in the first degree satisfactory to the Body & passed in the Negative. Nem. Con.

Whereas a Number of the Merchants in this Province have Inadvertently imported Tea from Great Britain, while it is subject to the Payment of a Duty imposed upon it by an Act of the British Parliament for that Purpose of raising a Revenue in America, and appropriately the same without the Consent of those who are required to pay for it:

Resolved, That in thus importing said Tea, they had justly incurr'd the Displeasure of our Brethren in the other Colonies.

And Resolved further, That if any Person or Persons shall hereafter import Tea from Great Britain, or any Master or Masters of any Vessel or Vessels of Great Britain shall take the same on Board to be imported to this Place until the said unrighteous Act shall be repealed, he or they shall be deem'd by the Body an Enemy to his Country; and we will prevent the Landing and Sale of the same, and the Payment of any Duty thereon. And we will effect the Return thereof to the Place from whence it shall come.

Resolve, That the foregoing Vote be printed and sent to England, and all the Sea-Ports in this Province.

Upon Motion made, Voted, That said Copies be taken of the whole Proceedings of the Meeting and transmitted to New-York & Philadelphia, And that Mr. Samuel Adams, Hon. John Hancock, Esq; William Phillips, Esq; John Rowe, Esq; Jonathan Williams, Esq; Be a Committee to transmit the same.

Voted, that the Committee of Corespondence for this Town, be desired to take Care that every other Vessel with Tea that arrives in this Harbour, have a proper Watch appointed for her ──── Also Voted, that those Persons who are desirous of making a Part of these Nightly Watches, be desired to give in their Names at Messieurs Clarke's Brigantine.

Voted, That those of this Body who belong to the Town of Boston do return their Thanks to the Brethren who have come from the Neighbouring Towns, for their Countenance and Union with the Body in this Exigence of our Affairs.

Voted, That the Thanks of the Meeting be given to Jonathan Williams, Esq; for his good service as Moderator.

Voted, That this Meeting be Dissolved ──── and it was accordingly Dissolved.

BOSTON Dec. 20. The following Notification was on Tuesday Morning the 14th Inst. posted up through this Town.

Friends! Brethren! Countrymen!

The perfidious Art of your restless Enemies to render ineffectual the late resolutions of the Body of People, demand your assembling at the Old South Meeting-House; precisely at two o'Clock This Day, at which the Bells will ring.

At the Meeting of the People of Boston, and the Neighbouring Towns, at the Old South Meeting-House in Boston on Tuesday December 14, 1773 and continued by Adjourment to Thursday the 16th of said Month occasioned by perfidious Acts of our restless Enemies, to render ineffectual the late Resolutions of the Body of the People.

Mr. Samuel Phillips Savage, A Gentleman of the Town of Western was chosen Moderator.

A Motion made and passed that Mr. Rotch, owner of Capt. Hall's Ship. be desired to give his Attendance.

Capt. Bruce, Master of one of the Ships with

Tea on Board, being present, it was moved that he might be asked, whether he will demand a Clearance for his Ship of the Custon House, and if refused, enter his protest, and then proceed on his voyage to London —— He replied that when all his Goods were landed, he would demand a Clearance, but if refused he was loth to stand the shot of thirty two pounders.

Mr. Rotch appeared, and was required at his peril to apply immediately to Mr. Collector Harrison for the Clearance for his ship; and Benjamin Knot, Esq; with nine other gentlemen, were appointed to proceed with him to the Collector's.

Mr. Rotch returned and aquainted the Body, that he had, accompanied by the said committee, waited on the Collector and required a clearance for his vessel, as directed; and this the Collector reply'd that he chose to see the Comptroller first; and at Ten o,Clock the next morning he should be ready to give hin an answer.

It was then moved that this meeting be adjourned to Thursday next at Ten o'clock A. M. and that Mr. Rotch and the committee be desired to wait upon the Collector at that time appointed. —— and the meeting was accordingly adjourned.

Thursday December 16 Ten o'Clock A. M. Met according to Adjournment.

The Committee to accompany Mr. Rotch to the Collector reported, that Mr. Rotch had made his demand in the following manner, viz. "I am required and compell'd at my peril by a body of people assembled at the old south meeting-house yesterday where Mr. Samuel Phillips Savage was President, to make a demand of you to give me a clearance for the ship Darthmouth for London in the situation she is now in with the Teas on board."

Upon which one of the committee observ'd that there were present, by order of the body, only as witnesses of the before mentioned demand and the answer should be given.

Thereupon Mr. Harrison the collector sair to Mr. Rotch (Mr. Hollowell the comptroller being present) 'then it is you make the demand;' Mr.

Mr. Rotch answered, 'yes, an am compell'd at my peril' Then Mr. Harrison said to Mr. Rotch 'your ship Dartmouth entered with me the 30th of November last with dutiable articles on board, for which the duties have not been paid, I cannot therefore give you a clearance until she is discharged of those aticles consistent to my duty.'

Mr. Rotch attending according to order, was informed, that this Body expect that he will immediately protest against the custom house and apply to the Governor for his pass for the Castle, and that his vessel shall this day proceed on her voyage for London.

Mr. Rotch reply'd to this, that he could not comply with their requirements, because it was impracticable.

Mr. Rotch was then told, that he had assured the Body that his vessel should sail within 20 days after arrival, which term would this day expire, and being asked whether he would order his vessel to sail this day, he emply'd that he would not.

The Body desired Mr. Rotch to make all possible dispatch in making a protest and procuring a pass for his vessel, and then adjourn'd till 3 o'clock P. M.

The People were informed, that several towns had lately come into measures to prevent the consumption of Tea, whereupon it was mentioned and Voted, That it is the sense of this Body that the use of Tea is improper and pernicious.

Upon a motion made, Voted, That it is the opinion of this Body, that it would be expedient for every town in this Province to appoint committees of inspection, to prevent this contested said tea from coming into any of the towns.

It was moved and question put, whether it be the sense and determination of this Body to abide by their former resolutions with respect to not suffering the Tea to be landed ——
Which passed in the affirmative Nem. Con.

It being now half past 4 o'clock, many were

desirous and even moved that the Meeting should be immediately Dissolved; but some Gentlemen of the Country informed the Body that their several Towns were so very anxious to have full information as to this matter, that they were quite desirous the Meeting should be continued until 6 o'clock especially as Mr. Rotch had been met with on his way to Milton for a pass, the motion was accordingly over ruled.

Mr. Rotch returned before 6 o'clock and inform'd the Body, that in pursuance of their directions he had waited upon the Governor Hutchinson, and demanded of him a Pass for his sailing by the Castle, and received for answer, "That he was willing to any thing consistent with the laws and his duty to the King, but that he could not give a pass unless the vessel was properly qualified from the Custom-House, but that he should make no distinction between this and any other Vessels provided she was properly cleared."——He further acquainted the Body that his protest against the Custom-House not being finished in season, he could not carry the same with him, but declared that he had informed the Governor of the steps he had and was taking as to Protest.

Mr. Rotch was then asked, Whether he would send his Vessel back with the Tea in her present circumstance? who answered that he could not possibly comply, as he apprehended a compliance would prove his ruin. —— He was further asked, Whether it was his intention to land the Tea? He replied that he had no business to do it unless he was called upon by the proper Persons, in which case he should attempt to land it for his own security.

The Body having manufactured an exemplary patience and caution in the method it had pursued to preserve the Tea, the property of the East India Company, without it being made saleable among us, which must have been counter worked by the Consignees of the Tea, and their Coadjutors, who have plainly manifested their inclination of throwing the Community in the most violent commotions, rather than relinquish and give up the project of a commission or contract, and that the advantages they have imagined from the establishment of an American Revenue; and no one being able to point out any thing further that it was the power of this Body to do, for the salutary purpose aforesaid —— It was moved and voted, That this Meeting immediately be Dissolved —— and it was accordingly.

Just before the Dissolution of the Meeting a Number of Brace resolute Men, dressed in the Indian Manner, approached near the Door of the Assembly, gave the War-Whoop, which rang thruogh the House, and was answered by some of the Galleries, but since being commanded, and a peaceable Deportment was again enjoyed, till the Dissolution: The Indians, as they were then called, repaired to the Wharf where the Ships lay that had the Tea on board, and were followed by hundreds of People to see the Event of the Transactions of those who made so grotesque an Appearance: They, the Indians, immediately repaired on board Capt. Hall's Ship, where they hoisted out the Chests of Tea, and when upon Deck stove the Chests and emptied the Tea overboard; having cleared this Ship they proceeded to Capt. Bruce's and then Capt. Coffin's Brig —— they applied themselves so dexterously to the Destruction of this Commodity that in the Space of three Hours they broke up 342 Chests, which was the whole Number in those Vessels, and discharged their Contents into the Docks; when the tide rose it floated the broken Chests and the Tea insomuch that the Surface upon the Water was filled therewith a considerable Way from the South Part of the Town to Dorchester-Neck, and lodged on Shore —— There was the greatest care taken to prevent the Tea from being purloined by the Populace: One or two being detected in endeavouring to pocket a small quantity stripped of their acquisitions and very roughly handled. —— It is worthy to Remark, that although a considerable quantity of Goods were still remaining on board the Vessels, no injury was sustained: Such attention to private Property was observed that a small Padlock belonging to the Captain of one of the Ships being broke, another was procured and sent to him.

—— The Town was very quiet during the whole Evening and the Night following: Those Persons who were from the Country, returned with merry Hearts, and the next Day Joy appeared in almost every countenance, some on occasion of the Destruction of the Tea others on account of the quietness with which it was affected.

BOSTON Dec. 27. At a Council held at the house of the honorable William Brattle Esq; in Cambridge on Tuesday 21, December 1773.

His Excellency Thomas Hutchinson, Esq; Governor. Samuel Danfort, Qilliam Brattle, James Pitt, Isaac Royall Esq; James Bowdwin, John Winthrop, John Erving and James Pussel Esqrs.

His Excellency acquainted the Council that the reason he had summoned them to meet at this time was that he might have their advice relating to the high handed riot of the evening of the 16th instant between the hours of six and nine o'clock, committed by persons disquised and unknown, on board three Vessels lately arrived from London then lying at a wharf in the Southerly part of the Town of Boston known by the name Griffin's Wharf —— After long debate it was advised. That the Attorney-General be directed to make diligent inquiry into the offence aforesaid in order to discover the offenders, and that he lay his discoveries before the Grand Jury for his Majesty's Superior Court of Judicature &c. for the County of Suffolk, at the next term, in order to prosecute.

BOSTON Dec. 27. The Printers are desired by a Committee of the Dealers of Tea in this Town, to insert the following authentic Copy of their Proceedings.

At a Meeting of a large Number of the principal Dealers in Teas in Boston, the 20th, and continued by adjournment to the 23d Dec. 1773.

Having maturely considered the many Evils that would inevitably flow from the execution of a late ministerial movement in favor of the East India Company, and that this flagrant attempt against our Liberties hast justly alarmed America, and excited a laudable spirit emulation in her Sons, to distinguish themselves opposing a measure which, if permitted to operate, would have drained the Colonies of the greater Part of their Specie, would have been constructed an aquiescence in the right assumed by the British Parliament to tax them, and might have ended in a total Privation of out just Rights.

Impress'd by an ardent solitude for our Country ourselves, and posterity, whose future welfare greatly depend on a repeal of the duty long complained of, and which hath been a principal cause, for the several years together, of an unhappy interruption of that reciprocal affection, that was wont to subsist between the parent State and the Colonies; the restoration of which is essential to the prosperity of both. Apprehending it may be in some degree in our power to facilitate that whish'd-for state, by our late connections, as sellers of the article thus burthen'd, and the consequent influence we must have in suppressing its use: This consideration hath begot an expectation in many of our fellow citizens and countrymen, that we do unite our endeavours wiht theirs in exterminating this destructive herb from the Province.

It must be evident to our friends and countrymen, in the seaports, and other towns, that a congruity of action, at this important crisis, is as necessary as a unanimity of sentiment; and that this instance of disinterestedness we are about to exhibit, by a voluntary surrender of an advantageous article of commerce, when opposed to the public good, will stimulate them to adopt similar to ours: In this confidence supported by a recollection of their inflexible virtue, frequently and recently manifested, we chearfully enter into the following Resolves:

1. That from and after the 20th of January 1774, we will suspend the sale of Teas, until the sense and determination of the inhabitants of the seaports and other towns, can be known, with respect to its total expulsion; or until a repeal of the revenue act make take place.

2. That we will not, in the mean time, purchase on our own Account, or receive on commission or otherwise, any Tea whatsoever.

3. That the Tea we have by us unsold, which

cost us 5s. shall be sold at no more than 4d. advance, until time, limited for suspending the sale.

4. That a Committee be appointed to apply to all Dealers in Tea in this Town to obtain their compliance to these Resolves, and make report of the same, with the Names of those who decline (if any there may be) in our next meeting.

5. That if, from the change of circumstances, or the intervention of other causes, any Ten of our number shall judge it necessary to call a meeting, to make any alterations, or to adopt other measures to effect the aforesaid purpose, they have our consent to do it.

N. B. ——— It is desired that all Persons concerned would consider the importance of a just determination, and be prepared to give answers to the committee, who will apply to them in a few days.

BOSTON Dec. 27. This last Week it was currently reported that his Excellency Governor Hutchinson, in conversation with some of the Council spoke of the late Proceedings here of the United Towns, as coming under the Denomination of Treason or Rebellion: ——— and intimated his Design that an attorney General should be heard upon the matter before the Council. ——— But the Matter not taking, his Excellency when he met his Council to do Business at the House of Brigadier Brattle in Cambridge, wisely changed his Tune; and Mr. Attorney wisely declined his Talk; and the Subject of Consideration turned upon burglary and Riots, instead of Treason and Rebellion; and Mr. Attorney gratified the Eyes of the honorable Board at Dinner instead of feasting their Ears in Council Chamber.

BOSTON Dec. 30. Monday evening Mr. Paul Revere returned from New York.

The News of the destruction of the Teas, as it was the only way left to prevent the chains prepared from being riveted, we are well informed, gave satisfaction to all the Friends of American Liberty, who heard of it.

The Tea ship was not arrived at New-York on Thursday last, when the post came away, and we are informed that Capt. Ascough, commander of the Swan, on that Station, has orders, when ever she arrives to supply her with necessaries, that she may immediately return from whence she came, with the Tea on board. On, receiving this intelligence and hearing likewise that the Tea had arrived at Charlestown South Carolina and that the Inhabitants there had determined it should return to London on the same bottom on which it came, all the bells in town were rung.

   It is said the behaviour of Governor Tryon at New-York with regard to the tea, will redound much of his honour ―――― whilst the conduct of a Hutchinson will be executed to the latest period of Time.

1774

BOSTON Jan. 10. Yesterday the Ship Dartmouth, Capt. Hall, sailed for London in whom went passengers, Francis Rotch, Mr. William Turner, Mr. James Henderson, Mr. David Black, Mr. John Dean Whitworth, and Mr. George Wilson.

BOSTON Jan. 17. On of the Tea Commissioners it is said narrowly escaped a Tarring and Feathering on day last week. Presumptuous men to think of gaining a footing in this Town again ——— to says every man, high and low, rich or poor.

It is said that some of the friends of the Tea Commissioners, that is hard upon them to be kept at the Castle, while two of the commissioners of the Custom who are more blameless are suffered to walk the streets at large.

BOSTON Jan. 24. Last Monday evening Elisha Hutchinson one of the Consignees arrived at the house of Col. Watson of Plymouth, his father-in-law. The people obtained knowledge of it, they tolled the bells in a solemn manner, and they were speedily a great appearance of them before the house, demanding Mr. Hutchinson's instant departure from the town; but through the interposition of the committee of correspondence, so much traduced, because so much dreaded by the tories, he was suffered to tarry until the next morning. In the morning the young gentleman, either oversleeping himself, or perhaps disposed to make an experiment on the tempers of the people, tarried beyond the limited time; but was fully convinced that his safety depended on his departure and he decamped in a snow storm; making the best of his way to Cheesemetuck to relate the melancholy adventure to the very sympathetic Chief Justice Hazelrod.

BOSTON Jan. 24. The weather for several days past has been severely cold; many persons have had their fingers, toes, &c. frost nipt.

The Harbour is so blocked up with ice, that our navigation is at a stand.

Last Monday Jemima Lewis, wife of Thomas Lewis, of this town, mariner, was found dead on the floor of her apartment. An inquisition was taken upon her body, and it was fully proved to the Jurors, that the preceding evening, she was intoxicated with spirituous liquor, being destitute of the common necessaries of life, and the weather being extreme cold, was frozen, and by that means came to her death.

BOSTON Jan. 27. Last Thursday afternoon as Mr. John Malcom was passing along the street, a lad with a sled ran by him and the sled bitting his feet, he pursued the boy with a cane in his hand to give him a blow, a Person near endeavouring to persuade him from it, upon which Malcom struck the man, and the people gathering together he got a sword, and made several pushes at him with it, and graz'd a man in his breast. A warrant was issued out by a magistrate against Malcom for a breach of the peace, and the constable went to his home to apprehend him, but he had confined himself, however he went to the back of the house and begged of the officer to let him alone till next morning, as he was afraid to venting out, so many people being enraged against him.

The officer then went away. In the evening a number surrounded his house, and entering, found him in the upper chamber, they got a rope and lowered him out of the window into a cart which they had prepared, then tore his clothes off, and tarr'd his head and body, and feathered him, then set him into a chair in the cart, and carried him through the main street into King Street, from thence they proceeded to Liberty Tree, and then to the Neck as far as the gallows, where they whipped him, beat him with sticks and threatened to hang him: having continued under the gallows about half an hour, they returned in the same manner surrounded by a vast concourse of people, and was carried to the most extreme part of the North End of the Town; and returned to his own house just before midnight: it is said he was near four hours in the condition above mentioned, and that he was so benum'd by the coldness of the weather, and his nakedness, and bruised in such a manner that his life is despaired of.

BOSTON Jan, 31. It is said Mr. Faneuil has determined to come up to Town this Week, being so tired with the treatment he receives from the beloved Soldiery, for which himself and brethren had such a Veneration and esteem, that he had rather run the risque of whether his Fellow Citizens may be disposed to inflict on him, than submit any longer to continual insults.

Remember Mr. Faneuil, this is the fault of your own Nursery. You laughed at Town-Meetings harangued against Military Tyranny. You are now perfectly welcomed to the Monopoly both of it and the Tea trade.

It is said Jack Frost has nearly compleated a Bridge from the Castle Island to the Main; so, that when finished, the Tea Consignees may, if dispos'd have the Opportunity of walking to land to see the Natives; or give them an Invitation to their City of Refuge.

BOSTON Feb. 7. Mess'rs Fleets, The Friends of the Agents for the East India Company beg leave through the channel of your Paper to assure the Publick, that the Insinuation published by Mess'rs Edes and Gill, in their Gazette on one of those Gentlemen having received any insult, or other ill Treatment from the soldiery at Castle William, is entirely groundless, and that, on the contrary all the Agents who have been at the Castle have been treated with the greatest Humanity and Politeness by the Honorble Gentlemen who command at that Fortress, and the other Gentlemen of the Military Corp.

BOSTON Feb. 14. Mess'rs Fleet,
  We'll have Freedom to call our own,
  Which shall depend on Heaven alone.

It is far beneath the character of the brave million of Freemen who inhabit this vast continent, to depend on any people but themselves, or present a petition for their Rights to anyone but the Lord who gave them being with the rights of humanity; and has told them that they who put their trust in Him shall never be confounded, but shall prosper.

It has vainly been expected by some, that petitioning the Rulers in Britain, would secure the liberties of America; but experience demonstrates their error, and confirms the general opinion, that Americans Liberty will forever depend upon American Virtues. The Patriots in Britain, are so far from being able to defend the Rights of America, that they cannot secure their own; and for the Americans to look for protection from a people who cannot protect themselves, would be the most consummate of all absurdities.

It has long been evident, that Britain declines in virtue, liberty and political wisdom; and there are many striking omens of her glory's hastening to a period. The virtue and liberty of America is her brightest hope; if this fails ruin stares her in the face. Therefore I would urge the Americans, by every argument which can move the human heart and by all the considerations of Virtue, Religion, and Liberty, to unite as one man animated with the highest ardour in the noblest cause, and stand firm to their purpose —— unalterably firm as the Mountains of America.

The preservation of the liberty and the progress of science in America, may rekindle the ancient British spirit, and old Albion may once more shine with the lustre of Freedom, —— her Sons being roused by Americans, may shake off the infamous shackles of arbitrary power, and no longer have masters instead of servants, to rule the state —— nor suffer themselves to be degraded below the scale of humanity, by being slaves to haughty lords, who do not suffer them to eat the fruit of their own labour, nor enjoy even the light of heaven without paying for it.* —— To establish the same usurpation and Tyranny in America, which have long plundered the unhappy Britons, has been the darling plan of corrupt ministers and their tools; but, under the smiles of Heaven, the Patriots in this country have proved superior to all the wicked machinations of their enemies. The Americam have merited the love and admiration of all the wise and virtuous, and every good man will offer up ardent vows to Heaven for them, that their patriotism may forever triumph over all the hated sons of Tyranny.

* In England and Ireland, the people are taxed for window light, and for almost every thing they eat, drink and wear; yet such is the unbounded luxury and bad policy of their rulers, the State is sinking in debt.

BOSTON Feb. 26. On Friday last the Governor sent out the following message to both Houses of Assembly viz.

"Gentlemen of the Council and the House of Representatives,
Having received discretionary leave from the King to go to England, I think proper new to acquaint you with this instance of his Majesty's most gracious condescension, and that I intend to avail myself of it as soon as his service will admit."

"I must desire you to give all the dispatch possible to such necessary public business as may yet lie before you, for I must soon, by an adjournment or prorogation, give the Court a recess, that I may attend to this preparation for my voyage which his Majesty's service and my personal affairs require, 24th. Feb. 1774.
T. Hutchinson."

BOSTON Feb. 28. As the Lamps for Illuminating the Streets of this Town are now setting up, the following Extract from a Late Law for the regulating of said Lamps is now printed, that the Public may be made more acquainted with the Fines and Penalty which will be incurred by such Person or Persons who either with design or by accident should any way destroy or damage these Lamps.

"Be it therefore enacted, that at any time after the publication of this Act, any Person or Persons shall and do willfully and maliciously break, throw down, or extinguish any Lamp that is or shall be hung or set up to light the Streets, Lanes, Allies and Passage-Ways, within said Town of Boston, either by said Town or private Inhabitant, or shall willfully or unwillfully damage the Post, Iron, or other Furniture thereof, every Person in offering thereof convicted by the lawful testimony of one or more Witness or witnesses, in any of his Majesty's Courts of General sessions of the Peace, to be thereafter held within and for the County of Sufflok, who are hereby empowered to hear and determine the offence, shall forfeit and pay the sum of Twenty Pounds, for each Lamp so broken or damaged, and the like sum for each Post or Iron or other Furniture be broken or damaged, and cost of Prosecution, and if any Person or Persons shall accidentally break, throw down, or otherwise damage any Post, Iron, or Furniture of such Lamp, he shall pay so much as in the Judgement of the Selectmen of said Town for the time being, shall fully repair the Damage done, into the hands of the Selectmen, or to such Person or Persons as they may appoint to receive the same; and if any such Person or Persons shall refuse to pay said Selectmen or the Person they shall appoint in a manner as aforesaid, the Treasurer of the Town of Boston is hereby empowered to prosecute any Person or Persons for said Damage, before any one of his Majesty's Justices of the Peace, in said County of Suffolk, who is hereby empowored to hear and determine the same; provided the double damages do not exceed Forty Shillings, if more, then to be recovered in any Court proper to try the same; and upon Conviction to give Judgement for double Damages and the cost of Prosecution, and award Execution accordingly. And if any Person or Persons sentenced to pay the aforesaid Fine of Twenty Pounds and Cost, shall refuse to pay the same, he or they shall be punished for the Offence by being imprisoned not exceeding six months, or by Whipping not exceeding twenty Stripes."

BOSTON March 3. Peter Oliver, Esq; hath ungratefully, falsely and maliciously laboured to lay imputations and scandal upon this his Majesty's government, insolently and contemptuously insinuating that the parsimony, injustice and ingratitude of said government, in which holding from him and adequate and due reward, for his services as a justice of the said superior court, he had been greatly impoverished, and that therefore he was obliged to take his Majesty's grant from the principal of justice due to his family and others. Whereas in fact, the reward granted him by the government, were always fully equal to the merit of his services as a justice of the said court as it is well known that the Peter Oliver, Esq; before his advancement to a seat in the superior court, had been usually employed in the business of trade, husbandry, and manufactures, to which he had applied his mind. And that he was appointed to said office without previous education and regular study in the law.

And the said Peter Oliver, Esq; by his conduct aforesaid, hath misrepresented and traduced this government, and endeavoured to alienate the hearts of his Majesty's liege people of this province from his Majesty, and set a division between them, to introduce into said court a partial and currupt administration of justice, destroy the present form of government in this province, and establish an arbitrary and tyranical government in its stead.

Whereas this house of representatives, in their name, and in the name of the inhabitants of this province, Do Impeach the said Peter Oliver, Esq; of the high crime of misdemeanors aforesaid. And saving to themselves by protestation the liberty of exhibiting at any time hereafter, to the governor and Council, or the Council only, and complaint of alligations against the said Peter Oliver, Esq; for incompetency, incapacity, or disability for the execution of his office; or any other accusation or impeachment against the said Peter Oliver, Esq; for any other crime and misdemeanours by him done and committed. Also of replying to the answers which said Peter Oliver, Esq; shall make to the said articles, or any of them; and of offering proof of the premises, or any of their impeachments, accusations and complaints that shall be exhibited by them, as the case shall require. They pray that the said Peter

Oliver, Esq; Chief Justice of the Superior Court of Judicature, Court of Assize and General Goal Delivery over this whole province, may be put to answer to all and every of the premesses; and that such proceedings, examinations, trials and judgements may be had and order thereon, as may be agreeable to law and justice.

BOSTON March 7. Last Thursday Morning died here the Honorable Andrew Oliver, Esq; Lieutenant-Governor of this Province, in the 68th Year of his Age, His Funeral is to be attended To-Morrow Afternoon, a Half after three o'clock, if the weather permits.

BOSTON March 10. Sunday last arrived in nine weeks from London, Captain Gorham, in the Brig Fortune, owned here, having on board 28½ chests of East India Company's Tea, consigned to sundry persons in this town.

The owners have published the following account, viz. That they gave express orders to the correspondent in London, that none of the East India Tea, should, on any terms be shipped on board said vessel, however advantageous the offer, or great the loss on the voyage. That on the vessel's arrival at Boston, they, the owners, freely, and publicly declared their willingness to send her back, loaded as she was, to London and run the risk of her being seized; but that many of the goods on board being much wanted in Boston, it was proposed to take these out, and send the tea only, back in the vessel; that she was accordingly reported at the Custom House, and a permit obtained for landing all the goods except the tea; but that notwithstanding all that could be said to the Custom House officers, they absolutely refused to furnish the papers necessary to authorize her return with the tea on board. This determination being publicly known, soon after, a number of men, having the appearance of Indians, entered the vessel, took out the tea, emptied every chest over board, and effectually destroyed the whole; after which they peaceably retired, without doing any further damage.

BOSTON March 14. His Majesty's Oknookortunkogog King of the Naraganset Tribe of Indians, on receiving information of the arrival of the arrival of another Cargo of the cursed weed tea, immediately summoned his Council at the Great Swamp by the River Jordan, who did advise and Consult to the immediate Destruction there of, after resolving that the Importation of the Herb, by any Persons whatever, as attended with pernicious consequences to the Lives and Properties of all the Subjects throughout America. Orders were then issued to the Seizor and Destroyer Generals and their Deputies to assemble the Executive Body under their Command to proceed directly to the Place where the noxious Herb was. They arrived last Monday Evening in Town and finding the Vessel, they emptied every Chest, into the Great Pacific Ocean, and effectually Destroyed the whole. (Twenty eight and a half) they are now returned to Naraganset to make a report of their doing to his Majesty's who we hear is determined to honour them with Commissions for the Peace.

BOSTON March 14. Wednesday His Excellency the Governor was pleased to send the following Message to both Houses, by the Secretary.

Gentlemen of the Council and Gentlemen of the House of Representatives,

I Have omitted nothing in my Power, consistent with my Duty to the King, which had a tendency to promote Harmony and good Agreement in the Legislature, the present Session. I have passed over without Notice the groundless, unkind Illiberal Charges and Insinuations made by each of the other Branches against the Governor, rather than any part of the public Business of the Province should be left unfinished, but as some of your Votes, Resolves and other Proceedings which you have suffered to be made public, strike directly at the Honor and Authority of the King and of Parliament, I may not neglect hearing public Testimony against them, and making use of the Power in me by the Constitution to prevent you from proceeding any further in the same Way.   Province-House, March 9th 1774.

T. Hutchinson.

After which the Secretary said, That it was his Excellency's Pleasure to prorogue to

Wednesday the 23th of April next.

BOSTON March 15. His Excellency has signed twenty public and private Acts, passed the late session of the General Assembly.

Refused. A Bill against Bribery and Corruption in the elections of Representatives.

Refused. A Bill for obliging the Sheriffs of several counties to give bond for the faithful discharge of their respective offices.

Refused. A Bill to prevent the further importation of Negroes.

BOSTON March 23. The following is an extract of a letter from Phillis, a Negro Girl of Mr. Wheatley's of this town, to the Reverend Sampson Accom. which we desire to insert as a specimen of her ingenuity. It is dated the 11th of February, 1774.

"Reverend and honored Sir,

I Have this day received your obliging, kind epistle, and am greatly, satisfied with your reason respecting the negroes, and think highly reasonable what you offer in vindication of their natural rights: Those that invade them cannot be insensible that the divine light is insensible chasing away the thick darkness which broods over the land of Africa, and the chaos which has reigned so long, in converting into beautiful order, and reveals more and more clearly, the glorious disposition of civil and religious liberties, which are so inseparably united, there is little or no enjoyment of one without the other: otherwise, perhaps the Israelites had been less solicitous for their freedom from Egyptian slavery: I do not say they would have been content without it, but no means, for in every human breast, God has Implanted a principle, which we call love of Freedom; it is impatient of oppression, and pants for deliverance; and by the leave of our modern Egyptians I will assert, that the same principle lives in us. God grant deliverance in his own way and time, and get his honour upon all those whose avarice impels them to countenance and help forward the calamities of their fellow creatures. This I desire not for their hurt, but to convince them the strange absurdity of their conduct whose words and actions are so diametrically opposed. How well the cry for liberty, and the reverse disposition for the exercise of oppressive power over others agree — I humbly think it does not require the penetration of a philosopher to determine."

BOSTON March 31. The Hon. John Hancock, Esq; having on account of health, declined serving as a fire-ward, it was voted unanimously, that the thanks of this town be given him for his good services in that office a number of years past.

BOSTON April 4. Massachusetts-Bay. By the Governor, a Proclamation for Dissolving the General Court.

Whereas the Great and General Court or Assembly now stands Prorogue to the 13th day of April next: I have thought it fit to order that the said Great and General Court of Assembly be Dissolved, and that the Members thereof be discharged from any further attendance.

And the Sheriffs of the several Counties, their Under Sheriffs or Deputies and the constables of the several Towns within the said Province are commanded to cause this Proclamation to be forthwith published and posted within the respective Precincts.

Given at Boston the Thirteeth Day of March, 1774, in the fourteeth Year of his Reign of our Sovereign Lord George the Third, by the Grace of God, of Great Britain, France and Ireland, King, Defender of the Faith, &c. T. Hutchinson. By His Excellency's Command,

                        Tho's Flucker, Secr'y.

BOSTON April 5. We hear from Cambridge that a person having been confined there a long time in goal, for debt, at the expense of one Samuel Carter, of Woburn, who on Thursday last paid the goaler ten dollars more, declaring his intention of keeping him in for life; a company, supposed, about seventy or eighty in number, in the Indian Habit, waited on Mr. Carter in the evening, and after breaking his windows and showing some of the marks of their dislike of his conduct, obliged him to walk with them to Cambridge, about seven miles, sign an instrument to release the man from confinement, and give him the cash he had a short time he deposited in the hands of the goaler, to bear his expenses home, as the man belonged to a neighbouring Town. —— The affair being thus settled three cheers were given, and the parties returned from whence they came.

BOSTON April 21. Last Monday se'nnight about eight o'clock a young man passing towards fore-street, through the boarded alley, was suddenly attacked by two men, supposed to be Irish; who asked who came there? The young man answered, a friend; they immediately seized him by each arm, and one of them drew out a uncommon long knife, and said, if you do not deliver what you have got, I will run you thro'; he replied, do what you will, I will not deliver any thing, the other took a very large club he had before concealed, and with one or two blows in the head knocked him down, they then kicked him in several parts of his body and ran off, leaving him much bruised, and very bloody on the ground, where he lay near half an hour almost senseless.

Last Thursday four young Lads went to Braintree in a Canoe, and on their return stopt to fish between Castle William and Dorchester Bay, but meeting with no success, in endeavouring to hoist up the Kellick they overset the Canoe, whereby one of them, an apprentice to Mr. Greyer, Stone-Cutter at the South End about 19 Years of age, was unfortunately drowned; the others were saved by a boat that was going to the Castle, who took them off from the Bottom of the Canoe, to which they had held till they were almost spent.

BOSTON April 21. A Passenger in Capt. Folger says, that as Lord Darthmouth was busily examining evidence concerning the destruction of the Tea at Boston, a Clerk of the House of Commons came to him and informed him the arrival of the Philadelphia Tea Ship, observed it was in vain to make further inquiries about it, for the continent was all in a flame; and upon this his Lordship immediately dismissed the Examination.

BOSTON May 5. Wanted a Man that writes a good

hand, understands merchant accounts, and can be well recommended. Enquire of the Printer.

BOSTON May 16. On Friday last there was a most numerous respectable Meeting of the Freeholders and other Inhabitants of this Town, legally warned and assembled in Faneuil-Hall, to consider the Edict lately passed by the British Parliament for shutting up the Harbour and other ways punishing the Inhabitants, and to determine upon proper measures to be taken by the Town thereon.

After making Choice of Samuel Adams Moderator of the Meeting, the Edict was distinctly read by the Clerk; and the Nature and Tendency as well as the Design of it being explained in the Observation of several Gentlemen upon it, the Town came into the following Vote. Nom. Com. Viz.

Voted, That it is the Opinion of the Town, that of the other Colonies come into a Joint Resolution to stop all Importations from Great Britain, and Exportation to Great Britain, and every part of the West Indies, till the Act of blocking up this Harbour be repealed, the same will prove the Salvation of North America and her Liberties: On the other Hand, if they continue their Exports and Imports, their is high reason to fear that Fraud, Power, and the most odious Oppression will triumphant over Right, Justice, social Happiness and Freedom. And Ordered, that this Vote be forthwith transmitted by the Moderator to all our Sister Colonies in the Name and behalf of this Town.

Then it was moved for Consideration, what Measures were proper for the Town to take on the present Emergency; whereupon several Judicious, spirited and manly Proposals were made; which being debated with a Candor, Moderation and Firmness, of Mind becoming a People resolved to preserve their Liberties, it was Voted, that the Moderator with John Rowe, Esq; Mr. Thomas Boylston, William Phillips, Esq; Doctor Joseph Warren, John Adams Esq; Josiah Quincy Esq; Thomas Cushing, Esq; Mr. Henderson Inches, Mr. William Mollineux, and Mr. Nathaniel Appleton, be a Committee to take the several Proposals that have been, and others that may be made, into consideration, and report to the Towns as soon as may be.

After which the Town made a choice of Mr. Aliver Wendell, Isaac Smith, Esq. Mr. William Dennie, Mr. William Powell, and Mr. John Pitts to repair immediately to the Town of Salem and Marblehead to communicate the Sentiments of this Metropolis to the Gentlemen there, consult with them, and make report at the Adjournment.

Then a Meeting was adjourned till Wednesday Next at Ten of the Clock in the Forenoon. The Meeting was open with an excellent Prayer by Rev. Dr. Cooper.

A Correspondent observed that there never were more unanimity than appeared in Faneuil-Hall last Friday; and he adds, that it was perfect as human Society can admit to.

It is an inexpressible Grief, that Mr. Hancock's ill state of Health would not permit his attendance in Farneuil-Hall on Friday last; We pray God he may be able to attend the General Assembly at the approaching Session.

It is said Faneuil-Hall was so throng'd last Friday that several hundred Persons were unable to attend the Meeting.

Last Saturday our worthy fellow Citizen Mr. Paul Revere, was dispatch'd by the Committee of Correspondence of this Town with important Letters to the Southern Colonies.

By Letters from Marblehead and Salem we are assured that several Capital Merchants in those Towns are resolved to haul up their Vessels till the Harbour of Boston shall be free.

Tuesday last the Freeholders and other Inhabitants of this Town met at Faneuil-Hall for the choice of Representatives; The Number of Votes were 536. The Hon. Thomas Cushing, Esq; had 524 votes. Mr. Samuel Adams, 535. Hon. John Hancock Esq; 536. William Phillips, Esq; 534.

Friday last arrived here his Majesty's Ship Lively, Capt. Bishop, in 26 Days from England, in whom came his Excellency General Gage, who is appointed Governor and Commander and Chief in this Province.

We are told that the Seat of Government is to be removed from this Town to Salem; that the

General Assembly, after Election, will be removed thither.

His Excellency landed at Castle William under a discharge of the cannon of the fortress. And we hear that the next day the following advice was given by his Majesty's council to his Excellency Governor Hutchinson. That General Gage's Commission for Governor of this Province be read on Tuesday next; the Boston Regiment the Troop of Guards and Cadet Company to be in Arms; His Excellency to land at the end of Long-Wharf, from thence to be escourted, attended by his Majesty's Council, to the Court-House; and an elegant dinner to be prepared at Farneuil-Hall.

BOSTON May 20. The Commissioners of his Majesty's Customs hereby give Notice, that from and after the first Day in June, 1774, the Officers of the Custom for this Port and Harbour, will be removed from the Town of Boston, to the Town of Plymouth, within the limits of the Port of Boston, them there proceed to carry on, in the usual Manner, the Business of their respective Departments, in the Collection and Management of his Majesty's Custom, and the Execution of the Laws of Trade: And no Officer of Customs will be permitted to remain in the Town or Harbour of Boston from and after the first Day of June next, during the Continuance and an Act passed in the present Year of his Majesty's Reign, entitled, an Act to discontinue in such Manner, and for such Time as are therein mentioned, the landing and discharging, landing or shipping of Goods, Wares and Merchandise, at the Town, and within the Harbour of Boston, in the Province of Massachusetts-Bay in North America.

By Order of the Commissioners.

Samuel Mather, pre. Secr'y.

BOSTON May 23. On Tuesday last, at 12 o'clock his Excellency Thomas Gage, appointed to the government of this province, landed at the Long-Wharf, where a number of his Majesty's Council, several members of the Common House of Assembly, many principal Gentlemen of the Town, and the Governor's or Cadet Company under arms, waited his arrival. The Cadet Company escorted his

Excellency (whose commission was borne before him) and the gentlemen aforesaid up the Long-Wharf, and through King-Street to the Council Chamber. The Troop of Horses, under the command of Major Snelling, the company of Artillery, commanded by Major Paddock, the company of Grenadiers commanded by Lieutenant Pierce, and the several companies of Militia, under the command of Colonel Erving, were under arms in King-Street; the respective officers saluted his Excellency as he passed, and he politely returned the salute.

After his arrival at the Council Chamber, his commission as Governor, and Vice-Admiral of the Province were read, and after the usual ceremonies were past his Excellency was sworn in by the Presindent of his Majesty's Council. His Excellency's Proclamation for continuing all Officers, &c. in their places till further orders was then read by the High Sheriff in the balcony of the State-House, which was answered by three huzzas, a firing of cannon from the batteries, and company of Artillery, and three vollies from the respective companies then ensued. His Excellency received the compliments of civil and military officers, and of other gentry, and after graciously receiving the Militia &c. was escorted by the Cadet company to Faneuil-Hall, (where an elegant entertainment was provided at the expence of the Province) attended by the members of his Majesty's Council, several of the honorable House of Representatives, a number of the Clergy, and other respectable Gentlemen. Many loyal toasts were drank, and the strictest harmony and decorum observed. After dinner his Excellency rode in a carriage to Province-House, where we hear he is to reside for a few days at least. Notwithstanding the rain, and badness of the day, there was a vast concourse of people assembled on the occasion.

BOSTON May 23. We hear his Excellency Mr. Hutchinson, Elisha Hutchinson, Esq; his second son, and Miss Hutchinson, his Excellency's youngest daughter, have engaged the elegant cabin of the ship Mineva, Capt. Callahan, which sails shortly for London.

BOSTON May 30. On Saturday last, Mr. Paul Revere returned here from Philadelphia, having been sent Express to the Southern Colonies with Intelligence of the later rash, impolitick and vindictive Measures of the British Parliament, who by the execrable Port-Bill have held out to us a most incontestable argument who ought to submit to Jurisdiction; and what rich Blessings we may secure to ourselves & Posterity, by absolute Acquiescence to their Lenity, Wisdom and Justice. Nothing can increase the Indignation with which our Brethren in Rhode Island, Connecticut, New-York and Philadelphia have received the Proof of Ministerial Madness.

They universally declare their Resolution to stand by us to the last extremity, they esteem the cause to their own, and highly applaud the Resolution of this People, not to be awed into Acquiescence by a mad Exertion of mere Power on the Part of our Enemies. ⸺ they adjure us for their sakes as well as our own to preserve; much approve of the plan of an entire Suspension of Trade with Great-Britain, and advise to the Committee of Merchants from the trading towns to convene at New-York, and there to form a restrictive plan for their trade to the West Indies. ⸺ Expresses are gone from Philadelphia for this Purpose to the Colonies Southward of them, who no doubt will concur in the same Measure and view the Subjugation of Boston, as in fact it is, the enslaving the whole.

This day Mr. Bradford is dispatched on his return to New-York and Philadelphia, from the Committee of Correspondence of this Town, and will probably tend to facilitate the Plan of Redemption from Ministerial Tyranny.

BOSTON June 6. The Seat of Government being for the present removed from this Town to Salem, in the County of Essex, his Excellency Gen. Gage on Wednesday last, at Noon, set out for that Place; and at the Invitation of Colonel Vassal, of Cambridge, dined with him, where he continued till Thursday Morning, where he breakfasted with Mr. Temple, at has Seat in Charlestown, and proceeded on his journey, accompanied by a Number of Gentlemen in their Carriages. His Excellency was met on the Road by the principal Gentlemen of Salem and Marblehead, who joined and formed a grand Procession to Colonel Brown's where he received their Congratulation on his appointment to the chief command of the Government of this Province, and where he, with many other Gentlemen, dined and tarried until Friday, when his Excellency went to the elegant Seat of the Hon. Robert Hooper, at Danvers, which he had politely offered for his Majesty's Residence. On Saturday it bring his Majesty's Birth Day, his Excellency returned to Salem and received the Compliments of a great Number of Gentlemen on that joyful Occasion and every Mark of respect from the People of all Ranks.

BOSTON June 6. We hear the Corporation of Harvard College have voted that considering the present dark Aspect of our public affairs ——— there will be no public Commencement this Year ——— and that the Candidates for the first and second Degrees, shall receive their Degrees in a general Diploma. Which Vote hath been concurred by the Overseers of the College.

The Meeting of the Overseers is adjourned to the 14th of July, so that they who do not apply before that Time, cannot have their Names inserted in the general Diploma, nor be admitted to their Degree this Year.

BOSTON June 26. His Majesty's Ships, Frigates and Schooners, are now placed in such a manner in the Harbour, as will prevent any Vessel from coming in or going out, so that the Act of Parliament for blocking up the Port of Boston, is now in all its parts carrying into Execution with the greatest Severity, many Vessels being already prevented from coming in, and Fishing Boats and other small Craft strictly search'd; so that we have reason to expect, that in a little time this Town will be in a truly distressed and melancholy Situation.

Al Business at the Custom House was finish last Wednesday at 12 o'Clock, and the Officers of the Customs the same Afternoon went to Plymouth; where the Office will again be opened.

BOSTON June 13. Last thursday arrived in

King-Road, and on Saturday came up into the Harbour, three Transports from Plymouth, having on board his Majesty's 4th Regiment. And this Morning the Vessels haul'd to the Long-Wharf, in order to land the Troops, who, it is said, are to encamp on the Common.

The Transports with the 43d Regiment on board, still remains below.

BOSTON June 20. We hear that the patriotic inhabitants of Philadelphia have generously Voted to give the Poor of this Town 1500 barrels of flour, 500 which, it is said may be soon expected.

Most of the stores on the Long-Wharf are now shut up; hundreds of the poor are out of employ, and many who lived generally will soon be reduced to the last Shilling. Yet under these unhappy circumstances people in general have that fortitude which did honour to the Ancient Romans.

"Undaunted by Tyranny we'll die or be Free."

We have heard of several neighbouring congregational churches who have set apart days of fasting and Prayer, on account of the present melancholy aspect of public affairs.

BOSTON June 20. In the House of Representatives. June 17, 1774.

Whereas the Town of Boston and Charlestown are at this Time suffering under the Hands of Power, by shutting up the Harbour by armed force which is the Opinion of the House in an Invasion of the said Town, evidently designed to compel the Inhabitants thereof to a Submission to the Taxes imposed upon them without their Consent; And whereas it appears to the House that this Attack upon the said Town for the purpose aforesaid is an Attack made upon this whole Province and Continent, which threatens the total destruction of the Liberties of all British Americans.

It is therefore, Resolved, as the clear opinion of the House, that the Inhabitants of the said towns ought to be relieved; and this House do recommend to all, and more especially to the Inhabitants of this Province to afford them speedy and constant relief in such a Way and

Manner as shall be most suitable to their circumstances, 'till the sense and Advice of our Sister Colonies shall be known in full confidence that they will exhibit Examples of Patience, Fortitude and Perseverance while they are thus called to endure this Oppression for the Preservation of the Liberties of this Country.

In the House of Representatives, June 17, 1774 Whereas this and his Majesty's other Colonies in North-America have long been struggling under the heavy Hand of Power; and our dutiful Petitions for the Redress of our intolerable Grievances have not only been disregarded and frowned upon but the Design totally alter the free Constitution of Civil Government in British America, and establish arbitrary Government and reduce the Inhabitants to Slavery appears more and more to be fixed and determined. It is therefore strongly recommended by this House to the Inhabitants of the Province that they renounce altogether the Consumption of India Teas, and as far as in them lies discontinue the use of all Goods and Manufactures whether that shall be imported from the East Indies and Great Britain until the public Grievances of America shall be radically and Totally redress. And it is also further recommended to all, that they give all possible Encouragement to the Manufactures of America. And it is moreover strongly recommended to the Inhabitants aforesaid, that they use their utmost endeavours to surpress Pedlers and Petty Chapmen (who are of late become a very great Nuisance) by putting in Execution the good and wholesome Laws of the Province for that Purpose.

[There were present in the House 129 Members, and only 12 Dissentients.]

Province of Massachusetts-Bay By the Governor. A Proclamation for Dessolving the General Court

Whereas the Proceeding of the House of Representatives, in the present Session, the General Court made it necessary for his Majesty's Service, that the above Said General Court should be dissolved.

I have therefore thought fit to dissolve the

said General Court, and the same is hereby dissolved accordingly, and the Members thereof are discharged from any further Attendance.

Given under my Hand at Salem, the 17th Day of June 1774, in the Fourteenth Year of his Majesty's Reign.   T. Gage.

By his Excellency's Command. Tho. Flucker Secr'y.

BOSTON June 27. Wednesday last a Troop Ship arrived here from Ireland, with Part of the 5th Regiment on Board; she sailed in Company with six others, with Troops, from whom she parted three or four Weeks ago.

Friday last two Soldiers, one of them named Low, the other Elliot, both belonging to the 6th Regiment, now garrison at Castle William having engaged in a boxing match, upon some supposed affront given, wherein the latter received so much Hurt that he died soon after; ——— A Jury of Inquest was sommoned from this Town, (by the desire of Col. Lesley, the commanding Officer,) who we hear bro't in their Verdict that his Death was occasioned by the Blows he received, and Low is since committed in Order for Trial.

Boston July 4. Province of Massachusetts-Bay by the Governor.

A Proclamation for discouraging Illegal Combinations.

Whereas certain Persons, calling themselves a Committee of Correspondence for the Town of Boston, have lately presumed to make or cause to be made, a certain unlawful instrument, purporting to be a solemn League of Covenant, intended to be signed by the Inhabitants of this Province; whereby they are most solemnly to covenant and engage to suspend all commercial Intercourse with the Island of Great Britain, until certain Acts of the British Parliament shall be repealed: And whereas printed Copies of the said unlawful Instrument have been transmitted, by the aforesaid Committee of Correspondence, so called, to the several Towns in this Province, accompanied with a scandalous, tratorous and seditious Letter, calculated to imflame the Minds of the People, to disturb them with ill-grounded Fears and Jalousies, and to excite them to enter into an unwarrantable, hostile, and traitorous combination, to distress the British Nation, by interrupting, obstructing, and destroying her Trade with the Colonies, contrary to their Allegiance due the King; and to the Form and effect of divers Statutes made for securing, encouraging, protecting, and regulating the said Trade; and destructive of the British Parliament, and the Peace, good Order, and safety of the Community. And whereas the Inhabitants of the Province, not duly considering the high Criminality, and dangerous Consequences to themselves of such alarming and unprecedented Combinations may incautiously be tempted to join in the aforesaid unlawful League and Covenant, and thereby expose themselves to fatal Consequences of being considered as the declared and open Enemies of the King, Parliament, and Kingdom of Great Britain.

In Observation therefore of my Duty to the King; in tenderness to the Inhabitants of this Province; and to the end that none who may hereafter engage in such dangerous Combinations, may plead in Excuse of their Conduct, that they were ignorant of the Crime in which they were involving themselves; I have thought fit to issue this Proclamation, hereby earnestly cautioning all Persons whatsoever within this province, against signing the aforesaid, or any similar Covenant or in any Manner entering into, or being concerned in such unlawful hostile, and traitorous Combinations, as they would avoid the Pains and Penalties due to such aggravated and dangerous Offences.

And I do hereby strictly enjoin and command all Magistrates, and other Officers, within the several Counties in this Province, that they take effectual Care to apprehend and secure for Trial, all and every Person who may hereafter presume to print or to publish, or offer to others to be signed, or shall themselves sign the aforesaid, abetting, advising, or assisting therein.

And the respective Sheriffs of the several Counties within this Province, are hereby required to cause this Proclamation forthwith to be posted out in some public Place, in each

Town, within their respective Districts.

Given under my Hand at Salem the 29th Day of June, 1774, in the fourteenth Year of his Majesty's Reign.   T. Gage.
By his Excellency's Command, Tho. Flecker Sec'ry.

Boston July 4. Since our last arrived a Number of Transports from Ireland, having on board the 5th and 30th Regiment of Foot.

Three Transports are sailed from hence, said to be gone to New-York, to bring hither the Regiment of Royal Fuzileers.

Friday last arrived here from England, Vice-Admiral Graves, in the Preston Man of War of 50 Guns.

On Saturday last a Company of the Royal train of Artillery with 8 Pieces of Cannon, landed here from the Castle, and are encamped on Powder House Hill in the Common.

Capt. Brown, in a Mast Ship, arrived at portsmouth last Week from London, and brought with him 27 Chests of the penicious and troublesome Commodity called Tea, which, upon it being certainly known to be on board, a Meeting of the Inhabitants was called, and the Committee chose to wait upon Mr. Parry the Consignee, to know whether he would consent to certain Proposals, made to him, that the Tea should not be landed but reshipped, who in a general manner gave them all the satisfaction they could desire, and a Watch of 15 Men was appointed to watch it, and the third Day it was put on board another Vessel and sent out of the Harbour, with a fair Wind, committed to the Waterly Elements.

It is reported that the above Tea is sent to Halifax.

BOSTON July 11. Letters from Virginia, Maryland, Pennsylvania, and other Places, mention that a considerable Quantities of Flour, Wheat, and other Grains, are collecting in those Governments, for the Relief of the Poor of this Town.

Several Loads of Wheat & Rye as a present from our Brethren in the Country, to the Poor of of this Place, arrived here last Week and are deposited in the Town Granary, and, on Friday last upwards of a Hundred Sheep were received here as a present from the Town of Pomfret in Connecticut, for the benefit of the Poor of this Town.

Advice from Annapolis in Maryland, mentions, That the Deputies of all the different Counties in that colony had met there the 22 instant, and after debating upon the Manner of Proceedings, and the Effect of the Boston Port and other Bills, they had resolved not to import from or export to Great-Britain any Goods or Merchandize, until those Acts were repealed; at which were present 93 Deputies.

BOSTON July 18. I believe every Friend of liberty feel the indignity and insult which have been offered to out patriotic brethren of New-Hampshire, the superlative impudence to send out their noxious teas to a people, who they knew had solemnly resolved that none should be landed among them. This infamous conduct of the India Company, is a full demonstration that they have abandoned liberty, justice and honor; and that they imagine the noble sons of New-Hampshire were as servile and base on themselves ——— but thanks to Heaven, the people of that province have given a demonstration to the world, that they are born in freedom, and in freedom they will live; ——— they have banished from their free land the duties and detested tea. May Heaven reward these Patriots with perpetual liberty ——— may America imitate this example, and share with them in Freedom.

Twenty Gentlemen of South Carolina have presented the industrious Poor of this devoted Town with 205 Tierces of Rice, which arrived at Salem last Monday. ——— for which the grateful Thanks are acknowledged.

BOSTON July 25. Letters from the Southern part of North Carolina assures us, "That the Inhabitants there will go as far in defence of American Liberty as can be expected: and recommend, if a Congress should be deemed the first step necessary to be taken, that Subscription, or rather Collections, be set on Foot throughout the Continent, to raise and remit a Sum of Money to the Community of Boston, for the Relief of their Distressed and suffering Brethren there, who must stand in equal Need of such Assistance as if their Town had been destroyed by Fire."

BOSTON Aug. 1. More than sixty days has expired, since Boston, by late Edict of the British Parliament, has been besieged by a British Fleet and Army, and its trade annihilated: The inhabitants now receive that insult and damage, which was never experienced in the hottest wars we have been engaged in with France and Spain, and their allies, the Savages of the American woods: The particulars of siege, and the maneuvers of our enemies, may in future be told by some able Historian. Suffice it is present to inform the world, that though wood and provisions have been allowed us by said Port-Act, the introduction of those articles has been attended with such loss of time and unnecessary charges as greatly to raise the price of fuel upon poor inhabitants: No wood can now be brought from the rivers and Bays included in our harbour, upon which we depended for a considerable part of our supply. No goods of any kind are suffered to be waterborne within the circle of 60 miles; No timber, boards, shingles, bricks, lime, sand &c. &c. are to be transported from one Wharf to another; and so even tradesmen, not immediately dependent upon shipping, are thrown out of business. No barrels of liquors, bread, flour, &c. are suffered to be brought a few rods to our row boats, or across our shortest ferries; and even the vessels on the stocks, which have for some time past been ready for launching, cannot be put into the water, without their being exposed to a threatened seizure.

Neither is the dry'd fish and oil, the charity of our Marblehead friends, nor rice, the generous present of the Carolinas, nor House-sand, to be brought us by water, but must be encumbered with great charge of land-carriage of about 30 miles: We are also cut off from the advantage and profit of supplying as usual an extent of sea coast on north and south of more than 100 leagues, even with British merchandize. ——— And when any of these hardships and distresses are mentioned to those insolents in office, the commissioners and their understrappers we are told it was the design of the act, and that it is not their intent to lessen those difficulties: —— This is the treatment meted out by the British ministers to a Town and Province, by whose exertions in the late war, the strong fortress of Louisburg was taken, which purchased the peace of Europe and and delivered Britons from their terrible apprehension of invasion by French flat-boats. What further cruelties we are to suffer we know not if whether America, or even this single town is in this way to be brought to the feet of Lord North, with the full surrender of their inestimable rights and liberties, time only can tell.

BOSTON Aug. 1. A cart load of new Pick-Axes were seen putting into a Store on Long-Wharf late Saturday. Query, What are we to apprehend from all these warlike Preparations? Is a Fort to be erected in good Earnest, and the Town to be awed into Submission by Cannon and Mortar? Forbid it, Heaven! Rather let it become a Heap, and be rais'd to its Foundation, that one mean Concession be means of its Preservation!

BOSTON Aug. 3. Last Tuesday Morning came to Town from Marblehead twelve Cart Loads of goods, Salt Fish, also a quantity of Oil, being the generous Donation of Sypathising Brethren of that Place. —— The above Provisions having been judged by the Revenue Officers not to be Victuals [the word of the Portbill] for the necessary Use and Sustenance of the inhabitants of the Town of Boston, it was therefore not permitted to be brought into this Port coastwise. ——The Benefaction of Rice fron South Carolina, has, since its arrival, remained there in the same Predicament; but we hear that it is now allowed to be an Article of Food, and not solely of Merchandize, and may be brought in by Water; also that Permission is given for launching the Vessels that are now on the Stocks here; which Liberty, for some time past, had been refused.

BOSTON Aug. 11. Yesterday morning the Hon. Thomas Cushing, Esq; Mr. Samuel Adams, John Adams and Robert Treat Paine Esqrs. the delegates, appointed by the Hon. House of Assembly, for this Province, to attend the general Congress to be holden at Philadelphia, some time next month, set out from hence, attended by a number of gentlemen, who accompanied them to Watertown, were met by many others, who provided an elegant entertainment for them; after dinner they proceeded on their journey, intending to reach Southborough last evening.

BOSTON Aug. 15. We hear that his Excellency Governor Gage desired the Attendance of the Selectmen of the Town at the Province House on Saturday last; when he informed them of that clause in the late act of parliament forbidding Town Meetings, without special Leave of the Governor, and gave the same to them to read; which being done, his Excellency told then he was ready on Application to give Liberty for a Town's-Meeting, if he should judge it expedient; and being told, that the Provincial Law had been the Rule of their Conduct in these Matters, he said he was determined to carry the Acts of Parliament into execution, and they must be answerable for any bad Consequence.

BOSTON Aug. 22. We hear that at a meeting of the Cadet Company last Week, a letter was laid before them from Mr. Flucker to Col. Hancock, acquainting him that the Governor had no further occasion for him as Commander of that Corps. Upon which the Company voted a Committee to wait on his Excellency with a message, informing him, that in consequence of his extraordinary dismission of their first Officer, they had judged proper to return the Standard, which as Commander and Chief he had presented the Company on his taking the Chair, and to acquaint him they no longer consider themselves the Governor's Independent Company of Cadets.

BOSTON Aug. 25. In the Massachusetts Spy, To his Excellency Governor Gage,

Sir,

You had some very plain hints from several writers who have been so good as to advise you of the temper of the people and nature of their business you are engaged in, whether you have profited by this price you put into your hand, you must answer to yourself at present and to some body else either in this life or another hereafter. You are ordered, as it is said, to enforce measures for an entire change of the free constitution of this colony, and thereby to shake the foundation of the liberties of all America. I tell you that it is out of your power to accomplish it, and the sooner you desist from the attempt the less guilt and disgrace you will incur. Had I lived to your years with a very moderate degree of reputation, I would have spurned the villains that proposed my under taking so dirty and wicked a jobb as that of robbing men of their rights, yes, I'd have thrown the commission in the face of proudest ministers of state that dared to offer it.

The Persons who advice you have followed since you came among us have no right to complain of censure so copiously powered upon them. Your Excellency might not have known the full extent of the drudgery to be performed when you left England. As your appointment was sudden you might not have known much about the right of Americans, and you may plead some excuse for what you have done when they, who you supposed knew the State of public affairs here, were continually filling your ears with stories of rebellious little faction on the town of Boston, especially when a number of men here among us have dared to swear destruction to the Charter of their country. But it is time to look for yourself and judge for yourself.

If you lose America to Briton, you tear the brightest jewel from your Sovereign's crown, and shake the very basis of a Solomon, not all the heroism of an Alexander can prevent your bringing destruction on yourself and the British empire, unless you very speedily turn onto the path which prudence and honour points out. Consider where you are and what you have to do. Do not trifle with the people. Tell them that you see their wrong. Tell them that it has been from misinformation that the late grievous acts of the British Parliament have passed. Assure them that you will do justice to their characters in your letters to Great Britain, Indeed, Sir, you must convince them that you are resolved that you will do your duty, and be their father and their friend. Delay not,* trust not your troops they are at best useless; if they act they will but insure your total defeat: hear no more of the Boston faction —— discard the wretches who mislead you —— look through the province which is under your care; observe the various ranks of people, all determined in one common cause; look through the continent —— take notice of their unanimity, and judge yourself whether those whose counsels you have hitherto followed are not deficient, infinitely deficient, both in honesty and ability.

Will you be dupe of a set of men who know that their all depends upon success of a mad, a desperate effort, to which they are urging you? Will you not reflect that if the measures of Administration should be frustrated, they will be reduced to absolute nothingness, and then the loss of the whole American world to Britain will not affect them so much as the loss of their places and pensions? Can you engage with such adventurers as these? You will be urged to the last extremity by the wretches who know their country will never forgive their treachery. Let their Counsel be far from you. I wish you may give a suitable attention to what I have wrote; but whether you hear, or whether you forebear, I know my Country will soon be free, and her incorrigible enemies will lick the dust.

Fabius.

* P. S. If I wish to destroy all connection between Great Britain and the Colonies, I would strongly persuade you to draw your troops into action, and order the fleet to bombard the town of Boston.

BOSTON Aug. 29. Wednesday arrived at Marblehead, Captain Perkins from Baltimore, with three thousand bushels of Indian corn, twenty barrels of rye meal, and twenty one barrels of bread, sent by the inhabitants of that place for the benefit of the poor of Boston; together with one thousand bushels of corn from Annapolis, sent in the same vessel, and for the same benevolent purpose.

BOSTON Aug. 29. A report having been industriously propagated in New-York, that principal inhabitants of this town are converting the donations of their brethren in the neighbouring colonies, which were intended for the relief of the suffering poor of this place, to their own private emolument, contrary to the charitable intentions of the benevolent contributions, and as such report is entirely without any manner of foundation, the public are desired not to credit it; the following narrative being of true state of the cause.

Our reception of the Boston Port Act, the chief concern of the principal Inhabitants was to provide relief for all such whose support depended on their daily labour: and, in the next place for those tradesmen, whose small funds, though sufficient for the common purposes of life, yet would soon be exhausted, if their resources were cut off. They considered the Employment of all these, especially the former, as a much more prudent measure than feeding them without any employment at all. They therefore adopted such a plan of business for their exercise, as were likely to be the most useful to the public, as well as most conducive to the health and good order of the employed. Accordingly the labourers were set to cleaning docks, making dykes, new laying of pavements in the public streets &c. These were all public concerns, and of no advantage to any individual, and further than as a member of the community to which he or she belonged. Not a single wharf, dock, dyke, or pavement, belonging to any individual, was ordered to be made or repaired, but only such, as the constant usage of the town, had always been supported at the expense of the public.

The principal inhabitants of the town have invariably considered the generous benefaction of their charitable and patriotic brethren in other colonies and given entirely for the relief of the indigent fellow citizens. But would it not be offering the greatest insult to good sense of their benevolent neighbours, to suppose that they intended to maintain a very great number of healthy, able bodied people in idleness, which must certainly be attended with great prejudice to them, as well as to the town in general, both now and hereafter? ——— or that, they regret to see and hear that our poor citizens are employed in the works which will be a public benefit?

Should the public interest of the Town of Boston be finally advanced by these services, in saving some future Taxes,* and they even become a small compensation for the inconceivable damage which it is now sustaining, by a suspension of all its principal businesses, can it be imagined that, there is a single person, in the almost endless list of contributors, who is sorry to find, that which he voluntarily gave, is like to be productive of the public advantage? It is much more candid, as well as charitable, to think that it must be a matter of the greatest satisfaction to every benevolent mind to hear, that what was only intended for one good purpose, has answered two.

A Friend of Boston.

* The experience of paving the streets in the town of Boston is always defrayed by a public tax on all the inhabitants.

BOSTON Sept. 8. On Wednesday last, the new divan (consisting of the wretched fugitives with whom the just indignation of their respective townsmen, by well-observed expulsion, have filled the capital) usurped the seats round the council board in Boston. Their deliberation have not hitherto transpired; and with equal secrecy, on Thursday morning at half after four, about 260 troops 11 boats at the Long-Wharf and proceeded up Medford river, to Temple's farm, where they landed, and went to the powder-house on Quarry-hill, in Charlestown bounds, whence they have taken 250 half barrels of powder, the store there, and carried it to the Castle.

A detachment from the corps went to Cambridge, and bro't off two field-pieces, which had lately been sent there for Col. Brattle's regiment. The preparation for this expedition caused much speculation, as some who were near the Governor gave out that he had sworn the committee of Salem should recognize or be imprisoned, nay, some said they would be put on board the vessel

Scarborough and sent to England forthwith. The committee of Boston sent off an express after ten on Wednesday evening to advise their brethren of Salem of what they apprehended was coming against them, who received their message with great politeness, and returned an answer purporting their readiness to receive any attack they might be exposed to for acting in pursuance of the laws and interest of their country as become men and christians.

From these several hostile appearances the county of Middlesex took the alarm, and on thursday evening began to collect in large bodies with their arms, provisions and ammunition, determining by some means to give a check to a power which so openly threatened their destruction, and in such a clandestine manner robb'd them of their means of defence, and on Friday morning some thousands of them had advanced to Cambridge, armed only with sticks, as they had left their fire arms, &c. at some distance behind. Some in deed had collected on Thursday evening and surrounded the attorney-general's house, who is also a judge of admiralty on the new plan for Nova Scotia, and being provoked by the firing of a pistol from a window, they broke some glass, but did little other mischief. The company however, concerned in this, were mostly boys and negroes, who soon dispersed.

On perceiving the concourse on Friday morning the committee of Cambridge sent express to Charlestown, who communicated the intelligence to Boston, and their respective committees proceeded to Cambridge without delay. When the first of the Boston committee came up, they found some thousands of people assembled before the Court-House, and judge Danfort standing on the steps speaking to the body, declaring in substance, that having now arrived at a very advanced age, and spent the greater part in the service of the public, it was a great mortification to him to find a step lately taken by him so disagreeable to his country, in which he conscientiously had meant to serve them; but finding their general sense against his holding a seat at the council board now upon the new establishment, he assured them that he had resigned said Office, and would never henceforth accept or act in the Office inconsistent with the charter rights of his country, and in conformation of said declaration, he delivered the following certificate, viz.

"Altho' I have this day made an open declaration to a great concourse of people who assembled at Cambridge, that I had resign'd my seat at the Council Board, yet for the future satisfaction of all; I do hereby declare under my hand, that such resignation has actually been made, and that it as my full purpose not to be any way concerned as Member of the Council at any time hereafter,'
September 2, 1774, S. Danforth.

Judge Lee was also on the Court-House steps, and delivered his mind to the body in terms similar to those used by judge Danforth, and delivered the following declaration, viz.
Cambridge 2d Sept. 1774.

"As great numbers of the inhabitants of the country are come into town, since my satisfying those who were met, not only by declaration, but by sending to them what I wrote to the Governor at my resignation, and being desirous to give the whole county and province full satisfaction of this matter, I hereby declare my resignation of a seat in the new constituted council, and my determination to give no further attendance.   Jos. Lee."

Upon this a vote was called for to see if the body was satisfied with the declarations and resignations aforesaid, and it passed in the affirmative, nem. con.

BOSTON Sept. 12. Last Monday the Selectmen of this Town waited on his Excellency Governor Gage, to acquaint him that the Inhabitants were much alarmed to find that he had ordered the breaking up the Ground near the Fortification on the Neck; and requested of his Excellency that extraordinary Movements, that they might thereby have it in their Power to quiet the Minds of the People; when his Excellency replied to the following purpose; That he had no intention of stopping up the Avenue to the Town or of obstructing the inhabitants or any of the Country People, coming in or going out of the Town as usual; that he had taken his measures and that he was to protect his Majesty's Subjects and his Majesty's Troops in this Town; and that he had no intention of any thing hostile against the Inhabitants.

On Friday last the Selectmen of this Town again waited upon his Excellency the Governor with the following Address. viz.

May it please your Excellency,

The Selectmen of Boston at the earnest Desire of a number of Gentlemen of the Town and County, again wait on your Excellency to acquaint you, that since our late Application the Apprehensions of the People not only this but of the neighbouring Towns are greatly increased by observing the Design of erecting a Fortress at the Entrance of the Town; and of reducing this Metropolis in other respect to the State of a Garrison. This with complaints lately made, of abuse from some of the Guards posted at that Quarter in assaulting and forcibly detaining several Persons who were peaceably passing in and out of the Town, may discourage the Market People from coming in with provisions as usual, and oblige the Inhabitants to abandon the Town. —— The Event we greatly deprecate, as it will produce Miseries which may hurry the Province into Acts of Desperation.

We should therefore think ourselves happy if we could satisfy the People that your excellency would suspend your Designs, and not add to the Distresses of the Inhabitants occasioned by the Port Act, that of garrisoning the Town,

John Scollay, chairman of the Selectmen.

The Governor's Answer.

Gentlemen,

When you lately applied to me respecting my ordering some cannon to be placed at the Entrance of the Town, which you term the erecting a fortress, I so fully expressed my Sentiments, that I thought you were satisfied the People had nothing to fear from that measure, as no use would by thereof, under their hostile proceedings should make it necessary; but as you have this Day acquainted me, that your Fears are rather increased, I have thought proper to assure, that I have no intention to prevent the free Egress and Regress of any Persons to and from the Town, or of reducing it to a Garrison neither shall I suffer any under my command to injure the Person or Property of any of his Majesty's Subjects. But as it is my Duty, so it shall be my Endeavours to preserve the Peace, and promote the Happiness of every Individual; and I earnestly recommend to you, and every Inhabitant, to cultivate the same spirit, and heartily wish they may live quietly and happily in the Town, Boston Sept. 9, 1774.

Tho's Gage.

Boston Sept. 12. The Town of Marblehead have agreed that their Regiment of Militia shall turn out four times a Week, with Arms and Ammunition According to Law in order to perfect themselves in Military Art.

Last Friday Morning, one Voluntine Ducket, a Deserter from the 65th Regiment, now at Halifax, was shot in the rear of the Camp in the Common, pursuant to the sentence of a Court Martial.

────── He was born at St. Peter's Parish in derbyshire, and was 21 Years of Age.

Saturday last most of the 59th Regiment march'd from Salem to this Place, and are now stationed on the Neck at the entrance of the Town; where great hostile Preparations are making as tho' an Enemy was approaching, when, it is tho't by some, the greatest Number is among ourselves.

BOSTON Sept. 19. The inhabitants of Georgia have published a set of Resolves upon the present disorded state of the Colonies, similar to those of many of the other Provinces; but non-Importation Measures are not mentioned; nor have they chosen Deputies to meet at the Congress.

THe 10th and 53d Regiments are ordered from Quebec, to join his Majesty's Troops in Boston.

BOSTON Sept. 26. By Mr. Paul Revere, who returned Express from Philadelphia last Friday Evening, we have the following, important Intelligence.

Philadelphia Sept. 17. 1774.

Sir,

Your Letter of the 11th Instant, together with the Resolutions of the County of Suffolk, and communicated the same to Congress: In consequence of which, they passed the several Resolutions which will be delivered you by Mr. Paul Revere together with a letter from the President. They highly applaud the wise, temperate and spirited Conduct of our People, in their oppression to the late Act for altering our Constitution. These Resolves will, we trust support and comfort our Friends and confound our Enemies. In Behalf of myself and Brethren,
   I am with Respect, your most humble Servant.
                              Thomas Cushing.
Joseph Warren, Esq;
                  Philadelphia 17th Sept. 1774.
Sir,
Your letter of the 11th Instant directed "To the Honorable Thomas Cushing, Member of the Massachusetts Bay," together with the Resolution entered into by the Delegates of the several Towns in the County of Suffolk, and their Addresses to his Excellency Governor Gage were communicated to the Congress, whereupon the Congress came into the following unanimous Resolves, which by their order I transmit to you to be communicated to the Committee od Correspondence for the Town of Boston.
   I am, Sir, your most obedient Servant.
                              Payton Randolph.
Joseph Warren Esq;
In Congress, Saturday Sept. 17, 1774.
A Letter from Dr. Joseph Warren, & sundry Resolutions entered into the County of Suffolk on Tuesday the 6th of this Instant, and an address from the Delegate of the said County to his Excellency Governor Gage, dated the 9th Instant was read. Whereupon, Resolved unanimously, that this Assembly deeply feels the suffering of their Countrymen in the Massachusetts Bay, under the Operation of the late unjust, cruel and oppressive Acts of the British Parliament.
——— That they most thoroughly approve the wisdom and Fortitude with which Opposition to these wicked Ministerial Measures has hitherto

been conducted, and they earnestly recommend to their Brethren a performance in the same firm and temperate Conduct, as expressed in the Resolutions determined upon at a Meeting of the Delegates for the County of Suffolk on Tuesday the sixth Instant; trusting that the Effects of the united Effects of North-America in their behalf, will carry such Conviction to the British Nation, of the unwise, unjust and ruinous Policy of the present Administration, as quickly to introduce better Men and wiser Measures.

Resolved unanimously, That Contributions from all the Colonies for the supplying the Necessities and alleviating the Distress of our Brethren at Boston, ought to be continued in such a manner and so long as their Occasion may require.

A true Extract from the Minutes.

Charles Thompson, Secry.

BOSTON Oct. 3. In Congress, Sept. 22, 1774.

Resolved, That the Congress request the Merchants and others, in the several Colonies, not to send to Great Britain any Orders for Goods; and to direct the Execution of all Orders already sent, to be delayed or suspended, until the Sense of the Congress on the means to be taken for the Preservation of the Liberties of America made public. Charles Thompson, Secry.

BOSTON Oct. 3. Extract of a letter from London, dated July 28, 1774.

"Whatever persons, whose interest is concerned to keep you in agitation, may assert, respecting the sense of the people here, in regard to American matters, you may be assured that your measures are almost universally disapproved, and that the popular tide is strongly in favor of coercive measures against the Bostoneans, I am more particular in this, because I have seen in your papers, extract letters, as from gentlemen in London, insinuating the opposition in America was greatly extolled by the Patriots of this country; whereas the contrary is true, and the ministry have been censured for their lenity, previously to the passing of the late Acts. Indeed, my dear friend, you can expect nothing from the popular voice in your favor, for even granting that it were so, Mr. Wilkes and his party have become so weak and contemptible, as only to furnish a subject of laughter and of triump to their enemies."

Extract from a letter from London, dated July 6, 1774.

"Do not be surprised if you should hear that other bills, worse if possible than those you have heard of, should pass next session of Parliament, as I am told there are some for dividing and separating the provinces, taking away the charters of some, and abolishing the Government of others and joining them to others."

BOSTON Oct. 10. Almost all empty Houses, out Houses, &c. in this Town, are now taken up for the Soldiery.

BOSTON Oct. 17. In the Provincial Congress at Concord, Oct. 14.

Resolved, That the several Constables and Collectors of Taxes theoughout the Province, who have or shall have Monies in their Hands, collected on Province Assessments, be advised not to pay the same or any Part thereof to the Hon. Harrison Gray, Esq; but that such Constables and Collectors, as also such Constables and Collectors as have or shall have any County Monies in their Hands, take and observe such Orders and Directions touching the same, as shall be given them by several Towns and Districts by whom they were chosen. And that the Sheriffs and the Deputy Sheriffs of the several Counties in the Privince, who have in their Hands any Province Monies be also advised not to pay the same to the said Harrison Gray, Esq; but that they retain the same in their Hands respectively, until further Advice of the Provincial Congress or Order from a constitutional assembly of the Province. And that the present Assessors of the several Towns and Districts in the Province be advised to proceed to make Assessments of the Tax granted by the Great and General Court of the Province at their last May Session, and that such Assessments be duly paid by the Person assessed, to such Person or Persons as shall be ordered by the said Towns and Districts respectively, and Congress recommend the Payment of Taxes accordingly.

A True Extract from the Minutes.
Benjamin Lincoln, Sec'y.
BOSTON Oct. 24. Grand American Congress, Philadelphia Oct. 8.
Resolved, That the Congress approve of the Opposition by the Inhabitants of the Massachusetts bay, to the Execution of the late Acts of Parliament, and if the same should be attempted to be carried into execution by force all America, in such Case, ought to support them in their Opposition.
In Congress October 10.
Resolved unanimously, That it is the Opinion of this Body, that the Removal of the People of Boston into the Country, would be not only extremely difficult in the execution, but so important in the Consequence, as to require the utmost Deliberation, before it is adopted; but in Case the Provincial Meeting of that Colony shall judge it absolutely necessary, it is the Opinion of the Congress, that all America ought to contribute towards Recompensing them for their Injury, they may thereby sustain, and it will be recommended accordingly.
Resolved, That every Person or Persons whatsoever, who shall take, accept or act, under the Commission, or Authority, in any wise desire from the Act of Parliament, passed last Session, changing the Form of Government, and violating the Charter of the Province of Massachusetts Bay, ought to be held in Detestation and Abhorrence by all good Men, and considered as the wicked Tools of the Despotism, which is preparing to destroy those Rights which God, Nature and Compact have given to America.
In Congress October 11.
As the Congress has given General Gage, an Assurance of the peaceable Disposition of the People of Boston,
Resolved unanimously, That they advised still to conduct themselves peaceably towards his Excellency General Gage, and his Majesty's Troops, now stationed in the Town of Boston, as far as can be possibly be consistent with their immediate Safety, and the Security of the Town, avoiding and Discountenancing every Violation

of his Majesty's Property, or any insult on his Troops; and that they peaceably and firmly preserve in the Line they are now conducting themselves, on the Defensive.

Resolved, That the Congress recommend to the Inhabitants of the Colony of Massachusetts Bay, to submit to a Suspension of the Administration of Justice, where it cannot be produced in a legal and peaceable Manner, under the Rules of the present charter, and Laws of the Colony found thereupon, until the Effect of their Application for a Repeal of the Act by which the Charter Rights are infringed, is known.

BOSTON Oct. 24. On Thursday last about 12 o'clock as Colonel Cleveland of the Royal artillery, and Captain Montresor, Engineer was returning together from the Neck, one Samuel Dyer, imperceptibly went up to the left of Colonel Cleveland and snatched his hanger from his side, and at the same time made a back stroke with it to his head, which was avoided; upon which he drew out a pistol and directed it at the Colonel, but it missed fired; and observing Captain Montresor with a kind of half dirk, coming up to him, he directed a pistol at the Captain's head at about three yards distance, which only flashed in the pan, and returned to the Colonel (who was disarmed) and made two or three strokes at him with his hanger, cutting a metal button almost asunder on his sleeve, cut his hat through, and made an incision behind his ear. On being pursued, he threw his pistols, which were taken up by Captain Montresor. He was the same afternoon committed to Cambridgr goal, and has been since removed to the goal in this town.

This Dyer says he was taken up last July, in a private manner, by order of Colonel Maddison, on suspicion of his enticing men to desert, and was sent to England on board Admiral Montegue's ship in irons ⎯⎯⎯ Upon his arrival he was examined before Lord North respecting the destruction of the tea, but nothing being found against him he was dismissed. ⎯⎯⎯ He then made his case known to the Lord Mayor, and the Sheriffs (Dayre & Lee) of London, who generously supplied him with money, and procured him a passage on board Captain Rogers for Newport, where he arrived about a forthnight since.

BOSTON Oct. 27. We are informed that Arnold Wells, Esq; owner of the vessel which brought a present wheat from our Brethren of Quebec has generously declined taking any thing on freight for the same.

A drove of sheep from our brethren of Scituate in the colony of Rhode Island for our suffering poor, were received last Saturday morning.

BOSTON oct. 31. From Baltimore, in Maryland we learn that a Vessel arrived there the 6th instant, sent by General Gage to purchase a load of Flour, a quantity of Blankets, &c. for the Troops under his Command in Boston, but that the Committee of Correspondence for that Place refused to furnish any of the Articles until they heard from the General Congress, where they had sent an express to receive directions how they should act upon the Occasion.

BOSTON Nov. 7. On Friday Evening last, in pursuing a Person who had been guilty of breaking the Peace in Charlestown, a barrel and bag of tea were stumbled on, which were immediately carried to the Training-Field and committed to Flames; after they were consumed it was suggested there were more in the same Place; upon which a search was made, and enough to fill a large Hogshead which was conveyed to a Place called the Green, before Cape-Briton Tavern, and a Quantity of Faggots laid round it, they were set on fire and the whole consumed; Every thing was conducted with such stillness and order, that many people there knew nothing of it until the next Morning. —— It is supposed the Quantity destroyed were between 4 and 500 weight.

We hear a gentleman belonging to Newburyport was very active in demolishing the above tea.

BOSTON Nov. 10. By the Governor a proclamation.

Whereas a number of persons, in the month of October last, calling themselves a Provincial Congress did, in the most open and dangerous terms, assumed to themselves to powers and authority of government, independent of, and repugnant to his Majesty's government, independent, legally ans constitutionally established within this province, and tending utterly to subvert the same; and did amongst other unlawful proceedings, take upon themselves to resolve and direct a new and uncostitutional regulation of militia, in high derogation of his Majesty's royal prerogative; and also elect and appoint Henry Gardner, Esq; of Stow, to be receiver-general, in the room of Harrison Gray Esq; then and still legally holding and executing that office; and also to order and direct the monies granted for his Majesty, to be paid into the hands of said Henry Gardner, and not said Harrison Gray, Esq; and further earnestly recommend to the inhabitants of the province to oblige and compel the several constables and collectors to comply with and execute the said directions, contrary to the oaths, and against the plain and express rules and directions of the law, all which proceedings have a most dangerous tendency to ensnare his Majesty's Subjects, the inhabitants of this province, and draw them into perjuries, riots, sedition, treason and rebellion. For the prevention of which evils, and the calamitous consequences thereof; I have thought it my duty to issue this proclamation, hereby earnestly exhorting, and in his Majesty's name strictly prohibiting all his liege subjects within this province, from complying in any degree with the said requisitions, recommendations, directions, or resolve of the aforesaid unlawfull assembly, as they regard his Majesty's highest displeasure, and wou'd avoid the pains and penalties of the law. And I do hereby charge and command all justices of the peace, sherriffs, constibles, collectors and other officers, in the several departments, to be vigilant and faithful in the execution of discharging of their duty, in their respective offices, agreeable to the well known established laws of the land; and the utmost of their power, by all lawful ways and means, to discountenance discourage, and prevent a compliance with such dangerous resolves of the abovementioned, or any other unlawful assembly whatsoever.

Given at Boston this 10th day of November, in the fifteenth year of the reign of his Majesty George the third, by the grace of God of Great Britain, France and Ireland, King, Defender of the faith &c. Annoque Dimini, 1774.

T. Gage.

BOSTON Nov. 14. Last Thursday an Inquisition was taken on the Body of Richard Cuitt, and the Jurors retorned the following Verdict, viz. That the said Cuitt was a Mariner on board the Thomas & Richard Transport ship, commanded by Cuthbert Park, lying in Hancock's Wharf, and did on the 10th day of November, between the Hours of 7 an 8 of the Clock in the Morning, cut through his Windpipe with a Razor, and then and there voluntarily and feloniously as a felon of himself, did kill and murder himself against the Peace of our Sovereign Lord the King, his Crown and Dignity.

The remains of this unhappy Person were immediately buried in the Manner and form, as by the law prescribes.

BOSTON Nov. 14. Last Wednesday evening arrived in town, the Hon. Thomas Cushing, esq; Mr. Samuel Adams, and John Adams, Esq; delegates from this province, to the late Grand American Congress. The people testified their joy at their safe arrival, by ringing of the bells &c.

Robert Treat Paine, Esq; the other Delegate from this Province, took passage at New-York and arrived at Rhode-Island last Week; from which, we hear he returned Home safe.

BOSTON Nov. 21. At a meeting of the Inhabitants of the town by adjournment, November 7th, the committee appointed for that purpose, made the following report, which was accepted by the Town.

Whereas, sundry regiments of his Majesty's troops are, contrary to law, and to the great annoyance and detriment of his Majesty's good subjects of this province, now stationed in the town of Boston, in a time of profound peace, for the avowed Purpose of carrying into execution sundry acts of the British Parliament, tending to enslave the people, and to subvert the constitution of the province, which it is our duty to protest against upon all occasions; yet nevertheless, we, the inhabitants of the town of Boston, in a town-meeting legally assembled, taking into serious consideration, the distressed circumstances of the metropolis, and being anxious still to use our best endeavours to preserve the decency and order for which the town has ever been remarkable, relying on the justice of our cause, and confiding in the united endeavours of the colonies, the wisdom of the Continental Congress, the justice and clemency of our sovereign, and smiles of divine providence, that our grievances will shortly be redressed, and our unalienable and precious rights, liberties and privileges be restored and secured to us upon a just and permanent basis. Therefore we recommend,

That as his Excellency the Governor has assured the town, that he will do in all his power to secure peace and good order of the town; That the town on their part will exert their best endeavoured to effect the same desirable purpose; and to the end would augment the town watch, and it is recommended to the selectmen of the town, that they increase the watch to the number of twelve men in each watch-house, for the security of the inhabitants, and that they be directed to patrole the streets of the town for the whole night the ensuing season.

And it is certainly desired that his majesty's justices of the peace, and other peace officers would exert their authority for the observance of the laws, and preserving of peace and order, and that when they hear any disturbance, they would not wait for a complaint, but call on the inhabitants, who will at all times be ready in assisting to disperse such persons or in bringing offenders of what rank or order soever to justice.

As in our present situation it is incumbent upon us particularly to attend to the peace and good order of the town, it is therefore earnestly recommended to the inhabitants to do all in their power to prevent or suppress any quarrels or disturbances, And it is seriously recommended to all masters of families that they restrain their children and servants for going abroad after nine o'clock in the evening, unless on necessary business.

And it is further recommended to the selectmen of the town, to join upon all retailers and taverners of the town, that they strictly conform to the laws of the province relating to disorderly persons.

      Attest. W. Cooper, Town Clerk.

BOSTON Nov. 21. Thursday last the Encampments here were broken up, and the troops are gone into houses, stores, &c. in different Parts of this town. We have eleven Regiments in this Town besides the Artillery. A Guard of 500 are every Day on Duty.

In the last Transpot that arrived here came a large Quantity of Powder, cannon, Balls, &c.

BOSTON Dec. 5. Extract of a letter from a gentleman of Veracity in Charlwstown South Carolina, November 6, 1774.

"A ship from London arrived here a few Days past, with 7 half Chests of Hyson and Bohia Teas; the owners of the Teas were obliged to go on board and throw it overboard themselves, in the sight of thousands of Spectators, and they think themselves very happy to come off without corporal Punishment."

Last Thursday and Inquisition was taken on the Body of John McDonald, a Soldier in the fourth Regiment, who was found dead that Morning on Boston Neck, and the jurors returned a Verdict in the following Words, viz. That the said John McDonald, being intoxicated with Liquor, did some time in the Evening of the 30th Day of November last, fall down upon the Beach, on the West Side of Boston Neck, and there expired by reason of Inclemency of the Weather, and by that Means to his death.

BOSTON Dec. 5. Last Saturday afternoon the Scaborough man of was, which was sent express from hence to England the beginning of September last, returned hither again, with dispatches for his Excellency the Governor, to contents of which have not transpired. The Scaborough sailed from Plymouth the 24th of October; and it is said, that three ships of the line, viz. The Asia, Boyne, and Sumerset, with the Hind frigate, and Falcon sloop of war with 500 marines on board each of the large ships, were to sail after for this place.

BOSTON Dec. 8. In the Provincial Congress, Cambridge, Dec. 1, 1774.

Whereas by rigorous operation of the Boston Port-Bill, the metropolis of this province and the neighbouriong town of Charlestown, have been brought into a most distressed state, many of their inhabitants being deprived of means of their subsistence, and reduced to the alternative of quitting their habitations, or perishing in them by famine, if they had not been supported by the free and generous contributions of our sister colonies, even from the remotest part of this continent.

Resolved, That the grateful acknowledgement of this Congress be returned to the several colonies for having so deeply interested themselves in behalf of said towns under their present suffering in the common cause; and that the Congress considered their donations not only as unexampled acts of benevolence of this province in general, which has also greatly suffered, and to charity to those towns in particular, but as convincing proof of the firm attachment of all the colonies to the glorious cause of liberty, and their determination to support them in the noble stand they are now making for the liberties of themselves and all America.

Signed by order of the Provincial Congress.

John Hancock, President.

In the Provincial Congress, Cambridge, Dec. 5, 1774.

Resolved, That the proceedings of the American Constitutional Congress, held at Philadelphia on the first of September last, and reported by the honourable delegates from this colony, have with the deliberation due to their high inportance been considered by us, and the American bill of rights therein contained, appear to be formed with the greatest ability and judgement; to be founded on the immutable laws of nature and reason, the priciples found in the English constitution, and respective charter and contitutions of the colonies; and to be worthy of their most vigorous support, as essentially necessary to liberty ——— Likewise the ruinous and iniquitous measures, which in violation of these rights at present convulse and threaten destruction of America, appears to be clearly pointed out, and judicious plans adopted for defeating them.

Resolved, That the most grateful acknowledgement are due to the truly honourable and patriotic members of the Continental Congress, for their wise and able exertions on the cause of American liberty: And this Congress in their names, in behalf of this colony, do hereby with the utmost sincerity express the same.

Resolved, That the Hon. John Hancock, Hon. Thomas Cushing, Esq; Mr. Samuel Adams, and John Adams, and Robert-Treat Pain, Esq; or any three of them be, and they hereby are, appointed and authorized to represent this colony, on the tenth of May next or sooner if necessary, at the American Congress to be held in Philadelphia; with full power with the delegates from the other American colonies, to concert, agree upon, direct and order such further measures, as shall to them appear to be best calculated for the recovery and establishment of American rights and liberties,and for the restoring harmony between Great-Britain and the colonies.

And whereas it is of the utmost importance that the salutary association of the Continental Congress be effectually executed; and the plans of foes to America defeated, who, aided by tyrannical power, intend to import goods, wares and merchandize prohibited by the association, which may clandestinely be vended as goods imported before the first of December instant, by assistance of such merchants and traders as to this intent shall basely prostitute themselves; and it will be extremely difficult to distinguish between goods imported before the said first of December and such as after said day shall, in violation of the association, be imported and secretly dispersed through the colony;

And whereas it is expressly recommended by the Continental Congress "to the provincial conventions, and to the committees in the respective colonies, to establish such further regulations as they may think proper for carrying into execution their association."

Resolved, That from and after the tenth day of October next, it will be indispensably necessary that all Goods, wares and merchandize, directly or indirectly imported from Great-Britain or Ireland, molasses, syrups, paneles, coffee or pimento from British plantations or from Dominica; wines from Madeira or the western islands; and foreign indigo, should cease to be sold or purchased in this colony, notwithstanding they have been imported before the first day of December aforesaid, unless the acts and parts of acts of the British Parliament (particularly enumerated in a paragraph of the American congress association subsequent to the fourteenth article) shall be repealed. And it is hereby strongly recommended to the inhabitants of the towns and districts in the colony, that from and after the tenth of October, they cease to sell or purchase, and prevent from being exposed to sale, within their respective limits, any goods, wares, merchandize, &c. above enumerated, which shall at any time have been imported into America, whether before or after the first of December aforesaid; unless said acts of Parliament shall be then repealed.

As it is likewise strongly recommended to the committees of inspection (which ought immediately, to be chosen agreeably to the said association by each town and district in the colony, not having already appointed such committees) that they exert themselves in causing the association as thereby directed to be strictly executed. And that after the said tenth day of October (unless the acts of parliament aforesaid are repealed_ they apply to all merchants and traders in the respective towns and districts, and take a full inventory of all goods, wares and merchandize aforesaid in their possessions, whether they shall have been imported before or after the first of December aforesaid;

require them to offer no more for sale, until said acts shall be repealed, and if any merchants, traders or others, shall refuse to have an inventory taken, or shall offer for sale after the said tenth of October, any such goods, wares or merchandize: It is expressly recommend- to the committees aforesaid, that they take their goods into their possessions to be stored at the risk of the proper owners until the repeal of the acts aforesaid, and publish the names of such refractory merchants, traders or purchasers, that they may meet with the merits of enemies to their country. And the towns and districts throughout the province are also advised, that they by no means fail vigorously to assist and support their committees, in discharging this as well as the other duties of their offices, and to cause this resolution to be executed by every measure which they shall think necessary.

Signed by order of the Provincial Congress,
John Hancock, President.
A true extract from the minutes,
Benjamin Lincoln, Secretary.

BOSTON Dec. 12. Our Brethren in the country are cautioned to beware of false brethren, as there are unfortunately such in almost every town. Could we possibly conceive that such monster of perfidy should inhabit any town of this province, as to become a spy and base betrayer of his brethren, when they are struggling to redeem not only themselves, but the very miscreant who abets the conspiracy against them from the soul fiend of Tyranny? I weep for the degeneracy of my countrymen! Reflect ye miserable hirelings! on the necessary consequence of your apostasy at this distressing juncture; and ye base Deserters of our Country's Cause, who are in League with the Enemies of America, who are preparing to revolt and cut the Throats of your Brethren, should the Hour of Hazard ever arrive; Ye are known; our Abhorrence of your conduct is enkindled, do not urge our patience to far, the Hour of Vengeance comes louring on, the Hand of Desperation, may urge a stroke Fatal to the Bosom that could harbour such infernal

Design:

Ye Sons of Peterham, Worcester, Woburn, &c. hear and forebear, and do no more so wickedly.

BOSTON Dec. 19. A letter from Quebec of the 26th of November mentions that "the interpreter, who, it was said, had been sent to the Six Nations to know if they would give their assistance to the King's Troops against the Colonies (should there be an occasion for them) have given an answer, that it is a family quarrel, and that they will by no means interfere between Parent and Children." The letter further adds that "they will also be very hard put to it to muster any Canadians for that purpose."

By a person lately arrived from Quebec, we learn further, that application had been made to the French Inhabitants of Canada to arm themselves against the Colonies; but they rejected the proposal with Indignation and declared that if any Canadian should be deluded so far as to go against their Sister Colonies, they would send ten to their relief.

BOSTON Dec. 19. The General Assembly of Rhode Island have ordered 40,000 flints, 300 Barrels of Gun Powder, 3 Tons of Lead, and 4 Brass field Pieces, to be procured for the use of that Colony.

Last Friday and Saturday se'nnight all the Cannon belonging to Fort George, in the Harbour of Newport, except four, was carried from thence to Providence, with the shot, &c. from whence they may be easily conveyed into the Country, to meet the Indians and Canadians with which the Colonies are threatened.

The People of the Province of New-Hampshire also thinking the Powder, &c. at the Fort at New-Castle, not safe any longer to remain there, last Week removed it, with small Arms and some Field Pieces, to a Place of more security.

BOSTON Dec. 19. In Provincial Congress, Cambridge, Dec. 9, 1774.

Whereas the Congress at the Session in October last, taking in Consideration the alarming state of the Colony, where, upon the most mature Deliberation fully convinced, that to provide against the Danger to which it was then exposed by a standing Army illegally posted in Boston; and from Time to Time reinforced, for the purpose of subverting our ancient Constitution and the Liberties of all North America; it was indispensably necessary that a considerable Sum of Money should be immediately laid out for the just Defence of this People; and whereas by a Resolve of the Congress, bearing Date 28th October, and published in the Papers, it among other Things earnestly recommended to the several Towns and Districts, that they would cause to be paid into the Hands of Henry Gardner, Esq; all province Monies due from them respectively, to supply the said pressing Exigencies of the Colony; and whereas the danger which then threatened the Province, is still continued and daily increasing: It is Resolved, and most earnestly recommended to all the Inhabitants of the Towns and Districts aforesaid, as they regard their own safety and the Preservation of their inestimable Rights and Liberties, that they cause the Monies aforesaid, to be paid forthwith to the said Henry Gardner, Esq; who has given Bonds with sufficient Sureties, the Satisfaction of the Congress; and they cause their respective proportion of the tax granted by the General Court in June last, and all other the Province Monies due from them respectively; to be supplied in some Way that shall be more expeditious than the usual Mode of collecting the Taxes, in Order to prevent any Delay in providing against the imminent Danger above mentioned ——— And the Members of the Congress are hereby desired to use their utmost industry for having this Resolve speedily and punctually complied with; and the Sheriffs and Deputy Sheriffs of the several Counties to pay the Province Monies in their respective Hands as had been already recommended.

    Signed by Order of the Provincial Congress.
                                          John Hancock Pres.
  A true Extract from the Minutes.
                Benjamin Lincoln, Secretary.
  BOSTON Dec. 22. Extract of a letter from Portsmouth, New-Hampshire, dated December 16.
  "We have been in confusion here for two days

on information that two regiments were coming to take possession of our Fort, ——— by beat of drum 200 men immediately assembled and went to the Castle in two gundalows who on their way were met with 150 more, and demanded the surrender of the Fort, which Capt. Cochran resisted; and fired three guns, but no lives were lost; ——— upon which they immediately scaled the walls, disarmed the Captain and his men, took possession of 97 barrels of powder ——— put it on board the gundalows, brought it up to town, and went off with it to some distance in the country. Yesterday the town was full of men, from the country, who marched in, in form; chose a committee to wait on the Governor, who offered that he knew of no such design to sending troops, ships, &c. This morning I hear there is a thousand or fifteen hundred on their march to town. The Governor and his Council sat yesterday on the affair, and are now meeting again. The men who came down, are those of the best property and note of the province."

BOSTON Dec. 26. A vessel with upwards of 1000 Bushels of Corn, from Rappahannock, in Virginia for the suffering Poor at Boston, hath been blown off the Coast, and is got to St. Eustatia, where the Cargo will be sold, and the Proceeds remitted hither.

A Donation of 8 Cords of Wood was received last Week from Yarmouth, in this Province.

Considerable Quantities of Goods have been given up in Pennsylvania, New-York, Connecticut and at different Ports in this Province, which arrived after the first of December to be disposed of agreeable to the Association of the Congress.

Last Saturday Morning one William Fergurson. aged 28 Years, a Soldier to his majesty's 10th Regiment, was shot at the bottom of the Common for Desertion, pursuant to Sentence of a Court Martial.

1775

BOSTON Jan. 2. The following vote expressing of the Gratitude of the Town for the benevolent Assistance received from the other Colonies under our present Calamities, and the Kind Recommendation of the late respectable Continental Congress for the future Support ——— Passed Nem. Con.

Whereas the Town of Boston in unfortunately become the most striking Monument of Ministerial Tyranny and Barbarity, and is particulary exhibited in the sudden shutting this Port. Thereby cruelly depriving the Inhabitants of the Metropolis of means they have hitherto used to support their Families, And whereas our Brethren in the other Colonies, well know that we are suffering in the common Cause of America and of Mankind, have from a generous and brotherly Disposition contributed largely towards our support in this time of our general Distress (without which many worthy and virtuous Citizens must have been in imminent danger of Perishing with Cold and Hunger) and whereas the Honourable Members of the Continental Congress have kindly recommended us to our Sister Colonies as worthy of future support from them, while the Iron Hand of unremitted Opresion lies heavy upon us: Therefore voted, that this Town, truly sensible of the generous Assistance they have received from their sympathizing Brethren, return their warmest and most sincere Thanks for the same and pray God, whose beneficence they so gloriously imitate, may bestow upon them the blessing he has promised to all those who feed the hungry and clothe the naked: and the Thanks of this Town are accordingly hereby given to our Benefactors aforementioned, and to the Honourable Members of the Continental

Congress for their Benevolence towards us expressed as aforesaid, which Support, if continued, cannot fail of animating us to remain steadfast in Defence of the Rights of America.

BOSTON Jan. 9. Extract from a letter from Philadelphia, Dec. 20, 1774.

"By accounts just received from Georgia, we are informed, that all the opposition to their concurrence with the other colonies have ceased, even the protectors have appeared openly at the poll, and voted for delegates to meet the next Congress; that they are fully resolved to retrieve their late neglect, and do heartily join in the association of the general congress: as proof of this, a subscription has been opened for Boston, and already makes respectable figre, no one subscribing less than 10 tierces of rice, which will be forwarded through this city to New-York, to your province ——— I dare say this account will give singular pleasure to all friends to liberty with you."

BOSTON 12. Whereas several persons have lately had their limbs and lives endangered, by the careless driving of wagons galloping of horses through the streets: ——— The following by-laws are in order of the town are inserted in this paper, by direction of the selectmen that every one may strictly conform himself to said orders, or expect a prosecution for the penalties that may hereafter be incurred by any breech of the same.

And it is further ordered, that henceforth no cart, dray, truck, or sled, drawn by either horse or horses, horse and oxen, shall be suffered to pass through any of the streets or lanes in this town, but with a Sufficient driver; who shall during such passage keep with his said cart, dray, truck, or sled, and carefully observe and attend such methods as may be best serve to keep said horse or horses or oxen under command, and shall have the thill horse by the head. And whatsoever carter or others understanding to drive any cart, dray, truck, or sled, shall during such passing through the streets or lanes as aforesaid, either ride in said cart, dray, truck or sled or otherwise neglect to observe and attend the rules prescribe to this order, such carters, drivers or owners for such cart, dray, truck, or sled, shall forfeit and pay the sum of eight shillings for each offence.

And it is further ordered, that no slay shall be drove in the streets of this town without bells fastened to the horses that dray the same; and whoever shall affend herein, shall forfeit and pay the sum of ten shillings for every offence.

Great danger arising often times form coaches, slays, and chairs and other carriages on the Lord's days as the people are going to, or coming from the several churches in the town being driven with great rapidity, and the public worship being ofter times much disturbed by such carriages driving by the side of the churches with great force in time thereof.

It is therefore voted and ordered, That no coach, slay, chair, chaise or other carriages, shall at such time be driven at a greater rate than a foot pace, on penalty of the sum of ten shillings, to be paid by the person driving, or if he be a servant or slave, by his master or mistress.

And it is further ordered, that no person whatsoever, shall at any time hereafter ride or drive a gallop or other pace, within any of the streets, lanes or alleys in this town, on penalty of forfeiting the sum of five shillings, for every such offence.

BOSTON Jan. 12. The following was left at the Massachusetts Spy for publication. viz.

Dearly beloved,
I cannot pass one hour more of my life, without thus publicly resigning the most odious office of any creature sustained, and publicly confessing my offence. I was born in the land of South Britain, and descended an ancient family, and was heir apparent to the office of master of the stag hounds, which is worth 2000 pounds sterling a year, in my minority to satisfy my roving disposition, shipped on board a brig, one Loring master for America, loaded with tea, hoping thereby to gain a perfect knowledge of

the pestiferous Sons of Liberty, that I might represent them to the ministry. But by a righteous providence the vessel was drove on shore upon the American coast and lost, with the cargo, though the people were saved, and I having the good fortune to meet with a venerable family who kindly received me, and still continue to support me with all necessaries of life, the house is known by the sign of the anchor, where I may be spoke with any time, as my determination is never to return to my native land, but renounce the said lucrative office for the pleasure and satisfaction I hope to enjoy among the glorious freemen of America. A particular detail of my first principles and design, is too lengthy to publish in a newspaper, I shall conclude by saying. I was a most wretched Tory, but now a staunch Whig, and I think my change is saving, as I hope for salvation no other way; a particular correspondence with freemen I reserve, and bid adieu to all slaves: Pardon this uncout appearance, and give me leave to subscribe myself a Son of Liberty and add my name.

Chance.

BOSTON Jan. 16. From Robbury, January 9, 1775, Yesterday although Lord's-Day, Numbers of the Officers of the Army were Traveling our streets (with scates either slung by their sides, or open in their Hands) on their Way to Jamaica Pond, (nearly 3 miles from the Boston Court-House) where having arrived they sported themselves in scateing for several hours in open view of one of the Meeting Houses, to the great Discomposure and Grief of the Pious and well disposed, and setting Example of Profaneness and Irreligion before the Young, too apt to be seduced by such Example. ———— But such practices being contrary to the Laws of God and the Laws of this Province and one of the articles of war (with the last of which at least, it is to be supposed those Gentlemen are acquainted) it is expected that his Excellency, to whom it is said Complaints will be made, will suppress such Profanation of the Sabbath in the future, more especially as his Excellency was pleased not long since to issue a Proclamation for the

Discouragement of Vice and Immorality, &c. which surely he will Discountenance in those immediately under his Command.

An Inhabitant.

BOSTON Jan. 23. There have been lately several Instances of flagrant Abuse by some of the Officers of the Army to the inhabitants of the Town without any Provocation. ——— A few Evening ago, two young Lads, Sons of Mr. Richard Hunnewell going to their Fathers office in Essex-Street, South-End were fired upon by an Officer from the Window of a House where he was; but happily the Shot with which the Musket was charged passed between the Lads without hurting either of them, and lodged in a Neighbouring fence. ——— And last Friday there was a high-handed Riot in King Street, occasioned, as we are informed, by a Number of Officers attempting to rescue a Prisoner out of the Hands of the Town-Watch. ——— An Inquisition is now making into this Affair before a Magistrate. ——— On Saturday Night last three Officers stopped at the Watch-House in King Street and insulted the Watch, threatening to have their Heart's Blood before Morning, &c. ——— two of the Selectmen waited on the Governor the same Evening, to inform him of the abuse.

BOSTON Jan. 23. The Public is hereby informed that a young Woman and a Child at the House of a Serjeant of the 59th Regiment, at the Head of Cross-Street, were Yesterday taken with the Small-Pox and soon after sent to the Hospital Ship in the Harbour: Upon a strict Enquiry no one has the Distemper in Town, By order of the Selectmen. William Cooper, Town Clerk. Jan. 12.

BOSTON Jan. 30. In our last we mentioned several Instances of the most flagrant Abuse offered to the Inhabitants of this Town by some of the Officers of the Army, especially a high-Handed Riot on the Evening of Friday the 22d Instant, the Particulars of which we deferred till the Matter had been enquired into by the Magistrates before whom the Complaints had been made by the Town-Watch.

On Tuesday and Wednesday last there was a full and impartial Examination of the Witnesses before the worshipful Edmund Quincy and John Hill Esquires, two of his Majesty's Justices of the Quorum for this County —— By the evidence it appeared as we are informed, that previous to the Riot the following Circumstances took place: A little after Ten o'Clock two young men passing down Mill-Street, near the Entrance into Long-Lane, they were accosted by an Officer not in English, but they supposed in another Language, which they did not understand; they asked him what he meant: he said he meant to tell them to go about their Business. They said they were going, and passed along into Long-Lane. They had not gone far before the Officer called to them to stop —— they stopped till he came to them, and angry Words ensued. The young Men, however, parted from him the second Time and went on their Way towards their Homes. The Officer followed and overtook them near the Head of the Lane, and stopped them again, telling them he supposed they were stiff Americans; to which one of them said, he gloried in the Character. Here again angry Words ensued, and the Officer drew his Sword, flourished it and struck one of the young Men on the Arm, who immediately seized him. —— at this juncture, three or four of the Town Watch, who were upon the patrole, come up and separated them, advising them to go home. The two young Men done so, but the Officer refused, saying, he was the Prisoner of the Watch and would go with them; they told him he was not their Prisoner, but might go where he pleas'd, and if he desired it they would see him safe home; but he insisted upon it that he was their Prisoner. —— The Watchmen went down the Lane towards their Head-Quarters in King-Street, where they had been going before, and the Officer accompanied them. In the way they met with several Persons, whom they took to be Servants of Officers, who supposing this Officer to be in custody of the Watch, attempted to rescue him, but he insisted upon being a Prisoner, and said the Watchmen were his Friends and he would go with them. They then went forward, and in Quaker-Lane, which leads into King-Street, they were met and assaulted by more than twenty Officers of the Army, who took the Watch-Poles from them and wounded some of them.

We thought it necessary thus far to give a detail of the affair, that our readers might know by what means this riot was introduced.

BOSTON Feb. 6. Extract of a Letter from New-York Jan. 27, 1775.

"As the Enemies of America are indefatigable, in giving the highest coloring to every event that has the least appearance of disunion among the Colonies, it is the duty of friends to counteract them. For this purpose I enclose you the late vote of our Assembly, in order that you may be fully informed of that fact, and be thereby enable to defeat their wicked Macination. ——— The meaning of the province question, in our Assembly's proceedings, is, that any motion or question proposed, shall not be then put; or, in other words, that the sense of the House shall not be taken on any such motion or question: Hence therefore, you will be able fully to understand the import of the determination of the House. ——— The present assembly has existed from 1769, and most of the members who are against any enquiry into the measures of Congress, as preparatory to the approbation of them, have long since forfeited their esteem of their constituents: And are therefore looking for favor from the Crown, for themselves and Families. Others of them were indisposed on, from meer ignorance, and some from fear; being frightened by designing men into apprehension that the Suffolk Resolves, which some call treason, would involve them in the guilt of it. ——— In short, Sir, no virtuous of spirited act could be expected from a House, which had, by its votes, violated the right of election, suspended the habeas corpus act, depriving the subject of his right to a trial by jury, and provide support, six years, for troops kept here for the express purpose of enslaving Americans. But although this miscreants are the legal representatives of the people; yet I can assure you, they are not their true representatives. And therefore you have no cause to fear that this city will depart from the association."

BOSTON Feb. 6. We hear from Plymouth, that 11 persons were chosen in that town on Friday se,nnight, to observe the actions of the Tories, and make reports from time to time, what they can hear and observe.

In the Provincial Congress at Cambridge, Feb. 7, 1775,

Whereas it appears to the Congress, that certain persons, are employed in diverse kinds of work for the army, now stationed in Boston, for the purpose of carrying into execution of the late acts of parliament, and in supplying them with iron for waggons, canvass, tent-poles, and other articles of field equipage, whereby said army be enable to take the field; and distress the inhabitants of the country,

Therefore, resolve, as the opinion of the Congress, and it is accordingly strongly recommended, to the inhabitants of the several Towns and Districts of this Province, that should any person or persons, presume to supply the troops now stationed in Boston, or elsewhere in said Province, with timber, boards, spars, pickets, tent-poles, canvass, bricks, iron, waggons, carts, carriages, entrenching tools; or any material for making any of the carriages, or implements aforesaid, with Horses or Oxen for draught, or any other materials whatsoever, which may enable them to annoy, or in any manner distres's said inhabitants, he or they so offending shall be held in the highest detestation, and deemed inveterate enemies to America, and ought to be prevented and opposed by all reasonable means whatever.

And whereas it appears to the Congress, that large quantities of straw will be wanted by the inhabitants of this Province, in case we should be driven to the hard necessity of taking up arms in our defence. ——— There resolve, That no person or persons ought to sell or dispose any straw, which he or they have on hand, except to the inhabitants of this province for their own private use, or the use of said province. And it is strongly recommended by the Congress to the Committee of Correspondence and that of

Inspection in the several Towns and Districts in this Province to see that the above Resolve be strictly and faithfully adhered to, till otherwise ordered by this or some other Provincial Congress, or House of Representatives.

A true Extract from the minutes,
                    Benjamin Lincoln, Secretary.

Boston Feb. 21. Extract from a Letter from New-Haven dated February 16, 1775.

"A man lately went from Hartford, to New-York to buy the town a stock of powder, and he was bringing it up by land, it was seized by a King's officer, and account of which got to Hartford last Saturday night, whereupon about twenty-eight persons immediately set out, well armed, in order to rescue it, and they arrived here towards Sabbath-day morning. They proceeded as far as Fairfield, and their they got it, for it was seized at Stamford; and Fairfield people had rescued it before the Hartford people had got there. They arrived here last night with the powder, and I suppose have set out for Hartford with it today. They had an attachment for the officer who seized it, and they intended to take and put him in goal for trial; whether they have effected it or not, I am not yet certain.

BOSTON Feb. 16. Yesterday forty-five loads of Wood were brought to town from Milton, being a present from that town to the suffering poor of this town.

BOSTON Feb. 20. Messieurs Fleets,

In giving the following thought a place in your next Paper you will oblige a constant Customer, and perhaps serve the cause of truth.

On reading the accounts of the battle between the brave Virginians and their savage neighbours, it brought to mind the keen resentment and mortifying reflections, that must naturally kindle in the breast of an experience General, brave Officers, and intrepid Soldiers, to remember the profest Design of Britain in maintaining standing armies in America, was protection of the Colonies; and yet know at the very moment the noble Virginians were bleeding, dying and winning the laurels of victory, they were confirm'd and basking in their tents, to execute one of the most inglorious designs that ever disgraced the name of a British Soldier, viz. enslaving a free Province, that has supported itself more than 150 years against savage foes. These resentments and reflections must still increase, when they fell and know the irresistible conviction this proceeding will give to every honest Man in Britain or America, of these two facts; first that the real design of keeping a standing army in America was not the protecting, but the enslaving the Colonies. The second thing thus demonstrated is, that the Colonies do not need or desire protection from these standing armies; but are able and willing to defend themselves; and therefore they must view there stay in America as useless and burdensome. ——— In this situation it is natural for America to imagine the honest generous souls of the Gentlemen of the Army will kindle to such a degree, when their inglorious and base employment is compared with that of the virtuous Virginians, gaining the art of war and glory of victory, that they would rather resign their commissions or lives, than suffer the eternal disgrace of having their names handed down to posterity, with these facts to fully some future page, in British or American story. Can we expect less from these generous spirits, than they let their currupt employers know the just indignation they feel at this abuse and disgrace that is and will be fixed eternally on their names, as the dupes of Tyranny?

                                      A Country Gentleman.

  BOSTON Feb. 27. The following is said to be an exact Copy of a Letter from one of the Officers of Rank, then in Boston to a noble Lord.

  My Lord,

Were your Lordship only a common Colonel of a regiment, I certainly should not have given myself the trouble of writing, nor you the trouble of reading this letter; but as you hold so high a rank, and will one day hold a still higher, I conceive to apologize for my seeming want of respect. As I have not waited on the General (for reason which he cannot. I think, disapprove)

I was not certain whether you might, in your military capacity, consider my writing as proper. But, as you are not merely a soldier, but a citizen of the first class and importance from your illustrious Family and fashion your vast property, and being destined by birth to be a Counsellor of the nation, I think some explanation of my conduct not only proper, but necessary, but I flatter myself, that, some time or other, your Lordship will not simply approve my conduct, but become a friend to the same cause. My Lord, I will venture to say that it is the cause of Great Britain as well as America; it is the cause of mankind. Were the principle of Taxing America without their consent admitted, Great Britain would that instant be ruined; the pecuniary influences of the Crown, and the army of placemen and pensioners, would be so increased that all opposition to the most iniquitous measures of the most iniquitous Ministers would be for ever borne down.

Your Lordship, I am sure, must be sensible that this pecuniary influence is already enormously too great, and the very wicked use is made of it. On these priciples every good Englishman (abstract of any particular regard for America) must oppose her being taxed by the Parliament of Great Britain, or more properly by the first Lord of the Treasury, for, in fact, The Parliament and Treasury have of late years, been one and the same thing. But, my Lord, I have, besides, a very particular regard for America: I was long amongst them, and know them to be most loyal, affectionate, Zealous subjects of the whole empire. General Gage himself must acknowledge the truth of what I advance. He was witness, through the course of the last war, and their Zeal, their ardour, their enthusiasm for whatever concerned the welfare, the interest, and the honour of the mother country. When I see, therefore, the extreme of calamities attempted to be brought down upon such a people by the intrigues of such persons as Bernard and Hutchinson; then I see the Ministers, violent and tyrannical, like North, mowing down whole constitution, merely to indulge his hereditary of liberty, and those who are attached to her, I think it the duty of every honest man, and friend of humanity, to exert his utmost to defeat the diabolical purpose. That these people have been totally misrepresented at home, that they have been most unjustly and cruelly treated, your Lordship will, I make no doubt, be sooner or latter convinced. But as for your present situation, and many circumstances, you will not probably fall into the way of truth so soon as I could wish, I beg leave to recommend to your perusal a sort of pamphlet, lately sent from England; it is entitled "A true state of the proceedings in the Parliament of Great-Britain, and in the Province of Massachusetts-Bay" Mr. ——— will furnish your Lordship with it, if you will make use of my name. It is a fair and candid relation of the whole process, from the beginning to end. When your Lordship has read it, you will be struck with compassion and horror, and I have great hopes, will become not a less warm (but more powerful) friend to this much injured country than myself. I take the liberty of recommending this method to your Lordship, and it is impossible you should gather any thing but misinformation from the men who, I find, surround head-quarters. The Sewels and Paxtons are not only interested to misrepresent, and calumniate, but to exterminate their country; there is no medium, their country must perish, or they meet with the desert of impious parricides. It was the misfortune of General Gage, from the beginning, to fall into such hands as these; had he not been deluded by men of this stamp, we should never have seen him acting in a capacity so incompatible with the excellence of his natural disposition. I must now, my Lord, entreat, that as fools and braves will, from misunderstanding and malice, probably disfigure my conduct, you will not suffer them to make any wrong impression, that you will be persuaded that I act not from any pique or disappointment (which I conclude will be insinuated) but from principle. I think my Lord, an English soldier owes a very great degree of reverence to the King as first magistrate, and third branch of the legislature, called to this mighty station by the voice of the people; but I think he owes still a great degree of reverence to the right and liberties of his country.

—— I think his country is every part of the empire, that in whatever part of the empire a sagacious minister manifestly invades those rights and liberties, whether in Great-Britain, Ireland, or America, every Englishman (soldier or not soldier) ought to consider their cause as his own: And that the rights and liberties of this country are invaded every man must see who has eyes, and is not determined to keep them shut. These, my Lord, are my principles; from these, I swear by all that is sacred and tremendous, I purely and solely act; and these I hope will rather serve than prejudice me in your Lordships opinion. I flatter myself farther: I flatter myself that you, my Lord, before it is long, will adopt them; that you will at least, in your letters to your father (who I have always been taught to esteem as an honest man, and friend to humanity) endeavour to undeceive the people at home. If the delusion is too strong, I can venture to affirm that you will feel consolation amidst calamities ready to fall upon your country, in the reflection that you had attempted to avert them. I shall now finish, my Lord, entreating that if any thing appears impertinent, either in the matter or length of this letter, you will attribute it to intemperate zeal in an honest cause, and that you will be assured I shou'd not have addressed it to a man who entertained an unfavourable opinion.

BOSTON March 2. Provincial Congress Cambridge Feb. 15, 1775.

Whereas the practice of peddlers and petty Chapmen, in going from town to town, selling East India goods and teas, and various sorts of European Manufactures, in direct opposition, to the good and wholesome laws of this province, whereby they are liable to the forfeiture of all their goods; besides being subjected to the penalty of twenty pounds, does manifestly tend to interrupt and defeat the measures necessary to recover and secure the rights and liberties of the inhabitants of these Colonies: And whereas the laws relating to the peddlers and petty Chapmen, cannot at present be effectually carried into execution.

It is therefore hereby earnestly recommended to the Committee of Inspection for the several towns and districts in this province, that they be very vigilant and industrious, to discover and find out when any peddlers and petty Chapmen, shall come into their respective towns and districts, for which such Committees is appointed, that such Committee without fail make a thorough and careful search and examination of the packs and baggages, and all the goods, wares and merchandizes of such peddlers and petty chapmen: and in case such Committee shall find India Teas or European Manufactures in the possession of such peddlers of petty chapmen, it is further recommended to such Committees to prevent by all reasonable means, such peddlers and petty chapmen, from vending any such teas and manufactures. And it is hereby recommended to the inhabitants not to trade with peddlers and petty chapmen for articles whatsoever.

Signed by order of the Provincial Congress.
John Hancock, Pres.
A true Extract from the minutes,
Benjamin Lincoln, Secretary.

BOSTON March 6. Messieurs Printers,
Nothing can be more unfair as to depreciate the valor of the British Troops, or of the Americans; both are from the same original Stock, and both have often demonstrated their heroism. ——— Englishmen love liberty, and have spirit to defend it; Americans are made of English blood, have the same love of liberty and equal spirit to defend it ——— then how ridiculous are all reflections upon either? ——— Shall these two parts of a great and brave nation ever contend to blood ——— Heaven forbid it. ——— Eternally cursed will its memory be, who endeavours to divide a gallant nation, who are united by all the sacred Ties of nature, to shed each other's blood! ——— Even Barbarians will join with Christians in execrating the horrid deed.

Now is the time for every man of honour who

loves the British nation, to hop forth, in defence of the rights of Englishmen in every part of the empire; he that is a friend to Britain will be a friend to liberty, and he that wishes liberty may prevail will be a friend to America and he who is not is to be pitied, for he wants Sentiment, virtue and Honour. ——— May such a character never hereafter be found in George's dominions.   William III.

BOSTON March 6. The following dispatch is dated Salem February 28, 1775.

"Last Sabbath the Peace of the Town was disturbed by the coming of a Regiment of the King's Troops the particulars relative to which are as follows. ——— A Transport arrived at Marblehead, apparently manned as usual, between two and three o'Clock (some people had gone to meeting) the Decks were covered with Soldiers, who having loaded and fixed their Bayonets, landed with great dispatch; and instantly marched off. Some of the Inhabitants suspecting they were bound for Salem, to seize some Materials there preparing for an Artillery, dispatched several Messengers to inform us of it. These Materials was on the North Side of the North River, and to come at them it was necessary to cross a Bridge, one Part of which was made to Draw up, for the Convenience of letting Vessels pass through. The Inhabitants kept a look-out for the Appearance of Troops. The Van Guard arrived, and took their Rout down in Town as far as the Long-Wharf, Perhaps to decoy the Inhabitants thither, away from the Place to which the main Body was destined. The main Body arrived soon after and halted a few Minutes by the Town House. It is said Inquiry was immediately made by some of the Officers for a Half-Brother of Col. Browne, the Mandamus Counsellor. Be this as it may, he was very soon whispering in the Colonel's Ear, in the front of the Regiment; and when he parted from the Colonel, the Regiment marched off with a quick Pace, in a direct Course for the North Bridge; just before their entrance upon which, the Draw-Bridge was pulled up. The Regiment however, pushed forward till they came to the Draw-Bridge not observing (as it seemed) that it was drawn up. The Colonel who led them expressed some surprize; and then turning about, ordered an Officer to face his Company to a Body of Men standing on the Wharf on the other side of the Draw-Bridge, and fire. One of the Townsmen (who had kept along Side the Colonel from the Time he marched from the Town House) instantly told him he had better not fire, that he had no Right to fire without further Orders "and if you do fire (said he) you will be all dead Men."——— The Company neither fired nor faced. ——— The Colonel then retired to the center of the Regiment, assembled his Officers and held a Consultation: Which being ended, the Colonel advanced a little, and declared he would maintain his ground, and go over the Bridge before he returned, if it was a month next. The same Townsman replied, he might stay as long as he pleased, no Body cared for that. The Half-Brother before mentioned (it is said) made towards the Bridge, but seeing the Draw-Bridge up says, "It is all over with us." He has since disappeared. Mean while two large Gondolas that lay aground (fot it was low-water) were scuttled lest they should cross the Channel in them. But whilst one Gentleman with his Assistants was scuttleling his own Gondola, a Party of about twenty Soldiers jumped into it, and with their Bayonets charged against our Townsmen (some of whom they pricked) compelling them quit it but before this a sufficient Hole had been made in the Bottom. This Attack of the Soldiers, and some other Occurances, occasioned a little Bickering, but by the Interposition of some of the Inhabitants the disputes subsided.

At lenght some Gentlemen asked the Colonel what was his Design in making this Movement, and why he would cross the Bridge? He said he had orders to cross it, and he would cross it if he lost his Life with the lives of his Men. And now (or before) asked why the King's Highway was obstructed? He was told it was not the King's Road, but the Property of the Inhabitalts who had a Right to do what they pleased with it. Finally, the Colonel said he must go over; and if the Draw-Bridge were let down so that he might pass, he pleged his Honour he would march not above thirty Rods beyond it, and then immediately return. The Regiment had now been at the Bridge an Hour and a Half; and every thing being secured, the Inhabitants directed the Draw-Bridge to be let down. The Regiment immediately passed over, marched a few Rods, returned, and with great Expedition went back again to Marblehead, where they embarked on board the Transport without delay.

Thr Regiment brought with them Lanthorns, Hatchets, Pick-Axes, Spades, Hand-Spikes, and several Coils of Rope.

When all the Circumstances are considered, there can remain no doubt that the sole purpose of the Manoeuvre was to steal away the Artillery Materials before mentioned. In the first Place the Regiment was taken from the Castle, so that the Inhabitants of Boston might be prevented giving us any Intellegence: The Transport arrived at Marblehead a considerable Time before the Regiment was landed, but the Men were kept from under the Hatches; As soon as the Inhabitants of Marblehead had got to Meeting, the troops landed and pushed on their March to Salem and proceeded to the very spot where the Materials for the Artillery were lodged. But meeting with this sad Rebuff, and finding their Plot was discovered, they made a Retreat. ——— Tis regretted that an Officer of Colonel Leslie's acknowledged Worth should be obliged in observance to his Orders, to come upon so painful an Errand.

Verious Reports were spread abroad respecting the Troops ——— the Country was alarmed; and one Company arrived in Arms from Danvers just as the Troops left Town. We immediately dispatched Messengers to the neighbouring Towns to save them the Trouble of coming in; but the Alarm flew like Lightning (and some doubtless magnified the first simple Report) so that a great Number were in Arms, and some on the March before the Messengers arrived.

BOSTON March 9. Last Saturday being the Anniversary of the horrid Massacre in King Street, Boston, 1770 perpetrated by a party of Soldiers (under the command of Captain Thomas Preston,) an elegant and spirited Oration was pronounced, at the Old South Meeting House in Boston, by Joseph Warren, Esq; in commemoration of that bloody tragedy.

BOSTON March 13. The act of Tarring and Feathering not repealed.

Last Thursday Morning, a Countryman was Tarr'd and Feather'd and carried thro' some of the Streets in this Town by a party of Soldiers, attended by some Officers: ——— The following is the Mans own Deposition, relative to that affair, sworn to before a Magistrate; upon which we shall make no Remarks, but leave the Public to judge of the Conduct of some of those who are said to have been sent among us to preserve the Peace and good Order, and to prevent Mobs, Tumults and other unlawful Assemblies.

"I Thomas Ditson, jun. of Bellerica, husbandman, testify and declare, that while walking in Fore-Street on the 8th of March in the Afternoon I enquired of some Townsmen who had any Guns to sell; one of whom I did not know, replied he had a very fine Gun to sell. The Man appear'd to be a Soldier, and I went with him to a House where one was, whom the Soldier called Serjeant, and seeing some old Cloaths about the House, I ask'd whether they sold such things; the serjeant replied that they did frequently; I then ask'd his price for an old red coat ript to pieces, he ask'd 3s. 6d. sterling, but I refused to give it, This one M'Clenchy, the Soldier I met with at first in the Street, said he had old cloath to sell, and sent his Wife out after them to a Man he called a Sergeant, as she soon brought an old Coat and an old Jacket; I then ask'd him if he had the right to sell them, and he said he would give a writing if he desired it, but said there was no Occasion. ——— then brought the said Coat and Jacket, and gave two Pistereens, and then put the Cloaths in a Bag, which was left behind; after which I went to M'Clenchy's to see the Gun, which he said was a very fine Piece; I ask'd him if he had any right to sell it, he reply'd he had and that the Gun was his to dispose of at any time; I then ask'd him whether he tho't the Centry would not take it from me at the Ferry, as I had heard that some Persons had had their Guns taken from them, but never tho't there were any Law against trading with Soldiers; he then told me he had stood Centry and that they frequently let them pass; he then ask'd me what I would give for the Gun; I told him I would give four Dollars if there was no risque in carrying it over the Ferry; he said there was not and that I might rely on his word. I agreed to give four Dollars for his Gun, but did not take it nor pay him the Money; going away he followed me down the stairs and says that there was a Serjeant who had an old rusty Piece that he would sell cheap; I ask'd him his price, he said he would sell it for one Dollar and a half if I would pay the Money down, and he urg'd me to take it; I then agreed to give him said sum. His Wife, as he called her, then came down and said M'Clenchy what are you going to do to bring that Man into a scrape; I then told them that if there was any difficulty to give me my Money again, but he refused, and replied his Wife made an oration for nothing, and that he had a right to sell his Gun to any body. I was afraid from her speaking that there was something not right in it and left the place, and coming away he followed me and urg'd the Guns upon me; I told him I had rather not take them for fear of what his Wife had said; he then declared there was no danger, for he had spoken to the Officers of Centry, who said he had a right to dispose of them, and urg'd me to pay the four Dollars I had offer'd for the Guns, which I then refused and desired I might have the one and half Dollars back which I had paid for the Gun, he refused, saying there was no danger and damn'd me for a Fool. I then paid him the four Dollars for the good Gun, but did not receive any one of them.

After I had paid the Money, he then said take care of yourself, and the first thing I saw was some Men coming up; I stept off to go after my great Coat but they followed and seized me and carried me to the Guard-House upon Foster's Wharf; this was about 6 or 7 o'clock in the

Evening. When I came into the Guard-House they read me a Law I never before saw or heard of. I was detained there till 7 in the Morning, when I should have been obliged to pay the .5 pounds mentioned in the Law read to me, and hired a Regular to carry a Letter to some Friends over the Ferry, which was to desire them to come to me as quick as possible with the Money to pay the Fine. Soon after the Serjeant came in and ordered me to strip; I then ask'd him what he was going to do with me, he said damn you I am going to serve you as you have served our Men; then came in a Soldier with a Bucket of Tar and a Pillow-bear of Feathers. I was then made to strip, which I did to my Breeches; they then tarr's and feather'd me, and while they were doing it an Officer who stood at the Door said tar and feather his Breeches which the accordingly did, and I was tarred and feathered from head to foot, and had a paper read to me, which was then tied round my Neck, but afterwards turned behind me, with the following words, wrote upon it, to best of my remembrance. [American Liberty or Liberty exemplified in a Villain who attempted to intice one of the Soldiers of his Majesty's 47th Regiment to desert and take up Arms with Rebels against the King and Country.]——— I was then ordered to walk out and get into a chair fastened upon Trucks, which I did, when a Number of the King's Soldiers, as I imagine, about 40 or 50, armed with Guns and fixed Bayonets, surrounded the Trucks, and they marched with a Number of Officers before them, one of who I have since heard was named Nesbit, together with a Number of Drums and Fifes from the Wharf up Kingstreet and and down Forestreet, and then thro' the Main-Street passing the Governor's House, until they came to Liberty-Tree, they then turned up Frog Lane and made a Halt, and a Serjeant, as I took him to be, said get down: I then asked which way I should go, and he said, where you please. Near to the Governor's House, the Inhabitants pressed in upon the Soldiers, the latter appeared to me to be angry, and I was afraid they would have fired, they being ordered to load their Muskets, which they did. Thomas Ditson, jun.

Suffolk fs. Boston, The above named Thomas Ditson, Junior, presently appearing, maketh solemn Oath to the truth of the foregoing Deposition by him subscriber, before

Edm. Quincy, J. Pecia.

Boston March 25. The Public are hereby informed, that on Thursday last a Lodger at the Royal Exchange Tavern was taken with the Small-Pox and immediately sent to the Hospital in West-Boston; three Children taken this Day at the Barracks in King-Street, were removed to the Hospital Ship at the Island-Wharf; which are the Places known to be infested with that Distemper in this Town.

By Order of the Selectmen,

William Cooper, Town Clerk.

BOSTON March 25. Extract of a Letter sent to New-York.

We are still without any of your favours, —— since the Army have found, that the Season is past for nature's forming a bridge from hence, their becoming abusive and insulting. —— They are now furnishing their fortification on the Neck, by picketing on each side. —— We propose to give you an account of the maneuvers of our adversaries as they may occur.

The 16th instant (being recommended by the Provincial Congress, to be observed as a day of fasting and prayer,) on the morning of this day, the society at the west end of Boston, were greatly disturbed by a party of Officers and Soldiers of the 4th, or King's own Regiment, when the people were assembling, they brought two market tents, and pitched them within about ten yards of the meeting-house; then sent three drums and three fifes, and kept them beating and playing till service was over; Colonel Maddison was present part of the time.

On the 17th in the Evening Colonel Hancock's elegant seat situated near the Common, was attacked by a number of officers, who, with their swords, cut and hacked the fence before his house in a most scandalous manner, and behaved very abusively, by breaking people's windows, and insulting almost every person they met.

On the 18th The Neck Guard seized 13,429, cartridges with ball, (we suppose thro' the information of some dirty scoundrel, of which we have many among us) and about 300 lb. of ball. which were carrying into the Country ——— this was private property ——— The owner applied to the General first but he absolutely refused to deliver it ——— They abused a teamster very much, and run a bayonet into his neck ——— The same evening a number of officers, heighten with liquor (as is said) with drawn swords, ran through the streets, like what they really were, madmen, cutting every one they met; the Stage Coach just arrived from Providence, passing by, they attacked it, broke the glass, and abused the passengers; the driver being a small fellow junped off his seat, caught one of them (Capt. Gore, of the 5th) and some blows passed ——— when the officer retired, not much to his Credit.

On the 19th, Colonel Hancock was again insulted by a number of inferior officers and privates, who entered his enclosure, and refused to retire after his requesting them so to do telling they telling him, that his house, stables, &c. would soon be their's and then they would do as they pleased ——— However on his application to the General he immediately sent one of his Aid de camps to the officer of the Guard at the bottom of the Common, to seize any officer or private, who should molest Colonel Hancock, or any inhabitant in their lawful calling. Your's &c.

BOSTON March 27. Wednesday last the Provincial Congress met at Concord ——— present 200 members.

In Provincial Congress March 24, 1775.

Whereas it is indispensably necessary for the safety of a free People, and the preservation of their Liberties, that they at all Times keep themselves in a State of actual Defence, against every Invasion of Depredation, and this Colony being threatened by a powerful Army posted in the Capital, with a professed Design of executing certains Acts of the British Parliament, calculated to destroy our invaluable Rights and Liberties, and the Government of this Colony as by the Charter and Law established therein:

Therefore, Resolved, That the Measure that have heretofore been recommended by this and former Provincial Congress, for Purpose of putting the Colony into a complete State of Defence, be still most vigorously pursued by the several Towns, as well as Individual Inhabitants: and that any Relaxation would be attended with the utmost Danger to the Liberties of the Colony and of all America; especially as the latest Advices from Great-Britain we had undoubted Reasons for Jealousy, that our implacable Enemies are unremitting in their Endeavours by fraud and Artifice, as well as by open Force, to subjugate this People; which is an additional Motive to the Inhabitants of the Colony to persevere in the Line of Conduct recommended by the Congress; and be ready to oppose with Firmness and Resolution, at the utmost Hazard, every attempt for that Purpose.

Signed by Order of the Provincial Congress,
John Hancock President.

A true Extract from the Minutes,
Benjamin Lincoln, Secretary.

BOSTON April 3. At a Meeting of the freeholders and other Inhabitants of the Town of Boston, duly qualified and legally warned in public Town-Meeting, assembled at Faneuil-Hall, on Tuesday the 28th Day of March, A. D. 1775.

The Selectmen laid before the Inhabitants the present state of the Small-Pox in this Town, whereby it appears, that there are on board the Hospital-Ship in the Harbour, thirty eight Persons with the Small-Pox, three of them were sent on board this Day. At the Hospital at West Boston, five Persons with the Distemper; two of them were sent from a Chamber in Mr. Rank's House at the Head of Cross Street, occupied by a Soldier; a Woman from the Lamb Tavern, at the South Part of the Town; a Man from his Dwelling near Dr. Byle's Meeting-House, and another Man from the Royal Exchange Tavern, in King Street; that Mr. Rank's Wife at his House at the Head of Cross Street, was taken with Distemper where Guards are placed to prevent a Communication of the infection; and that the Hospital-Ship was this forenoon, removed to some distance from the Wharf. ——— The Town having duly considered the foregoing, and all the Circumstances relative to the Small-Pox among us, and being of opinion, that the Probability was in Favor of Destemper's spreading.

Voted, Nom. Con. That the Selectmen of the Town be desired to continue the same Vigilance they have hitherto shewn, to prevent the spreading of the Small-Pox, in this Place.

Also Voted, Nom. Con. That the Selectmen be desired to see that the law, relative to the concealing and spreading of infectious Distempers, be put into Execution against any Persons who shall make an attempt of that Nature, by Inoculations; or any other way. ——— And that no one may plead Ignorance of the said Law: It was further voted, That the Town-Clerk be directed to publish such Paragraph or Paragraphs of the Law, which affixes the Penalty, for concealing and spreading infectious Distempers, also the Proceeding of this Meeting, relative to the Small-Pox.

Attst. William Cooper, Town Clerk.

BOSTON April 10. Extract of a letter from New-York April 3, 1775.

"I am really under the greatest anxiety for the fate of you and your distressed citizens, as such great quantities of Military stores have been carried from hence to your Town, as well as boards, hay, straw, bran, harnesses, &c. &c. which added to the 300 horses that we are told are sent from Canada, portent the worse of designs. It is suspected that the troops really mean to take to the field, and attempt to open the Courts under the new regulations, or make a force march to Worcester.

Others imagine that they will march 5 or 10 miles at a time, in order to compel you to commence hostilities first: whilst some think that nothing will be attempted 'till the Parliament has decided on the grand controversy. However I am not clear but that orders to prosecute the Ministry's intentions till the Parliament decides otherwise, there is no doubt that the Parliament itself would justify such conduct,

Tho' as the expense of much blood and treasure. For Heaven sakes be watchful as all, under God depends on your conduct at this time.

BOSTON April 10. The Army of this town seem to be preparing for a march; a considerable numbers of waggons are made and now ready for their use, several blacksmiths, we are informed, are employed in making crowsfeet, &c.

BOSTON April 17. The Provincial Congress adjourn'd last Saturday Afternoon, to the 10th of May next; but if necessary, to meet earlier.

—— And we have it from undoubted Authority, that a perfect Unanimity prevail'd in all the important Measures and Deliberations which came before them.

A Letter from Taunton Dated last Friday, mentions, "That on the Monday before, Parties of Minute Men, &c. from every Town in the County, with arms and ammunition, meet at Freetown early that Morning in order to take Col. Gilbert, but he had fled on board the Man of War at Newport; They then devided in parties, and took 29 Tories who had signed enlistments and received arms in the Colonel's Company, to join the King's troops; they also took 35 Muskets, a Case Bottles of Powder, & a Basket of Bullets. all of which they bro't to Taunton the same afternoon, where the Prisoners were separately examined, 18 of whom made such humble acknowledgement of their past bad conduct, and solemn promised to behave better for the future, they were discharged; but 11 being obstinate and insulting, a party was ordered to carry them to Simsbury Mines; but they were sufficiently humble before they had got 14 miles on their way thither; upon which they were bro't back the next day, and after signing proper articles to behave better for the future, were escorted to Freetown. —— There was upward of 2000 Men embodied there last Monday.

BOSTON April 17. In Provincial Congress, at Concord April 14, 1775.

Whereas Numbers of Persons from the unhappy situation in the Town of Boston, are removing with their Effects. —— It is recommended to the good People of the Province, that they would rent their Houses, and assist such Persons with Teams for their Removal, Provisions for their Support, and all the Necessaries upon as easy easy and cheap Terms as they can possibly afford; and that all goods and Merchandize be sold in the like Manner, agreeable to the Spirit of the Continental Association.

By order of the Provincial Congress.

John Hancock, President.

BOSTON April 17. Capt. Collins brings advice, That the Act for restraining the Trade, and blocking up all the ports of New-England had passed the House of Commons: That Lord Chatham, with a number of his patriotic Friends, finding their Efforts, for saving the Nation from Tyranny and Horror of a Civil War, arose from their Seats, and abruptly left the House of Lords, giving a reason for their Conduct; that they would have no further Concerns in the Legislature who were involving the Nation in Blood and Slaughter.

Boston April 24. The unhappy Transaction of last week are so variously related that we shall not at present undertake to give any particulars Accounts thereof.

The Printers of the Boston Evening Post hereby informs the Town that they shall desist publishing their paper after this day, till Matters are in a more settled State.

Printers Thomas & John Fleet.

ESSEX GAZETTE, SALEM April 25. Last Wednesday the 19th of April the Troops of his Britannic Majesty commenced Hostilities upon the People of this Province, attend with Circumstances of Cruelty not less brutal than what our venerable Ancestors received from the vilest Savages of the Wilderness. The Particulars relative to this Interesting Event, by which we are involved in all the Horror of a Civil War, we have endeavoured to collect as well as the present confused State of affairs will admit.

On Tuesday Evening a Detachment from the army, consisting, it is said, of 8 or 900 Men, commanded by Lieut. Col. Smith, embarked at the Bottom of the Common in Boston, on board a Number of Boats, and landed at Phip's Farm, a little Way up Charles River, from whence they proceeded with Silence and Expedition, on their way to Concord, about 18 Miles from Boston.

The People were soon alarmed, and began to Assemble, in several Towns, before Day-Light, in order to watch the Motion of the Troops.

At Lexington, 6 Miles below Concord, a Company of Militia, of about 100 Men, mustered near the Meeting-House; The Troops came in sight of them just before Sun-rise; and running within a few Rods of them, the Commanding Officer accosted the Militia in words to this Effect. ——'Disperse you Rebels —— Damn you throw down your Arms and Disperse.' Upon which the Troops huzza'd, and immediately one or two Officers discharged their Pistols, and were instantly followed by the firing of 4 or 5 of the Soldiers and then there seemed to be a general Discharge from the whole Body: Eight of our Men were killed, and nine Wounded. In a few Minutes after this Action the Enemy renewed their March for Concord; at which Place they destroyed several Carriages, and Carriage Wheels, and about 20 Barrels of Flour, belonging to the Province.

Here about 150 Men going towards a Bridge, of which the Enemy were in Possession, the latter fired and killed 2 of our Men, who then returned the Fire, and obliged the Enemy to retreat back to Lexington, where they met Lord Percy, with a large Reinforcement, with two Pieces of Cannon. The Enemy now having a Body of about 1800 Men, made a Halt, picked up many of the Dead, and took care of the Wounded. At Menotomy, a few of our Men attacked a Party of twelve of the Enemy, (carrying some Stores and Provisions to the Troops) killed one of them, wounded several, made the rest Prisoners, and took Possession of all their Arms, Stores, Provisions, &c. without any loss on our side.

The Enemy halted one or two Hours at Lexington, found it necessary to make a second retreat, carrying with them many of the Dead and the Wounded, who they put in Chaises and on Horses that they found standing in the Road. They continued their Retreat from Lexington to Charlestown with great Precipitation; & notwithstanding their field Pieces, our People continued the pursuit firing at them till they got to Charlestown Neck, (which they reached at a little after Sunset) over which the Enemy passed, proceeded up Bunker's Hill, and soon afterwards went into Town, under the Protection of the Sumerset Man of War of 64 Guns.

In Lexington the Enemy set Fire to Deacon Loring's House and Barn, Mrs. Muliken's House and Shop, Mr. Joshua Bond's House and Shop, which were all consumed. They also set Fire to several other Houses, but our People extinguished the Flames. They pillaged almost every House they passed by, breaking and destroying Doors, Windows, Glasses, &c. and carrying off Cloathing and other valuable Effects. It appears to be their Design to burn and destoy all before them; and nothing but our vigorous Pursuit prevented their infernal Purpose from being put in Execution. But the savage Barbarity exercised upon the Bodies of our unfortunate Brethren who fell, is almost incredible; Not content with shooting down unarmed, aged and infirm, they disregarded the Cries of the wounded, killed without Mercy, and mangling their Bodies in the most shocking Manner.

We have the Pleasure to say, that, notwithstanding the highest Provocations given by the Enemy, not one Instant of Cruelty, that we have heard of, was committed by our victorious Militia: but, Listening to the merciful Dictates of the Christian Religion, they "Breathed higher Sentiments of Humanity."

New-York Journal May 4. Mr. Holt, please to insert the following in your next paper, and you will oblige many of our readers, and particularly your humble servant.

"On the 18th of instant April, the humane and benevolent General Gage, ordered a select number of about 1200 of his Grenadiers and best troops, in a most secret manner, to march up the country as Concord, (as supposed) to seize Col. Hancock and Mr. Samuel Adams. The first exploit they performed, was, in their way to Lexington; they found about 30 men exercising, and without provocation, fired upon them for about 15 minutes

killed 6 men, and wounded several when they were
retreating as fast as possible ——— then the
troops proceeded in their way to Concord; on the
road they killed a man on horseback, and killed
geese, and hogs, cattle and every living creature they came across: They came to a house
where said Hancock and Adams lodges, (who luckily escaped them) they searched the house and
when they could not find them, these barbarians
killed the woman of the house and all the children, in cold blood and then set the house on
fire."

Alas! would not heathen, in all their savage
barbarity and cruelty, blush at such horrid
murder, and worse the brutal rage! is this the
bravery of British troops? Is this the native
courage, and intrepidity of English soldiers,
so much boasted of? is it not rather the ferocity of a mad wild beast from whom they cannot
be supposed to differ, only in shape? Let every
American hear and abhor; let every inhabitant
consider what he is like to suffer if he falls
into the hands of such cruel and merciless
wretches; what miseries and calamities shall we
not be subject to the unrighteous and tyrannical
claims of the parliament, of taking what we call
our own, when, and in what manner they please,
without consent; don't this teach us, that a
body of men, as well as a particular person,
may tyrannically oppress? Let every American
consider, what interest have we in George the
third, or what inheritance have we in the parliament of Great Britain? have they not declared that all of the New-England colonies are
rebels, and have ordered and commanded blood
thirsty soldiers, to cut the throats of men,
women and children, and are they not at this
instant, endeavouring to carry their bloody decree into execution? And how long (besure not a
great while) before the rest of the Americans
will meet with the same, unless they tamely
give up their all into their hands, to be taken
by them as they please, without the colony's
consent; but be thanked, the soldiery have met
with a check. And what is all this rage and
duty? for no other cause, but that we are slow

to believe the power of Parliament in incompetent; and that they have a right to depose of us, and all we have as they please, without our consent. Surely no man in his senses, or that hath any notion of preserving his person or property, but what will without hesitancy, resolve and determine to sell his life as dear as he can, rather then submit to such a slavish and abject condition ——— therefore my countrymen think, and by thinking, you will necessarily, be led to determine, that now or never you may be free; if once you lose this opportunity and submit, it is not probable you will ever have another. If any should say we had better try conciliatory measures, and again petition for relief, from the King and Parliament, I ask to what purpose can it be? Have not particular colonies tried petitions by themselves, and not all colonies united in a petition of relief? and to what effect? Have they not been disdainfully and contemptuously trampled upon and treated with scorn and called nothing but factious complaints? Doth it not plainly appear, that both the King and the ministry, are so fixed and determined at all hazard, to destroy American liberty, as that it is to a little purpose to complain, or reason with them, as it is to reason with irrational creatures? Therefore it seems there is nothing for us to do, but to appeal unto God, in the use of what force and strength we have, in defence of liberties and prosperities, and rely on his almighty aid for help to repeal this Tyrant's rage.

An ODE on LIBERTY

Happy's the man, who unconstrain'd
  Obey but nature's equal laws,
Who fears no power, but might maintain'd,
  And boldly vindicates his country's cause.
Fortune's attack, secure he braves;
  Firmly prepar'd for any chance;
None tremble at her frowns, but slaves;
  Whose dastard fears their abject hopes enhance.
His roving steps, uncurb'd by dread,
  From clime to clime can freely roam:
He goes where choice, or fortune lead,
  Freedom his guide; and all the world his home.
Concious of worth, his generous soul,
  To stoop to lawless power disclaims:
No threats of force his thoughts controul,
  He e'en enjoys his liberty in chains.

Connecticut Courant
May 1, 1775.

FULLNAME INDEX

ABBOT, Samuel 350
ADAMS, 449 Abijah 21 John
  304 341 381 394 411 415
  Mr 39 173 249 291-292
  Samuel 16 62 101 107 151
  168 204 248 291 331 350
  360 381-382 394 411 415
  448
ALBY, Samuel 307
ALDEN, John 205
ALEING, Mr 345
ALFORD, William 90
ALLEN, Elizabeth 1
AMES, Levi 343-344 Richard
  126
ANDERSON, Robt 314
ANDREW, Joseph 42
APPLETON, Nathanial 350
  Nathaniel 381
APTHORP, Madam 194 Mr 126
ARCHBALD, Edward 199
  Francis 199
ASCOUGH, Capt 367
ASHLIN, Lee 13
ATTUCKS, 241 Crispus 201
  206 229 240 326
ATTWOOD, Joseph 343-344
ATWOOD, Samuel 200
AUCHMUTY, Robert 71
AUCMUTY, Robert 151
AUSTIN, Samuel 75
AVERY, John Jr 162
AYERS, Joseph 205
BADGER, 138-140 146 151
  Abel 137-138
BAKER, John 117 292
BALDWIN, Cyrus 162
BALL, Capt 49
BANKS, Mrs 11
BARNES, 213 Henry 14 185
BARRET, John 77

BAUTINEAU, James 304
BAXTER, Paul 89
BAYLEY, Samuel 89
BEACH, William 36
BEAL, Capt 24
BEAMIS, Philip 212
BEBBER, Abraham Van 132
BEDGE, Stephen 209
BEETLE, William 155
BELL, Christian 320 James
  320-321 325
BENNET, Capt 226
BENNETT, Capt 53 Mrs 342
BENTON, Mr 300
BERNARD, 239 294 299 306
  331 333 Francis 15-16 86
  95 114 118 151 153 156
  158-161 165-166 183 193
  286-287 Gov 64 88 99 111
  146 220 233 247 259 John
  162 184 Mr 135 Shute 99
BERRY, 42
BEVER, William 30
BICKER, Martin 343-344
BICKERS, Mr 344
BIGLEY, 261
BIGNAL, "Widow" 255
BILLINGS, Joseph 162 Seth
  162
BINGLEY, 258
BINNEY, Capt 24
BIRD, Mr 45
BISHOP, Capt 382
BLACK, David 369
BLACKMAN, Benjamin 24
BLAKE, Capt 42 Increase 89
BLAKEY, 40
BLANCHER, Ebenezer 208
BOLFINCH, Mr 49
BOLLAN, Mr 175
BOND, Joshua 448

452

BONKER, 100
BOTINEAU, James 178
BOURGATTE, Charles 240 242
BOURNE, Malatiah 77
　Maletiah 75
BOUTINEAU, James 303 Nancy
　178
BOWDWIN, James 365
BOWER, Col 324
BOWMAN, Mr 39
BOXLEY, William 300
BOYLSTON, Thomas 381
BRADFORD, Capt 96 177
　Joseph 212 Mr 385
BRADLEY, Samuel 97
BRADSHAW, Thomas 321
BRATTLE, Col 399 Maj Gen
　307 Qilliam 365 William
　52 365
BRAY, George 49
BRECK, Robert 199
BRETT, James 185 Thomas 177
BRIDGE, Ralph 155
BROWER, Sampson Saltes 304
BROWN, Capt 391 Col 39 386
　John 120 Jonathan 296
　Maj 27 Mr 122-123
　Nicholas 296 William 177
BROWNE, Col 435
BRUCE, Capt 117 357-358 360
　364
BRYAN, John 292
BUFF, Elisha 225
BURCH, 166 Mr 168 173
　William 165
BURNET, David 63
BURROWS, John 68
BUTE, 239
BUTLER, Phineas 97
BUTMAN, Thomas 190
BYLE, Dr 443
CAHOUN, Capt 24
CALDWELL, Capt 151 James
　201 229 326
CALEF, Capt 345 W 198
CALLAHAN, Capt 384
CAMBIER, Com 256
CAMDEN, Lord 135
CAMERON, John 155
CAMPBELL, Duncan 131
　William 129
CANANT, Daniel 97

CARMICHAEL, 139-140 146 151
　Thomas 137-138 140
CARR, 241 Col 157 Lt Col
　121 Patrick 202 229 326
CARTER, Michael 158 Mr 379
CHAMPION, 223
CHAPMAN, Mrs 326
CHARLES, 1st King OF Great
　Britain 261 2nd King Of
　Great Britain 261 King
　Of Great Britain 306
CHATHAM, Lord 51 135 446
CHECKLEY, Mr 11 41
CHEESMAN, Elizabeth 311
　George 311
CHEVALIER, Nicholas 342
CHREVER, Ezekiel 357
CHURCH, Dr 124
CHUSHING, Thomas 249
CICERO, 263
CLARK, Capt 36 352 Dr 23
　208 218 John 202 314
　John Newington 209 Jonas
　343
CLARKE, 350 355 360 Dr 117
　Joseph 30 Mr 354 Richard
　162 347 349-352 355
　Thomas 28
CLARKES, 357
CLEVELAND, Col 408
CLIFFORD, Michael 155
COCHRAN, 142 Capt 420
COFFIN, Capt 357 364
COLDWELL, 241 James 206
COLEMAN, Mathew 155
COLLECTOR, Dudley 130
COLLINS, Capt 446
COLLSWORTHY, Samuel 66
COMIELKBAKER, Everet 30
CONANTS, Natanial 97
CONNER, Capt 93 107 William
　154
CONVERS, Joseph 98
COOK, Capt 223 346
　Middlecot 77
COOKSON, Capt 102 112
COOLIDGE, Mr 336
COOPER, Mr 42 Rev Dr 382 W
　413 William 77 93 211
　311 425 441 444
COPLEY, Mr 354 357-359
COPPER, Thomas 155

CORBET, 149-150
CORBOT, Michael 154
CORNER, Capt 110-112 129
CORNNELL, George 175
CORNOR, Capt 110
COSSIN, Capt 358
COTTER, Joffrey 99
COX, 42
CRAFTS, Capt 34 Edward 205
CRISPIN, Capt 318
CROFTS, John 155
CROMWELL, Oliver 239
CUITT, Richard 411
CUMMINGS, Ann 184-185
   Elizabeth 184-185
CURTIS, John 131
CUSHING, Tho 331 Thomas 62
   75 101 107 151 210 248
   291 381-382 394 404 411
   415
CUSHINGS, Thomas 16
CUTLER, Ebenezer 216 Mr 216
DALRYMPLE, Col 203-204 206
   Lt Col 117 221
DALY, John 314
DALYRMPLE, Lt Col 121
DANA, Justice 127 181
   Richard 126 177 195
DANFORT, Judge 400 Samuel
   365
DANFORTH, S 401
DARLING, Celeb 307
DARTMOUTH, Earl Of 305 Lord
   380
DAUGHETY, 100
DAVENPORT, Mr 49
DAVERSON, Capt 223
DAVIS, Capt 14 Deacon
   Thomas 187 Jacob 187
   Robert 309
DAWSON, Capt 183
DAY, Jean 56
DAYRE, 408
DEBERDT, Mr 59 89
DEBLOES, Stephen 35
DEBLOIS, Gilbert 162
DENMISON, Patrick 155
DENNIE, John 100 William
   382
DERBY, Capt 324
DEXTER, 102 Mr 39 Samuel 67
DICKASON, 223

DITSON, Thomas Jr 438 441
DOANE, Capt 312
DODDINGTON, Lt 300
DOLBEARE, Benjamin 41
DONNELLY, 138-140 146 151
   Bryan 137-138
DOWSE, Joseph 125
DOYLE, 98 Capt 29
DRAPER, Mr 78 183 Samuel 98
DUBLOIS, Mr 290
DUDDINGSTON, Lt 293
DUDDINGTON, Mr 300
DUNN, Capt 24 226
DURANT, Mr 68
DYER, Peter 132 Samuel 408
EDDY, Mr 202
EDEDS, 275
EDES, 54 56 60 65 69 71 82
   91 93 103 110 127-128
   140 143 172 174 198 221
   246 261 271 273 281 299
   318 371 Jacob 245
   Messier 7
EDWARD, I King Of Great
   Britain 102
EDWARDS, Alexander 329 Capt
   187
ELIOT, Mr 12
ELLIOT, 389 William 73
EMERY, John 120
EMMONS, Jacob 49
EMTROISTLE, Archibald 155
ERVING, Col 384 John 365
EVERDEN, Elizabeth 99
EVEREDEN, Benjamin 2
EVERS, Capt 19 Thomas 19
FALSON, Junathan 19
FANEUIL, 350 Benj 351 Benj
   Jr 350 Benja Jr 355
   Benjamin 349 Mr 371
   Richard 347
FANNING, Pierce 154
FELLOWS, 154 Samuel 152-153
   257
FERGURSON, William 420
FIELD, Malchy 93 Mr 202
FINNEY, Mr 346
FISSENDEN, Mrs Nathaniel
   212 Nathaniel 212
FITCH, Samuel 304 341
FLECKER, Tho 391 Tho's 285
   356 Thomas 242

FLEET, 163 John 446 Thomas 446
FLEETS, 52 55 69 124 142 190 195 282 371
FLEMING, 172 178 181
FLEMMING, 167
FLUCKER, Mr 395 Tho 277 294 389 Tho' 276 Tho's 262 271 379 Thomas 266
FOLGER, Capt 380
FOLGIER, Timothy 98
FORDYKE, C 155
FORREST, Mr 126
FOWLER, Mr 296
FRANKLIN, Benjamin 35 Dr 133
FREBODY, Capt 317
FREEMAN, Patrick 185 209
FURNASS, John 88
GAGE, G 128 Gen 30 32 117 128 145 331 382-383 385 407 409 432 448 Gov 395 401 404 Lt Gen 242 T 389 391 411 Tho's 403 Thomas 383
GAINES, Robert 155
GAMBIER, Com 235 251 James 256
GARDINER, William 20
GARDNER, Capt 217 307 Henry 410 419 Isaac 151 James 301 Justice 321 S 123
GEORGE, 227 "Great" 13 3rd King Of Great Britain 6 278 379 411 3rd Lord 242 King Of Great Britain 114-115 134 269 435 Lord 285
GILBERT, Col 445
GILL, 54 56 60 65 69 71 82 91 93 103 110 127-128 140 143 172 174 198 221 246 261 271 273 275 281 299 318 371 John 100 Messeir 7
GMLE, Mr 103
GOLDTHWAIT, Joseph 258
GOLDTHWART, Ezekial 77 Ezekiel 113
GOLDTWALT, Sarah 290
GOODANOW, Jonathan 99
GOODHUE, William 61

GORE, Capt 442 John 194 Mr 195 Sammy 194
GORHAM, Capt 376
GOWDY, John 78-79
GRAHAM, 131
GRAY, 233-234 241 Benjamin 206 Harrison 406 410 James 197 Mr 227 Samuel 201 206 229 326
GREAT, Britain King Of 51 95-96 135 158 161 258 262 279 281 309 327 341 363 373 390 450
GREEN, 42 168 172 Hammond 234 James 97 John 202 Maj 126 Nathanial 41 Rufus 16
GREENLAW, John 163
GREENLEAF, John 276 Joseph 266 270 275 277 279 283 S 16 William 45 75 328
GREENLEAY, Sheriff 355
GREENVILLE, George 65 Mr 135
GREENWOOD, Mr 202 Thomas 234
GREYER, Mr 380
GRIDLEY, John 167 Mr 176
GRIFFITH, John 49
GVDE, Mr 103
HAINES, Matthew 286
HALL, Capt 262 352-354 357-358 360 364 369 Jonathan 88 Mr 39 221 238
HAMMET, Benjamin 88
HAMMUND, Mr 332
HANCOCK, 449 Col 297 343 354 395 441-442 448 John 14 16 21 49 101 104 107 128 145 151 164 189 204 210 236 248 251 291-292 331 341 348 350 360 379 414-415 417 419 434 443 446 Mr 39 96 127-128 163-164 227 249 255 337 382
HANDCOCK, John 164
HARDWICK, Richard 329
HARRIMAN, David 1
HARRIS, Stephen 62
HARRISON, Capt 19 David 18 Mr 174 361-362

HARTLEY, Mr 45
HARTSHORN, Aaron 217
HATCH, Nailer 11
HATHORNE, Capt 6
HAYES, James 97
HAZELROD, Chief Justice 369
HENDERSON, James 369
HENSAW, Joshua 75 204
HERSEY, Mr 252
HICKS, John 199
HIDE, Mr 180
HILL, John 426 Justice 197-198
HILLHOUSE, Capt 345
HILLSBOROUGH, 239 Earl Of 117 242 259 261 313 Lord 221 260 262 300 304
HOLLOWELL, Mr 361
HOLME, Capt 142
HOLT, Mr 448
HOMANS, Mr 302
HOOD, Com 129 157 160 223 Joseph 164 Samuel 134
HOOKER, John 36
HOOPER, Robert 386
HORSMANDER, Daniel 317
HOWARD, Capt 202
HOWE, Joseph 299 Joshua 98
HUBBARD, Mr 12 T 38 Thomas 155 341
HUCHINSON, Tho 355
HULTON, 166 173 Henry 165 Mr 168
HUMMAN, William 319
HUNNEWELL, Richard 425
HUNT, William 25
HUNTER, Capt 1
HUTCHINGSON, T 310
HUTCHINSON, 333 347 351 368 Edward 252 Elisha 162 349-350 355 369 384 Gov 256 260 262 338 354 363 383 Justice Foster 140 Lt Gov 196 Mr 247 264-266 268-269 300-301 306 384 T 192 210 245 250 285 324 334-335 337 356 373 377 379 Thomas 52 241 245 288 337 349 365 Thomas Jr 162 Thos Jr 351 William Sanford 248
HUTCHISON, Thomas 305

HUTCHSON, T 242
INCHES, Henderson 291 381 Hendreson 77 Mr 289
INDIAN, Noadgawwerremet 15 Oknookortunkogog 376
INGERSOOL, Mr 249
JACKSON, Joseph 190 Mr 199 William 198 314
JACOBSON, Capt 182
JARVIS, Capt 103 257
JAVIS, Capt 10
JEPSON, Benjamin 352
JOHNSON, John 100
JOHNSTONE, 190
JONES, 20 132 Benjamin 253 John 184 Robert 155
JOY, Benjamin 88
KEELER, Capt 316 Robert 329
KELLOG, William 30
KENT, 312 John 39
KILROI, 232-233
KILROY, 229
KING, 330 John 228 Joseph 329
KNIGHT, Thomas 68
KNOWLES, 20
KNOX, Mr 194 Thomas 193
LANGDON, John 208
LAURENS, Philip 342
LEAR, Henry 2
LEAT, James 146
LEDYARD, Dr 20
LEE, 408 Charles 209 Jos 401 Judge 401 Thomas 8
LEECH, John 199
LEIGH, Benjamin 201
LESLEY, Col 389
LESLIE, Col 437 Lt Col 338
LEWIS, Jemina 370 Thomas 370
LIGHTGOW, William 15
LILLIE, Mr 194 216 Theophilus 162 193
LINCOLN, Benjamin 329 407 417 419 434 443
LINGEE, Capt 300
LITTLE, Thomas 100
LIVINGSTON, Mr 26
LLOYD, Henry 12
LOCKE, 318 Samuel 263
LORD, 20
LORING, Dr 199

LOW, 389
LOWDER, Jonathan 179 Mr 180
LOWTHER, James 246
LYDE, Capt 64
M'CLENCHY, 438-439
M'COWEN, Capt 142
M'NEIL, Archibald 198
MACKAY, Brig Gen 159 Maj
  Gen 155 157 Mungo 177
MACLAY, Col 130
MADDISON, Col 408
MADISON, Col 441
MAGNO, Francis 120
MAJOR, John 62
MALCOM, Capt 57 145 John
  370
MALTBY, Capt 346
MANSFIELD, Lord 68
MANWARING, 242 Edward 234
  240
MARSHAL, Capt 14 James 2
  John 14
MARTIN, Joseph 34
MARTUM, Roger 69
MATHER, Samuel 383
MAVERICK, 241 Mary 207
  Samuel 201 206 229 326
MAVERIUCK, 227
MAYOR, Lord 408
MCDONALD, John 413
MCINTIRE, Leonard 99
MCLAREY, 40
MCMASTERS, 212-213 215
  James 162 John 184
  Patrick 184
MECHER, Robert 30
MEEK, Moses 90
MEIN, 167 172 178 181 James
  184 John 100 162 176 180
  182-183 Mr 163-164
MEINS, Mr 164
MELLENS, Mr 31
MERCHANT, William 199
MERRILL, 153-154 Josiah 153
MILINEUX, William 204
MILLARD, Thomas 30
MILLER, William 111
MILLS, John 89 Susannah
  238
MOLESWORTH, Capt 151 Sukey
  151
MOLINEAUX, William 350

MOLINEUX, W 101
MOLLINEAUX, William 381
MOLTON, William 37
MOLYNEAUX, William 126
MONK, Cristopher 202 228
MONRO, John 240
MONTAGU, Adm 315-316 320
MONTAGUE, Adm 338
MONTEGUE, Adm 408
MONTGOMERY, 229
MONTRESOR, Capt 408
MOORE, Henry 61 85
MORSE, Benjamin 37 Capt 324
MORTON, Capt 1 18-19 201
MOULTON, 330 Joseph Jr 329
MULIKEN, Mrs 448
MUNFORD, Samuel 160
MUNRO, John 234
MURRAY, 199 David 255 257
NAGLE, James 155
NESBIT, 440
NEWMAN, John 90
NICHOL, Mr 130
NICHOLS, 102
NICKERSON, Ansell 315 341
NIKERSON, 311-312 Capt 312
  340 Thomas 315
NIXON, James 87
NOBLE, Capt 27 Robert 30
NORTH, Lord 408
OGLETHORPE, Gen 220
OLIVER, 333 A 16 151 Andrew
  241 337 376 Mr 260-261
  Peter 317 374-376 Sec
  261 Thomas 292-293
OLNEY, Richard 68
OTIS, Abigail 10 James 10
  16 74 101 107 151 165-
  166 176-177 190 211 235
  248 253 302-304 311
  James Jr 168 Joseph 79
  Mr 39 96 167 169-174 178
  249
PACKARD, Elijah 2
PACKWODD, Capt 160
PACKWOOD, Joseph 159
PADDOCK, Adino 65 257 Capt
  251 Maj 297 343 384 Mr
  17
PAIN, Robert Treat 415
PAINE, Mr 38 Robert Treat
  394 411

PALFREY, Wm 164
PANTON, Lt 151-152 154-155 157-158 Mr 148-150
PARK, Cuthbert 411
PARKER, Benjamin 97 Daniel 39 Davis 202 Gidion 97 Jeremia 97
PARKS, John 302 314
PARKWOOD, Capt 159
PARRY, Mr 391
PARSONS, Jacob 152-153
PATTERSON, Robert 202
PAXTON, 166 333 Charles 165
PAYNE, Edward 75 77 202
PEACOCK, Mr 158
PECIA, J 441
PEMBERTON, Sam 177 Samuel 195
PEMBORTON, Samuel 204
PENDERGAST, 27
PERCY, Lord 447
PERKINS, Abigail 43 Capt 397
PETTY, James 146
PHILIPS, 27 William 291 Wm 331
PHILLIPS, Col 67 William 204 360 381-382
PIERCE, Lt 384
PITCHER, Moses 88
PITT, "Patriot" 13 James 365 Mr 51
PITTEE, Seth 63
PITTS, John 350 382
POLEY, Simeon 111 Simion 111
POMEROY, Brig Gen 157 Col 129
POPE, William 36
PORTLAND, Duke Of 246
POWELL, William 350 382
POWER, Thomas 147
PRATT, Magaret 79
PRESTON, Capt 200 203 221 227-228 258 Thomas 438
PRICE, Capt 113 Ezekiel 126 130 Henry 14 Job 308
PROCTOR, Edward 193 354 Mr 194
PUSSEL, James 365
QUICK, Alice 66 Mrs 67
QUINCY, Edm 441 Edmond 195

QUINCY (cont.)
   Edmund 75 426 Josiah 381 Josiah Jr 341
QWIN, Capt 24
RAND, John 97
RANDOLPH, Payton 404
RANK, Mr 443
RANSLEAR, 33 John Van 25 Robert 33 Robert Van 30 32
RAYNOLDS, Edward 155
READ, Capt 159-160
REDDISH, John 155
REEVE, Mr 168-169 173 Richard 157
REID, Capt 159
REMICK, Joseph 89
RENKEN, Mr 2
RENSELEAR, 26 Col 27 Mr 26-27
REVERE, Paul 117 208 218 367 382 385 403-404
RHODES, William 97
RICHARD, Owen 253
RICHARDS, 211
RICHARDSON, 194-195 228 257 305 Abigail 271 Ebenezer 193 208-210 286 330-331 Esquire 271
RICHARSON, 202
RIORDON, Capt 193
RITCHIE, John 42
ROACH, 34
ROBINSOMN, John 235
ROBINSON, 166 174 177 Brother 173 John 165-167 172 177-178 190 207 253 302-304 Mr 167 169-171 175-176
ROGERS, Capt 409 Daniel 155 Nathaniel 162 213
ROTCH, Francis 369 Mr 354 357-358 360-363
ROWE, John 16 75 357-358 360 381 Mr 116
ROYALL, Isaac 365
RUDDOCK, 127 John 16 75 126 Justice 195
RUGGLES, Brigadier 12
RUSSEL, John 227
RUSSELL, 172 J 13 156
RYAN, Joseph 154

SABIN, Thomas 68
SAGE, Syez 69
SAUNDERS, Adm 259
SAVAGE, Samuel Phillips
   360-361
SAVILL, Jeffe 227
SAVILLE, Jeffe 156
SAWYER, Dutch 99
SCAEVOLA, Micius 266 Mucius
   263 265-266 269 279 283
SCHUYLER, Hermanus 25
SCHYLER, 31 Herman 30 32
SCOLLAY, James 87 John 87
   402
SCOTT, Capt 210 223
SCULLAY, John 355
SCULLEY, John 355
SEARCHER, Mr 330
SEBIN, Thomas 68
SENNET, John 257 285 292
SEVER, Ebenezer 315
SEWALL, Jonathan 71
SHARP, 50
SHAW, Elizabeth 34
SHEAFFE, Capt 39 Edward 52
   Sukey 151 William 151
SHELBURNE, Lord 59 89
SHEPARD, John 199
SHORT, John 285
SIDNEY, 318
SILLBY, Mr 200
SIMMS, Capt 46
SKINNER, Richard 97
SLAVE, Phillis 345 378
   Polidore 314
SLOPER, Samuel 158
SMETBURST, Joseph 97
SMITH, 332 Abijah 186 238
   Beth 292 Capt 251 298
   338 Ed 31 Elizabeth 286
   Ichabod 100 Isaac 39 382
   Lt Col 446 Richard 209
   William 100
SMYTH, Frederick 317
SNELLING, Maj 384
SNIDER, 208 228 241 286
   Christopher 209-210
   Cristopher 194
SNOW, John 99 Mr 41
SNYDER, 331
SODEN, Mr 141
SPAWHAWK, John 190

SPEAR, Pool 89
SPENCER, Mr 96
SPIER, Paul 115
SPOOR, Isaac 33
SPRAGUE, J 290
SPRING, Henry 97
STALKER, Andrew 30
STEADMAN, Capt 250
STEEL, John 18
STODDARD, Justice 126
STONE, John 319
STOODY, William 285
STORY, Mr 299
STUDLY, Mr 25
SULLIVAN, Thomas 155
SUMMERS, Samuel 17-18
SWEANEY, Capt 131
TACKER, Lt 307
TALCORT, Col 20
TARBET, Hugh 292
TAYER, Capt 249 Mr 343
TAYLER, Arodi 71
TAYLOR, Edward 100
TEMPLE, Mr 385
TENBROOK, Conolius 27
THARTER, Col 324
THAYER, Nathanial 112
   Nathaniel 113
THEXTER, Col 324
THOMAS, Isaiah 265 270 277
   Mr 262 266 279 291 301
   326 348
THOMPSON, Capt 161 Charles
   405 Paul 319 William 42
THORP, John 313
THURSTON, Peter 98
TILLOCK, John 31
TIMMINS, Mr 357-358
TOWNSEND, Isaac 36
TRIAL, Robert 130
TRICKMAN, Mac 35
TRYPE, Richard 36
TUDOR, Deacon 342
TURELL, Joseph 252
TURNER, 246 Capt 289 Lewis
   289 Mr 125 290 William
   369
TYLER, James 20 Royal 67
TYNG, William 257
TYRON, Gov 368
VALENTINE, Capt 42
VASSAL, Col 385

VICKERY, Joseph 119-120 Mr 121
VIRGIL, 263
WADE, Abner 29
WAITE, John 45
WALKER, 42 Capt 332 Mr 164 202
WARD, Col 96 John 1 16
WARDEN, William 258
WARREN, Dr 195 James 210 Joseph 204 350 381 404 438 Robert 30
WATERHOUSE, John 319 Sam 2
WATERMAN, Capt 107 Robert 41
WATKINS, Hugh 155
WATSON, Col 369
WATTS, Capt 37
WELLES, Samuel 315
WELLINGTON, Josiah 325
WELLS, Arnold 409
WENDELL, Aliver 382
WENTWORT, David 28
WENTWORTH, Gov 85 157 253
WHEATLEY, John 29 Mr 378
WHEATLY, John 345
WHEELER, David 28 31
WHITE, George 209 John 3d 97 Nathaniel 10 Samuel

WHITE (cont.) 302
WHITTEMORE, Betty 320 Jabez 300
WHITWOOD, Capt 31
WHITWORTH, John Dean 369
WIER, Capt 64-65
WILKES, Mr 405
WILLIAM, 62 3rd 435
WILLIAMS, Capt 238 Foster 186 John Foster 237 Jonathan 49 75 77 353 356 360 Mr 302
WILLSON, John 257
WILMOT, George 194 209-210
WILSON, 255 Capt 121 George 369
WING, Dingly 89
WINSLOW, Joshua 350-351 355
WINTHROP, John 365 Samuel 303-304
WITTEMORE, Mr 300 Mrs 300
WOFE, Gen 235
WOOD, John 63
WRAY, Capt 21
YOUNG, James 198 Mr 137
ZELOTES, Simon 301

Other Heritage Books by the author:

1767 Chronicle

Boston, the Red Coats, and the Homespun Patriots, 1766-1775

Central Colonies Chronicle: The Freeman, the Servants, and the Government, 1722-1732

French and Indian War Notices Abstracted from Colonial Newspapers
Volume 2: 1756-1757
Volume 3: January 1, 1758 to September 17, 1759
Volume 4: September 17, 1759 to December 30, 1760
Volume 5: January 1, 1761 to January 17, 1793

Jolly Old England

Journal of Occurrences: Patriot Propaganda on the British Occupation of Boston, 1768-1769

Newspaper Datelines of the American Revolution
Volume 1: April 18, 1775 to November 1, 1775
Volume 2: November 1, 1775 to April 30, 1776
Volume 3: May 1, 1776 to November 1, 1776
Volume 4: November 1, 1776 to January 30, 1777

Pontiac's Conspiracy and Other Indian Affairs: Notices Abstracted from Colonial Newspapers, 1763-1765

www.ingramcontent.com/pod-product-compliance
Lightning Source LLC
Chambersburg PA
CBHW050322230426
43663CB00010B/1715